本书出版获中央高校基本科研业务费
以及上海外国语大学学术著作出版资助

『红楼梦』

会话引导语英译研究

——基于语料库的多元视角分析

李 颖◎著

当代翻译跨学科研究文库

上海交通大学出版社

SHANGHAI JIAO TONG UNIVERSITY PRESS

**内容提要**

本书为当代翻译跨学科研究文库系列之一,以自建"《红楼梦》原文－霍译本－杨译本平行语料库"为基础,采用定量统计与定性分析相结合的方法,对《红楼梦》原文、霍译本、杨译本中的会话引导语进行分析考察。全书共五章,绪论部分介绍了本书研究的缘起、背景、采用的研究方法,以及研究意义。第一章对该研究的相关学术成果进行了梳理,并提出了本书研究的必要性和重要性。第三、第四和第五章分别对《红楼梦》原文会话引导语、英译文会话引导语和会话引导语的英译作了相关研究与论证。结语部分给出了本书研究的意义和启示。本书适合文学、翻译学、语言学相关专业学者参考使用,也适合《红楼梦》英译爱好者阅读使用。

**图书在版编目(CIP)数据**

《红楼梦》会话引导语英译研究:基于语料库的多元视角分析 / 李颖著. —上海:上海交通大学出版社,2023.12

(当代翻译跨学科研究文库)

ISBN 978‐7‐313‐25840‐3

Ⅰ.①红… Ⅱ.①李… Ⅲ.①《红楼梦》-英语-翻译-研究 Ⅳ.①H315.9

中国版本图书馆 CIP 数据核字(2021)第 249182 号

**《红楼梦》会话引导语英译研究——基于语料库的多元视角分析**

《HONGLOUMENG》HUIHUA YINDAOYU YINGYI YANJIU——JIYU YULIAOKU DE DUOYUAN SHIJIAO FENXI

著　　者:李　颖

出版发行:上海交通大学出版社　　　　地　　址:上海市番禺路 951 号

邮政编码:200030　　　　　　　　　　电　　话:021‐64071208

印　　刷:上海万卷印刷股份有限公司　经　　销:全国新华书店

开　　本:710mm×1000mm　1/16　　印　　张:23.25

字　　数:484 千字

版　　次:2023 年 12 月第 1 版　　　　印　　次:2023 年 12 月第 1 次印刷

书　　号:ISBN 978‐7‐313‐25840‐3

定　　价:78.00 元

# 序

　　《红楼梦》是中国古典小说的巅峰之作。它把时代前沿的思想和完美的艺术形象高度融合在一起，体现中华文化的特色亮点，追寻人类生命、生活的意义与价值，吸引了一代代学人不懈研究探索。对于《红楼梦》这样一部奇书，"人们已经说过了千言万语，大概也还有千言万语要说"（李泽厚，《美的历程》）。在这已经说过的千言万语之中，最精辟的要数鲁迅先生的那句："总之自有《红楼梦》出来以后，传统的思想和写法都打破了。"（鲁迅，《中国小说的历史的变迁》）这可谓迄今为止对《红楼梦》思想艺术成就所作的最言简意赅的概括。

　　《红楼梦》深刻的思想性和精湛的艺术性也受到外国读者的关注和喜爱，是最具影响力的中国著作之一。在世界文学史上，《红楼梦》与《伊利亚特》《奥德赛》《神曲》《悲惨世界》《浮士德》《战争与和平》等著名典籍一道，共同构成了人类文明共有的精神高度坐标。法国文学评论家曾这样评价曹雪芹：他的目光和布鲁斯特一样敏锐；他具有托尔斯泰的同情心；他具有缪西尔的才智和幽默，同时他还具有巴尔扎克对自上而下社会各阶层的洞察力。正是因为《红楼梦》广泛的国际影响力，其迄今为止已被翻译成英文、俄文、德文、日文、法文、意大利文等30余种语言。这一中西文化交流的成果无疑是可喜的，已然"成为中国文学史上一道独特而灿烂的风景"。

　　《红楼梦》用诗一般的笔法叙述故事，人物关系复杂，诗的平仄对仗和用典涉及中华汉字语文、诗词传统的独特性。因此，向西方读者介绍《红楼梦》，既是一项有意义的工作，又是一项极富挑战的工作。比如，元春、迎春、探春、惜春，都预先埋伏着人物命运，蕴含着中华文化；又如，林黛玉所住之潇湘馆，传说中潇湘竹上的斑点是泪痕所化。要在翻译中最大限度保留和传达这些文化精要，绝非易事。在英语中，往往没有一个单词（word）能与汉字的某个词语密合相当、精恰无疑，这也许是译者翻译包括《红楼梦》在内的中国文化典籍时感到棘手的一个缘由。对于西方读者来说，无法接触中文原本，只靠翻译，而且通常是不附加注解的"白文"译本。如果没有高超翻译水平和"音美、形美、意美"的审美艺术，读者难免会坠入云雾，茫茫然不知所云，难以体味中华文化的博大精深、美妙绝伦。

近些年,《红楼梦》的翻译已成为红学的有机组成部分,研究内容全面深入,呈现出精专与广博并存的局面,研究方法与研究视角也日趋多样化。李颖博士的《〈红楼梦〉会话引导语英译研究——基于语料库的多元视角分析》独辟蹊径,选取《红楼梦》中的会话引导语进行系统分析,拓展了《红楼梦》英译研究视角,是对中国古典白话小说会话引导语英译研究的有益探索。

总的来说,我认为本书有三方面特色值得肯定。一是分析方法上,基于语料库的定性、定量分析相结合。本书以公认最优秀的《红楼梦》翻译作品——英国汉学家、翻译家大卫·霍克思(David Hawkes)与约翰·闵福德(John Minford)共同翻译的全译本《石头记》(The Story of the Stone)和我国著名翻译家杨宪益与戴乃迭夫妇翻译的英文全译本《红楼梦》(A Dream of Red Mansions)为原本,创建了全新版"《红楼梦》原文—霍译本—杨译本平行语料库",借助文本分析软件提取原文和译文中的会话引导语,力求从整体上把握会话引导语的英译方法与特色。二是研究对象上,以人物语言会话及内心独白前的引导语作为研究对象。在《红楼梦》中,曹雪芹不厌其烦地使用简单的"道""说""笑道"等引导语,与会话的丰富多样形成鲜明对比。尽管这些会话引导语形式单纯,但主语不尽相同,语境多种多样,使用时的情感更是千差万别。因此,看似一样的动词实际上暗含了不同的信息和意义。三是研究论证上,从《红楼梦》会话引导语英译中探讨古典文学翻译的规律性方法。本书分析了中西译者对于会话引导语翻译的不同处理方式,并在英文原版小说中寻求参照及支撑,研究结果比较客观地反映了中西方会话引导语使用文化的差异,将对中国文化典籍的翻译提供有益的借鉴。

在全球化语境中,中国文化"走出去"是一项涉及诸多方面的宏伟工程。期待更多的学界同仁加入新时代《红楼梦》英译研究,以文载道、以文传声、以文化人,向世界阐释推介更多具有中国特色、体现中国精神、蕴藏中国智慧的优秀文化瑰宝。

是为序。

冯庆华
上海外国语大学教授、博士生导师
2023 年 10 月

# 前　言

　　《红楼梦》是中国古典文学作品中的瑰宝,是举世公认的中国古典小说巅峰之作。这部诞生于封建社会后期的鸿篇巨制,堪称"封建社会的百科全书",是中华传统文化的集大成者,拥有深厚的思想文化内涵和极高的艺术审美价值。《红楼梦》问世两百多年来,深受读者喜爱和推崇,对社会生活产生了深远影响。作为一部长篇章回体小说,《红楼梦》处处体现了汉语语言的文化特色和独特魅力。作者曹雪芹在继承中国优秀文学传统的基础上,通过个性化的语言描写和塑造了诸多生动、经典、耐人寻味的人物形象,使该著作成为中国古典文学史上一座难以逾越的高峰。不仅如此,《红楼梦》在世界文坛也拥有举足轻重的地位,被誉为"世界文坛的一块丰碑"。《红楼梦》是翻译语言最多的世界25部名著之一,目前译本已涉及英、法、日、韩、俄、德等20多种不同文字,主要有摘译、节译、全译三种形式,数量不下60种,在中华优秀传统文化的对外传播中发挥着不可替代的作用。

　　本书源于笔者对《红楼梦》及其英译本日益深入的研究及愈发浓厚的兴趣。与众多"80后"一样,笔者对于《红楼梦》最初的认识来源于王扶林导演拍摄的1987年版《红楼梦》连续剧;中学时代曾在父亲引领下两次通读《红楼梦》,深感晦涩难懂,一度望而却步。自2007年起,笔者有幸在硕士及博士研究阶段师从"红译专家"冯庆华教授,不仅在导师指导下数次重读《红楼梦》原文,对于《红楼梦》的理解从主观零碎的感性认识提升到系统科学的理性认识,更有机会接触并深入研究杨宪益、戴乃迭译本和霍克思译本两部经典作品。笔者在不断学习和研究《红楼梦》原文及其译文过程中发现,曹雪芹作为语言艺术大师,喜欢用较多的笔墨来描写人物的会话和行动,以此凸显人物个性。《红楼梦》中的会话内容精彩绝伦,而引导人物会话的引导语却非常单一和程式化,作者只是不厌其烦地使用"道""说""笑道"等引导语,与会话的丰富多样形成了鲜明对比。此外,两个经典译本的译者对原文中会话引导语的处理方式也引人深思——崇尚归化、尽可能将原文信息明晰化的译者霍克思似乎并没有比杨宪益夫妇使用更多样化的方式来处理单一的会话引导语。这背后究竟有什么样的原因和文化背景呢？

　　带着上述疑问，笔者自行创建了全新版的"《红楼梦》原文—霍译本—杨译本平行语料库"，采用定量统计与定性分析相结合的方法，对《红楼梦》原文、霍译本、杨译本中的会话引导语进行分析考察。首先，分析《红楼梦》原文中会话引导语的特色及历史背景；其次，总结《红楼梦》霍译本和杨译本中会话引导语的语言特征，并分析其原因；最后，通过将《红楼梦》原文与译文对照研究，总结和探寻会话引导语的翻译策略和翻译方法，以期在一定程度上拓展《红楼梦》会话引导语领域的英译研究，为译者风格研究提供新的切入角度。

　　本著述的创新点有四：第一，研究方法新。笔者自行创建《红楼梦》平行语料库，在确保语料选取更加客观公正的基础上，从总体上对原文及其英译文进行语料库翻译学和文化等角度的多元分析对比。第二，研究文本新。笔者选取上海外语教育出版社 2012 年发行的汉英对照版《红楼梦》为底本，创建出一个全新的《红楼梦》汉英双语平行语料库。第三，研究对象新。本书首次对《红楼梦》原文中的会话引导语进行系统分类和特色分析，并对会话引导语的英译进行全面、系统、深入的剖析。第四，研究结果新。本书探讨中西译者对会话引导语翻译的不同处理方式，反映中西方会话引导语使用的文化差异，这将对中国学生的翻译及英语写作教学提供一定的启示和方向。

　　本书共分六个部分，其中第三、第四和第五部分为全书的核心。绪论部分简述研究缘起、研究背景及创新意义，明确研究目标、研究方法以及全文的框架。第一章介绍了各学派研究的重点。第二章是对《红楼梦》原文中会话引导语的研究。第三章是对《红楼梦》译文中会话引导语的研究。第四章基于《红楼梦》原文以及译文中会话引导语的研究，着重分析了《红楼梦》会话引导语的翻译问题。结论部分总结了本书的意义和启示，指出存在的不足，并就后续研究提出建议。

　　《红楼梦》翻译研究任重道远，常研常新。由于本人知识视野与研究能力有限，本书难免存在局限性及错漏之处，恳请各位专家学者和读者朋友们不吝赐教。

李　颖

2023 年 7 月于上海

# 目　录

# 绪　论

　　《红楼梦》堪称中国古今第一奇书，是我国古典白话小说的巅峰之作，其创作覆盖了当时自然学科与社会学科的方方面面，堪称"中国封建社会的百科全书"。该书问世不久，即以手抄本的形式广为流传。程伟元在《红楼梦序》中写道："好事者每传抄一部，置庙市中，昂其价得数十金，可谓不胫而走者矣。"嘉庆年间刊行的《京都竹枝词》曾载"开谈不说《红楼梦》，纵读诗书也枉然"。自问世两百多年来，《红楼梦》始终备受世人的青睐与推崇，经久不衰的"红楼文化"已深深融入国人生活中的各个层面——从文学、影视、戏曲，到说书、弹词、插画，从剪纸、挂历、明信片，到书签、纸扇、扑克牌，皆可寻觅到"红楼"的踪迹。

　　《红楼梦》深刻的社会意义和巨大的美学价值同样受到外国读者的关注与喜爱，是最具影响力的中国著作之一。这颗世界文学宝库的璀璨明珠，愈来愈多地得到世界各国人民的接受和欣赏。国外学者把"红学"与"甲骨学""敦煌学"并列为关于中国的三门世界性的"显学"。《红楼梦》也是翻译语言最多的世界25部名著之一。《红楼梦》目前已被翻译成英、法、日、韩、俄、德等20多种不同语种，海外的《红楼梦》译本有摘译、节译、全译3种形式，数量不下60种，仅全译本就有20多种。[①]

　　《红楼梦》的英译始于1816年，英国传教士马礼逊（Robert Morrison）第一次翻译了《红楼梦》选段，内容是第三十一回里宝玉和袭人的对话。此后还有其他传教士英译了《红楼梦》的选段，大多被用于汉语教学和传播领域。在1830—1987年的150多年里，《红楼梦》共出现过9种英译本，由此"成为中国文学史上一道独特而灿烂的风景"（陈宏薇、江帆，2004）。20世纪70年代出现了《红楼梦》的两种英文全译本。英国汉学家、翻译家大卫·霍克思（David Hawkes）与女婿约翰·闵福德（John Minford）共同翻译了一百二十回共五卷全译本《石头记》（*The Story of the Stone*），于1973—1986年由企鹅出版集团

---

　　① 参见"红楼"译本知多少——《红楼梦》海外传播情况，载《文汇报》2003年10月21日，http://www.china.com.cn/international/txt/2003-10/21/content_7430964.htm。

(Penguin Group)陆续出版。1978—1980年,我国著名翻译家杨宪益与戴乃迭夫妇翻译的英文全译本《红楼梦》(*A Dream of Red Mansions*)由中国外文出版社分三卷出版发行(为方便起见,下文中将这两部译本分别简称为霍译本和杨译本)。霍译本和杨译本是《红楼梦》英译史上真正的英文全译本,出版以来一直被公认为是优秀的翻译作品。本专著即选取该两部优秀全译本来探讨《红楼梦》会话引导语的英译问题。

## 一、研究缘起

本著述方向的确定主要源于三方面的因素:

第一,"红楼情结"。与众多"80后"一样,笔者对于《红楼梦》最初的认识来源于王扶林先生导演的1987年版《红楼梦》连续剧。精致的服饰与布景、传神动人的表演、精彩生动的对话,在幼小的心灵里播撒了"红楼情结"的种子。中学时代和本科时代曾在父亲的引领下两次通读《红楼梦》,深感晦涩难唔,一度望而却步,敬畏仰止。直到2007年笔者有幸师从"红译专家"冯庆华教授开始硕士研究生阶段的学习,不仅得以数次重读《红楼梦》原文,更有机会接触到了杨译本和霍译本两部经典作品,如获至宝,原本压抑的"红楼情结"被再次激发,对于《红楼梦》的理解也从主观零碎的感性认识得以提升到系统科学的理性认识。在攻读博士学位期间,冯教授开设的红楼梦翻译艺术研究课程,系统阐述了该研究领域各种内容和方法,为笔者将个人热情倾注到翻译研究提供了非常重要的前提和基础。

第二,困惑思考。此次研究基于笔者数次阅读《红楼梦》原文以及译文过程中的一些困惑和思考。作为古典白话小说的杰出代表,《红楼梦》的文学成就是多方面的,其中最被人津津乐道的特点之一是其语言方面的成就。我们知道,小说语言通常由叙述人语言和人物语言组成。通常古典白话小说中叙述人语言在数量上比较多,对语言风格起主导作用。而《红楼梦》则不同,人物语言(主要是人物会话,也包括少量的内心独白)例外地占了大部分篇幅。据冯庆华教授研究,《红楼梦》原著中有700多个人物,其中最主要的60个人物的会话与独白文本占全文文本的35.35%。曹雪芹作为语言艺术大师,其对话写作技巧炉火纯青,堪称典范。他用较少的篇幅描写周围环境、刻画人物外貌,而较多地把笔墨用来描写人物的会话和行动以直接揭示人物的思想性格,语言生动活泼,凸显人物个性。鲁迅先生曾在《中国小说史略》(中华书局,2010年)中说,自有《红楼梦》以来,传统的思想和写法都打破了。然而,笔者却在阅读中发现,尽管《红楼梦》会话内容精彩绝伦,引导人物会话的会话引导语却非常单一和程式化,语言大师曹雪芹只是不厌其烦地使用简单的"道""说""笑道"等引导语,与会话的丰富多样形成了鲜明对比。这背后究竟有什么样的原因和背景?译者在译文中又会作何处理呢?

　　第三,不平则鸣。笔者带着疑惑和好奇心对杨译本和霍译本的会话引导语翻译进行了特别关注和考察。在查阅《红楼梦》会话引导语英译研究方面资料的过程中,发现相对于《红楼梦》会话研究的累累硕果而言,会话引导语的研究寥寥无几,且零散滞后。人物会话的内容固然重要,可引导会话的方式对于人物形象的塑造同样非常有意义。我们在原文中很容易发现,这些会话引导语尽管形式单纯,主语却不尽相同,语境多种多样,使用时的方式情感更是千差万别,因此看似平凡的动词实际暗含了数不尽的信息和意义。两个译本的译者对于原文的处理方式也有一定的差别,崇尚归化、尽可能将原文信息明晰化的译者霍克思似乎并没有比杨译使用更多样化的方法来处理单一的会话引导语。事实确实如此吗? 又是什么原因导致了这种现象的出现? 会话引导语英译研究领域的荒凉召唤着我们对该领域给予更多的关注和钻研。

## 二、研究意义

　　本研究在前人零星研究的基础上对我国古典白话小说《红楼梦》中的会话引导语进行系统分析,并对其中最为常见的会话(包括语言会话和内心独白)引导语英译进行基于语料库的定量和定性分析考察,以期在一定程度上拓展《红楼梦》会话引导语领域的英译研究,为译者风格研究提供新的切入角度。

　　在考察分析《红楼梦》会话引导语的特色及分类、霍译本和杨译本如何处理以及原因时,研究体现出描写性特征,但在探讨新时代背景下会话引导语应当如何翻译时则在一定程度上体现出规约性特点。因此,本研究是一项描写性和规约性相辅相成的理论探讨。

　　此次"会话引导语英译研究"以我国古典白话小说西渐和文化传播为依托,以全球多元化背景下中华文化"走出去"战略的实施为落脚点,试图为新时代我国典籍英译提供一定参考借鉴,具有鲜明时代感和现实意义。

## 三、研究内容

　　本研究基于平行语料库的研究范式,通过对《红楼梦》会话引导语翻译的全面系统的对比研究,尝试回答如下问题:

　　(1)《红楼梦》原文中的会话引导语有什么特色? 其历史背景是什么?

　　(2)《红楼梦》霍译本和杨译本中有关会话引导语的英译文本各呈现出什么特征? 形成这些语言特征的原因是什么?

　　(3)通过将《红楼梦》原文与译文对照研究,总结会话引导语的翻译策略和翻译方法。

　　对上述问题的研究能够从总体上概括《红楼梦》两个译本对于会话引导语

的翻译特征,并探索出不同译者的翻译策略和翻译方法,解答在跨文化背景下不同翻译特征的意义,从而为《红楼梦》英译研究提供新的视角和思路。

## 四、研究方法

### (一)基于语料库的定量定性相结合

笔者自行创建了全新版"《红楼梦》原文—霍译本—杨译本平行语料库",借助文本分析软件提取原文和译文中的会话引导语,在确保语料选取客观公正的基础上,从总体上对两个译本,以及原文和译文进行分析对比,力求从整体上把握《红楼梦》会话引导语的英译方法与特色。

### (二)多元视角分析探究

引语现象与会话引导语涉及叙事学与小说文体学等理论,会话引导语及其英译研究涉及语料库翻译学和文化等数个领域,对于译文中会话引导语再现的策略方法探究涉及现代译学相关理论、多元文化理论等。

## 五、研究创新点

本研究的创新之处可大致归结为以下四点:

### (一)研究方法创新

笔者自行创建《红楼梦》平行语料库,在确保语料选取更加客观公正的基础上,从总体上对研究对象及其英译文进行语料库翻译学和文化等角度的多元分析对比,力求从整体上把握《红楼梦》会话引导语在霍译本和杨译本中的传译特色,改变了以往零碎、粗浅的主观分析性研究模式,使研究结果更具科学性和说服力。

### (二)研究文本创新

鉴于《红楼梦》原文版本杂多[①],加之杨译本和霍译本参照的《红楼梦》底本不同,"绝对不能轻率地拿一个通行的本子来充当译者据以翻译的底本"(洪涛,2006)。但是,《红楼梦》英译研究中原文又是最基础、最关键的前提。为了确保研究的准确性和可信度,我们需要设法在可能的情况下寻求原文和译本之间,以及两个译本内容之间的最大近似值。

笔者在本研究中选取上海外语教育出版社 2012 年出版的《红楼梦》汉英对

---

① 有关《红楼梦》底本问题本书不再赘述。

照版里的中文部分①("霍本"②)作为原文底本,这可以确保霍克思译文与原文的完全对应,再将杨译本的相关内容核查后录入,有出入的内容用红色字体标出(构建平行语料库时仅保留杨译本中与"霍本"中文对应的部分,删除多余的部分,以确保语料库"中文—霍译本—杨译本"的完全对应),由此创作出一个全新的《红楼梦》汉英双语平行语料库。该语料库的构建不仅为此次研究提供了崭新的素材,也为今后的《红楼梦》英译研究贡献了一份语料支持。

(三)研究对象创新

本书的研究对象为《红楼梦》中的人物会话引导语,包括所有人物语言会话及内心独白(可看作是自己与自己的会话)前的引导语,如"黛玉道:""宝玉笑道:""王夫人说:""贾母命:""宝钗暗自思道:""内心自忖道:"等,不包括"写道:""诗云:""词曰:""念道:""唱道:""联道:"等后面引出文字(如对联、诗词、书信、圣旨等)的引导语。

本书首次对《红楼梦》会话引导语的英译进行全面、系统、深入的剖析。对原文会话引导语(包括人物会话和内心独白)的系统分类和特色分析,以及对会话引导语英译的深入探究,将拓宽《红楼梦》英译研究视角,扩展《红楼梦》译者风格研究领域,有效改善《红楼梦》会话引导语乃至中国古典白话小说会话引导语英译研究中的零散局面。

(四)研究结果创新

本书将探讨中西译者对于会话引导语翻译的不同处理方式,并试图在英文原版小说中寻求参照及支撑,研究结果将比较客观地反映中西方会话引导语使用的文化差异。翻译与写作密不可分,此项研究结果必将对中国学生的翻译与英语写作教学提供一定的启示和取向。

## 六、本书结构

本书共分六个部分:

绪论部分介绍了本次研究的背景及意义、研究内容、研究方法及全文的

---

①　范圣宇"汉英对照版《红楼梦》校勘说明"有清晰的表述:前八十回中文部分以人民文学出版社1964年竖排版(启功校注)为底本,主要参校《红楼梦八十回校本》(俞平伯校本)、《脂砚斋重评石头记》(庚辰本)、《脂砚斋甲戌抄阅再评石头记》(甲戌本)、《戚蓼生序本石头记》(有正本)、《乾隆抄本百廿回红楼梦稿》(梦稿本);英文部分以霍克思先生翻译的企鹅出版社《石头记》1973年版第一卷、1977年版第二卷、1980年版第三卷为底本,参照霍克思先生《红楼梦英译笔记》(香港岭南大学文学与翻译研究中心,2000年)及相关日记、书信,对现有译文作了全面系统的校订。后四十回中文部分以人民文学出版社1964年竖排版为底本;英文部分以闵福德教授翻译的企鹅出版社《石头记》1982年版第四卷、1986年版第五卷为底本。

②　范圣宇在"汉英对照版《红楼梦》校勘说明"中写道:霍克思在翻译时参考过诸多版本,最终形成与现存各版本均不一样的本子,我们姑且称作"霍本"。

框架。

第一章归纳总结与《红楼梦》会话引导语英译研究相关领域的研究成果,指出目前研究的匮乏以及存在的问题,阐明开展此次研究的必要性和重要性。

第二章分别从《红楼梦》原文会话引导语与非引导语对比、《红楼梦》与古典作品会话引导语对比、《红楼梦》与现代作品会话引导语对比、《红楼梦》前八十回与后四十回会话引导语对比等方面展开对原文中会话引导语的语言特点的分析和研究。

第三章对霍译本和杨译本这两部优秀译文中的会话引导语进行数据统计和特色分析,研究层面包括:将两部译本的会话引导语文本分别与其非会话引导语文本进行对比、将两部译本的会话引导语文本分别与原版英文小说中的会话引导语进行对比、将两部译本中的会话引导语进行详细对比、将霍译本中前八十回与后四十回会话引导语进行对比等。

第四章在对《红楼梦》原文以及译文中会话引导语研究的基础上,着重分析研究《红楼梦》会话引导语的翻译问题。笔者将《红楼梦》的会话引导语划分为几个大的类别进行翻译研究:"说道"类会话引导语、"笑道"类会话引导语、"哭道"类会话引导语、"骂道"类会话引导语和"啐道"类会话引导语等。

本书最后总结本研究的意义和启示,指出此次研究存在的不足之处,并就后续研究提出建议。

# 第一章　经久不衰的多学派研究

本章论述旨在归纳总结与《红楼梦》会话引导语英译研究相关领域的研究成果,采取由总到分、从面至点的方式梳理了引语、引导语、《红楼梦》会话引导语及其英译的研究,为本专著的开展提供了重要的理论前提和实践基础。

## 第一节　"会话引导语"的多学派研究

纵观国内外现存的有关"引导语"研究,均是与"引语"紧密相连,学者们将"引导语"作为一个与"引语"相对的概念。人物会话是小说的重要组成部分。叙述者为了增强话语表达的效果经常会采用多种不同的表达人物话语的方式。其中引语就是经常被使用的表达方式之一。引语分为两个部分,一部分是人物的话语,即被引用的部分;另一部分是引出人物话语的句子,即我们所研究的引导语。鉴于此,我们有必要先就国内外关于"引语"方面的研究进行梳理,这些研究中不同程度地涉及了有关引导语的讨论。

### 一、"引语"研究回顾

引语在修辞中被称为"引用",是指对他人的话语、典籍或文章的引用。引语这种特殊的语言使用形式很早以前就受到中外学者的关注,而且在研究视角、研究方法、研究重点上不尽相同。

修辞学对引语的研究成果颇丰。引用作为一种修辞格,其作用早已为大家所了解:在文章中引用别人的话、典故、名言、诗文、故事或俗语,利用一般人对大众意见的尊重与对权威的崇拜,来增加自己言论的说服力,达到使人信服的目的。孔子曰,"述而不作,信而好古"[1],意为自己的著述只是传承旧说而不是创立新义,信奉并喜欢古时候的准则。这样的传统影响了一代又一代的中国文人,因此引用修辞格在中国早已被广泛应用。我国汉代文论《文心雕龙》中将

---

① 出自《论语·述而》,原文是:"子曰:述而不作,信而好古,窃比于我老彭。"

"引语"阐释为"盖文章之外,据事以类义,援古以证今者也",可见已将引语置于语境中加以考察,只可惜缺少系统的描写。

在西方的古典时期,亚里士多德已经认识到引语的作用,他在《修辞学》中做了比较详细的阐述。语法学上对引语的探讨,多集中于直接引语如何通过语法形式的转化变为间接引语。传统语法学通常这样来界定引语:说者向听者转告他人或者本人说过的话,称为"转述";它可以是直接转述,保持原语句的内容和形式并放入引号内,称为"直接引语";也可以是间接转述,说者用自己的话进行转述,称为"间接引语"。直接引语和间接引语共同构成被转述小句,它与引导语或者转述小句一起组成转述句。

随着文体学和叙事学的兴起,西方语言学家对英语文学作品中的引语现象进行了大量的研究,有了长足的发展,如英国批评家 Norman Page(1973)将小说话语的表达方式归纳为直接引语、间接引语、被覆盖的引语、"平行的"引语、"带特色"的引语、自由间接引语、自由直接引语、从间接引语"滑入"直接引语等八种。英国语言学家 Leech 和 Short(1981)根据叙述者介入的不同程度对引语形式进行了有规则的排列:间接引语或间接思想、自由间接引语或自由间接思想、直接引语或直接思想、自由直接引语或自由直接思想、语言行为或思想行为的叙事转述。

语义学的研究开始摆脱拘泥于引语间转化时语法形式和句子结果变化的传统做法,而转向语义角度。其中影响极大的是 Halliday(2000)从功能语义和功能结构的角度运用"投射"对引语进行了专门描述:"投射指的是一种逻辑语义关系,在这种关系中一个小句的功能不是对(非语言的)经验的直接表述,而是对(语言的)表述的表述。"他同时区分了投射的两种类型:并列和主从;还区分了言语和思维的不同表达方式,体现为述说和观点。从结构上看,并列投射为直接引语,主从投射为间接引语;从语义上看,被言语投射为述说,被思维(心理)投射为观点。

我国也有一些学者注意到引语这种特殊的语言使用现象,并进行了相关的研究,如赵毅衡、刘大为、申丹、徐赳赳、张荣健等。赵毅衡(1987)的《小说叙述中的转述语》是较早探讨转述(引语)现象的文章,作者从叙事学和文体学的角度出发,对小说叙述中的转述语进行研究。他认为以前学者对引语的分类过于复杂,缺乏明显的划分规律,建议把引语划分为直接式与间接式、引语式与自由式,这样简单的划分互相组合就构成了四个小类,即直接引语式、间接引语式、间接自由式和直接自由式,这也是目前学术界通常采用的四个类型。他还指出之所以转述语分为这么多的类型,是由于引导语的存在与否以及人称的变化造成的,也是叙述语境对于引语的压力,也是叙述者介入(控制)人物话语的结果。刘大为(1991)通过言说动词句的概念来讨论言语行为和言语交际的关系,将言说动词句分为言语行为的被述句、言语行为的实示句和言语行为的自述句三类,指出话语一旦离开现场实示即被转述的本质;除直接、间接转述外,他还提到了概括、指称等诸多转述类型,将转述问题的研究上升到语言哲学的高度。申丹(1991)评述了英国批评家诺曼·佩奇(Norman Page)对小说人物话语的表达方式进行的八种分类和归纳,指出他的分类过于烦琐,并以中英文小说中的引语为语料对比分析了自由直接引语、直接引语、间接引语及"言语行为的叙述体"的语用功能,指出不同的表达方式具有其独特的功能和优势。徐赳赳(1996)以报刊上的 355 篇叙述文为语料,系统且详尽地分析了现代汉语叙述文中的直接引语这种特殊语言使用形式的分类、功能及应用原则;总结出直接引语有结构重叠和结构分离两种结构,并从口语直接引语和书面直接引语、直接引语的指称、直接引语和管领词,以及直接引语和间接引语四个方面分析归纳了直接引语的特征,在此基础上总结出直接引语的五大功能:逐字复制功能、责任分离功能、同一性功能、不易描写的功能和吸引的功能。作者还指出,引语的用法,都应从修辞的角度、需要的角度来考虑。依据 Tannen(1989)提出的"建构式对话"理论,张荣健(2000)详细讨论了书面语和会话中引语的不同类型和功能。他认为在会话中,引语,特别是直接引语,并非仅仅是"转述他人的话语",而是"转述话语行为的众多其他方面"。张荣建在徐赳赳总结的直接引语的五大功能的基础上又提出直接引语还能产生用引号表现的音响的效果,最后他指出无论是在会话还是书面语中,直接引语和间接引语都是话语或思维的两个不同表现方式。戴连云(2004)研究发现传统的汉语小说的直接引语的模式只有一种,即说话者—引述词—话语内容,而英语的直接引语排列顺序不同于传统的汉语,比较多样,有五种不同的模式。她还指出直接引语在小说中有三种作用:直接引语是分析、评价人物形象的依据;直接引语与其他表达方式配合使用,可以产生非凡的音响效果;直接引语给人一种"事件重现"的印象,使读者产生身临其境的感觉。辛斌(2009)总结了关于引语的几种主要理论,指出传统的引语理论可以分为两大类,一类从语义的角度而另一类则从语用的角度出发,作者比较倾向于把引语作为一个整体对待,对其做出认知语用上的解释。王艺(2004)将对引语的研究放在言语行为理论的视角下进行,就引语本质、产生机制、使用效果、功能实现、表现形式以及在日常生活和文学语言中的各种变体进行了系统化的论述。黄冠颖(2007)以邢福义先生的"小三角"理论为基础,对中国古典白话小说中的直接引语进行详细的描述。倪广妍(2014)对《歧路灯》引语的分类、结构、功能特点、发展变化等进行了封闭性研究分析。

此外,学者们还从其他不同视角和领域对引语进行了研究。辛斌(1998)从批评语言学的角度,分析了新闻报道中引语的语篇语用功能,并考察了报道者如何运用它们来传达自己的观点,影响着读者对引语的理解;同时他还进一步从转述言语角度考察新闻语篇的对话性,把新闻语篇分为事件性消息(event news)和转述性消息(speech-reporting news),指出按其对话性程度分为独白式和对话式(dialogism)。贾中恒(2000)关注的是对转述内容起着引导和介绍作用的转述引语及其语用功能,提出引语本身只要具备一定的语境因素,其潜在的某些言语行为就可能被激活。唐青叶(2004)侧重对比了所收集的自然学科和人文学科的学术语料中引用的使用现象,认为系统功能语法中的原话引用(quote)和间接引用(report)在学术语篇中集中出现在引言部分,并要求标注包括被引用人姓名、出版年份直至页码的引用源,在整个语篇生成过程中作者、被引用人、读者乃至研究对象之间均形成了功能性互动关系,使得语篇具有了互文性(intertextuality);学术语篇中对原文引用的处理依据传统的分类可以具化成完整引用(integral structure)和不完整引用(non-integral structure),即前者将被引用者姓名、出版日期和页码等完整信息全部标注在句中。陈润(2007)从言语行为理论出发,对引语问题进行了论述,结合对外汉语课堂教学,对引语的教学内容、练习设计及教师引用技巧运用提出了自己的看法。黄勤(2008)结合批评话语分析和翻译的视角,对新闻语篇中的引语及其翻译的语篇和语用功能进行了研究。杨颖莉、林正军(2008)从功能和语用两个层面探讨了直接引语和间接引语在信息传递上的特征与差异,并从语用层面探索直接引语向间接引语转换的理据,最后强调要根据场合、文体、转述对象等选择得体恰当的转述方式。

在语言认知研究方面,彭建武(2008)探究了引语的性质和认知因素是如何影响引语的生成和使用的,比如人对世界的感知经验,观察事物的方式是如何影响人们对引语的使用的,特别是在同样符合语言规范的条件下人们该如何选择不同的引语来表达非客观的意义,引语的意义在大脑中究竟是怎样构建的。黄友(2009)考察了引语的性质、类型、各类引语的规则和策略、引语的忠实度以及制约忠实度的修辞动因。吕晶晶(2011)从多个维度对引语现象进行了考察,指出目前我国引语研究虽已提出功能视角的导向,但研究对象趋于静态和单一,对于形式和功能的复杂匹配认识过于简单,忽略了引语作为一个完整的言语行为框架,具有原型性和形式功能多维性特征,其中任何一个参数的变化都会导致忠实度、目的和功能的变化。高小丽(2013)从引语类型、引导语和消息来源三个方面对汉英报纸新闻语篇中的引语进行定量和定性的比较分析,发现在汉英报纸中,间接引语的出现频率均为最高,其次是直接引语;就引导语而言,英汉语报纸中的中性引导语、心理引导语和言语行为引导语均存在显著差异,英语报纸中这三类引导语的出现频率均高于汉语。与汉语相比,英语中的言语行为引导语更为丰富多样,而汉语较单一,汉语标题中偏爱使用"强调"这个词,并且这个引导语的逻辑主语几乎都指称领导者,这使本来非常普通的一个引导语具有了"权力"的特性。

## 二、"引导语"研究回顾

无论是从语言学、文学、叙事学，还是哲学、心理学角度，引导语的研究时常伴随着引语的研究出现。

不同时期的学者尝试对引导语按照不同标准进行了分类。Thompson 和 Ye(1991)根据引导语的外延和评价潜势把引导语分为语篇动词、心理动词和研究动词三大类。此后 Hyland(2000)又对此分类和描述进行了进一步的修正，提出了研究动词、认知动词和语篇动词三类引导语。Biber 等(2000)也把动词按语义域进行了归类：表行动和事件的活动动词如 buy 等；表交际行为的交际动词如 ask 等；表认知和情感的思维动词如 think 等；表引导事件的物质动词如 become，等等。张荣建(2000)提出：按照话语和思维性质划分，引导语可以分成引导话语和引导思想两大类，如 say、tell、explain 均可在直接和间接引语中用来引导话语，而 think、suppose、assume 则用来引导思想。贺灿文、周江林(2001)仿照汤姆森的分类方法，把引导语分为现实类(类似于研究类)、语篇类、思维类和状态类等四大类。唐青叶(2004)又在汤姆森的基础上把引导语分为表示作者引用行为和被引用者言语行为的动词，且根据这些引导语所包含的评价潜势将其分为表作者立场和被引用者立场的动词。

关于引导语的作用和价值，贾中桓(2000)以言语行为理论为基础对引导语的语用功能做了探究，他将由引导语构成的语境称为即时语境，即时语境在一定程度上弥补了引用所造成的原话语的语境缺失。Thompson(2000)也指出，引导语的使用表达了作者对引用内容的态度，能增强观点的说服力。由此可见，引导语除了在语法上起到连接作用外，还具有帮助作者实现有效交际的语用价值。辛斌(2008)认为，引导语构成引语最直接的语境，具有预示和支配其理解的功能。

与引导语相关的研究内容比较多样。Bergler(1992)以及陈明(2002)均对新闻语篇中的引导语进行了研究。黄谊军(2001)对科技论文引言中的引导语与主语搭配情况作了分析。王艺(2004)专门考察了直接引语的引导语，包括汉语中的言说动词、引导语的特点和功能。高天霞(2010)将关注重点从直接引语转向了放在直接引语前的"曰"与"说"。姚毅(2012)结合认知语用的相关理论对引导语进行解析，从认知语用角度揭示书面问题语篇中引导语的功能。他认为引导语是认知思维与言语行为的融合，隐藏着作者对引用内容和观点的态度、视角。在书面文体语篇中引导语的选用具有激活局部语篇或整个语篇的功能，所以英语书面文体语篇引导语的使用应基于交际目的而灵活运用。

引语的研究除涉及其定义、分类、语用功能等基本理论研究之外，不同学科的学术论文之间的对比研究以及不同作者群体之间的对比研究也是引导语研究的主要内容。Thompson 和 Ye(1991)研究了非母语学习者在学术英语(English for Academic Purposes,EAP)写作中引导语的使用情况。他们根据语义内涵和评价潜势对引导语进行了分类,考察了语义内涵和评价潜势之间的互动以及即时语境对学生使用引导语的影响,最后提出了引导语使用模型,这一模型有助于学生理解引语与引用以及更好地在学术论文中进行引用和发表评论。Hyland(2000)对比分析了自然科学和人文科学学术论文中的引用现象,发现在两类论文中引用的使用频数以及作者对引语的描述存在很大差异,人文科学论文作者更多地引用以往的研究成果,也更多地使用引导语,并对引用内容做出评价。唐青叶(2004)通过对 6 个学科共 30 篇论文的引导语的统计分析,发现引导语出现的频率顺序为应用语言学、社会学、哲学、医学、物理学、生物学,同时从引导语的分类及使用可以看出这些动词是认知思维与言语行为的融合,隐藏着作者对引用内容和观点的态度、视角。比如:confirm 强调研究结果的重要性,而 indicate、suggest 只是一种推测性结论;point out 表明同意被转述人的观点;state 则没有表明作者的观点;非人称结构如 it is said to be 暗示这个主张不一定属实;claim 暗含了作者"不同意"或至少内容不真实,只是被转述人"自称"而已,信息的真实性有待证实,这种用法表明转述人置身事外,不承担责任,往往在后一句跟着表示转折的词 however,暗示作者引出不同意见。这些引导语不仅揭示了作者的观点、态度,也具有激活局部小语篇或整个语篇的功能。胡志清(2007)发现中国硕士研究生论文中的引导语使用比较单一集中,外国硕士研究生论文中的引导语使用则比较灵活宽泛。捷克学者 Olga(2008)通过研究大学生和研究生学术论文中的引导语后发现两类学术均较多地使用嵌入式(integral)引用。辛斌(2008)对比研究了中外新闻语篇中的引导语,指出新闻语篇中的引导语选择范围比较狭窄,含有"指示""要求""强调"等意思的动词比较多,且每个引导语的管辖范围明确,边界清楚;他认为中外新闻报道中引导语使用的差异主要取决于新闻报道的内容、目的和报道者的态度,因此对于引用的研究应建立在具体的语篇和语境之上。陈建林(2011)通过对比中国英语专业学生与美国学生的论说文语料研究了前者论说文中引导语的使用特点,指出中国学生的引导语使用比较模糊、笼统,引语结构比较单一,引语来源不太确定。以上这些研究为针对不同语境和不同体裁中的引导语研究提供了理论基础。

## 三、"言说动词"研究回顾

笔者在资料搜集过程中发现,在与会话引导语相关的一些研究中,言说动词是一个很重要的部分。言说动词与人物的会话密切相关。迄今国内学界对于汉语言说动词的研究已取得一定的进展和成果。现简要归纳如下：

1898年出版的《马氏文通》是中国关于汉语语法的第一部系统性著作，开创了中国的语法学。言说动词作为表述言说行为的一类特殊动词，也逐渐进入了学者们的研究视野。有关"言说动词"的概念，我国著名语言文字学家黎锦熙教授早在1924年的专著《新著国语文法》中就有涉及，他曾把动词分为外动词、内动词、助动词、同动词的四分法来划分动词，然后再依据意义把外动词区分为处分事物、经验方法、交接物品、交涉人事、认定名义、变更事物、情意作用、表示关系等八种，其中交涉人事、认定名义、情意作用等三类中涉及了大量的言说动词，如劝、嘱咐、叫、称许、批评、笑骂等。但黎锦熙教授并未明确提出"言说动词"这一概念。60余年之后，语文学家尹世超先生才明确指出"全能动词"里面含有一个"表示言语行为的"小类，譬如，说、询问、告发、表白等。直到1991年，刘大为在《言语行为与言说动词句》一文中才正式提出"有一类词专门用于把语言作为一种行为来谈论，这就是言说动词，如'说''通知''承认''问''请求''劝告''预言'等。由于人不可能对未表现为语言的对象进行思考，思考活动就其整体而言也就是一种内部言语行为，言说动词因而应该包括'想''认为''相信''知道'等心理动词"。

进入21世纪以来，有关言说动词的研究明显增多，吴剑锋（2009）收集了20篇相关文献并按研究范式差异分三块介绍了这一领域的研究状况。方寅、夏燕舞（2012）收集了更加丰富的文献，尤其是吴文发表之后出现的新的文献资料，从句法、语义、语用及个案研究四个方面对该领域的研究进行了梳理。笔者试图就目前所能查阅到的资料大致作一下梳理和总结：

第一类是历时共时研究。汪维辉（2003）指出，现代汉语方言的"说类词"主要有三个，北方话的"说"，南方方言的"话"和中部方言的"讲"。作为"说类词"，它们的确立都是近代汉语阶段的事："话"大约形成于唐代；"说"则定型于唐宋之际；"讲"在历史文献中只能追溯到元代，它的产生时间和扩散过程还有待进一步研究。杨凤仙（2007）选取上古时期汉语言说类动词作为研究对象，考察这些词语在上古文献的使用情况；通过对言说类动词词义进行共时词义系统的分析和历时词义演变、词汇兴替的考察，对义场词项的增减和词义的演变作出解释，从而揭示言说类动词演变的规律。田源（2007）以汉语中的说类动词"言""语""曰""云""道"等为研究对象，主要研究言说义动词的上位词，以"两个三角"的理论框架为指导，对说类动词从古到今的嬗变过程、说类动词在方言中的分布、说类动词的句法语义等方面进行了多角度考察，主要分析了说类动词的历时演变、共时分布和句法语义搭配规律，试图从历时和共时角度揭示说类动词的特征和规律。蔡俊杰（2008）从言语行为理论的角度对现代汉语言说类动词进行定义，并通过系统的考察揭示该类动词在句法、语义、语用等方面的特点,探讨它们在现代汉语中的一些使用规律。郭颖洁、李诗(2011)从"曰""言"和"说"所具有的"说话"这一基本词义入手,阐释三者的起源,总结三者在语义和使用方面的区别,统计历代文献中"曰""言""说"的使用情况,并对统计结果进行分析,陈述三者在使用上逐渐分化的原因。

第二类是句法、语义和语用研究。吴剑锋(2006)着重分析了句类的充分必要标记——言说动词以及其他可选择性标记,并分析了它们在划分句类中的地位和作用。王展(2008)基于菲尔摩(Fillmore)的框架语义学理论,对汉语言说类动词进行了分类研究。徐默凡(2008)根据能否在显性施为句中明示把言说动词分为三类:语义逻辑上不能明示的内隐性言说动词、使用习惯上不能明示的描述性言说动词和能够明示的自指性言说动词。内隐性言说动词不能明示的原因与行事修辞意图有关,是对行事行为真诚规则和本质规则的违反,又可分为欺骗类和转移类。描述性言说动词不能明示的原因和表达修辞意图有关,主要是礼貌意图压倒了明示意图,可分为负面类、无礼类和施惠类。自指性言说动词可明示,在实际使用中的隐显取决于表达修辞意图。马云霞(2010)阐释了修辞动因下言说动词的扩展,认为表示身体行为的动词可以通过隐喻或者转喻引申出言说类语义,进入言说的语义域,体现出具体语义类与抽象语义类之间的系统关联。肖珊(2011)以"词群—词位变体"理论为背景,结合"语义基元结构"理念,建立了较为完整的现代汉语言说动词语义概念系统,并对系统内部语义结构进行了全面的考察和解释。

第三类是个案研究。鞠彩萍(2006)以《祖堂集》谓语动词为平台,从历时和共时角度考察了"言、语、曰、云、说、话、谓、道"八个言说动词的句法和语义特点,指出现代汉语常用词"说"和"道"在以《祖堂集》为代表的唐五代时期发展已趋成熟;在考察言说动词的频率差异时,指出《祖堂集》文献文本属性方面的某些特点;此外还考察了《祖堂集》特色言说动词,指出禅宗典籍中有一类"问"不表示询问义,它们只相当于一般言说动词"曰"或"说"。易丹(2009)针对母语是英语的留学生在对对象类介词"跟、向、对"与言说类动词搭配使用的过程中常见偏误的种类和原因,对对象类介词"跟、向、对"与言说类动词的选择搭配关系进行分析和讨论,找出其选择搭配的一般规律。米婷婷(2011)列举了《生经》中的"言说类词"的成员,如"语""言""曰""说""谓""告""白""启"等,指出它们相互之间的连用情况颇多,并从共时角度出发,采用描写和解释相结合的方法,揭示它们在句法功能和语义色彩等方面的特点,探讨它们的使用规律、频率以及使用环境等。翟雪艳(2013)分析了《国语》中全部言说动词的使用情况,分节重点解析了言说动词"问"和"曰",并与《左传》中相应的言说动词的用法进行了比较。

第四类是虚化、语法化和话语标记研究。刘丹青(2004)认为汉语的"道"已经虚化为一个谓语补足语从句的标记,简称为"标句词"。赵询思(2006)从词汇和句子两个层面说明了言说动词"说"在现代汉语使用中的虚化,揭示出其职能改变但又有保留本身含义,并进一步分析了新句式中其使用及形成的原因。随利芳(2007)指出言说动词"说"和"道"可以与其他动词结合构成"Ⅴ说/Ⅴ道"格式,充当标句词,引出小句宾语。但"说"比"道"在语法化的道路上走得更远,可以置于连词后,与动词的结合面也比"道"广。郑青(2011)对现代汉语和现代日语的言说动词"说"和イウ的语法化过程进行了考察和对比。玄玥(2011)提出位于句首的"说"的用法之一是引导客观叙述的标记词,表明其后内容的非主观性。以往对"说"及其他言说动词的语法化和词汇化等研究中尚未注意到这种语言现象。此外,还有一些学者从方言的角度考察言说动词的语法化,如方梅(2003)以北京口语材料为研究对象,考察言说动词"说"在共时层面的种种变异,以及相关的历时线索,提出在现代汉语北京话中,"说"作为言说动词的语义和功能发生了虚化,产生了新的语法功能——从句标记(subordinator)。从这方面进行撰文的还有王健(2013)、黄映琼(2013)、范一文(2013)等。

对于英语中言说动词的研究材料比较稀缺,笔者能够查阅到的只有何心(2008)列举了一些英语的"言说类"动词,并指出英语的"言说类"动词几乎都以单纯词为主,如 say、speak、tell、talk 等。文章对比了汉英"言说"类动词在构词方式、语义类别、认知模式、文化内涵等方面的异同。还有裴文娟(2010)也涉及了中英言说动词的对比,以及原著中如何使用不同的言说动词来表示说话时具体的细化的方式。

综上所述,我们可以看到,尽管有关言说动词的研究在新时期获得了巨大的发展,但相对来说研究比较零散,缺乏系统性,研究的广度、深度、力度仍有很大的提升空间。

## 第二节 《红楼梦》会话引导语及其英译相关研究

### 一、《红楼梦》会话引导语相关研究

关于《红楼梦》会话研究的成果非常之多,笔者在 CNKI 中国知网"全文"检索模式下输入"《红楼梦》会话/对话",总共搜寻到 9 890 条结果。而当笔者输入"《红楼梦》会话/对话引导语"时,总共搜寻到 88 条结果,且只是初步检索结果,后经过筛选及核查,仅有以下 3 篇学位论文与《红楼梦》的会话引导语相关,但均未对该领域作重点深入的探究。

卢惠惠(2004)的博士论文中有一节关于"单调划一的'引导式'引言句"的内容,以《红楼梦》为例论述了古典白话小说"引导式"引言方式,并把这种现象

称为白话小说与现当代小说最大的风格区别特征之一。黄冠颖（2007）探讨了古典小说中的直接引语的引导语，语料包括唐代传奇《莺莺传》、宋元话本《错斩崔宁》以及《水浒传》《三国演义》《西游记》《儒林外史》《红楼梦》《儿女英雄传》《老残游记》《孽海花》等古典白话小说。作者探讨了引导语的类型、位置、使用与否，对会话引导词的使用频率进行了统计。张蕾（2008）提到了《红楼梦》人物内心独白的引导句式的特色，即不再仅仅局限于"她/他想道"等引导语，出现了自由直接思想引语模式。

冯庆华（2015）不仅对《红楼梦》原文中的引语句（引导语）进行了句频分析，展现了曹雪芹与高鹗之间的差异与各自的风格，还将引语句分成了"笑道"，"哭道"与"泣道"，"叹道"，"骂"与"骂道"，"啐道"及"喝道"等六大类进行研究。此外作者还认识到了不同引导语与人物性别、性格之间的关系。

## 二、《红楼梦》会话引导语英译相关研究

迄今为止，国内外对于《红楼梦》会话引导语英译的研究文章非常稀少，甚至对于中国古典白话小说会话引导语的英译研究材料都非常匮乏。

关于古典白话小说会话引导语的研究，高磊（2009）选用了《三国演义》的罗译本中的会话引导语为案例分析，尝试将韩礼德（M. A. K. Halliday）的"投射理论"应用到中国小说的人物会话翻译中去，同时引用了约翰·奥斯汀（John L. Austin）提出的相关言语行为理论的观点，最终总结出小说会话翻译中引导语翻译的制约性因素，如译者主体性、交换信息、被投射句的功能、言语行为类型等。刘克强（2013）对《水浒传》中的会话引导语"道"进行了分类，并基于自建的《水浒传》汉英平行语料库，利用 ParaConc 检索软件就《水浒传》的四个译本关于"道"的翻译进行对比考察，研究发现沙博理的译文会话引导语最为丰富、多样，赛珍珠的译本最为单调、简单。此外，赛珍珠译文的独特会话引导语也最少，沙博理译文的独特会话引导语则最多。

不得不提的是，杜学敏（2009）选用理雅各、辜鸿铭以及刘殿爵三位翻译家的译本，借助平行语料库对《论语》中"说类词"的翻译进行对比研究，分析三个译本的翻译特点及其所采用的翻译策略，也能为本研究提供些许借鉴和参考。裴文娟（2010）尝试用框架语义学研究小说《哈利·波特与魔法石》中言说动词的英译汉，可以从反方向为我们会话引导语的汉译英研究提供线索和思路。

关于《红楼梦》会话引导语研究，除了冯庆华教授分别于 2012 年和 2015 年出版的两部专著中有专题研究外，目前的研究绝大多数是围绕个别引导语展开的，如"道""笑道"等，对于《红楼梦》会话引导语进行较为全面考察的期刊或论文几乎为零。

冯庆华（2012）在专著《思维模式下的译文词汇》中有一节专门考察人物会

话引导语的内容,为后续的研究提供了翔实的语料和宝贵的思路。冯庆华统计了《红楼梦》人物会话中所有词频在 4 次以上的各类引导语,并将霍译本、杨译本中的引导语与其他 5 个不同的文本(英国小说合集、美国小说合集等,篇幅均与霍译本相当)对比分析,发现霍译与杨译在处理引导语时风格迥异,例如杨译用了很多其他动词或动词词组来处理原文中的"说"和"道",如 asked、told、cried 等,而霍译的替代词无论类别还是次数都比杨译少得多,使用 said 的次数为杨译的 2.7 倍,且这一数据得到了英国小说合集(包括《大卫·科波菲尔》《傲慢与偏见》《简·爱》等 10 部英国小说原著)和美国小说合集(包括《飘》《嘉莉妹妹》《红字》等 5 部美国小说原著)的有力支持;在"笑道"的翻译中,霍译用了更多的 smilingly 这个词语,且大多出现在谓语之前,而杨译更多使用 laughingly,且经常放在谓语之后。冯庆华(2015)在专著《思维模式下的译文句式》中也有关于引语句(会话引导语)翻译的考察,不仅对原文中的引导语进行了句频分析和分类,也对杨译本、霍译本关于引导语处理的独特词句与特色词句进行了对比研究,借助英美小说和英国国家语料库(British National Corpus, BNC)提供数据支持,此外还按照会话引导语的分类对原文与译文进行了对照研究,研究结果表明:杨译尽管语言十分简洁,但是在翻译引语句方面使用了各种各样的动词来取代 said 一词,收到了生动形象的效果,让英美读者能够深刻地理解说话人的情感与语气;而霍译用英语小说传统的表述方式,以 said 为绝对主要词语来进行处理,且不放过原文里字里行间、言里言外的任何细节,既忠实于原文的内容,又最大限度地做到译文的可读性与情节的合理性,这是其母语思维模式的结果,同时也是其交际翻译法的结果。

赵朝永(2014)旨在考察邦斯尔(B. S. Bonsall)《红楼梦》译本的译者风格,在篇章层面有专门关于叙述风格的探讨,通过会话引导语类型与位置的统计与会话引导词"笑道"的叙事方式差异,考察邦译本《红楼梦》在直接引语叙述风格上的风格特点及其与霍、杨译本的差异性。邦译本引导语的翻译基本是"拷贝"了原文的表达方式,译文相对霍、杨译本较为明显的动词显化趋势却呈现出相反的动作意义"隐含化"特点;关于对会话引导词"笑道"的英译模式较为固定,较为严格地模拟了原文章回小说会话引导词"单一化""模式化"的特点,译文风格受到原文风格的较大影响,译文的显化程度相对较低,叙述方式也相对单一。相对而言,霍、杨译本的文学更为灵活多样,无论是小句类型、位置还是叙述方式均倾向于译语的表达习惯,译文的显化程度明显高于邦译文。

刘泽权、闫继苗(2010)对《红楼梦》原文语料库中前五十六回的报道动词(会话引导词)"道"及三个英译本(杨译、霍译和邦译)的翻译进行描述性研究,通过"道"的最频繁报道形式"(某人)道"的翻译,考察三位译者的翻译风格和策略。结果表明,译者对报道动词的选择受报道方式和话语内容等多方面影响,数据统计结果印证了报道动词反映译者风格、翻译策略呈显化趋势的假设。高磊(2013)从标记理论的角度对古典白话小说中典型会话引导语"道"的英译进行了考察和分析,发现其英译对应词带有明显的显化倾向,呈现出标记性特点,并指出语义标记本身所具有的不对称性是导致英译过程中"道"的语义显化的内在成因。

国内学者关于会话引导语"笑道"的英译研究相对较多。在相关的学位论文中,叶常青(2002)通过观察"笑道"在原文中所处的语境,确定说话者"如何""笑道",然后对英译文中对应"笑"和"道"的词所包含的语义成分,判定译者有没有把"笑道"在上下文中的确切含义表达出来,略谈了几个有关翻译原则和翻译批评方法的问题;讨论了重译和翻译批评的问题,认为重译是必要的,除了传统上从文学的角度进行翻译批评之外,还可以利用多种语言学的工具,例如语料库的统计方法,语义学中的语义成分分析,叙述学的原理等多角度多层次地进行。张明晗(2012)以《红楼梦》及其三个英译本(杨译、霍译和邦译)前五十六章的会话引导语"笑道"为语料,以维索尔伦(Verschueren)的语境顺应论为理论,探讨三个译本中"笑道"的译法,通过数量和举例对比来分析三位译者所译的"笑道"能否忠实传达和忠于原著中具体人物的出身、性格、身份、教养、地位和个性等。作者认为杨宪益夫妇全面把握人物的社会地位、性情、人物关系、场合,并积极顺应言语产生时的社交世界、物理世界和心理世界,通过翻译"笑道",准确、鲜明、灵活、形象地再现了原语文化。此外,关于"笑道"研究的期刊论文也较多,其中叶造就(1988)撰写的《〈红楼梦〉中"笑道"英译种种》是笔者目前所能查阅到最早对"笑道"的英译做出分析的学者,此后陆续有其他学者借助语境顺应论、语义学、语料库翻译学等理论,采用定性或定量的方法对"笑道"一词的英译进行了对比和分析,如肖维青(2006)、袁夕娣(2008)、孙雁冰(2008)、胡启好(2009)、张迎海(2009)、曹雪梅和沈映梅(2010)、冯全功(2011)、王三(2012)等。顾晓波(2011)基于自建红楼梦语料库,运用定性分析与定量分析相结合的方法,通过计算机统计手段,细致而深入地探讨杨译本中"冷笑"一词的翻译,借以探求杨译本在"冷笑"翻译方面的特点。研究发现《红楼梦》原文中抽象、模糊、单调的"冷笑"在杨译本中96%都得以译出,且更加具体、清晰、丰富。翁林颖(2014)以《红楼梦》前八十回中凤姐重复和模糊的"忙笑""陪笑"和"冷笑"三种笑态为例,以直译、功能对等的阐释和锦上添花式的增译三种显化英译策略,论证大卫·霍克思采用细节显化翻译原则英译《红楼梦》的体态语。通过霍克思具体清晰地英译三种笑态,得出霍克思采用细节显化翻译原则取决于译者专业汉学家身份、译者翻译目的、《红楼梦》小说本身因素与当时社会历史背景,但未从会话引导语角度进行分析。

上述理论研究也再次印证了本专著研究的意义。首先,迄今为止尚未有关于《红楼梦》原文会话引导语非常全面、系统的分析研究出现,这意味着《红楼梦》会话引导语的英译研究没有一个科学、完善的基础和前提。

其次,从研究内容上讲,《红楼梦》会话引导语英译的相关研究内容绝大多数比较单一,以个别词语为研究对象的居多,即单个会话引导语(主要是"道"和"笑道")的英译研究占很大比例,尚未出现将《红楼梦》一百二十回全部会话引导语以及两部优秀译本均囊括分析的先例。研究呈现出零散、缺乏系统性的特点,广度亟须拓宽。

最后,从研究方法来看,目前定性分析居多,主观性的分析和鉴赏占主流,很少有借助科学统计手段和文本分析工具进行的定量研究,使得研究始终流于表面,难以得出科学的、令人信服的结论,研究深度和细节化有待进一步加强。

# 第二章　《红楼梦》原文会话引导语研究

　　《红楼梦》原文在艺术上取得了辉煌的成就,其博大精深在中国文学史上是罕见的。《红楼梦》最主要的成就之一就在于其丰富、深厚、逼真和自然的语言。人物语言(主要是人物会话,也包括少量的内心独白)在《红楼梦》原文中占据了相当高的比例,而每一段人物会话前都有会话引导语的出现。冯庆华教授在其2012年出版的《思维模式下的译文词汇》中曾做过相关研究,"最主要的 60 个人物的会话与独白文本占全文文本的 35.35%;引导语总词频达到 11 377,平均每一回里都有 95 个引导语"(冯庆华,2012:53)。对《红楼梦》原文中的会话引导语开展分析和研究是我们进行其英译研究的重要基础和根本前提。本章中笔者将着重分析描写《红楼梦》原文中会话引导语的语言特点。

## 第一节　《红楼梦》原文会话引导语与非引导语对比研究

　　为了凸显《红楼梦》原文会话引导语的特色,笔者首先采取将其中的会话引导语内容与非会话引导语内容作对比研究。会话引导语内容的筛选是基于笔者自行创建的"《红楼梦》汉英双语平行语料库",格式为"中文—霍译本—杨译本",该语料库的文本依据是上海外语教育出版社 2012 年出版发行的汉英对照版《红楼梦》。关于该汉英对照本的版本问题,前文已作说明,此处不再赘述。

### 一、《红楼梦》会话引导语语料的提取

　　笔者自行创建了"《红楼梦》汉英双语平行语料库",具体的创建方法为:首先,以霍译本的句子为划分单位,按照霍译本的英文句子来拆分对应的中文原文内容;其次,在中文内容与霍译本句子对应的基础上进一步将会话引导语和人物会话分开;最后,按照"中文—霍译本"语料库切分好的中文格式将杨译文一一对照进去,舍弃杨译本比霍译本多余的内容。

　　创建后的语料库格式如表 2-1 所示:

表 2－1 《红楼梦》汉英双语平行语料库样表

| 原文 | 霍译 | 杨译 | 章回 |
|---|---|---|---|
| 第四十一回 | Chapter 41 | Chapter 41 | 第四十一回 |
| 贾宝玉品茶栊翠庵 | Jia Bao-yu tastes some superior tea at Green Bower Hermitage | Baoyu Sips Tea in Green Lattice Nunnery | 第四十一回 |
| 刘老老醉卧怡红院 | And Grannie Liu samples the sleeping accommodation at Green Delights | Granny Liu Succumbs to Wine in Happy Red Court | 第四十一回 |
| 话说刘老老两只手比着说道：// "花儿落了结个大倭瓜。" | 'This flower will to a pumpkin grow.' // As Grannie Liu of the flower-studded hair said this, gesturing with her hands to suggest the size of the full-grown pumpkin， | Granny Liu's gestures and response，// "A huge pumpkin forms when the flowers fall，" | 第四十一回 |
| 众人听了,哄堂大笑起来。 | a shout of laughter rose from all those present. | caused a fresh glee of mirth. | 第四十一回 |
| 于是吃过门杯, | She drank the 'pass' cup. | After tossing off the cup of wine， | 第四十一回 |
| 因又斗趣,笑道：// "今儿实说罢,我的手脚子粗,又喝了酒,仔细失手打了这磁杯; | 'To be truthful,' she said, aiming for another laugh, 'I'm but a clumsy body at the best of times, and having drunk so much, I'm scared of breaking this pretty cup you've given me. | in the hope of wine，in the hope of raising another laugh she observed：// "To tell the truth，I'm clumsy. And now that I'm tipsy, unless I'm very careful，I may smash this porcelain cup. | 第四十一回 |
| 有木头的杯取个来, | You should have given me a wooden one； | If you'd given me a wooden one | 第四十一回 |
| 我就失了手,掉了地下,也无碍。" | then if I dropped it，it wouldn't matter.' | it wouldn't matter even if I dropped it." | 第四十一回 |
| 众人听了又笑起来。 | The others laughed； | Once more everybody laughed. | 第四十一回 |
| 凤姐儿听如此说,便忙笑道：// "果真要木头的,我就取了来, | but Xi-feng pretended to take her seriously：// 'If you really want a wooden cup to drink out of, I can find you one. | "If you really prefer wooden cups I'll fetch some," offered Xifeng. | 第四十一回 |

（续表）

| 原文 | 霍译 | 杨译 | 章回 |
|------|------|------|------|
| ——可有一句话先说下: | But I'd better warn you. | "But first I must warn you | 第四十一回 |
| 这木头的可比不得磁的, | The wooden ones aren't like these porcelain ones; | that the wooden cups aren't like porcelain ones; | 第四十一回 |
| 那都是一套,定要吃遍一套才算呢。" | they come in sets of different sizes, and if we get them out for you, you'll have to drink out of every one in the set.' | they come in a set, and you must drink from every cup in the set." | 第四十一回 |
| 刘老老听了,心下战敠道: // "我方才不过是趣话取笑儿, | Granule Liu calculated. // 'I was only joking,' she thought. | The old woman thought: // I was only trying to raise a laugh, | 第四十一回 |
| 谁知他果真竟有, | 'I didn't think they'd really have any. | but it seems they really do have them. | 第四十一回 |
| 我时常在乡绅大家也赴过席,金杯银杯倒都也见过,从没见有木头杯的。 | When I've dined with the gentry back home, I've seen many a gold and silver cup in their houses, but never a wooden one. | When I've dined with the village gentry I've seen plenty of gold and silver cups, never any made of wood. | 第四十一回 |

　　基于"《红楼梦》汉英双语平行语料库"筛选出会话引导语主要历经如下几个步骤:

　　(1)确定会话引导语的范围:本研究围绕"会话引导语"(conversation introducer)展开,研究的核心内容决定了引导语的筛选必须以"引出实际发声行为以及具体言辞表述,旨在开展和维系人与人之间的会话及交流的语言成分"为标准。因此,笔者列入考察范围的引导语必须满足如下几个条件:第一,引导语的主语必须是人物,动物(如鹦鹉)的发声行为不在研究之列;第二,引导的内容必须是经口头表达的,描写的或落笔的内容不在研究之列;第三,口头表达必须有会话的对象,而非单纯的吟哦或念诵。有一点需要说明的是,人物的内心独白也被列入笔的考察范围,因为内心独白可以看作自己与自己的会话,且同时满足以上几个必要条件。

　　(2)在明确了遴选标准后,笔者首先在"《红楼梦》汉英双语平行语料库"中筛选出所有带":"的表格,在此基础上进行如下筛除:第一,引导内容明显是书面体的引导语,如"写道:""联道:""曰:""云:""正是:"等;第二,引导内容为陈述某种常识或事实、本质实为插入语、起提醒作用的引导语,如"知道:""看官:"等;第三,引导内容并非以会话为目的的引导语,如"念道:""唱道:""吟道:"等。

(3)在按照相对统一的标准进行初步遴选后,笔者又将剩余的内容逐条筛选分析,将其余的非会话引导语内容剔除出去,这些内容多无特定格式,表达方式非常自由,只能采取人工一一筛选的方式,这些内容如:

- 也有立在桌上拍着手乱笑、喝着声儿叫打的:
- 黛玉感戴不尽,以后便亦如宝钗之称呼,连宝钗前亦直以"姐姐"呼之,宝琴前直以"妹妹"呼之:
- 又常对着跟他的小厮们说:
- 后来听得里面女儿们拿他取笑:
- 看官听说:
- 又改题:
- 所叹者:
- 那鹦哥又飞上架去,便叫:
- 薛姨妈笑着应了。于是凤姐放下四双筯:
- 因此吩咐了他老子连摆三日酒:
- 宝玉听了,又喜,又气,又叹:
- 那都是傻想头:
- 又注着:
- 亦长在宁荣二府走动惯熟,都给他起了个混号,唤他做"王一贴":
- 独喜得时上什么辛金为贵,什么巳中"正官""禄马"独旺:
- 第一件:
- 第三件:

(4)在多次反复确认核对后,笔者初步得到了《红楼梦》会话引导语语料的A版本,该版本是原文—霍译本—杨译本对照的双语版本。

(5)将A版本中的原文内容单独列出,并进行简化和核心内容提取,原则上只保留同一个句子单位里面与会话引导核心动词直接相关的内容。按照此方法最终遴选出精简版的《红楼梦》原文会话引导语内容(简称B版本)。

在此需要说明的是:与A版本不同,B版本仅仅包含《红楼梦》原文中精简会话引导语的内容,而无霍译本和杨译本的英文部分。B版本中总共有11 633个条目,总字数为99 252。《红楼梦》原文总字数为856 637,会话引导语的内容为全文内容的11.6%。本章中进行的所有数据统计分析均是以B版本为基础和对象。

## 二、《红楼梦》会话引导语高频字、搭配研究

字频是汉字的出现频率,指某个汉字在一定语料中使用或出现的次数与样本总字数的比率。基于某种语料库,利用一定手段分别统计每个字在某特定的语料库中使用或出现的频次,频次居于前列的就是高频字。高频字可以展示该文本用字的偏好和倾向性,对于我们研究作品和作者的语言风格、语体特点有非常重大的意义。本章将统计《红楼梦》原文中的一字符字频到五字符字频,然后挑选典型的、具有代表性的高频字进行研究。

(一)《红楼梦》会话引导语高频字研究

笔者先对《红楼梦》会话引导语进行字频方面的研究,从一字符字频到五字符字频不等。在开展具体研究之前,有几个问题需要说明:

(1)研究是以"字符"为统计单位,除了汉字之外,":""""",等标点符号也包含在内,因为标点符号也有重要的研究意义,尤其是":"作为会话的重要标识,对于会话引导语的研究至关重要。

(2)为了精确起见,笔者还把单纯的汉字(如"道")和"汉字+:"(如"道:")分别做统计和处理,因为"道"的出现未必一定是作为会话引导语,有可能是"道人"等名词中的用字,而"道:"就一定是会话引导语的形式,"笑道""笑说""便问"等形式也是同样情况。

(3)厘清"语义搭配"(semantic collocation)与"自然搭配"(natural collocation)的概念:"语义搭配"的出发点是"语义",指字符与字符之间存在一定的语法关系,搭配具有逻辑性,且搭配后的词语能够清晰地表达特定的意义。而"自然搭配"的出发点是"形式",字符与字符之间因为存在某种位置上的关系而组合搭配在一起,但不保证这种搭配具有逻辑性或产生特定的意义。因此"自然搭配"包括"语义搭配"和"非语义搭配"(non-semantic collocation)。以"道"前面的字符搭配为例,"笑道""说道"等搭配符合逻辑、具有特定含义,属于语义搭配;而"玉道""母道"等搭配的形成仅仅是因为原文中出现了"宝玉道""贾母道",因此属于被机械地截取出的二字搭配,本身无实际语义,必须借助其他结构成分才能表达意义,因此应属于"自然搭配"中的"非语义搭配"范畴。本章列举的所有一字符以上的搭配均选取语义搭配,特此说明。

**1. 一字符字频**

一字字符出现次数在 2 次以上的有 1399 个。限于篇幅,在此只列举字频位于前 50 位的字符。

| | | | |
|---|---|---|---|
| :(11 634) | 说(3112) | 玉(2217) | 贾(1918) |
| 道(9116) | 笑(2958) | 宝(2099) | 人(1857) |

| | | | |
|---|---|---|---|
| 了（1692） | 见（862） | 袭（510） | 薛（343） |
| 便（1260） | 凤（840） | 王（504） | 里（338） |
| 一（1205） | 母（783） | 不（481） | 上（335） |
| 来（1150） | 忙（753） | 钗（477） | 平（324） |
| 又（990） | 因（689） | 那（468） | 都（322） |
| 的（974） | 黛（587） | 政（406） | 个（321） |
| 儿（972） | 他（567） | 众（390） | 琏（312） |
| 姐（936） | 头（566） | 子（384） | 起（303） |
| 问（900） | 只（550） | 老（375） | 在（303） |
| 听（882） | 回（538） | 想（374） | |
| 着（881） | 夫（513） | 春（369） | |

**2. 二字符字频**

《红楼梦》会话引导语二字符的自然搭配出现次数在 2 次以上的多达 5996 个。限于篇幅，在此仅列举字频位于前 50 位的语义搭配。

| | | | |
|---|---|---|---|
| 道：（9008） | 众人（342） | 说着（182） | 又说（124） |
| 笑道（2399） | 贾琏（312） | 鸳鸯（163） | 出来（115） |
| 宝玉（1540） | 平儿（312） | 一个（152） | 冷笑（115） |
| 说：（1491） | 问道（300） | 便问（146） | 便道（110） |
| 说道（960） | 便说（261） | 笑说（145） | 听说（108） |
| 凤姐（826） | 只见（233） | 尤氏（145） | 麝月（107） |
| 贾母（740） | 探春（226） | 因说（141） | 听见（105） |
| 黛玉（586） | 湘云（218） | 起来（139） | 又道（99） |
| 袭人（510） | 丫头（211） | 因问（139） | 薛蟠（98） |
| 宝钗（477） | 一面（200） | 晴雯（129） | 回说（95） |
| 听了（468） | 紫鹃（185） | 婆子（128） | 点头（91） |
| 贾政（406） | 李纨（184） | 回道（125） | |
| 问：（352） | 进来（183） | 贾珍（125） | |

**3. 三字符字频**

《红楼梦》会话引导语三字符的自然搭配出现次数在 2 次以上的多达 7235 个。限于篇幅，在此仅列举字频位于前 50 位的语义搭配。

| | | | |
|---|---|---|---|
| 笑道：（2399） | 说道：（960） | 宝玉道（478） | 王夫人（394） |

| | | | |
|---|---|---|---|
| 问道：(300) | 回道：(125) | 便说道(92) | 袭人笑(71) |
| 宝玉笑(250) | 贾母笑(120) | 回说：(92) | 李纨道(68) |
| 凤姐儿(223) | 便道：(109) | 邢夫人(84) | 想道：(68) |
| 薛姨妈(204) | 小丫头(109) | 忙道：(81) | 鸳鸯道(66) |
| 贾母道(195) | 贾琏道(107) | 又说：(79) | 便问：(64) |
| 凤姐道(178) | 宝钗笑(106) | 平儿道(78) | 忙笑道(63) |
| 袭人道(177) | 冷笑道(105) | 叹道：(77) | 因笑道(63) |
| 黛玉道(175) | 又道：(99) | 因说道(77) | 因说：(61) |
| 贾政道(171) | 宝玉听(98) | 因问：(75) | 正说着(61) |
| 便说：(161) | 凤姐笑(97) | 来说：(74) | 探春道(60) |
| 刘老老(149) | 笑说：(96) | 湘云道(74) | |
| 宝钗道(135) | 黛玉笑(95) | 众人道(73) | |

**4. 四字符字频**

　　《红楼梦》会话引导语四字符的自然搭配出现次数在 2 次以上的多达 5423 个。限于篇幅,在此仅列举字频位于前 50 位的语义搭配。

| | | |
|---|---|---|
| 宝玉道：(478) | 平儿道：(78) | 便笑道：(50) |
| 宝玉笑道(231) | 因说道：(77) | 笑说道：(49) |
| 贾母道：(194) | 湘云道：(74) | 刘老老道(48) |
| 凤姐道：(178) | 众人道：(72) | 凤姐儿笑(47) |
| 袭人道：(176) | 宝玉听了(70) | 平儿笑道(47) |
| 黛玉道：(175) | 李纨道：(68) | 贾珍道：(46) |
| 贾政道：(171) | 袭人笑道(68) | 湘云笑道(46) |
| 王夫人道(136) | 鸳鸯道：(66) | 又笑道：(44) |
| 宝钗道：(135) | 忙笑道：(63) | 尤氏道：(42) |
| 贾琏道：(107) | 因笑道：(63) | 晴雯道：(41) |
| 贾母笑道(105) | 薛姨妈道(62) | 麝月道：(41) |
| 冷笑道：(105) | 探春道：(60) | 陪笑道：(39) |
| 宝钗笑道(101) | 都笑道：(52) | 听了这话(38) |
| 便说道：(92) | 凤姐儿道(52) | 想了一想(38) |
| 凤姐笑道(92) | 紫鹃道：(52) | 笑问道：(38) |
| 黛玉笑道(84) | 探春笑道(51) | 众人都道(37) |
| 周瑞家的(83) | 便问道：(50) | |

**5. 五字符字频**

《红楼梦》会话引导语五字符的自然搭配出现次数在 2 次以上的多达 3024 个。限于篇幅,在此仅列举字频位于前 50 位的语义搭配。

宝玉笑道:(231)　　薛姨妈笑道(27)　　麝月笑道:(15)
王夫人道:(136)　　众人笑道:(27)　　宝琴笑道:(14)
贾母笑道:(105)　　贾琏笑道:(26)　　宝玉忙道:(14)
宝钗笑道:(101)　　尤氏笑道:(26)　　众人都说:(14)
凤姐笑道:(92)　　冯紫英道:(25)　　宝玉又道:(13)
黛玉笑道:(84)　　贾政笑道:(25)　　点头叹道:(13)
袭人笑道:(68)　　王夫人听了(24)　　点头笑道:(13)
薛姨妈道:(62)　　周瑞家的道(24)　　刘老老笑道(13)
凤姐儿道:(52)　　紫鹃笑道:(21)　　王善保家的(13)
探春笑道:(51)　　王夫人笑道(20)　　心里想道:(13)
刘老老道:(48)　　听了笑道:(19)　　众人都笑道(13)
平儿笑道:(47)　　向宝玉道:(18)　　贾母便说:(12)
凤姐儿笑道(46)　　邢夫人道:(18)　　陪笑说道:(12)
湘云笑道:(46)　　拍手笑道:(17)　　贾母便问:(11)
众人都道:(37)　　晴雯笑道:(17)　　那丫头道:(11)
林之孝家的(34)　　一个小丫头(16)　　悄悄的笑道(11)
李纨笑道:(33)　　鸳鸯笑道:(15)

通过以上列举的《红楼梦》原文会话引导语文本中一字符到五字符的前 50 位语义搭配,我们不仅可以看到各种会话引导词的使用情况,也可以根据主语清晰地判断出会话的几个主要人物。

在会话引导词方面,"道:"的使用次数最多,有 9008 次(包含"笑道:""说道:"等);其次是"笑道:"(含"冷笑道:"等)2399 次、"说道:"960 次、"问道:"300 次。我们还应该发现"笑道"和"笑道:"及"说道"和"说道:"的检索数量分别完全一致,而"道"和"道:"的数量则相差 108 个,再次证明了我们将检索单位精确到字符的必要性。

如将作主语的人物进行分析,则"宝玉道:"数量最多,有 478 次;其次是"宝玉笑道:"(231 次)、"贾母道:"(194 次)、"凤姐道:"(178 次)、"袭人道:"(176 次)、"黛玉道:"(175 次)、"贾政道:"(171 次),等等。这些统计数据对于我们分析人物话语权、考察会话引导语对于人物角色的塑造等具有非常重要的意义。

以上是针对《红楼梦》原文会话引导语文本整体进行的字频统计。下面将以":"为核心和立足点,对":"左侧的语义搭配字符进行研究。

### (二)《红楼梦》会话引导语搭配研究

本书使用 PowerConc 软件对会话引导语(精简版)进行检索,检索内容是":"前的一字符至五字符的语义搭配。

#### 1. 一字符搭配

":"左侧的一字搭配字符出现次数在 2 次以上的有 75 个,其中字频在 10 次以上的有 20 个:

| | | | |
|---|---|---|---|
| 道(9008) | 他(64) | 儿(25) | 玉(18) |
| 说(1491) | 命(46) | 着(22) | 起(16) |
| 问(352) | 人(40) | 们(20) | 报(13) |
| 想(70) | 回(37) | 来(19) | 声(11) |
| 叫(69) | 是(27) | 咐(18) | 骂(10) |

#### 2. 二字符搭配

":"左侧的二字搭配字符出现次数在 2 次以上的,自然搭配有 420 个,语义搭配有 183 个,其中字频在 10 次以上的有 47 个:

| | | | |
|---|---|---|---|
| 笑道(2399) | 因问(75) | 又问(41) | 喝道(15) |
| 说道(960) | 想道(68) | 叫道(36) | 想着(15) |
| 问道(300) | 便问(64) | 啐道(35) | 吩咐(14) |
| 便说(161) | 因说(61) | 问他(34) | 还说(14) |
| 回道(125) | 忙问(53) | 答道(31) | 笑问(14) |
| 便道(109) | 都说(52) | 嚷道(24) | 便命(11) |
| 又道(99) | 都道(51) | 说是(21) | 急道(11) |
| 笑说(96) | 哭道(50) | 应道(21) | 平儿(11) |
| 回说(92) | 只说(49) | 人回(20) | 因道(11) |
| 忙道(81) | 骂道(48) | 心想(18) | 又叫(11) |
| 又说(79) | 劝道(48) | 一想(18) | 便叫(10) |
| 叹道(77) | 忙说(41) | 宝玉(16) | |

#### 3. 三字符搭配

":"左侧的三字搭配字符出现次数在 2 次以上的,自然搭配有 913 个,语义搭配有 392 个,其中字频在 10 次以上的有 86 个:

宝玉道(478)  陪笑道(39)  翠缕道(15)
贾母道(194)  来说道(38)  答应道(15)
凤姐道(178)  笑问道(38)  宝蟾道(14)
袭人道(176)  薛蟠道(35)  忙说道(14)
黛玉道(175)  惜春道(34)  秋纹道(14)
贾政道(171)  又说道(32)  笑着道(14)
宝钗道(135)  婆子道(31)  吩咐道(13)
贾琏道(107)  也笑道(31)  贾环道(13)
冷笑道(105)  点头道(29)  起来道(13)
便说道(92)   丫头道(29)  代儒道(12)
平儿道(78)   焙茗道(25)  贾母说(12)
因说道(77)   妙玉道(24)  贾赦道(12)
湘云道(74)   贾芸道(23)  接口道(12)
众人道(72)   那人道(23)  忙劝道(12)
李纨道(68)   雪雁道(22)  笑回道(12)
鸳鸯道(66)   因问道(21)  包勇道(11)
忙笑道(63)   又问道(20)  宝玉说(11)
因笑道(63)   都笑说(19)  贾蔷道(11)
探春道(60)   贾蓉道(19)  拍手道(11)
都笑道(52)   进来说(19)  微笑道(11)
紫鹃道(52)   听了道(19)  先笑道(11)
便问道(50)   香菱道(19)  小厮道(11)
便笑道(50)   湘莲道(19)  贾瑞道(10)
笑说道(49)   雨村道(18)  来问道(10)
贾珍道(46)   忙问道(17)  强笑道(10)
又笑道(44)   小红道(17)  薛蝌道(10)
尤氏道(42)   莺儿道(17)  迎春道(10)
晴雯道(41)   咤异道(17)  有的说(10)
麝月道(41)   金桂道(16)

### 4. 四字符搭配

":"左侧的四字搭配字符出现次数在 2 次以上的,自然搭配有 930 个,语义搭配有 471 个,其中字频在 10 次以上的有 47 个:

宝玉笑道(231)　　　王夫人道(136)　　　贾母笑道(105)

| | | |
|---|---|---|
| 宝钗笑道（101） | 冯紫英道（25） | 点头笑道（13） |
| 凤姐笑道（92） | 贾政笑道（25） | 心里想道（13） |
| 黛玉笑道（84） | 紫鹃笑道（21） | 贾母便说（12） |
| 袭人笑道（68） | 听了笑道（19） | 陪笑说道（12） |
| 薛姨妈道（62） | 向宝玉道（18） | 贾母便问（11） |
| 凤姐儿道（52） | 邢夫人道（18） | 那丫头道（11） |
| 探春笑道（51） | 拍手笑道（17） | 香菱笑道（11） |
| 刘老老道（48） | 晴雯笑道（17） | 一面笑道（11） |
| 平儿笑道（47） | 鸳鸯笑道（15） | 贾珍笑道（10） |
| 湘云笑道（46） | 麝月笑道（15） | 进来回道（10） |
| 众人都道（37） | 宝琴笑道（14） | 进来回说（10） |
| 李纨笑道（33） | 宝玉忙道（14） | 小丫头道（10） |
| 众人笑道（27） | 众人都说（14） | 笑着说道（10） |
| 贾琏笑道（26） | 宝玉又道（13） | 一面说道（10） |
| 尤氏笑道（26） | 点头叹道（13） | |

### 5. 五字符搭配

"："左侧的五字搭配字符出现次数在 2 次以上的，自然搭配有 494 个，语义搭配有 220 个，其中字频在 10 次以上的只有 7 个：

| | | |
|---|---|---|
| 凤姐儿笑道（46） | 王夫人笑道（20） | 悄悄的笑道（11） |
| 薛姨妈笑道（27） | 刘老老笑道（13） | |
| 周瑞家的道（24） | 众人都笑道（13） | |

现将《红楼梦》会话引导语文本中"："左侧的从一字符到五字符、出现次数在 2 次以上的语义搭配统计列表如下（见表 2-2）。

表 2-2 《红楼梦》会话引导语"："左侧语义搭配统计

| 类别 | 数量 | 百分比 |
|---|---|---|
| 一字符搭配 | 75 | 5.59 |
| 二字符搭配 | 183 | 13.65 |
| 三字符搭配 | 392 | 29.23 |
| 四字符搭配 | 471 | 35.12 |
| 五字符搭配 | 220 | 16.41 |
| 合计 | 1341 | 100.00 |

经列举对比后我们可以看到,《红楼梦》会话引导语文本中":"左侧的四字符语义搭配数量最多,占到了总搭配的 1/3 以上;其次是三字符、五字符、二字符语义搭配;一字符语义搭配数量最少,仅有总搭配的 5.59%。

### 三、《红楼梦》会话引导语与非引导语字频对比研究

通过对精简版的《红楼梦》原文会话引导语文本的字频进行统计,得出字频在前 100 位的汉字,同时列出这 100 个汉字在《红楼梦》原文总文本的字频以及非引导语中的字频,以供对比研究(见表 2 - 3)。

表 2 - 3　会话引导语字频前 100 位汉字及其在非引导语及全文中的字频统计

| 排序 | 汉字 | 引导语字频 | 百分比 | 非引导语字频 | 百分比 | 原文总字频 | 百分比 |
|---|---|---|---|---|---|---|---|
| 1 | 道 | 9116 | 9.185 | 1976 | 0.261 | 11 092 | 1.293 |
| 2 | 说 | 3112 | 3.136 | 6475 | 0.855 | 9587 | 1.117 |
| 3 | 笑 | 2958 | 2.98 | 955 | 0.126 | 3913 | 0.456 |
| 4 | 玉 | 2217 | 2.234 | 3759 | 0.496 | 5976 | 0.696 |
| 5 | 宝 | 2099 | 2.115 | 3704 | 0.489 | 5803 | 0.676 |
| 6 | 贾 | 1918 | 1.933 | 3243 | 0.428 | 5161 | 0.601 |
| 7 | 人 | 1857 | 1.871 | 8481 | 1.120 | 10 338 | 1.205 |
| 8 | 了 | 1692 | 1.705 | 19 396 | 2.561 | 21 088 | 2.458 |
| 9 | 便 | 1260 | 1.27 | 2428 | 0.321 | 3688 | 0.43 |
| 10 | 一 | 1205 | 1.214 | 10 469 | 1.382 | 11 674 | 1.361 |
| 11 | 来 | 1150 | 1.159 | 10 071 | 1.330 | 11 221 | 1.308 |
| 12 | 又 | 990 | 0.998 | 4098 | 0.541 | 5088 | 0.593 |
| 13 | 的 | 974 | 0.981 | 14 634 | 1.932 | 15 608 | 1.819 |
| 14 | 儿 | 972 | 0.979 | 5979 | 0.789 | 6951 | 0.81 |
| 15 | 姐 | 936 | 0.943 | 2635 | 0.348 | 3571 | 0.416 |
| 16 | 问 | 900 | 0.907 | 1077 | 0.142 | 1977 | 0.23 |
| 17 | 听 | 882 | 0.889 | 2351 | 0.310 | 3233 | 0.377 |
| 18 | 着 | 881 | 0.888 | 5697 | 0.752 | 6578 | 0.767 |
| 19 | 见 | 862 | 0.869 | 3927 | 0.518 | 4789 | 0.558 |
| 20 | 凤 | 840 | 0.846 | 1123 | 0.148 | 1963 | 0.229 |

| 排序 | 汉字 | 引导语字频 | 百分比 | 非引导语字频 | 百分比 | 原文总字频 | 百分比 |
|------|------|------------|--------|--------------|--------|------------|--------|
| 21 | 母 | 783 | 0.789 | 1393 | 0.184 | 2176 | 0.254 |
| 22 | 忙 | 753 | 0.759 | 1015 | 0.134 | 1768 | 0.206 |
| 23 | 因 | 689 | 0.694 | 1185 | 0.156 | 1874 | 0.218 |
| 24 | 黛 | 587 | 0.591 | 784 | 0.104 | 1371 | 0.16 |
| 25 | 他 | 567 | 0.571 | 6945 | 0.917 | 7512 | 0.875 |
| 26 | 头 | 566 | 0.57 | 2932 | 0.387 | 3498 | 0.408 |
| 27 | 只 | 550 | 0.554 | 4041 | 0.534 | 4591 | 0.535 |
| 28 | 回 | 538 | 0.542 | 2513 | 0.332 | 3051 | 0.356 |
| 29 | 夫 | 513 | 0.517 | 1244 | 0.164 | 1757 | 0.205 |
| 30 | 袭 | 510 | 0.514 | 688 | 0.091 | 1198 | 0.14 |
| 31 | 王 | 504 | 0.508 | 1137 | 0.150 | 1641 | 0.191 |
| 32 | 不 | 481 | 0.485 | 14 005 | 1.849 | 14 486 | 1.688 |
| 33 | 钗 | 477 | 0.481 | 630 | 0.083 | 1107 | 0.129 |
| 34 | 那 | 468 | 0.472 | 4468 | 0.590 | 4936 | 0.575 |
| 35 | 政 | 406 | 0.409 | 569 | 0.075 | 975 | 0.114 |
| 36 | 众 | 390 | 0.393 | 787 | 0.104 | 1177 | 0.137 |
| 37 | 子 | 384 | 0.387 | 5033 | 0.665 | 5417 | 0.631 |
| 38 | 老 | 375 | 0.378 | 2860 | 0.378 | 3235 | 0.377 |
| 39 | 想 | 374 | 0.377 | 1420 | 0.187 | 1794 | 0.209 |
| 40 | 春 | 369 | 0.372 | 639 | 0.084 | 1008 | 0.117 |
| 41 | 薛 | 343 | 0.346 | 615 | 0.081 | 958 | 0.112 |
| 42 | 里 | 338 | 0.341 | 4983 | 0.658 | 5321 | 0.62 |
| 43 | 上 | 335 | 0.338 | 3458 | 0.457 | 3793 | 0.442 |
| 44 | 平 | 324 | 0.326 | 585 | 0.077 | 909 | 0.106 |
| 45 | 都 | 322 | 0.324 | 2350 | 0.310 | 2672 | 0.311 |
| 46 | 个 | 321 | 0.323 | 5283 | 0.698 | 5604 | 0.653 |
| 47 | 琏 | 312 | 0.314 | 571 | 0.075 | 883 | 0.103 |
| 48 | 起 | 303 | 0.305 | 2184 | 0.288 | 2487 | 0.29 |

（续表）

| 排序 | 汉字 | 引导语字频 | 百分比 | 非引导语字频 | 百分比 | 原文总字频 | 百分比 |
|---|---|---|---|---|---|---|---|
| 49 | 在 | 303 | 0.305 | 3608 | 0.476 | 3911 | 0.456 |
| 50 | 向 | 298 | 0.3 | 290 | 0.038 | 588 | 0.069 |
| 51 | 面 | 286 | 0.288 | 1457 | 0.192 | 1743 | 0.203 |
| 52 | 家 | 282 | 0.284 | 3583 | 0.473 | 3865 | 0.45 |
| 53 | 也 | 280 | 0.282 | 5779 | 0.763 | 6059 | 0.706 |
| 54 | 这 | 273 | 0.275 | 7381 | 0.975 | 7654 | 0.892 |
| 55 | 叫 | 271 | 0.273 | 2169 | 0.286 | 2440 | 0.284 |
| 56 | 李 | 271 | 0.273 | 404 | 0.053 | 675 | 0.079 |
| 57 | 湘 | 261 | 0.263 | 340 | 0.045 | 601 | 0.07 |
| 58 | 心 | 261 | 0.263 | 2340 | 0.309 | 2601 | 0.303 |
| 59 | 小 | 258 | 0.26 | 1745 | 0.230 | 2003 | 0.233 |
| 60 | 姨 | 254 | 0.256 | 683 | 0.090 | 937 | 0.109 |
| 61 | 话 | 251 | 0.253 | 2202 | 0.291 | 2453 | 0.286 |
| 62 | 进 | 246 | 0.248 | 1296 | 0.171 | 1542 | 0.18 |
| 63 | 丫 | 245 | 0.247 | 978 | 0.129 | 1223 | 0.143 |
| 64 | 云 | 240 | 0.242 | 443 | 0.058 | 683 | 0.08 |
| 65 | 看 | 236 | 0.238 | 2144 | 0.283 | 2380 | 0.277 |
| 66 | 紫 | 232 | 0.234 | 331 | 0.044 | 563 | 0.066 |
| 67 | 探 | 230 | 0.232 | 283 | 0.037 | 513 | 0.06 |
| 68 | 妈 | 227 | 0.229 | 801 | 0.106 | 1028 | 0.12 |
| 69 | 下 | 227 | 0.229 | 2501 | 0.330 | 2728 | 0.318 |
| 70 | 正 | 225 | 0.227 | 1154 | 0.152 | 1379 | 0.161 |
| 71 | 出 | 217 | 0.219 | 2936 | 0.388 | 3153 | 0.367 |
| 72 | 是 | 217 | 0.219 | 9711 | 1.282 | 9928 | 1.157 |
| 73 | 手 | 209 | 0.211 | 801 | 0.106 | 1010 | 0.118 |
| 74 | 得 | 204 | 0.206 | 3102 | 0.410 | 3306 | 0.385 |
| 75 | 去 | 191 | 0.192 | 5822 | 0.769 | 6013 | 0.701 |
| 76 | 走 | 190 | 0.191 | 1047 | 0.138 | 1237 | 0.144 |

| 排序 | 汉字 | 引导语字频 | 百分比 | 非引导语字频 | 百分比 | 原文总字频 | 百分比 |
|------|------|------------|--------|--------------|--------|------------|--------|
| 77 | 大 | 189 | 0.19 | 3208 | 0.424 | 3397 | 0.396 |
| 78 | 悄 | 188 | 0.189 | 236 | 0.031 | 424 | 0.049 |
| 79 | 鹃 | 185 | 0.186 | 260 | 0.034 | 445 | 0.052 |
| 80 | 纨 | 184 | 0.185 | 201 | 0.027 | 385 | 0.045 |
| 81 | 氏 | 180 | 0.181 | 309 | 0.041 | 489 | 0.057 |
| 82 | 有 | 180 | 0.181 | 5633 | 0.744 | 5813 | 0.677 |
| 83 | 等 | 173 | 0.174 | 1674 | 0.221 | 1847 | 0.215 |
| 84 | 时 | 172 | 0.173 | 1927 | 0.254 | 2099 | 0.245 |
| 85 | 尤 | 172 | 0.173 | 283 | 0.037 | 455 | 0.053 |
| 86 | 莺 | 165 | 0.166 | 258 | 0.034 | 423 | 0.049 |
| 87 | 二 | 164 | 0.165 | 2428 | 0.321 | 2592 | 0.302 |
| 88 | 鸳 | 164 | 0.165 | 266 | 0.035 | 430 | 0.05 |
| 89 | 口 | 163 | 0.164 | 581 | 0.077 | 744 | 0.087 |
| 90 | 自 | 163 | 0.164 | 2201 | 0.291 | 2364 | 0.276 |
| 91 | 身 | 160 | 0.161 | 950 | 0.125 | 1110 | 0.129 |
| 92 | 婆 | 157 | 0.158 | 434 | 0.057 | 591 | 0.069 |
| 93 | 刘 | 151 | 0.152 | 157 | 0.021 | 308 | 0.036 |
| 94 | 命 | 149 | 0.15 | 798 | 0.105 | 947 | 0.11 |
| 95 | 到 | 148 | 0.149 | 2152 | 0.284 | 2300 | 0.268 |
| 96 | 过 | 145 | 0.146 | 2385 | 0.315 | 2530 | 0.295 |
| 97 | 两 | 138 | 0.139 | 2058 | 0.272 | 2196 | 0.256 |
| 98 | 门 | 137 | 0.138 | 1101 | 0.145 | 1238 | 0.144 |
| 99 | 声 | 136 | 0.137 | 602 | 0.079 | 738 | 0.086 |
| 100 | 忽 | 135 | 0.136 | 287 | 0.038 | 422 | 0.049 |

　　在上述会话引导语字频与中文原文总字频以及非引导语字频对比的表格中我们可以看到，会话引导语文本中字频位于前列的字在与非引导语文本的对比中依旧存在优势。现选取前10名做一下对比（见图2-1）。

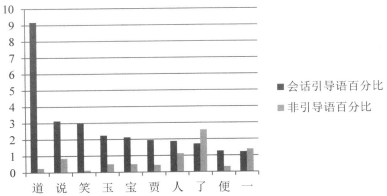

图 2 - 1 《红楼梦》会话引导字频前 10 位汉字及其在非引导语中的字频统计

"道"字在会话引导语中出现的频率非常高,有 9116 个,占会话引导语总容量的 9.185%,而在原文总文本中只占 1.293%,非引导语中更是仅占 0.261%。可以说,"道"字在会话引导语中占了绝对优势,是非引导语的 35 倍。《红楼梦》原文总字数为 856 637,每 1000 个字里就有 11 个作为会话引导语的"道"字。

字频高居第二的"说"字的对比也非常明显。"说"在会话引导语中的字频为 3112,占会话引导语总容量的 3.136%,仅次于"道",而在中文原文中只占 1.117%,非引导语中仅占 0.855%,会话引导语中的"说"字是非会话引导语中的 3.7 倍。值得注意的是,"说"在非引导语中的字频很高,为 6475 个,远远大于"道"在非引导语中的字频 1976,这与《红楼梦》原文写作的拟书场风格有密切关系。

"笑"字在会话引导语字频中位列第三,有 2958 个,占会话引导语总容量的 2.98%,这与其在原文总字频中 0.456% 的比例形成鲜明的对比,更是其在非引导语中比例的 23.7 倍,充分说明了"笑"是非常值得我们关注的重要会话引导语之一。

此外,"问"字也是《红楼梦》原文中一个重要的会话引导语,字频为 900,比例为 0.907%,是其在非引导语中所占比例 0.142% 的 6.4 倍。据此我们可以初步判断出在《红楼梦》原文中带有询问性质的会话数量也比较多。

我们在统计过程中还发现,会话引导语中"便""忙""因"等修饰性质的副词比例远远高于它们在非引导语中的比例,分别为 4 倍、5.7 倍和 4.4 倍。这些副词的使用代表了人物的态度,也是会话引导语中非常重要的内容(见图 2 - 2)。

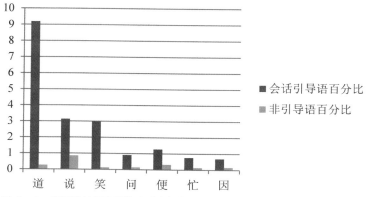

图 2 - 2 "便""忙""因"等在会话引导语及非会话引导语中的字频对比

## 四、《红楼梦》会话引导语特色字研究

笔者使用文本分析软件 AntConc 对《红楼梦》会话引导语文本与《红楼梦》原文文本进行比较,提取会话引导语相对于原文总文本的特色字。统计结果显示,会话引导语文本相对于中文总文本共有 58 个特色字(见表 2 - 4)。

表 2 - 4  会话引导语特色字

| 排序 | 字符 | 字频 | 关键度 | 排序 | 字符 | 字频 | 关键度 |
|---|---|---|---|---|---|---|---|
| 1 | 道 | 9116 | 16 087.302 | 15 | 钗 | 477 | 473.315 |
| 2 | 笑 | 2958 | 4923.375 | 16 | 听 | 882 | 439.343 |
| 3 | 说 | 3112 | 2102.933 | 17 | 姐 | 936 | 430.202 |
| 4 | 玉 | 2217 | 1821.486 | 18 | 政 | 406 | 386.813 |
| 5 | 宝 | 2099 | 1665.402 | 19 | 向 | 298 | 352.602 |
| 6 | 贾 | 1918 | 1579.577 | 20 | 王 | 504 | 311.234 |
| 7 | 问 | 900 | 950.742 | 21 | 春 | 369 | 297.686 |
| 8 | 便 | 1260 | 920.806 | 22 | 夫 | 513 | 290.155 |
| 9 | 凤 | 840 | 826.756 | 23 | 人 | 1857 | 288.533 |
| 10 | 忙 | 753 | 737.019 | 24 | 众 | 390 | 272.118 |
| 11 | 母 | 783 | 616.747 | 25 | 薛 | 343 | 268.273 |
| 12 | 黛 | 587 | 578.124 | 26 | 湘 | 261 | 261.353 |
| 13 | 因 | 689 | 559.170 | 27 | 平 | 324 | 251.809 |
| 14 | 袭 | 510 | 498.905 | 28 | 李 | 271 | 246.845 |

（续表）

| 排序 | 字符 | 字频 | 关键度 | 排序 | 字符 | 字频 | 关键度 |
|------|------|------|--------|------|------|------|--------|
| 29 | 珘 | 312 | 239.486 | 44 | 姨 | 254 | 124.948 |
| 30 | 探 | 230 | 238.859 | 45 | 嬷 | 116 | 112.733 |
| 31 | 紫 | 232 | 218.245 | 46 | 雯 | 133 | 111.578 |
| 32 | 又 | 990 | 207.203 | 47 | 麝 | 107 | 109.900 |
| 33 | 纨 | 184 | 204.907 | 48 | 晴 | 129 | 105.047 |
| 34 | 悄 | 188 | 192.805 | 49 | 瑞 | 118 | 104.281 |
| 35 | 云 | 240 | 182.761 | 50 | 想 | 374 | 97.536 |
| 36 | 鹃 | 185 | 175.909 | 51 | 啐 | 53 | 92.061 |
| 37 | 刘 | 151 | 172.713 | 52 | 忽 | 135 | 89.136 |
| 38 | 叹 | 124 | 152.687 | 53 | 拍 | 57 | 88.276 |
| 39 | 氏 | 180 | 146.319 | 54 | 冷 | 117 | 86.420 |
| 40 | 尤 | 172 | 144.937 | 55 | 拉 | 127 | 86.251 |
| 41 | 莺 | 165 | 144.880 | 56 | 骂 | 96 | 84.342 |
| 42 | 鸳 | 164 | 139.834 | 57 | 陪 | 96 | 82.591 |
| 43 | 见 | 862 | 135.052 | 58 | 咐 | 97 | 80.305 |

反之,《红楼梦》总文本相对于会话引导语文本而言的独特字有 218 个,为便于对比起见,现同样选取前 58 个列举如下(见表 2 - 5)。

表 2 - 5 全文与会话引导语相比之独特字

| 排序 | 字符 | 字频 | 关键度 | 排序 | 字符 | 字频 | 关键度 |
|------|------|------|--------|------|------|------|--------|
| 1 | 我 | 11 | 1828.827 | 10 | 有 | 180 | 462.153 |
| 2 | 你 | 1 | 1515.309 | 11 | 呢 | 5 | 415.259 |
| 3 | 不 | 481 | 1074.177 | 12 | 的 | 974 | 403.769 |
| 4 | 是 | 217 | 1040.411 | 13 | 好 | 96 | 402.078 |
| 5 | 么 | 21 | 712.614 | 14 | 就 | 73 | 365.158 |
| 6 | 太 | 60 | 575.991 | 15 | 什 | 16 | 300.186 |
| 7 | 这 | 273 | 525.101 | 16 | 罢 | 5 | 298.258 |
| 8 | 们 | 112 | 493.211 | 17 | 也 | 280 | 292.749 |
| 9 | 去 | 191 | 466.358 | 18 | 今 | 24 | 285.164 |

（续表）

| 排序 | 字符 | 字频 | 关键度 | 排序 | 字符 | 字频 | 关键度 |
|---|---|---|---|---|---|---|---|
| 19 | 爷 | 16 | 281.637 | 39 | 样 | 25 | 150.939 |
| 20 | 奶 | 22 | 275.728 | 40 | 再 | 21 | 148.357 |
| 21 | 事 | 62 | 244.206 | 41 | 做 | 13 | 139.953 |
| 22 | 还 | 68 | 227.785 | 42 | 倒 | 39 | 137.631 |
| 23 | 没 | 59 | 218.878 | 43 | 多 | 18 | 136.047 |
| 24 | 了 | 1692 | 217.967 | 44 | 谁 | 8 | 135.949 |
| 25 | 可 | 32 | 207.669 | 45 | 哥 | 2 | 132.444 |
| 26 | 怎 | 8 | 202.152 | 46 | 里 | 338 | 131.110 |
| 27 | 姑 | 21 | 183.891 | 47 | 天 | 35 | 129.003 |
| 28 | 要 | 120 | 182.631 | 48 | 咱 | 1 | 124.196 |
| 29 | 个 | 321 | 179.308 | 49 | 为 | 31 | 118.414 |
| 30 | 别 | 17 | 174.256 | 50 | 大 | 189 | 115.978 |
| 31 | 如 | 66 | 174.225 | 51 | 死 | 831 | 112.787 |
| 32 | 日 | 114 | 172.577 | 52 | 竟 | 595 | 111.194 |
| 33 | 年 | 7 | 167.996 | 53 | 东 | 820 | 110.696 |
| 34 | 以 | 10 | 167.506 | 54 | 或 | 492 | 106.566 |
| 35 | 知 | 120 | 162.907 | 55 | 娘 | 1938 | 105.170 |
| 36 | 妹 | 16 | 161.634 | 56 | 才 | 1822 | 104.544 |
| 37 | 些 | 70 | 160.702 | 57 | 所 | 901 | 103.248 |
| 38 | 若 | 1 | 154.542 | 58 | 他 | 7512 | 102.760 |

下面将对会话引导语文本中几个重要的、典型的特色字"道""笑""说""因"等分别进行详细的研究。

（一）关于"道"字的研究

"道"字是《红楼梦》会话引导语的第一大特色字，关键度高达 16 087.302，因此我们非常有必要首先开展关于"道"字的专题研究。

我们使用 PowerConc 软件对会话引导语"道"的搭配进行研究。正如前面所提到的，在古典白话小说中，会话引导语总是位于会话之前，因此会话引导语"道"后面的内容属于会话的范畴，在此不多做研究。关于"道"的搭配问题仅限于"道"字前面的（左侧的）内容。

需要特别说明的是,笔者在筛选搭配字符时,只选取与"道"构成语义搭配的字符,那些构成非语义搭配的自然搭配字符不在统计之列,之后关于"笑""说"等的统计也是如此。

**1. "道"字的一字搭配**

我们检索"道"字左侧的第一个搭配字符。与"道"构成语义搭配的、字频在 2 次以上的搭配字符有 61 个,其中字频在 10 次以上的有 24 个:

| | | | |
|---|---|---|---|
| 笑(2399) | 忙(81) | 劝(48) | 知(20) |
| 说(960) | 叹(77) | 叫(36) | 喝(16) |
| 问(300) | 想(68) | 啐(35) | 告(13) |
| 回(125) | 都(51) | 答(31) | 气(13) |
| 便(110) | 哭(51) | 嚷(24) | 急(11) |
| 又(99) | 骂(49) | 应(21) | 因(11) |

通过前文所列可以看出,在与"道"的一字搭配中,语义搭配有 61 个。其中"笑道"的频率最高,为 2399 次,其次为"说道"960 次,"问道"300 次,"回道"125 次,"便道"110 次,"又道"99 次,"忙道"81 次,"想道"68 次,"都道"和"哭道"各 51 次,"骂道"49 次,"叫道"36 次,"嚷道"24 次。

**2. "道"字的二字搭配**

我们检索"道"字左侧的 2 个搭配字符,并筛选出语义搭配,字频在 2 次以上的语义搭配字符有 265 个,其中字频在 10 次以上的有 80 个:

| | | | |
|---|---|---|---|
| 宝玉(478) | 众人(73) | 尤氏(42) | 焙茗(25) |
| 贾母(195) | 李纨(68) | 晴雯(41) | 妙玉(24) |
| 凤姐(178) | 鸳鸯(66) | 麝月(41) | 贾芸(23) |
| 袭人(177) | 忙笑(63) | 陪笑(39) | 那人(23) |
| 黛玉(175) | 因笑(63) | 笑问(38) | 雪雁(22) |
| 贾政(171) | 探春(60) | 薛蟠(35) | 因问(21) |
| 宝钗(135) | 都笑(52) | 惜春(34) | 又问(20) |
| 贾琏(107) | 紫鹃(52) | 纨笑(33) | 贾蓉(19) |
| 冷笑(105) | 便问(50) | 又说(32) | 听了(19) |
| 便说(92) | 便笑(50) | 婆子(31) | 香菱(19) |
| 平儿(78) | 笑说(49) | 也笑(31) | 湘莲(19) |
| 因说(77) | 贾珍(46) | 点头(29) | 雨村(18) |
| 湘云(74) | 又笑(44) | 丫头(29) | 忙问(17) |

| | | | |
|---|---|---|---|
| 小红(17) | 忙说(14) | 贾赦(12) | 微笑(11) |
| 莺儿(17) | 秋纹(14) | 接口(12) | 先笑(11) |
| 咤异(17) | 笑着(14) | 忙劝(12) | 小厮(11) |
| 金桂(16) | 吩咐(13) | 笑回(12) | 贾瑞(10) |
| 翠缕(15) | 贾环(13) | 包勇(11) | 强笑(10) |
| 答应(15) | 起来(13) | 贾蔷(11) | 薛蟠(10) |
| 宝蟾(14) | 代儒(12) | 拍手(11) | 迎春(10) |

"道"字左侧的二字语义搭配字符高达 265 个,其中出现了许多二字人物名称,如"贾母道""凤姐道""黛玉道""贾政道""贾琏道",等等。此外还有一些重要的引导语搭配也凸显出来,首先是与"笑"搭配的动词,如"冷笑道"(词频高达105)、"笑说道""笑问道""微笑道""陪笑道"等;还有其他说话的方式,如"咤异道""点头道""拍手道""吩咐道""答应道"等;一些修饰性副词的搭配也有相当多的数量,如"因说道""因笑道""因问道""又问道""又笑道""忙笑道""都笑道"等。

**3. "道"字的三字搭配**

我们检索"道"字左侧的三字搭配字符,并筛选出有意义的语义搭配,字频在 2 次以上的语义搭配字符有 368 个,其中字频在 10 次以上的有 43 个:

| | | |
|---|---|---|
| 宝玉笑(231) | 众人笑(27) | 宝玉又(13) |
| 王夫人(136) | 贾琏笑(26) | 点头叹(13) |
| 贾母笑(105) | 尤氏笑(26) | 点头笑(13) |
| 宝钗笑(101) | 冯紫英(25) | 心里想(13) |
| 凤姐笑(92) | 贾政笑(25) | 陪笑说(12) |
| 黛玉笑(84) | 紫鹃笑(21) | 那丫头(11) |
| 袭人笑(68) | 听了笑(19) | 香菱笑(11) |
| 薛姨妈(62) | 向宝玉(18) | 一面笑(11) |
| 凤姐儿(52) | 邢夫人(18) | 贾珍笑(10) |
| 探春笑(51) | 拍手笑(17) | 进来回(10) |
| 刘老老(48) | 晴雯笑(17) | 小丫头(10) |
| 平儿笑(47) | 鸳鸯笑(15) | 笑着说(10) |
| 湘云笑(46) | 麝月笑(15) | 一面说(10) |
| 众人都(37) | 宝琴笑(14) | |
| 李纨笑(33) | 宝玉忙(14) | |

在与"道"相关的 368 个三字语义搭配中出现了多个三字的人物名称,如"王夫人道""凤姐儿道""薛姨妈道""刘老老道""冯紫英道""赵姨娘道""史湘云道"等。二字人物与"笑道"的搭配也很多,如"贾母笑道""凤姐笑道""黛玉笑道""平儿笑道""湘云笑道"等。此外,关于说话时的方式和态度描写更加充分,出现了"拍手笑道""点头笑道""悄悄说道""走来说道""起身笑道"等词语;说话的对象性也进一步明确,如"向黛玉道""向平儿道""向众人道"等。描写内心会话的引导语有"心里想道"和"心中想道"。

### 4. "道"字的四字搭配

我们进一步检索"道"字左侧的四字语义搭配字符,检索结果较二字、三字搭配字符有所减少,字频在 2 次以上的语义搭配字符有 197 个,其中字频在 10 次以上的仅有 7 个:

| | | |
|---|---|---|
| 凤姐儿笑(46) | 王夫人笑(20) | 悄悄的笑(11) |
| 薛姨妈笑(27) | 刘老老笑(13) | |
| 周瑞家的(24) | 众人都笑(13) | |

在本次检索结果中,首先是出现了四字人物姓名与"道"的搭配,这些人物姓名多是描述性和指代性的,如"周瑞家的道""门上的人道""那老婆子道"等。其次是三字人名与"笑道"的搭配,如"凤姐儿笑道""薛姨妈笑道""王夫人笑道""乌进孝笑道"等。修饰性副词的搭配也比较明显,如"众人都笑道""黛玉忙笑道""凤姐忙问道""忙起身笑道"等。描写性词语也因为字数的增加而更加丰富,如"微微的笑道""哈哈的笑道""拍着手笑道""悄悄的问道""轻轻的叫道"等。心理会话描写出现了"心下自思道"。

### 5. "道"字的五字搭配

最后我们检索了"道"字左侧的五字语义搭配字符,发现数量显著减少,字频在 2 次以上的语义搭配字符有 54 个,其中字频在 10 次以上的仅有 1 个:

| | | |
|---|---|---|
| 林之孝家的(11) | 刘老老忙笑(3) | 便轻轻的叫(2) |
| 王善保家的(5) | 抿着嘴儿笑(3) | 便向王夫人(2) |
| 周瑞家的笑(4) | 王夫人点头(3) | 颤巍巍的说(2) |
| 宝玉听了笑(3) | 笑嘻嘻的说(3) | 长府官冷笑(2) |
| 喘吁吁的说(3) | 周瑞家的又(3) | 凤姐儿都笑(2) |
| 凤姐儿忙笑(3) | 宝玉点头叹(2) | 凤姐儿接着(2) |
| 凤姐听了笑(3) | 背后有人说(2) | 和王夫人说(2) |
| 贾母点头叹(3) | 便和王夫人(2) | 后面有人叫(2) |

| | | |
|---|---|---|
| 贾母等都说（2） | 旺儿媳妇笑（2） | 一个丫头说（2） |
| 贾母听了笑（2） | 向平儿冷笑（2） | 因又笑着说（2） |
| 拉他的手笑（2） | 向王夫人笑（2） | 又向贾母笑（2） |
| 来回王夫人（2） | 向薛姨妈笑（2） | 又向小红笑（2） |
| 赖大家的笑（2） | 小红进来回（2） | 又转念一想（2） |
| 刘老老也笑（2） | 笑着向宝钗（2） | 指着宝玉笑（2） |
| 刘老老咤异（2） | 邢王二夫人（2） | 只得勉强说（2） |
| 南安太妃笑（2） | 薛蝌进来说（2） | 众人都咤异（2） |
| 秋纹走来说（2） | 雪芹先生笑（2） | 周瑞家的便（2） |
| 叹了一口气（2） | 也悄悄的笑（2） | 抿着嘴儿说（2） |

在与"道"相关的五字语义搭配字符中已经不存在单纯的人名，仅有两个以上人物的共同会话引导语，如"邢王二夫人道"。"笑道"与"说道"的搭配仍然是比较核心的部分，如"周瑞家的笑道""贾母等都说道""刘老老也笑道""雪芹先生笑道"等。描述性的引导语新增加了"抿着嘴儿笑道""抿着嘴儿说道""薛蝌进来说道"等。修饰性副词搭配仍然围绕"忙""又""因"展开，如"凤姐儿忙笑道""周瑞家的又道""因又笑着说道""又向贾母笑道"等。

**6. "道"字搭配研究小结**

通过表2-6我们可以看出，在字频大于2次的与"道"字相关语义搭配中，三字搭配的数量最多，占38.94%；其次是二字搭配，占28.04%；四字搭配占20.85%；数量较少的是一字搭配和五字搭配，分别仅有6.46%和5.71%。

表2-6　会话引导语"道"字搭配统计

| 类别 | 数量 | 百分比 |
|---|---|---|
| 一字搭配 | 61 | 6.46 |
| 二字搭配 | 265 | 28.04 |
| 三字搭配 | 368 | 38.94 |
| 四字搭配 | 197 | 20.85 |
| 五字搭配 | 54 | 5.71 |
| 合计 | 945 | 100.00 |

**（二）关于"笑"字的研究**

会话引导语"笑"的字频位列第三位，为2958个，仅次于"道"和"说"，而在特色字的排名中，其关键度却超越"说"字，跃居第二位，为4923.375。下面我们来着重分析"笑"这一关键会话引导语。"笑"与"道"的分析方法有所不同——

"道"作为会话引导语时后面一定是直接加":"和会话内容,而"笑"则不然,前后都可以有其他内容,如前面加"冷"字构成"冷笑"、后面加"说"或"道"构成"笑说""笑道"等。因此我们需要使用 PowerConc 软件分别对会话引导语"笑"的前后搭配进行研究,将所有与"笑"构成语义搭配的、字频在 2 次以上的左右两侧字符筛选出来。

### 1. "笑"字的一字符搭配

我们检索"笑"字左侧的第一个搭配字符,将字频在 2 次以上的语义搭配字符列举如下:

| | | | |
|---|---|---|---|
| ,(285) | 便(75) | 微(12) | 还(2) |
| 冷(115) | 又(65) | 好(10) | 皆(2) |
| 都(85) | 也(42) | 悄(8) | 乃(2) |
| 陪(80) | 含(14) | 方(7) | 玩(2) |
| 因(79) | 先(14) | 说(6) | 亦(2) |
| 忙(78) | 强(12) | 取(4) | 赳(2) |

"笑"字前面的一字语义搭配字符字频在 2 次以上的共有 24 个。之所以也将","列举出来,是因为逗号","在"笑"字之前的频率很高,这种搭配出现的背景一般是主语之后有一部分描述性的内容,然后用逗号隔开,再接"笑道""笑问"等,如"那僧托于掌上,笑道:""却说甄士隐俱听得明白,遂不禁上前施礼,笑问道:""门子忙上前请安,笑问:"等。此外,我们可以发现"冷笑""都笑""陪笑""因笑""忙笑""便笑""又笑"的频率也很高。

"笑"字右侧的第一个搭配字符,字频在 2 次以上的语义搭配字符有:

| | | | |
|---|---|---|---|
| 道(2399) | 问(61) | 央(7) | 让(5) |
| 说(145) | 了(33) | 骂(6) | 推(4) |
| 着(76) | 回(20) | 指(6) | 拉(2) |
| ,(62) | 劝(7) | 答(5) | 谢(2) |

"笑"字后面的一字语义搭配字符数量并不是很多,仅 16 个,且字频差异巨大。其中"笑道"的搭配频率非常高,有 2399 次,远超接下来的"笑说"(145),成为会话引导语的最重要搭配之一。"笑着"作为伴随状语出现的频率较高。其他与动词的搭配还有"笑问""笑回""笑劝""笑骂""笑答""笑让"等。我们这里同样将"笑"字之后的 62 个","搭配列举出来,因为逗号","在"笑"字之后的频率也较高,一般是在"笑"的动作完成之后,以逗号做分隔,后面再接"说道""说"

"道"等言说动词,这种用法与直接使用"笑道"和"笑说"相比较,似乎更能强调先"笑"后"说"的状态。如:"躬身低头含笑,因说:""喜的眉开眼笑,忙说道:""相视而笑,都说是:"等。

**2. "笑"字的二字符搭配**

与"笑"字搭配的二字字符中,左侧字频在 2 次以上的语义搭配字符有:

| | | | |
|---|---|---|---|
| 宝玉(250) | 婆子(10) | 媳妇(4) | 走来(3) |
| 贾母(120) | 贾芸(9) | 湘莲(4) | 茗烟(3) |
| 宝钗(106) | 薛蟠(9) | 小厮(4) | 琥珀(3) |
| 凤姐(97) | 二姐(8) | 兴儿(4) | 不住(2) |
| 黛玉(95) | 妙玉(8) | 丫头(4) | 窗外(2) |
| 袭人(71) | 陪着(7) | 丫鬟(4) | 翠缕(2) |
| 平儿(53) | 秋纹(7) | 也都(4) | 翠墨(2) |
| 探春(53) | 小红(7) | 一个(4) | 代儒(2) |
| 湘云(49) | 迎春(7) | 一旁(4) | 都大(2) |
| 李纨(35) | 岫烟(7) | 只得(4) | 堆着(2) |
| 众人(33) | 便冷(6) | 子兴(4) | 二人(2) |
| 贾琏(29) | 口内(6) | 宝蟾(3) | 哈哈(2) |
| 尤氏(29) | 惜春(6) | 焙茗(3) | 贾蔷(2) |
| 贾政(27) | 又好(6) | 便忙(3) | 金荣(2) |
| 紫鹃(22) | 那僧(5) | 大家(3) | 李纹(2) |
| 忙陪(21) | 秦钟(5) | 道人(3) | 那人(2) |
| 拍手(19) | 上来(5) | 道士(3) | 忍着(2) |
| 听了(19) | 四人(5) | 过来(3) | 蕊官(2) |
| 一面(19) | 微微(5) | 忽然(3) | 上去(2) |
| 晴雯(18) | 摇头(5) | 贾蓉(3) | 喜的(2) |
| 麝月(18) | 又陪(5) | 贾瑞(3) | 因便(2) |
| 鸳鸯(15) | 雨村(5) | 金桂(3) | 因冷(2) |
| 宝琴(14) | 莺儿(5) | 忙又(3) | 因陪(2) |
| 点头(14) | 春燕(4) | 门子(3) | 又冷(2) |
| 贾珍(13) | 芳官(4) | 起来(3) | 又悄(2) |
| 因又(13) | 回头(4) | 悄悄(3) | 詹光(2) |
| 香菱(12) | 进来(4) | 先生(3) | 坠儿(2) |
| 起身(11) | 秦氏(4) | 也忙(3) | |
| 勉强(10) | 士隐(4) | 在旁(3) | |

"笑"字前面的二字语义搭配字符共有 114 个。从前文我们可以推断出,宝玉是"笑"得最多的人物,其次是贾母、宝钗、凤姐、黛玉、袭人、平儿等。此外"笑"还有诸多伴随动作,如"拍手笑""点头笑""听了笑"等。

右侧字频在 2 次以上的语义二字搭配字符有:

| | | | |
|---|---|---|---|
| 道:(2399) | 着道(14) | 骂道(5) | 让:(3) |
| 说:(96) | 着说(13) | 劝道(5) | 问他(3) |
| 说道(49) | 回道(12) | 着回(4) | 央道(3) |
| 问道(38) | 起来(12) | 回:(3) | 着问(3) |
| 嘻嘻(21) | 答道(5) | 几声(3) | 谢道(2) |
| 问:(14) | 回说(5) | 两声(3) | 央告(2) |

"笑"字后面的二字语义搭配字符数量不多,仅有 24 个。遥遥领先的依然是会话引导语"笑道:",其次是"笑说:""笑说道""笑问道""笑问:""笑着道""笑回道"等。此外还有对于笑的具体补充描述,如"笑嘻嘻""笑几声""笑两声"等。

**3. "笑"字的三字符搭配**

与"笑"字搭配的三字字符中,左侧字频在 2 次以上的语义搭配字符有:

| | | |
|---|---|---|
| 凤姐儿(47) | 金桂冷(6) | 平儿冷(4) |
| 听了,(32) | 拉住,(6) | 晴雯冷(4) |
| 薛姨妈(29) | 探春冷(6) | 他嫂子(4) |
| 众人都(24) | 微微的(6) | 听了冷(4) |
| 王夫人(21) | 袭人冷(6) | 凤姐陪(3) |
| 笑了一(16) | 黛玉忙(6) | 哈哈的(3) |
| 进来,(14) | 宝玉便(5) | 贾母忙(3) |
| 悄悄的(14) | 宝钗因(5) | 贾母也(3) |
| 刘老老(13) | 凤姐冷(5) | 贾母又(3) |
| 宝玉忙(10) | 眉开眼(5) | 拦住,(3) |
| 出来,(10) | 嘻嘻的(5) | 柳家的(3) |
| 起来,(10) | 邢夫人(5) | 勉强陪(3) |
| 走来,(9) | 凤姐忙(4) | 那人冷(3) |
| 听说,(8) | 贾政冷(4) | 拍着手(3) |
| 宝玉冷(7) | 贾政陪(4) | 平儿忙(3) |
| 黛玉冷(7) | 连忙陪(4) | 探春又(3) |
| 冯紫英(6) | 忙起身(4) | 乌进孝(3) |

| | | |
|---|---|---|
| 袭人等(3) | 呵呵大(2) | 袭人也(2) |
| 向宝玉(3) | 回来,(2) | 湘莲冷(2) |
| 向黛玉(3) | 会意,(2) | 湘云冷(2) |
| 尤二姐(3) | 贾母便(2) | 湘云先(2) |
| 只得陪(3) | 贾母因(2) | 向宝钗(2) |
| 坐下,(3) | 贾琏冷(2) | 向贾母(2) |
| 黛玉先(3) | 贾琏也(2) | 向贾琏(2) |
| 宝玉陪(2) | 接了,(2) | 向平儿(2) |
| 宝玉又(2) | 进去,(2) | 向小红(2) |
| 宝钗冷(2) | 看了,(2) | 小丫头(2) |
| 宝钗又(2) | 李纨等(2) | 也进来(2) |
| 北静王(2) | 李纨因(2) | 尤三姐(2) |
| 便拍手(2) | 搂着他(2) | 玉钏儿(2) |
| 都点头(2) | 忙陪着(2) | 在窗外(2) |
| 都起身(2) | 妙玉冷(2) | 站起来(2) |
| 二姐儿(2) | 那道人(2) | 张道士(2) |
| 二人都(2) | 那小厮(2) | 众婆子(2) |
| 凤姐又(2) | 平儿便(2) | 作揖,(2) |
| 躬身陪(2) | 王一贴(2) | 莺儿便(2) |
| 哈哈大(2) | 惜春冷(2) | 黛玉也(2) |

　　"笑"字前面的三字语义搭配字符数量有111个。其中三字人名与"笑"字的搭配很多,如"凤姐儿笑""薛姨妈笑""王夫人笑""刘老老笑""冯紫英笑"等。二字人名一般搭配"冷笑"或其他修饰词语,如"宝玉冷笑""黛玉冷笑""金桂冷笑""探春冷笑""袭人冷笑""众人都笑""宝玉忙笑""黛玉忙笑""宝钗因笑"等。还有一类重要搭配为"动词+逗号(,)+笑",表示在某个其他动作之后又出现了"笑"的动作或状态,如"听了,笑""进来,笑""起来,笑""走来,笑""听说,笑""拉住,笑"等。这种表述方式同时强调前面的动作和"笑"的动作,为"笑"的含义分析提供背景状态。

　　与"笑"字搭配的三字字符中,右侧字频在2次以上的语义搭配字符有:

| | | |
|---|---|---|
| 说道:(49) | 着道:(14) | 答道:(5) |
| 问道:(38) | 回道:(12) | 骂道:(5) |
| 嘻嘻的(18) | ,说道(10) | 劝道:(5) |
| 了一笑(16) | 着说道(10) | ,道:(4) |

| | | |
|---|---|---|
| ，因说(4) | 向贾母(3) | 问他：(2) |
| 回说：(4) | 央道：(3) | 谢道：(2) |
| 着回道(4) | 着进来(3) | 着点头(2) |
| ，忙说(3) | 着说：(3) | 着问道(2) |
| 个不住(3) | 不笑的(2) | 着央告(2) |
| 了一回(3) | 两声道(2) | 着站起(2) |
| 了一声(3) | 了两声(2) | |
| 向宝钗(3) | 起来了(2) | |

"笑"字后面的三字语义搭配字符数量有 34 个。"笑说道："作为会话引导语的频率最高，有 49 个，其次为"笑问道：""笑着道：""笑回道：""笑着说道""笑答道：""笑骂道：""笑劝道：""笑回说：""笑着回道""笑央道：""笑着说：""笑谢道：""笑两声道""笑问他：""笑着问道"等。关于"笑"的描述也因为总字符的增加而变得更加生动，如"笑嘻嘻的""笑了一笑""笑个不住""笑了一回""笑了一声""笑了两声"，与其他动词搭配使用有"笑着进来"和"笑着点头"等。此外，"笑＋逗号（，）＋言说动词"的搭配也是"笑"字三字语义搭配的特色之一，强调"笑"的动作发生在"说话"之前，更加突出"笑"的优先性和开口说话时的情境。

**4. "笑"字的四字符搭配**

与"笑"字搭配的四字字符中，左侧字频在 2 次以上的语义搭配字符有 55 个：

| | | |
|---|---|---|
| 红了脸，(9) | 迎出来，(3) | 刘老老也(2) |
| 听了，都(9) | 迎上去，(3) | 南安太妃(2) |
| 听了，冷(5) | 站起来，(3) | 起来，因(2) |
| 听了，忙(5) | 只见宝玉(3) | 起来了，(2) |
| 周瑞家的(4) | 便悄悄的(2) | 手一撒，(2) |
| 走进来，(4) | 出来，都(2) | 说着，又(2) |
| 宝玉听了(3) | 会意，因(2) | 跳出来，(2) |
| 长府官冷(3) | 贾母听了(2) | 听了，又(2) |
| 凤姐儿忙(3) | 进来，便(2) | 听说，忙(2) |
| 凤姐听了(3) | 进来，都(2) | 王夫人忙(2) |
| 刘老老忙(3) | 进来，陪(2) | 旺儿媳妇(2) |
| 抿着嘴儿(3) | 拉他的手(2) | 袭人勉强(2) |
| 跑进来，(3) | 赖大家的(2) | 想毕，便(2) |
| 听说，便(3) | 连忙陪着(2) | 想毕，因(2) |

| | | |
|---|---|---|
| 想了想,(2) | 薛姨妈也(2) | 又向贾母(2) |
| 想一想,(2) | 雪芹先生(2) | 又向小红(2) |
| 向平儿冷(2) | 也悄悄的(2) | 指着宝玉(2) |
| 向王夫人(2) | 一个丫鬟(2) | |
| 向薛姨妈(2) | 一想,也(2) | |

"笑"字前面的四字语义搭配字符主要描写"笑"这个动作前发生的动作,交代"笑"发生的背景或伴随状态,中间常用逗号隔开,如"红了脸,笑""听了,都笑""听了,冷笑""听了,忙笑""走进来,笑""跑进来,笑""听说,便笑""迎出来,笑""迎上去,笑""站起来,笑""进来,陪笑""进来,便笑""进来,都笑"等。四字人物姓名搭配只有"周瑞家的笑",三字或二字人名后一般有修饰成分再加上"笑",如"宝玉听了笑""凤姐听了笑""贾母听了笑""长府官冷笑""凤姐儿忙笑""刘老老忙笑"等。对于"笑"的具体描写有"抿着嘴儿笑"等。

与"笑"字搭配的四字字符中,右侧字频在2次以上的语义搭配字符数量较少,仅有20个:

| | | |
|---|---|---|
| ,说道:(10) | ,忙说道(2) | 向贾珍道(2) |
| 着说道(10) | 几声,说(2) | 向李纨道(2) |
| 起来,说(7) | 两声道:(2) | 向薛姨妈(2) |
| 嘻嘻的道(4) | 了,说:(2) | 向众人道(2) |
| 着回道(4) | 了一笑道(2) | 着问道:(2) |
| ,因说:(3) | 起来了,(2) | 着站起来(2) |
| 嘻嘻的说(3) | 向宝玉道(2) | |

"笑"字右侧的四字语义搭配中,作为会话引导语的"笑着说道:"数量最多,有10个,其次是"笑嘻嘻的道""笑着回道:""笑嘻嘻的说""笑两声道:""笑了一笑道:""笑着问道:"等。该类型搭配与之前相比一个显著的特点是"对象性"更加明确,出现了多次"笑向××道"的搭配,如"笑向宝玉道""笑向贾珍道""笑向李纨道""笑向众人道"等。此外依旧有几个"笑+逗号(,)+言说动词"的搭配,强调"笑"的动作和随后发生的"说话"动作。

### 5."笑"字的五字符搭配

最后我们考察了"笑"字的五字符搭配情况。先来看左侧的五字字符搭配,字频在2次以上的语义搭配字符有:

| | | |
|---|---|---|
| 贾母听了,(6) | 想了一想,(6) | 喜的眉开眼(5) |

| | | |
|---|---|---|
| "嗤"的一(3) | 答应了，又(2) | 忙站起来，(2) |
| 宝玉听了，(3) | 芳官听了，(2) | 那雪芹先生(2) |
| 那长府官冷(3) | 凤姐听了，(2) | 说的众人都(2) |
| 一把拉住，(3) | 贾母听说，(2) | 听了，点头(2) |
| 黛玉听了，(3) | 将手一撒，(2) | 听了，拍手(2) |
| 黛玉笑了一(3) | 林之孝家的(2) | 想了半日，(2) |
| 宝玉笑了一(2) | 忙跑进来，(2) | 又指着宝玉(2) |
| 宝钗走来，(2) | 忙迎出来，(2) | 走到跟前，(2) |

"笑"字前面的五字语义搭配字符数量有 27 个。在该类搭配中，"笑"字前的修饰成分更加丰富多彩，以"听"和"想"为关键字的衔接表述较多，如"贾母听了，笑""宝玉听了，笑""黛玉听了，笑""凤姐听了，笑""芳官听了，笑""贾母听说，笑""听了，点头笑""听了，拍手笑""想了一想，笑""想了半日，笑"等。其他伴随的动作有"一把拉住，笑""将手一撒，笑""忙跑进来，笑""忙迎出来，笑""忙站起来，笑""又指着宝玉笑"等。此外，五字的人物名称包括"林之孝家的笑"和"那雪芹先生笑"等。

与"笑"字搭配的五字字符中，右侧字频在 2 次以上的语义搭配字符数量较少，仅有 15 个，且出现最多的只有 5 次：

| | | |
|---|---|---|
| 起来，说：(5) | 了一笑，说(2) | 向宝玉道：(2) |
| 嘻嘻的道：(4) | 了一笑道：(2) | 向贾珍道：(2) |
| 嘻嘻的说道(3) | 起来，说道(2) | 向李纨道：(2) |
| ，忙说道：(2) | 起来了，说(2) | 向众人道：(2) |
| 了一笑，道(2) | 嘻嘻的走来(2) | 着向宝钗道(2) |

"笑"字后面的五字语义搭配字符包含"笑嘻嘻的道："笑嘻嘻的说道""笑了一笑道："等。"对象性"明确的"笑向××道"也有 5 个，分别为"笑向宝玉道："笑向贾珍道："笑向李纨道："笑向众人道："笑着向宝钗道"等。"笑＋逗号（，）＋言说动词"的搭配有 6 个，包括"笑起来，说："笑，忙说道："笑了一笑，道""笑了一笑，说""笑起来，说道"和"笑起来了，说"等。

### 6. "笑"字搭配研究小结

通过表 2 - 7 我们可以看出，在字频大于 2 次的与"笑"字相关语义搭配中，左侧二字符的语义搭配的数量最多，占比超过 25%；其次是左侧三字符的语义搭配，也占 25%；左侧四字符的搭配占 12% 左右；其余搭配的比例均不超过 10%。

表 2 - 7　会话引导语"笑"字搭配统计

| 类别 | 数量 | 百分比 |
|------|------|--------|
| 一字符搭配(左) | 24 | 5.45 |
| 一字符搭配(右) | 16 | 3.64 |
| 二字符搭配(左) | 114 | 25.91 |
| 二字符搭配(右) | 24 | 5.45 |
| 三字符搭配(左) | 111 | 25.23 |
| 三字符搭配(右) | 34 | 7.73 |
| 四字符搭配(左) | 55 | 12.50 |
| 四字符搭配(右) | 20 | 4.55 |
| 五字符搭配(左) | 27 | 6.14 |
| 五字符搭配(右) | 15 | 3.41 |
| 合计 | 440 | 100.00 |

（三）关于"说"字的研究

"说"字在《红楼梦》会话引导语文本中排名第二,字频为3112,在会话引导语文本相对于原文总文本的特色字中位居第三,关键度为2102.933。"说"字也是《红楼梦》原著中仅次于"道"的一个非常重要的会话引导语。下面我们依旧使用 PowerConc 软件来着重分析"说"这一关键会话引导语的前后搭配情况,将所有与"说"字构成语义搭配的、字频在2次以上的左、右两侧字符筛选出来。

**1. "说"字的一字符搭配**

检索"说"字左侧的第一个搭配字符,将字频在2次以上的语义搭配字符列举如下:

| | | | |
|------|------|------|------|
| ,(577) | 都(65) | 却(13) | 叹(5) |
| 便(261) | 忙(55) | 方(9) | 也(5) |
| 笑(145) | 只(53) | 解(9) | 并(4) |
| 因(141) | 他(38) | 悄(9) | 喊(4) |
| 又(124) | 话(33) | 就(8) | 禀(4) |
| 来(112) | 且(21) | 去(8) | 反(3) |
| 听(108) | 还(16) | 报(5) | 接(3) |
| 回(95) | 才(15) | 劝(5) | 乃(3) |
| 正(71) | 见(13) | 嚷(5) | 先(3) |

| 常（2） | 改（2） | 连（2） | 再（2） |
|---|---|---|---|
| 传（2） | 敢（2） | 乱（2） | |
| 答（2） | 皆（2） | 求（2） | |

　　"说"字前面的一字语义搭配字符有 46 个。从上述内容我们可以发现，位于"说"字左侧字频最高的是逗号"，"，有 577 个。这种搭配大多情况是主语后面加一系列叙述性或说明性的内容，然后加逗号，随后加"说"字直接来引导会话，或使用"说道：""说笑道："等。如："宝钗想了想，说："咳嗽了两声，说道："等。其次是"便说""因说""又说""都说""忙说"等修饰成分与"说"字的搭配。动词与"说"的搭配有"笑说""回说"等。此外，"话说""且说"的搭配使用频率较高，这与以《红楼梦》为代表的古典白话小说的拟书场风格密切相关。

　　"说"字右侧字频在 2 次以上的语义搭配一字字符有：

| ：（1491） | 话（29） | 他（11） | 笑（6） |
|---|---|---|---|
| 道（960） | 了（28） | 出（10） | 破（2） |
| 着（182） | 是（22） | 毕（9） | |
| 完（38） | 到（15） | 起（6） | |

　　"说"字后面的一字语义搭配字符数量不多，仅 14 个，且字频之间跨度很大。其中最多的是"："，高达 1491 个，这充分说明了"说："直接作为会话引导语的频率是最高的；其次为"说道"960 个、"说是"22 个。"说笑"不能直接作为会话引导语，除非后面再加上一个"道"字。

　　**2. "说"字的二字符搭配**

　　检索"说"字左侧的二字搭配字符，将字频在 2 次以上的语义搭配字符列举如下：

| 一面（27） | 宝钗（13） | 凤姐（8） | 有人（7） |
|---|---|---|---|
| 宝玉（24） | 笑着（13） | 过来（8） | 只得（7） |
| 进来（22） | 走来（12） | 黛玉（8） | 便回（6） |
| 如此（21） | 平儿（11） | 方欲（7） | 便笑（6） |
| 都笑（19） | 起来（11） | 口里（7） | 出来（6） |
| 陪笑（19） | 袭人（11） | 起身（7） | 含泪（6） |
| 贾母（18） | 因又（10） | 悄悄（7） | 回头（6） |
| 回来（15） | 有的（10） | 上来（7） | 贾蓉（6） |
| 来回（15） | 口内（9） | 尤氏（7） | 丫头（6） |

| | | | |
|---|---|---|---|
| 一个(6) | 向他(4) | 不便(2) | 齐声(2) |
| 又听(6) | 因笑(4) | 不敢(2) | 气的(2) |
| 众人(6) | 滴泪(3) | 才要(2) | 取笑(2) |
| 不好(5) | 点头(3) | 出去(2) | 劝他(2) |
| 贾琏(5) | 芳官(3) | 大家(2) | 商议(2) |
| 接着(5) | 故意(3) | 大声(2) | 上去(2) |
| 忙笑(5) | 跪下(3) | 道人(2) | 上头(2) |
| 跑来(5) | 含笑(3) | 分辩(2) | 拭泪(2) |
| 推他(5) | 急的(3) | 赶着(2) | 司棋(2) |
| 笑回(5) | 贾政(3) | 告诉(2) | 太监(2) |
| 摇头(5) | 贾芸(3) | 和尚(2) | 叹气(2) |
| 在旁(5) | 连忙(3) | 家人(2) | 听人(2) |
| 紫鹃(5) | 那人(3) | 贾蔷(2) | 屋里(2) |
| 半日(4) | 听他(3) | 近前(2) | 惜春(2) |
| 抱怨(4) | 外面(3) | 就回(2) | 喜欢(2) |
| 便又(4) | 外头(3) | 拉他(2) | 先回(2) |
| 高声(4) | 媳妇(3) | 来又(2) | 小厮(2) |
| 贾珍(4) | 心里(3) | 来禀(2) | 兴儿(2) |
| 哭着(4) | 薛蟠(3) | 里面(2) | 绣橘(2) |
| 赖大(4) | 又笑(3) | 忙回(2) | 也笑(2) |
| 勉强(4) | 鸳鸯(3) | 忙解(2) | 又回(2) |
| 婆子(4) | 嘴里(3) | 那僧(2) | |
| 他又(4) | 半晌(2) | 念佛(2) | |
| 湘云(4) | 焙茗(2) | 碰头(2) | |

　　"说"字前面的二字语义搭配字符数量比一字字符显著增多,字频在2次以上的有129个。在"说"字前面出现了许多二字人物名称,如"宝玉说""贾母说""宝钗说""平儿说""袭人说""凤姐说""黛玉说"等。还有与"笑"搭配的几种用法,如"都笑说""陪笑说""笑着说"等。添加伴随动作的搭配有"一面说""进来说""如此说""回来说""走来说""起来说""过来说"等。此外还有表示"说"的方式和目的的搭配,如"来回说""人回说"等。"口内说"和"口里说"等搭配并无具体的意义,仅仅是为了强调"口头说"这一动作。

　　位于"说"字右侧的字频在2次以上的语义搭配二字字符有:

| | | | |
|---|---|---|---|
| 道:(960) | 是:(21) | 到这(11) | 不出(4) |

| | | | |
|---|---|---|---|
| 出来(4) | 他:(4) | 这话(3) | 完了(2) |
| 话时(4) | 起:(3) | 着便(3) | 之间(2) |

我们可以看到"说"字后面的二字语义搭配字符数量很少,仅有 12 个。"说道:"作为会话引导语的频率很高,有 960 次;"说是:"用得比较少,仅有 21 次,此外还有 4 次"说他:"和 3 次"说起:"的用法,比较少见。此类搭配中出现了"说"字组成的几种插入语,如"说到这""说话时""说着便""说完了""说之间"等,这时的"说"已经不再侧重讲话的内容是什么,而更多地具备了一种插入语和话语标记的性质。

**3."说"字的三字符搭配**

检索"说"字左侧的三字搭配字符,将字频在 2 次以上的语义搭配字符列举如下:

| | | | |
|---|---|---|---|
| 起来,(23) | 听如此(5) | 出去,(3) | 黛玉便(3) |
| 宝玉听(17) | 向袭人(5) | 道谢,(3) | 半日才(2) |
| 进来,(17) | 黛玉听(5) | 凤姐听(3) | 宝玉见(2) |
| 众人都(15) | 凤姐便(4) | 赶来,(3) | 宝玉因(2) |
| 贾母听(14) | 告诉他(4) | 赶上来(3) | 宝玉又(2) |
| 贾母便(13) | 见如此(4) | 急了,(3) | 北静王(2) |
| 凤姐儿(11) | 磕头,(4) | 贾政听(3) | 便起身(2) |
| 贾母因(11) | 口内笑(4) | 贾琏便(3) | 便悄悄(2) |
| 王夫人(11) | 忙陪笑(4) | 贾琏听(3) | 便上来(2) |
| 进来回(10) | 探春听(4) | 李十儿(3) | 便推他(2) |
| 走来,(10) | 听宝玉(4) | 忙起身(3) | 不等人(2) |
| 听了,(9) | 袭人见(4) | 他母亲(3) | 不等他(2) |
| 站起来(9) | 向宝玉(4) | 袭人听(3) | 传进来(2) |
| 过来,(8) | 邢夫人(4) | 向贾蓉(3) | 大喜,(2) |
| 宝玉便(7) | 薛姨妈(4) | 笑了,(3) | 道喜,(2) |
| 悄悄的(7) | 薛蟠听(4) | 丫头们(3) | 二人忙(2) |
| 宝钗听(6) | 一个又(4) | 丫鬟来(3) | 凤姐笑(2) |
| 出来,(6) | 众人听(4) | 一面笑(3) | 跪下,(2) |
| 回来,(6) | 众人笑(4) | 有人回(3) | 和平儿(2) |
| 轻轻的(6) | 宝玉忙(3) | 又不好(3) | 和众人(2) |
| 下来,(6) | 宝钗便(3) | 又笑着(3) | 慌了,(2) |
| 乱嚷,(5) | 宝钗因(3) | 雨村听(3) | 回话,(2) |

| | | | |
|---|---|---|---|
| 回贾母(2) | 那婆子(2) | 探春便(2) | 一个人(2) |
| 贾环便(2) | 那丫头(2) | 探春因(2) | 一齐都(2) |
| 贾母笑(2) | 跑进来(2) | 听见,(2) | 有人来(2) |
| 贾琏又(2) | 陪酒的(2) | 外面人(2) | 有一个(2) |
| 进来笑(2) | 陪笑回(2) | 袭人便(2) | 鸳鸯听(2) |
| 口内只(2) | 平儿回(2) | 喜儿便(2) | 这个又(2) |
| 拦住,(2) | 平儿笑(2) | 香菱便(2) | 这一个(2) |
| 老婆们(2) | 婆子便(2) | 湘云因(2) | 只不好(2) |
| 连忙解(2) | 起身,(2) | 向宝钗(2) | 众人便(2) |
| 林之孝(2) | 起身来(2) | 向贾母(2) | 众人回(2) |
| 刘老老(2) | 起身笑(2) | 向绣橘(2) | 走过来(2) |
| 乱叫,(2) | 晴雯听(2) | 向紫鹃(2) | 黛玉笑(2) |
| 马道婆(2) | 晴雯因(2) | 小丫头(2) | 黛玉因(2) |
| 忙过来(2) | 请安,(2) | 丫头便(2) | 黛玉又(2) |
| 忙拉他(2) | 嚷进来(2) | 丫头来(2) | |
| 那个又(2) | 上来,(2) | 摇手儿(2) | |
| 那两个(2) | 四人回(2) | 也不敢(2) | |

"说"字前面的三字语义搭配字符字频在 2 次以上的有 153 个。此次筛选中出现了许多三字人名与"说"的搭配,如"凤姐儿说""王夫人说"等。"××听说"的格式也很突出,如"宝玉听说""贾母听说""宝钗听说""黛玉听说""探春听说"等。表示伴随动作或状态的搭配有:"进来回说""悄悄的说""轻轻的说""口内笑说"等。"说"的对象性也得以明确,如"向袭人说""告诉他说""向宝玉说"等。此外,与"笑"字的搭配一样,"说"字也有一类重要的搭配为"动词+逗号(,)+说",表示在某个动作之后又出现了"说"的动作,如"起来,说""进来,说""走来,说""听了,说""过来,说""出来,说""回来,说"等。这种表述方式同时强调前面的动作和"说"的动作,交代"说话"时的前提和背景。

位于"说"字右侧的字频在 2 次以上的语义搭配三字字符有:

| | | | |
|---|---|---|---|
| 到这里(9) | 不出来(3) | 了一遍(2) | 了一声(2) |
| 了几句(6) | 到这句(2) | 了一句(2) | 着又问(2) |

"说"字后面的三字语义搭配字符仅有 8 个,大多是作为插入语或表示伴随状态,如"说到这里""说到这句""说着又问"等。

**4. "说"字的四字符搭配**

检索"说"字左侧的四字搭配字符,将字频在 2 次以上的语义搭配字符列举如下:

| | | |
|---|---|---|
| 众人都笑(9) | 出来,因(2) | 袭人等忙(2) |
| 听了,都(7) | 打发人来(2) | 想一想,(2) |
| 笑起来,(7) | 都笑了,(2) | 向王夫人(2) |
| 红了脸,(5) | 凤姐儿又(2) | 笑几声,(2) |
| 听了,便(5) | 躬身陪笑(2) | 邢夫人因(2) |
| 哭起来,(4) | 和王夫人(2) | 薛姨妈听(2) |
| 听见如此(4) | 黄了脸,(2) | 薛蝌进来(2) |
| 王夫人因(4) | 贾母等都(2) | 丫头回来(2) |
| 想了想,(4) | 贾母如此(2) | 丫头们都(2) |
| 周瑞家的(4) | 见他如此(2) | 丫头们回(2) |
| 半日回来(3) | 进来,回(2) | 丫头跑来(2) |
| 出来,笑(3) | 进来,笑(2) | 丫鬟们回(2) |
| 喘吁吁的(3) | 进来了,(2) | 一个丫头(2) |
| 凤姐儿听(3) | 看了,都(2) | 一句话没(2) |
| 刘老老便(3) | 忙走来,(2) | 一面回头(2) |
| 秋纹走来(3) | 那陪酒的(2) | 因又笑着(2) |
| 听了,忙(3) | 那一个又(2) | 迎上来,(2) |
| 小丫头子(3) | 女先儿回(2) | 与众人都(2) |
| 笑嘻嘻的(3) | 起来,因(2) | 站起来,(2) |
| 宝玉不便(2) | 起来,只(2) | 赵姨娘便(2) |
| 宝玉忙笑(2) | 听说,便(2) | 只得勉强(2) |
| 背后有人(2) | 王夫人等(2) | 呷着嘴儿(2) |
| 便站起来(2) | 王夫人听(2) | |
| 颤巍巍的(2) | 西平王便(2) | |

"说"字前面的四字语义搭配字符有 70 个,其中出现了许多形象的四字词语来修饰"说",且格式一致,均使用了叠字手法,富有节奏感,如"喘吁吁的说""笑嘻嘻的说""颤巍巍的说""咭哝哝的说"。除了常规的修饰性词语如"众人都说""王夫人因说""宝玉忙笑说""凤姐儿又说""刘老老便说"等,也有非常自由的表达方式,如"半日回来说""打发人来说""躬身陪笑说"等。"动词+逗号(,)+说"形式的例子也很多,且在"说"之前多了一些修饰成分,如"听了,都说"

"听了,便说""出来,因说""起来,只说"等。

"说"字右侧的四字符搭配,字频大于 2 的搭配字符仅有 4 个,即"说到这句话"(2 次)、"说了几句话"(2 次)、"说了一句道"(2 次)、"说着又问:"(2 次)。

**5. "说"字的五字符搭配**

检索"说"字左侧的五字搭配字符,将字频在 2 次以上的语义搭配字符列举如下:

| | | |
|---|---|---|
| 啐了一口,(4) | 婆子进来回(2) | 掀帘进来,(2) |
| 传进话来,(3) | 请了安,便(2) | 小丫头回来(2) |
| 都笑起来,(3) | 伤起心来,(2) | 小丫头跑来(2) |
| 想了一想,(3) | 叹了口气,(2) | 笑了一笑,(2) |
| 便红了脸,(2) | 听了大喜,(2) | 笑起来了,(2) |
| 咕咕哝哝的(2) | 王善保家的(2) | 写出来,因(2) |
| 唬了一跳,(2) | 袭人忙拉他(2) | 丫头来请,(2) |
| 贾母听了,(2) | 袭人走来,(2) | 饮了门杯,(2) |
| 冷笑几声,(2) | 吓了一跳,(2) | 迎出来,笑(2) |

"说"字前面的五字语义搭配字符有 27 个,除了五字人物名称(如"王善保家的")与"说"的搭配外,最大的特色是"动词＋逗号(,)＋说"的表达,且形式、内容丰富多彩,将"说"字前的人物神态和会话环境描写得非常细致传神,如"啐了一口,说""都笑起来,说""便红了脸,说""唬/吓了一跳,说""伤起心来,说""叹了口气,说""听了大喜,说""笑起来了,说""请了安,便说""掀帘进来,说""饮了门杯,说""迎出来,笑说"等。

"说"字右侧的五字符搭配,字频大于 2 的搭配字符仅有 2 个:"说着,人回:"(4 次)和"说了一句道"(2 次)。

**6. "说"字搭配研究小结**

通过表 2-8 我们可以看出,在字频大于 2 的与"说"字相关语义搭配中,左侧三字符的搭配数量最多,约占总搭配的近 33%;其次为左侧二字符搭配,约占 28%,左侧四字符搭配占 15%;数量最少的是右侧四字符和五字符搭配,均占总搭配的 1% 不到。

表 2-8 会话引导语"说"字搭配统计

| 类别 | 数量 | 百分比 |
|---|---|---|
| 一字符搭配(左) | 46 | 9.89 |
| 一字符搭配(右) | 14 | 3.01 |

(续表)

| 类别 | 数量 | 百分比 |
|---|---|---|
| 二字符搭配(左) | 129 | 27.74 |
| 二字符搭配(右) | 12 | 2.58 |
| 三字符搭配(左) | 153 | 32.90 |
| 三字符搭配(右) | 8 | 1.72 |
| 四字符搭配(左) | 70 | 15.05 |
| 四字符搭配(右) | 4 | 0.86 |
| 五字符搭配(左) | 27 | 5.81 |
| 五字符搭配(右) | 2 | 0.43 |
| 合计 | 465 | 100.00 |

## (四) 关于"因"字的研究

"因"字也是《红楼梦》会话引导语文本的特色字之一,在会话引导语文本中的字频为 689,占总文本的 0.694%,在非会话引导语文本中的字频为 1185,占总文本的 0.156%。会话引导语中的比例是非会话引导语中比例的 4.5 倍。

《新华字典》中对于"因"的解释有:①〈名词〉原因;理由;机会;②〈动词〉依靠,凭借;沿袭,承袭;连接;顺应;③〈介词〉由于,因为;趁着,乘便;④〈形容词〉亲近;⑤〈连词〉于是,就;因而。

"因"字在《红楼梦》中绝大多数是作为连词来用的,用于会话引导语中很少表示"因为"的意思,大多表达"于是""就"或"因而"之意,有承上启下的作用,如:

- 士隐听了,不便再问,因笑道:"玄机固不可泄露……"(第一回)
- 雨村因问:"近日都中可有新闻没有?"(第二回)
- 众人见黛玉年纪虽小,其举止言谈不俗,身体面貌虽弱不胜衣,却有一段风流态度,便知他有不足之症,因问:"常服何药?为何不治好了?"(第三回)
- 警幻见宝玉甚无趣味,因叹:"痴儿竟尚未悟!"(第五回)
- 凤姐早已明白了,听他不会说话,因笑道:"不必说了,我知道了。"因问周瑞家的道:"这老老不知用了早饭没有呢?"(第六回)

此外,《红楼梦》中的"因"还有一类特殊的用法值得我们关注,那就是"因Y,因G"。在这个组合里"因"既有"因为"之义,也有"因此、于是"之义。需要特别指出的是,在古代汉语中,"因"属于因果类复句关联标记的范畴,既可标示原因又可标示结果;而在现代汉语里,"因"仅用来标示原因。《红楼梦》中显然采用的是"因"在古代汉语中的用法,既标示原因又标示结果,相当于现代汉语中的"因为 Y,所以 G"句式。"因"标因和"因"标果结合在一起,构成一个"同表异里"的因果句式(邢福义,1993:39)。

在"因 Y,因 G"的句式中,"因 G"是会话引导语成分,核心动词常用"说"类动词,而 Y 的核心动词常用"见"类动词。因此"因见……因说……"的说法在《红楼梦》中非常常见,例如:

- 凤姐等至净室更衣净手毕,因见智能儿越发长高了,模样儿越发出息的水灵了,因说道:"你们师徒怎么这些日子也不往我们那里去?"(第十五回)

- 那时天色将晚,因见袭人去了,却有两三个丫鬟伺候,此时并无呼唤之事,因说道:"你们且去梳洗,等我叫时再来。"(第三十四回)

- 因见尤氏进来,不似方才和蔼,只呆呆的坐着,李纨因问道:"你过来了,可吃些东西? 只怕饿了?"(第七十五回)

- 贾母因见月至天中,比先越发精彩可爱,因说:"如此好月,不可不闻笛。"(第七十六回)

当然,也有些时候只在 G 里出现"说"类动词,而在 Y 里不出现"见"类动词。如:

因此时薛姨妈李婶娘都在座,邢夫人及尤氏等也都过来请安,还未过去,贾母因向王夫人等说道:"今日我才说这话,素日我不说:……"(第五十二回)

## 第二节 《红楼梦》与古典白话小说会话引导语对比研究

《红楼梦》与《水浒传》《三国演义》《西游记》是公认的中国古典文学四大名著。这四部著作历久不衰,是汉语文学中不可多得的杰出作品。《红楼梦》创作于 18 世纪中叶的清朝,距今 200 多年,位居四大名著之首。《水浒传》创作于元末明初,距今 600 多年;《三国演义》略晚,与《水浒传》属于同时期作品;《西游记》成书于明朝中期,距今 400 多年。《金瓶梅》虽不是四大名著之一,但它是中国第一部文人独立创作的长篇白话世情章回小说,成书于明朝晚期,距今约 400 年,比《红楼梦》早一个多世纪。《红楼梦》中多有借鉴《金瓶梅》的痕迹,两书存在较明显的继承关系①。因此,《水浒传》《三国演义》《西游记》和《金瓶梅》都与《红楼梦》有着很大的关联和可比性。此部分我们将对《红楼梦》与《三国演义》《水浒传》《西游记》《金瓶梅》中的会话引导语作对比研究。

---

① 脂砚斋曾在《红楼梦》庚辰本第十三回眉批中云:"《红楼梦》深得《金瓶》壶奥"。

## 一、古典白话小说中的会话引导语特色

以《红楼梦》为代表的章回体小说由话本小说发展而来,使用的是日常白话,在表现对话场景时可以利用自己言、文一致的语体优势尽力"再现"情境,创造另一种生动、逼真的艺术效果。一般来说,白话语体可以极大程度"模仿"人物会话,真切再现人物的会话情景,从而使作品带上鲜活、逼真的艺术风格。古典白话小说的叙述者时而叙述事件的发展过程,时而模仿人物口吻进行会话,为了把叙述语与人物会话分开,在行文中不得不在每一段人物会话甚至每一段内心独白之前加上引导性词句,并且尽可能使用直接式,引导语只能加在前面,不能放到任何其他地方,以免引起误解。

在中国古典小说中,由于当时没有标点符号,为了将叙述语和人物话语分开,作家必须使用"某某道""某某曰"的格式,即采用直接引语形式;另外,由说书话本发展而来的中国小说喜好模仿人物原话,这对中国古典小说的叙事体裁有较大的影响(申丹,2001:290)。

古典白话小说采用的基本上都是"引导式"引言方式。这也成为白话小说与现当代小说最大的风格区别特征之一。如:

- 宝玉道:"我怎么没有见过他,你带他来我瞧瞧。"(《红楼梦》第五回)
- 秦氏笑道:"我这屋子大约神仙也可以住得了。"(《红楼梦》第五回)
- 贾母便说:"你们去罢,让我们自在说说话儿。"(《红楼梦》第五回)

每一个人发话之前都加上了"说""道""问"等引导语,且都位于会话之前。这种一成不变的记言方式一直延续到20世纪以后的一些民族传统风格的作品,例如赵树理的《小二黑结婚》《李有才板话》等,仍只采用一种引导式的"说:……""道:……"记言方式。在现当代小说中的会话引导语形式非常灵活,除了"追加式""插入式",还出现了完全依赖话轮分配及上下文语境的没有引导语的"无标记"记言方式,而这在没有现代标点符号隔断的古典白话小说中是不可想象的方式。

古典白话小说与现代小说对话引导语位置不一的主要原因在于,中文原来只有简单的点断,在引入现代标点符号之前,不仅没有引号,没有逗号、句号,甚至不能分段。缺乏标点和分段的古典格式使叙述中的引语一直是直接引语,中国古典白话小说中使用直接引语的现象是极为显著的,这几乎成了中国古典小说最为显著的叙述语式标志。

此外,古典白话小说具有拟书场风格,说书人一般喜好模仿人物原话,因此较多使用直接引用方式。

为了充分地实现表现人民大众情感、使大众情感获得情感体验与满足这一初衷,古代白话小说除了依靠"话须通俗方传远,语必关风始动人"(冯梦龙)来

迎合"里耳",还依赖于相对固定的程式结构和类型化描写来强化。这种程式化不仅表现在内容、情节的安排方面;也表现在艺术体制上,如开场诗、得胜头回、正话、收场诗的结构方式;更表现在语言形式上。(卢惠惠,2007:253)

## 二、《红楼梦》会话引导语与古典白话小说对比研究

为了分析《红楼梦》中会话引导语的特色,我们将《红楼梦》会话引导语中字频在前 50 的高频字筛选出来(主要人物的人名用字不计算在内),然后按照会话引导语的字频顺序将这 50 字在《红楼梦》中的字频与在《三国演义》《水浒传》《西游记》《金瓶梅》中的字频做比较研究。

经筛选,《红楼梦》会话引导语文本中前 50 个高频字如表 2-9 所示。

表 2-9　会话引导语前 50 位高频字

| 排序 | 字符 | 字频 | 百分比 | 排序 | 字符 | 字频 | 百分比 |
|---|---|---|---|---|---|---|---|
| 1 | 道 | 9116 | 9.185 | 21 | 那 | 468 | 0.472 |
| 2 | 说 | 3112 | 3.136 | 22 | 众 | 390 | 0.393 |
| 3 | 笑 | 2958 | 2.98 | 23 | 子 | 384 | 0.387 |
| 4 | 了 | 1692 | 1.705 | 24 | 想 | 374 | 0.377 |
| 5 | 便 | 1260 | 1.27 | 25 | 里 | 338 | 0.341 |
| 6 | 一 | 1205 | 1.214 | 26 | 上 | 335 | 0.338 |
| 7 | 来 | 1150 | 1.159 | 27 | 都 | 322 | 0.324 |
| 8 | 又 | 990 | 0.998 | 28 | 个 | 321 | 0.323 |
| 9 | 的 | 974 | 0.981 | 29 | 起 | 303 | 0.305 |
| 10 | 问 | 900 | 0.907 | 30 | 在 | 303 | 0.305 |
| 11 | 听 | 882 | 0.889 | 31 | 向 | 298 | 0.3 |
| 12 | 着 | 881 | 0.888 | 32 | 面 | 286 | 0.288 |
| 13 | 见 | 862 | 0.869 | 33 | 家 | 282 | 0.284 |
| 14 | 忙 | 753 | 0.759 | 34 | 也 | 280 | 0.282 |
| 15 | 因 | 689 | 0.694 | 35 | 这 | 273 | 0.275 |
| 16 | 他 | 567 | 0.571 | 36 | 叫 | 271 | 0.273 |
| 17 | 头 | 566 | 0.57 | 37 | 心 | 261 | 0.263 |
| 18 | 只 | 550 | 0.554 | 38 | 小 | 258 | 0.26 |
| 19 | 回 | 538 | 0.542 | 39 | 话 | 251 | 0.253 |
| 20 | 不 | 481 | 0.485 | 40 | 进 | 246 | 0.248 |

（续表）

| 排序 | 字符 | 字频 | 百分比 | 排序 | 字符 | 字频 | 百分比 |
|------|------|------|--------|------|------|------|--------|
| 41 | 丫 | 245 | 0.247 | 46 | 是 | 217 | 0.219 |
| 42 | 看 | 236 | 0.238 | 47 | 手 | 209 | 0.211 |
| 43 | 下 | 227 | 0.229 | 48 | 得 | 204 | 0.206 |
| 44 | 正 | 225 | 0.227 | 49 | 去 | 191 | 0.192 |
| 45 | 出 | 217 | 0.219 | 50 | 走 | 190 | 0.191 |

　　笔者检索了以上 50 个字在《红楼梦》原文总文本及分别在《三国演义》《水浒传》《西游记》和《金瓶梅》中的字频及百分比如表 2 - 10 所示。

表 2 - 10　会话引导语前 50 位高频字在三部古典白话小说中的字频统计

| 排序 | 字符 | 会话引导语 | 百分比 | 《红楼梦》 | 百分比 | 《金瓶梅》 | 百分比 | 《西游记》 | 百分比 | 《三国演义》 | 百分比 | 《水浒传》 | 百分比 |
|------|------|------------|--------|------------|--------|------------|--------|------------|--------|--------------|--------|------------|--------|
| 1 | 道 | 9116 | 9.185 | 11 092 | 1.293 | 9672 | 1.279 | 10 991 | 1.541 | 546 | 0.092 | 9790 | 1.212 |
| 2 | 说 | 3112 | 3.136 | 9587 | 1.117 | 6264 | 0.829 | 2314 | 0.324 | 1396 | 0.235 | 3393 | 0.420 |
| 3 | 笑 | 2958 | 2.98 | 3913 | 0.456 | 1209 | 0.160 | 1016 | 0.142 | 482 | 0.081 | 540 | 0.067 |
| 4 | 了 | 1692 | 1.705 | 21 088 | 2.458 | 13 963 | 1.847 | 7690 | 1.078 | 1417 | 0.238 | 10840 | 1.342 |
| 5 | 便 | 1260 | 1.27 | 3688 | 0.43 | 1786 | 0.236 | 753 | 0.106 | 905 | 0.152 | 4123 | 0.510 |
| 6 | 一 | 1205 | 1.214 | 11674 | 1.361 | 1864 | 0.247 | 7895 | 1.107 | 4026 | 0.677 | 9332 | 1.155 |
| 7 | 来 | 1150 | 1.159 | 11221 | 1.308 | 10 627 | 1.406 | 5928 | 0.831 | 3285 | 0.553 | 9351 | 1.157 |
| 8 | 又 | 990 | 0.998 | 5088 | 0.593 | 2689 | 0.356 | 2476 | 0.347 | 1190 | 0.200 | 1936 | 0.240 |
| 9 | 的 | 974 | 0.981 | 15608 | 1.819 | 7882 | 1.043 | 5388 | 0.755 | 154 | 0.026 | 4104 | 0.508 |
| 10 | 问 | 900 | 0.907 | 1977 | 0.23 | 1717 | 0.227 | 915 | 0.128 | 1024 | 0.172 | 1020 | 0.126 |
| 11 | 听 | 882 | 0.889 | 3233 | 0.377 | 1179 | 0.156 | 979 | 0.137 | 628 | 0.106 | 1610 | 0.199 |
| 12 | 着 | 881 | 0.888 | 6578 | 0.767 | 3832 | 0.507 | 2478 | 0.347 | 288 | 0.048 | 2742 | 0.339 |
| 13 | 见 | 862 | 0.869 | 4789 | 0.558 | 3537 | 0.468 | 3392 | 0.476 | 2546 | 0.428 | 4322 | 0.535 |
| 14 | 忙 | 753 | 0.759 | 1768 | 0.206 | 488 | 0.065 | 306 | 0.043 | 149 | 0.025 | 399 | 0.049 |
| 15 | 因 | 689 | 0.694 | 1874 | 0.218 | 957 | 0.127 | 480 | 0.067 | 470 | 0.079 | 706 | 0.087 |
| 16 | 他 | 567 | 0.571 | 7512 | 0.875 | 7794 | 1.031 | 5718 | 0.802 | 396 | 0.067 | 3068 | 0.380 |

| 排序 | 字符 | 会话引导语 | 百分比 | 《红楼梦》 | 百分比 | 《金瓶梅》 | 百分比 | 《西游记》 | 百分比 | 《三国演义》 | 百分比 | 《水浒传》 | 百分比 |
|---|---|---|---|---|---|---|---|---|---|---|---|---|---|
| 17 | 头 | 566 | 0.57 | 3498 | 0.408 | 2357 | 0.312 | 2136 | 0.299 | 463 | 0.078 | 2817 | 0.349 |
| 18 | 只 | 550 | 0.554 | 4591 | 0.535 | 3094 | 0.409 | 2478 | 0.347 | 1179 | 0.198 | 4261 | 0.527 |
| 19 | 回 | 538 | 0.542 | 3051 | 0.356 | 1565 | 0.207 | 1283 | 0.180 | 1719 | 0.289 | 2011 | 0.249 |
| 20 | 不 | 481 | 0.485 | 14486 | 1.688 | 10 420 | 1.378 | 8825 | 1.237 | 6730 | 1.133 | 8089 | 1.001 |
| 21 | 那 | 468 | 0.472 | 4936 | 0.575 | 4036 | 0.534 | 7335 | 1.028 | 210 | 0.035 | 4515 | 0.559 |
| 22 | 众 | 390 | 0.393 | 1177 | 0.137 | 682 | 0.090 | 1175 | 0.165 | 1142 | 0.192 | 1783 | 0.221 |
| 23 | 子 | 384 | 0.387 | 5417 | 0.631 | 6729 | 0.890 | 2942 | 0.412 | 1377 | 0.232 | 2890 | 0.358 |
| 24 | 想 | 374 | 0.377 | 1794 | 0.209 | 518 | 0.069 | 486 | 0.068 | 125 | 0.021 | 387 | 0.048 |
| 25 | 里 | 338 | 0.341 | 5321 | 0.62 | 4512 | 0.597 | 2822 | 0.396 | 500 | 0.084 | 5150 | 0.637 |
| 26 | 上 | 335 | 0.338 | 3793 | 0.442 | 4556 | 0.603 | 3691 | 0.517 | 2048 | 0.345 | 5601 | 0.693 |
| 27 | 都 | 322 | 0.324 | 2672 | 0.311 | 1646 | 0.218 | 1173 | 0.164 | 754 | 0.127 | 2763 | 0.342 |
| 28 | 个 | 321 | 0.323 | 5604 | 0.653 | 4589 | 0.607 | 5682 | 0.797 | 258 | 0.043 | 6346 | 0.785 |
| 29 | 起 | 303 | 0.305 | 2487 | 0.29 | 1616 | 0.214 | 1067 | 0.150 | 993 | 0.167 | 1991 | 0.246 |
| 30 | 在 | 303 | 0.305 | 3911 | 0.456 | 5144 | 0.680 | 3317 | 0.465 | 1625 | 0.273 | 4331 | 0.536 |
| 31 | 向 | 298 | 0.3 | 588 | 0.069 | 722 | 0.096 | 352 | 0.049 | 225 | 0.038 | 417 | 0.052 |
| 32 | 面 | 286 | 0.288 | 1743 | 0.203 | 1501 | 0.199 | 951 | 0.133 | 807 | 0.136 | 2079 | 0.257 |
| 33 | 家 | 282 | 0.284 | 3865 | 0.45 | 4760 | 0.630 | 1265 | 0.177 | 494 | 0.083 | 2047 | 0.253 |
| 34 | 也 | 280 | 0.282 | 6059 | 0.706 | 2851 | 0.377 | 2927 | 0.410 | 2263 | 0.381 | 1831 | 0.227 |
| 35 | 这 | 273 | 0.275 | 7654 | 0.892 | 4322 | 0.572 | 3782 | 0.530 | 133 | 0.022 | 3951 | 0.489 |
| 36 | 叫 | 271 | 0.273 | 2440 | 0.284 | 1671 | 0.221 | 1408 | 0.197 | 297 | 0.050 | 1538 | 0.190 |
| 37 | 心 | 261 | 0.263 | 2601 | 0.303 | 1584 | 0.210 | 1458 | 0.204 | 1019 | 0.171 | 1450 | 0.179 |
| 38 | 小 | 258 | 0.26 | 2003 | 0.233 | 2781 | 0.368 | 1516 | 0.213 | 656 | 0.110 | 3035 | 0.376 |
| 39 | 话 | 251 | 0.253 | 2453 | 0.286 | 1264 | 0.167 | 511 | 0.072 | 88 | 0.015 | 911 | 0.113 |
| 40 | 进 | 246 | 0.248 | 1542 | 0.18 | 1158 | 0.153 | 775 | 0.109 | 808 | 0.136 | 1204 | 0.149 |
| 41 | 丫 | 245 | 0.247 | 1223 | 0.143 | 419 | 0.055 | 34 | 0.005 | 0 | 0 | 43 | 0.005 |
| 42 | 看 | 236 | 0.238 | 2380 | 0.277 | 2203 | 0.291 | 2031 | 0.285 | 517 | 0.087 | 2313 | 0.286 |

（续表）

| 排序 | 字符 | 会话引导语 | 百分比 | 《红楼梦》 | 百分比 | 《金瓶梅》 | 百分比 | 《西游记》 | 百分比 | 《三国演义》 | 百分比 | 《水浒传》 | 百分比 |
|---|---|---|---|---|---|---|---|---|---|---|---|---|---|
| 43 | 下 | 227 | 0.229 | 2728 | 0.318 | 3678 | 0.487 | 2960 | 0.415 | 2776 | 0.467 | 4503 | 0.557 |
| 44 | 正 | 225 | 0.227 | 1379 | 0.161 | 1293 | 0.171 | 1284 | 0.180 | 1106 | 0.186 | 1750 | 0.217 |
| 45 | 出 | 217 | 0.219 | 3153 | 0.367 | 2632 | 0.348 | 2267 | 0.318 | 2342 | 0.394 | 2756 | 0.341 |
| 46 | 是 | 217 | 0.219 | 9928 | 1.157 | 5530 | 0.732 | 6463 | 0.906 | 1610 | 0.271 | 5698 | 0.705 |
| 47 | 手 | 209 | 0.211 | 1010 | 0.118 | 1093 | 0.145 | 1367 | 0.192 | 626 | 0.105 | 1476 | 0.183 |
| 48 | 得 | 204 | 0.206 | 3306 | 0.385 | 1627 | 0.215 | 3805 | 0.533 | 1570 | 0.264 | 4653 | 0.576 |
| 49 | 去 | 191 | 0.192 | 6013 | 0.701 | 5084 | 0.673 | 3668 | 0.514 | 1844 | 0.310 | 5247 | 0.649 |
| 50 | 走 | 190 | 0.191 | 1237 | 0.144 | 1476 | 0.195 | 1282 | 0.180 | 791 | 0.133 | 1336 | 0.165 |

　　随即笔者考察了《红楼梦》会话引导语相对于四部古典名著的独特字和特色字。方法是使用 AntConc 软件中的 Word List 和 Keyword List 功能，将《水浒传》《三国演义》《西游记》和《金瓶梅》四部著作合并成一个文本进行分析比较。

　　《红楼梦》中的会话引导语相对于四部古典名著来讲，独特字有 25 个：

| | | | |
|---|---|---|---|
| 琏(312) | 唻(4) | 螯(2) | 箈(1) |
| 雯(133) | 扔(4) | 噔(1) | 蘅(1) |
| 嬷(116) | 诧(4) | 墅(1) | 锞(1) |
| 碰(12) | 哟(3) | 掰(1) | 㬎(1) |
| 詹(12) | 喊(2) | 瓢(1) | |
| 嘟(7) | 戤(2) | 畸(1) | |
| 撂(7) | 蛔(2) | 硼(1) | |

　　特色字有 3 个：琏（字频 312，关键度 5137.672）、雯（字频 133，关键度 2190.098）、嬷（字频 116，关键度 1910.160）。

　　独特字中，去除"琏""雯""詹"等人名用字，以及"戤""蛔""墅"等名词，出现频率最高的独特字是"嬷"。该字在《水浒传》《三国演义》《西游记》和《金瓶梅》中一次都没有使用过。特色字中"琏"和"雯"均为人名用字，唯一有参考意义的也是"嬷"字。

下面将对《红楼梦》会话引导语中具有代表性的独特字"嬷""嘟""诧""哧""喊"和"嗌"进行分析。

**（一）关于"嬷"字的研究**

《新华字典》对"嬷"的解释是：①称呼老年妇女；②旧时称呼奶妈。在《红楼梦》里，曹雪芹对于嬷嬷们虽然着墨不多，但也是见血见肉，人物形象丰满：嬷嬷有在府上的老年女仆人，如宋嬷嬷，更多的是奶妈兼仆人，如李嬷嬷、赵嬷嬷等，最显贵的则可以算赖嬷嬷了。我们知道，奶嬷嬷的地位在古代还是相对高的，至少在她哺乳的对象面前是有一定话语权的。这也解释了为什么"嬷"字在《红楼梦》的会话引导语中可以占有一席之地。此外，曹雪芹的曾祖母曾做过康熙皇帝的"嬷嬷"，这或许也成为曹公不惜分出笔墨来对嬷嬷们进行描写刻画、赋予她们话语权的原因之一。

本研究使用 AntConc 软件中的 Concordance Plot 功能搜寻"嬷"字在《红楼梦》一百二十回会话引导语中的分布，发现"嬷"字最后一次出现是在全文约三分之二处，此后再也没有出现。图 2-3 是检测结果。

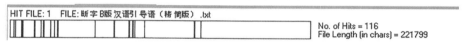

**图 2-3　"嬷"字在各章回会话引导语的分布情况**

事实上，经核查后发现，"嬷"字最后一次使用是在第七十七回中的"李嬷嬷指道："。据此可以初步判断，嬷嬷们在《红楼梦》的后三分之一部分（确切地说是在第七十七回以后）的话语权和角色身份已经较之前淡化了许多。

**（二）关于"嘟"字和"诧"字的研究**

《现代汉语词典》对于"嘟"的定义为：①象声词：汽车喇叭～地响了一声；②（嘴）向前突出、撅着：弟弟听说不让他去，气得～起了嘴。③（～囔）自言自语，含抱怨的意思，如"别瞎～了"（"囔"读轻声）。

《红楼梦》会话引导语中的 7 个"嘟"字都以"嘟囔"或"嘟嚷"的形式出现，多表示不满情绪：

钱来，口内 嘟 囔说：　　　　　　　说酒令，嘟 嘟 嚷嚷说：
几画，口内 嘟 嘟囔囔的，　　　　　几下，口里 嘟 嘟囔囔的骂
画，口内嘟 嘟 囔囔的，又　　　　　下，口里嘟 嘟 囔囔的骂道
语说酒令，嘟 嘟囔囔说：

《红楼梦》会话引导语中的独特字"诧"全部是以"诧异"的形式出现：

| | |
|---|---|
| 听了,十分诧异,因说道 | 人听了,都诧异道: |
| 宝玉诧异道: | 听了,又是诧异,又笑道 |

《红楼梦》原文中表示"感到惊奇或奇怪"的意思时,有两种不同的写法,"咤异"和"诧异",其中"咤异"的用法较多,有 29 个。在《水浒传》《三国演义》《西游记》和《金瓶梅》全文中均没有出现"诧"字;"咤"字倒是出现了 12 次,且有 11 次都是在《西游记》中,表"大叫""怒吼"之意:

| | | | |
|---|---|---|---|
| 金瓶梅 | 阵上将军叱咤献威风; | 西游 | 那怪看得眼咤,小龙丢了 |
| 西游 | 一声叱咤如雷吼,两 | 西游 | 闻得行者叱咤一声道:" |
| 西游 | 刀强弓,大咤一声道:" | 西游 | 喊声叱咤振山川,吆 |
| 西游 | 见了他,大咤一声"休走 | 西游 | 一声"唵吽咤唎",即使 |
| 西游 | 至面前,大咤一声道:" | 西游 | 里容得,大咤一声,现了 |
| 西游 | 妖杖诚然凶咤。 | 西游 | 头模样,叱咤一声,喝道 |

（三）关于拟声字"咻""喊"和"噔"的研究

《红楼梦》中使用了大量的拟声字词,这对刻画人物性格、渲染环境气氛起到了非常重要的作用。在《红楼梦》会话引导语相对于四部古典名著的独特词里,就出现了诸如"咻""喊"和"噔"之类的拟声字:

| | |
|---|---|
| ,鼻孔里"咻咻"两声, | 屋子的人,喊喊喳喳的说 |
| 鼻孔里"咻咻"两声,冷 | 子的人,喊喊喳喳的说: |
| 在床上"扑咻"的一声笑 | 只听"咯噔"的一声门 |
| 凤姐"扑咻"的一笑: | |

以上"咻""喊"和"噔"都属于拟声字,直接模拟人物或事物的声音,使语言更加具体、生动和形象,给人以如闻其声、身临其境的感觉。其中"咻"指的是"发出咝咝的声音",常与"笑"的动作连用;"喊"形容细碎的说话声,含有"众人七嘴八舌"的蕴意;"噔"表示"沉重的东西落地或撞击物体的声音",可以产生独特的音响效果。

## 三、汉语言说动词"道"的演变

汉语从古到今言说动词很多。据不完全统计,仅不太冷僻的单音词就不下一百个,如果加上复音词,数量就更大。汪维辉(2003)曾对"说类词"做过统计,包括言、云、曰、语、说、道、讲、话、咟等上位词,以及话、谈、论、议、评、谋、谓、白、告、诏、报、诉等下位词。汪维辉(2003)指出:动词语义场中有上位词和下位词之分,上位词是只有核心义素而无限定义素的词,如"说"的义素可以分析为:+使用+言语+表达+意义;下位词则是在核心义素的基础上加上各种各样限定义素的词,如"骂"的义素为:+使用+(粗野/恶意的)言语+表达+(侮辱/斥责等)意思,他认为一个多义词可以既是上位词也是下位词,如现代汉语中的"说"以表示"责备、批评"的意思出现时,就成了"说类词"下位词。这些言说动词,不仅在汉语历史上数量相当多,而且用法也是错综复杂的。

黄冠颖(2007)曾在其硕士论文《直接引语现象分析》中对《莺莺传》《错斩崔宁》《水浒传》《三国演义》《西游记》和《红楼梦》中的会话引导词进行了研究,发现在古典白话小说中使用最多的四个会话引导词依次是:道(57%)＞曰(16%)＞说(3%)＞问(2%)。

"道"字在《红楼梦》《金瓶梅》《西游记》和《水浒传》中的数量都很大,分别为11 092(1.29%)、9672(1.28%)、1099(1.54%)和9790(1.21%),唯独在《三国演义》中比例非常低,总共只有546个,占总文本的0.09%。《三国演义》中字频最高的是"曰"字(8755个),人物会话大多以"曰"来引导,与其他几个文本有显著差异。如第一回中取几个例子:

- 角拜问姓名,老人曰:"吾乃南华老仙也。"
- 靖曰:"贼兵众,我兵寡,明公宜作速招军应敌。"
- 玄德幼时,与乡中小儿戏于树下,曰:"我为天子,当乘此车盖。"
- 随后一人厉声言曰:"大丈夫不与国家出力,何故长叹?"
- 时人有桥玄者谓操曰:"天下将乱,非命世之才不能济。能安之者,其在君乎?"

上古汉语中用于直接引语前的言说动词主要是"曰",如经典作品《论语》中的"子曰"等,都是"曰+直接引语"的用法。从先秦到隋,"曰+直接引语"一直是最主要的表达形式,如:

- 王占曰:"其有来艰,其胃丙不吉。"(郭沫若《殷契料编》一一三六)
- 庞恭与太子质于邯郸,谓魏王曰:"今一人言市有虎,王信之乎?"(《韩非子》)

"道"出现的频率很低。根据汪维辉(2003)考察,《论语》中"道"字出现的总次数为89次,用作"说"2次,《孟子》为150次中出现5例,《吕氏春秋》为245次中出现1例。

直到东汉到隋的中古汉语时期,"说"和"道"作为言说动词才开始活跃起来,表现出强大的生命力。唐宋时期"说"成为言说动词的核心词,但"说"带直接引语的用例不是很多,带直接引语的用法通常是由"言""道"和书面语词汇"云""曰"充当。蒋绍愚(1993)在《白居易诗中与"口"有关的动词》一文中指出,

"说"和"道"都可以加助词"着"。"说"还可以在后面加介词"向",说明"说"和"道"口语化的程度较高。"道"与"说"在词义和用法上都很相近,有时在同一段文章里"说"与"道"杂用,或者"道说"连用。"道"跟"说"在词义上的区别大致是:"说"是一般地说,强调的是"说话"这一行为;"道"则是详细地说,把事情说清楚,有时还加上主观的阐述或评论。如:

- 李靖本是个少年英锐、胆粗气豪的人,闻了此言,略无疑畏,但道:"我乃凡人,如何可代龙神行雨?"老夫人道:"君若肯代行,自有行雨之法。"《隋唐演义》

到了元明清时期,"说"和"道"带直接引语的用法开始大量出现。"道"与单纯的言说动词组合搭配,如"言道""说道"。因为"言""说"等动词本身的言说意义已经很强,所以"道"的功能发生转变,主要作用为介引直接引语。如:

- 张飞离了玄德,言道:"要知端的,除是根问去!"去于后槽根底,见亲随二人,便问,不肯实说。(《三国志评话》)
- 金生是要在里头的,答道:"只怕小生才能浅薄,不称将军任使。岂敢推辞?"(《二刻拍案惊奇》)

这也印证了"道"字在《红楼梦》原文会话引导语中的绝对优势地位。

## 第三节  《红楼梦》与现代小说会话引导语对比研究

在第二节中,我们将《红楼梦》会话引导语与古典名著《三国演义》《水浒传》《西游记》和《金瓶梅》的会话引导语进行了对比研究,属于共时研究的范畴。为了彰显《红楼梦》会话引导语的时代特色,我们认为有必要同时开展历时研究,将《红楼梦》与现代作品中的会话引导语进行比较分析。

笔者选取了鲁迅的小说集《呐喊》和《彷徨》、巴金的长篇小说《家》、矛盾的长篇小说《子夜》、莫言的长篇小说《丰乳肥臀》做对比研究,这些文学名著堪称现代作品中的精品。《呐喊》是鲁迅的第一部小说集,写于 1918—1922 年"五四"运动前后,《彷徨》写于"五四"运动后新文化阵营分化的时期。《家》于 1933 年 5 月出版首本单行本,《子夜》的出版时间是 1933 年 1 月,《丰乳肥臀》最早出版于 1995 年。

### 一、《红楼梦》会话引导语与现代小说字频统计

与前一节的考察方式一致,我们检索了《红楼梦》会话引导语文本中字频排名前 50 的高频字分别在《呐喊》和《彷徨》,以及《家》《子夜》和《丰乳肥臀》中的字频及百分比(见表 2 - 11)。

表 2-11  会话引导语前 50 位高频字在几部现代小说中的字频统计

| 排序 | 字符 | 会话引导语 | 百分比 | 《红楼梦》 | 百分比 | 《呐喊》＋《彷徨》 | 百分比 | 《家》 | 百分比 | 《子夜》 | 百分比 | 《丰乳肥臀》 | 百分比 |
|---|---|---|---|---|---|---|---|---|---|---|---|---|---|
| 1 | 道 | 9116 | 9.185 | 11092 | 1.293 | 494 | 0.368 | 813 | 0.354 | 814 | 0.312 | 1188 | 0.256 |
| 2 | 说 | 3112 | 3.136 | 9587 | 1.117 | 943 | 0.703 | 1933 | 0.843 | 1526 | 0.585 | 2573 | 0.555 |
| 3 | 笑 | 2958 | 2.98 | 3913 | 0.456 | 186 | 0.139 | 660 | 0.288 | 897 | 0.344 | 376 | 0.081 |
| 4 | 了 | 1692 | 1.705 | 21088 | 2.458 | 2833 | 2.111 | 5233 | 2.281 | 5446 | 2.088 | 7303 | 1.574 |
| 5 | 便 | 1260 | 1.27 | 3688 | 0.43 | 614 | 0.458 | 494 | 0.215 | 258 | 0.099 | 635 | 0.137 |
| 6 | 一 | 1205 | 1.214 | 11674 | 1.361 | 2459 | 1.832 | 4002 | 1.744 | 4915 | 1.884 | 7811 | 1.683 |
| 7 | 来 | 1150 | 1.159 | 11221 | 1.308 | 1245 | 0.928 | 2184 | 0.952 | 2409 | 0.923 | 3115 | 0.671 |
| 8 | 又 | 990 | 0.998 | 5088 | 0.593 | 553 | 0.412 | 993 | 0.433 | 1148 | 0.440 | 698 | 0.150 |
| 9 | 的 | 974 | 0.981 | 15608 | 1.819 | 5233 | 3.899 | 8328 | 3.630 | 8636 | 3.310 | 18863 | 4.065 |
| 10 | 问 | 900 | 0.907 | 1977 | 0.23 | 158 | 0.118 | 360 | 0.157 | 317 | 0.122 | 379 | 0.082 |
| 11 | 听 | 882 | 0.889 | 3233 | 0.377 | 223 | 0.166 | 359 | 0.156 | 373 | 0.143 | 385 | 0.083 |
| 12 | 着 | 881 | 0.888 | 6578 | 0.767 | 945 | 0.704 | 1783 | 0.777 | 1762 | 0.675 | 7386 | 1.592 |
| 13 | 见 | 862 | 0.869 | 4789 | 0.558 | 442 | 0.329 | 831 | 0.362 | 426 | 0.163 | 221 | 0.048 |
| 14 | 忙 | 753 | 0.759 | 1768 | 0.206 | 87 | 0.065 | 161 | 0.070 | 81 | 0.031 | 122 | 0.026 |
| 15 | 因 | 689 | 0.694 | 1874 | 0.218 | 205 | 0.153 | 180 | 0.078 | 121 | 0.046 | 187 | 0.040 |
| 16 | 他 | 567 | 0.571 | 7512 | 0.875 | 1837 | 1.369 | 4445 | 1.938 | 2957 | 1.133 | 4349 | 0.937 |
| 17 | 头 | 566 | 0.57 | 3498 | 0.408 | 434 | 0.323 | 669 | 0.292 | 972 | 0.373 | 2149 | 0.463 |
| 18 | 只 | 550 | 0.554 | 4591 | 0.535 | 448 | 0.334 | 556 | 0.242 | 542 | 0.208 | 1034 | 0.223 |
| 19 | 回 | 538 | 0.542 | 3051 | 0.356 | 347 | 0.259 | 559 | 0.244 | 623 | 0.239 | 551 | 0.119 |
| 20 | 不 | 481 | 0.485 | 14486 | 1.688 | 2002 | 1.492 | 3538 | 1.542 | 3556 | 1.363 | 3544 | 0.764 |
| 21 | 那 | 468 | 0.472 | 4936 | 0.575 | 594 | 0.443 | 806 | 0.351 | 2077 | 0.796 | 2135 | 0.460 |
| 22 | 众 | 390 | 0.393 | 1177 | 0.137 | 18 | 0.013 | 154 | 0.067 | 76 | 0.029 | 80 | 0.017 |
| 23 | 子 | 384 | 0.387 | 5417 | 0.631 | 888 | 0.662 | 918 | 0.400 | 1201 | 0.460 | 4280 | 0.922 |
| 24 | 想 | 374 | 0.377 | 1794 | 0.209 | 354 | 0.264 | 606 | 0.264 | 563 | 0.216 | 640 | 0.138 |

（续表）

| 排序 | 字符 | 会话引导语 | 百分比 | 《红楼梦》 | 百分比 | 《呐喊》+《彷徨》 | 百分比 | 《家》 | 百分比 | 《子夜》 | 百分比 | 《丰乳肥臀》 | 百分比 |
|---|---|---|---|---|---|---|---|---|---|---|---|---|---|
| 25 | 里 | 338 | 0.341 | 5321 | 0.62 | 798 | 0.595 | 1624 | 0.708 | 1553 | 0.595 | 2968 | 0.640 |
| 26 | 上 | 335 | 0.338 | 3793 | 0.442 | 778 | 0.580 | 1535 | 0.669 | 1632 | 0.626 | 5895 | 1.270 |
| 27 | 都 | 322 | 0.324 | 2672 | 0.311 | 455 | 0.339 | 552 | 0.241 | 645 | 0.247 | 941 | 0.203 |
| 28 | 个 | 321 | 0.323 | 5604 | 0.653 | 681 | 0.507 | 1832 | 0.799 | 1484 | 0.569 | 3065 | 0.661 |
| 29 | 起 | 303 | 0.305 | 2487 | 0.29 | 434 | 0.323 | 843 | 0.367 | 871 | 0.334 | 1732 | 0.373 |
| 30 | 在 | 303 | 0.305 | 3911 | 0.456 | 1257 | 0.937 | 2880 | 1.255 | 2317 | 0.888 | 4176 | 0.900 |
| 31 | 向 | 298 | 0.3 | 588 | 0.069 | 159 | 0.118 | 264 | 0.115 | 210 | 0.080 | 323 | 0.070 |
| 32 | 面 | 286 | 0.288 | 1743 | 0.203 | 390 | 0.291 | 1069 | 0.466 | 619 | 0.237 | 664 | 0.143 |
| 33 | 家 | 282 | 0.284 | 3865 | 0.45 | 437 | 0.326 | 707 | 0.308 | 514 | 0.197 | 1090 | 0.235 |
| 34 | 也 | 280 | 0.282 | 6059 | 0.706 | 1229 | 0.916 | 1205 | 0.525 | 1494 | 0.573 | 1146 | 0.247 |
| 35 | 这 | 273 | 0.275 | 7654 | 0.892 | 1183 | 0.882 | 2223 | 0.969 | 2000 | 0.767 | 1992 | 0.429 |
| 36 | 叫 | 271 | 0.273 | 2440 | 0.284 | 171 | 0.127 | 261 | 0.114 | 346 | 0.133 | 605 | 0.130 |
| 37 | 心 | 261 | 0.263 | 2601 | 0.303 | 257 | 0.192 | 669 | 0.292 | 697 | 0.267 | 689 | 0.148 |
| 38 | 小 | 258 | 0.26 | 2003 | 0.233 | 378 | 0.282 | 345 | 0.150 | 773 | 0.296 | 1592 | 0.343 |
| 39 | 话 | 251 | 0.253 | 2453 | 0.286 | 234 | 0.174 | 833 | 0.363 | 773 | 0.296 | 356 | 0.077 |
| 40 | 进 | 246 | 0.248 | 1542 | 0.18 | 183 | 0.136 | 368 | 0.160 | 408 | 0.156 | 785 | 0.169 |
| 41 | 丫 | 245 | 0.247 | 1223 | 0.143 | 3 | 0.002 | 26 | 0.011 | 0 | 0 | 0 | 0 |
| 42 | 看 | 236 | 0.238 | 2380 | 0.277 | 633 | 0.472 | 1084 | 0.473 | 1087 | 0.417 | 1226 | 0.264 |
| 43 | 下 | 227 | 0.229 | 2728 | 0.318 | 429 | 0.320 | 849 | 0.370 | 868 | 0.333 | 1949 | 0.420 |
| 44 | 正 | 225 | 0.227 | 1379 | 0.161 | 201 | 0.150 | 234 | 0.102 | 274 | 0.105 | 367 | 0.079 |
| 45 | 出 | 217 | 0.219 | 3153 | 0.367 | 544 | 0.405 | 970 | 0.423 | 956 | 0.366 | 2017 | 0.435 |
| 46 | 是 | 217 | 0.219 | 9928 | 1.157 | 2142 | 1.596 | 2747 | 1.197 | 4139 | 1.587 | 3649 | 0.786 |
| 47 | 手 | 209 | 0.211 | 1010 | 0.118 | 235 | 0.175 | 379 | 0.165 | 598 | 0.229 | 1411 | 0.304 |
| 48 | 得 | 204 | 0.206 | 3306 | 0.385 | 749 | 0.558 | 1138 | 0.496 | 1109 | 0.425 | 1156 | 0.249 |

（续表）

| 排序 | 字符 | 会话引导语 | 百分比 | 《红楼梦》 | 百分比 | 《呐喊》+《彷徨》 | 百分比 | 《家》 | 百分比 | 《子夜》 | 百分比 | 《丰乳肥臀》 | 百分比 |
|---|---|---|---|---|---|---|---|---|---|---|---|---|---|
| 49 | 去 | 191 | 0.192 | 6013 | 0.701 | 792 | 0.590 | 1527 | 0.666 | 1132 | 0.434 | 1395 | 0.301 |
| 50 | 走 | 190 | 0.191 | 1237 | 0.144 | 302 | 0.225 | 920 | 0.401 | 423 | 0.162 | 728 | 0.157 |

《红楼梦》中的会话引导语相对于《呐喊》与《彷徨》，以及《家》《子夜》和《丰乳肥臀》来讲，独特字有 62 个：

| | | | |
|---|---|---|---|
| 琏(312) | 乜(4) | 戍(1) | 蘅(1) |
| 雯(133) | 俞(3) | 旬(1) | 虬(1) |
| 嬷(116) | 茜(3) | 枇(1) | 衾(1) |
| 麝(107) | 跂(3) | 棠(1) | 袂(1) |
| 邢(100) | 咛(2) | 槲(1) | 跐(1) |
| 茗(70) | 怄(2) | 湫(1) | 醒(1) |
| 菱(66) | 戥(2) | 琮(1) | 醐(1) |
| 莺(54) | 掭(2) | 盥(1) | 铰(1) |
| 焙(53) | 琪(2) | 硼(1) | 猓(1) |
| 蟾(38) | 螯(2) | 禧(1) | 靓(1) |
| 岫(24) | 偕(1) | 秉(1) | 颖(1) |
| 钏(22) | 嗟(1) | 缥(1) | 饧(1) |
| 橘(12) | 噔(1) | 臻(1) | 鲞(1) |
| 詹(12) | 墅(1) | 苓(1) | 㳠(1) |
| 倪(11) | 娄(1) | 茯(1) | |
| 摺(7) | 寅(1) | 藩(1) | |

特色字有 64 个，其字频和关键度如表 2-12 所示：

表 2-12 《红楼梦》会话引导语的特色字的字频和关键度

| 排序 | 字符 | 字频 | 关键度 | 排序 | 字符 | 字频 | 关键度 |
|---|---|---|---|---|---|---|---|
| 1 | 道 | 9116 | 32 341.549 | 3 | 宝 | 2099 | 9059.987 |
| 2 | 贾 | 1918 | 9688.572 | 4 | 玉 | 2217 | 9048.601 |

（续表）

| 排序 | 字符 | 字频 | 关键度 | 排序 | 字符 | 字频 | 关键度 |
|---|---|---|---|---|---|---|---|
| 5 | 笑 | 2958 | 8441.513 | 33 | 莺 | 165 | 798.966 |
| 6 | 说 | 3112 | 4458.184 | 34 | 鸳 | 164 | 793.947 |
| 7 | 黛 | 587 | 2948.293 | 35 | 紫 | 232 | 683.593 |
| 8 | 凤 | 840 | 2898.236 | 36 | 雯 | 133 | 673.994 |
| 9 | 钗 | 477 | 2391.682 | 37 | 探 | 230 | 673.824 |
| 10 | 袭 | 510 | 2374.866 | 38 | 尤 | 172 | 645.883 |
| 11 | 便 | 1260 | 2365.253 | 39 | 姨 | 254 | 643.712 |
| 12 | 忙 | 753 | 2297.969 | 40 | 嬷 | 116 | 587.845 |
| 13 | 问 | 900 | 1877.801 | 41 | 平 | 324 | 570.568 |
| 14 | 听 | 882 | 1705.970 | 42 | 晴 | 129 | 547.398 |
| 15 | 因 | 689 | 1690.344 | 43 | 麝 | 107 | 542.236 |
| 16 | 姐 | 936 | 1644.924 | 44 | 李 | 271 | 524.783 |
| 17 | 琏 | 312 | 1581.099 | 45 | 邢 | 100 | 506.763 |
| 18 | 薛 | 343 | 1506.193 | 46 | 蟠 | 99 | 490.660 |
| 19 | 王 | 504 | 1383.419 | 47 | 悄 | 188 | 488.098 |
| 20 | 儿 | 972 | 1383.097 | 48 | 妈 | 227 | 445.801 |
| 21 | 春 | 369 | 1350.147 | 49 | 回 | 538 | 410.798 |
| 22 | 湘 | 261 | 1290.317 | 50 | 芸 | 81 | 391.954 |
| 23 | 夫 | 513 | 1273.254 | 51 | 刘 | 151 | 382.785 |
| 24 | 人 | 1857 | 1247.375 | 52 | 珍 | 132 | 380.791 |
| 25 | 见 | 862 | 1241.788 | 53 | 蓉 | 78 | 370.108 |
| 26 | 政 | 406 | 1219.826 | 54 | 茗 | 70 | 354.734 |
| 27 | 众 | 390 | 1040.614 | 55 | 菱 | 66 | 334.463 |
| 28 | 丫 | 245 | 1016.991 | 56 | 只 | 550 | 303.938 |
| 29 | 母 | 783 | 984.806 | 57 | 云 | 240 | 301.371 |
| 30 | 纨 | 184 | 920.173 | 58 | 向 | 298 | 292.994 |
| 31 | 鹃 | 185 | 907.228 | 59 | 莺 | 54 | 273.652 |
| 32 | 又 | 990 | 895.218 | 60 | 焙 | 53 | 268.584 |

（续表）

| 排序 | 字符 | 字频 | 关键度 | 排序 | 字符 | 字频 | 关键度 |
|---|---|---|---|---|---|---|---|
| 61 | 陪 | 96 | 262.948 | 63 | 氏 | 180 | 244.787 |
| 62 | 咐 | 97 | 244.896 | 64 | 叹 | 124 | 231.095 |

接着使用 AntConc 软件中的"negative keyword"功能，检索出 5 部现代小说相对于《红楼梦》会话引导语而言的特色字有 264 个，限于篇幅并便于对比，此处也仅列举前 64 个，其中的字频指的是《红楼梦》会话引导语的字频（见表 2－13）：

表 2－13　几部现代小说相对于《红楼梦》会话引导语的特色字分析

| 排序 | 字符 | 字频 | 关键度 | 排序 | 字符 | 字频 | 关键度 |
|---|---|---|---|---|---|---|---|
| 1 | 的 | 974 | 2466.560 | 21 | 而 | 13 | 255.624 |
| 2 | 我 | 11 | 1730.495 | 22 | 天 | 35 | 251.715 |
| 3 | 她 | 1 | 1209.433 | 23 | 这 | 273 | 249.345 |
| 4 | 地 | 31 | 1143.505 | 24 | 什 | 16 | 244.364 |
| 5 | 你 | 1 | 1033.632 | 25 | 马 | 25 | 227.363 |
| 6 | 是 | 217 | 992.934 | 26 | 对 | 23 | 212.644 |
| 7 | 们 | 112 | 576.534 | 27 | 还 | 68 | 209.950 |
| 8 | 在 | 303 | 522.780 | 28 | 现 | 1 | 207.303 |
| 9 | 么 | 21 | 504.664 | 29 | 觉 | 58 | 206.560 |
| 10 | 有 | 180 | 441.061 | 30 | 可 | 32 | 200.197 |
| 11 | 就 | 73 | 428.093 | 31 | 白 | 13 | 196.892 |
| 12 | 不 | 481 | 403.104 | 32 | 生 | 31 | 195.715 |
| 13 | 上 | 335 | 378.899 | 33 | 以 | 10 | 193.386 |
| 14 | 他 | 567 | 360.719 | 34 | 没 | 59 | 190.408 |
| 15 | 到 | 148 | 332.750 | 35 | 多 | 18 | 186.615 |
| 16 | 样 | 25 | 328.144 | 36 | 成 | 7 | 186.393 |
| 17 | 大 | 189 | 286.341 | 37 | 年 | 7 | 186.082 |
| 18 | 很 | 3 | 277.223 | 38 | 为 | 31 | 185.028 |
| 19 | 但 | 6 | 271.281 | 39 | 水 | 9 | 172.947 |
| 20 | 然 | 61 | 262.302 | 40 | 从 | 30 | 169.648 |

| 排序 | 字符 | 字频 | 关键度 | 排序 | 字符 | 字频 | 关键度 |
|------|------|------|--------|------|------|------|--------|
| 41 | 经 | 13 | 166.728 | 53 | 光 | 28 | 139.664 |
| 42 | 亲 | 44 | 165.413 | 54 | 弟 | 5 | 139.062 |
| 43 | 个 | 321 | 153.680 | 55 | 新 | 11 | 138.889 |
| 44 | 吴 | 5 | 152.828 | 56 | 工 | 3 | 135.402 |
| 45 | 开 | 37 | 152.676 | 57 | 黑 | 2 | 131.969 |
| 46 | 用 | 28 | 152.661 | 58 | 全 | 1 | 127.364 |
| 47 | 长 | 21 | 151.476 | 59 | 里 | 338 | 125.610 |
| 48 | 能 | 15 | 148.354 | 60 | 一 | 1205 | 124.890 |
| 49 | 要 | 120 | 146.081 | 61 | 情 | 15 | 122.120 |
| 50 | 去 | 191 | 144.588 | 62 | 把 | 101 | 122.109 |
| 51 | 公 | 3 | 141.456 | 63 | 于 | 15 | 121.695 |
| 52 | 慧 | 1 | 140.084 | 64 | 眼 | 94 | 119.096 |

## 二、《红楼梦》会话引导语与现代小说特色字研究

通过以上将《红楼梦》会话引导语与 5 部现代小说的字频、独特字、特色字对比分析,我们可以清楚地发现《红楼梦》会话引导语与现代小说作品的特色。接下来我们将挑选有代表性的几个特色字进行具体的分析研究。

(一)关于"的"字的研究

"的"是 5 部现代小说相对于《红楼梦》会话引导语而言的第一大特色字,关键度高达 2466.560。从图 2-4 我们可以看到,在这 5 部现代小说中,"的"字有41 060 个,占文本总量的 3.8%。其中鲁迅小说集《呐喊》和《彷徨》总字数为134 207(检索时为方便表述,此处统一用"鲁迅小说"代替,下文不一一表述),其中"的"字有 5233 个,占总文本的 3.90%;《家》的总字数为 229 422,其中"的"字有 8328 个,占总文本的 3.63%;《子夜》的总字数为 26 0881,其中"的"字有8636 个,占总文本的 3.31%;《丰乳肥臀》的总字数为 464 970,其中"的"字有18 863 个,占总文本的 4.06%。而《红楼梦》的会话引导语文本仅有 974 个"的",比例还不到总文本的 1%。"的"字可以看作是汉语发展的一个缩影,自"五四"新文化运动以来,白话文蓬勃发展并普遍应用,"的"在文章中所占的比例也呈现上升趋势。

| No. | Search Terms | Freq. | File Count | 1.丰乳肥臀 | 2.家 | 3.鲁迅小说 | 4.子夜 |
|---|---|---|---|---|---|---|---|
| | Size | 1089480 | 4 | 464970 | 229422 | 134207 | 260881 |
| | Tokens | 41060 | 4 | 18863 | 8328 | 5233 | 8636 |
| | Types | 1 | 4 | 1 | 1 | 1 | 1 |
| 1 | 的 | 41060 | 4 | 18863 | 8328 | 5233 | 8636 |

图2-4 "的"字在几部现代小说中的字频分布统计

**（二）关于"道"字的研究**

"道"字在5部现代小说中总共仅有3309个，所占比例最高的只有0.37%。笔者检索了"道："的数量，以期分析"道"作为会话引导语在几部现代小说中出现的频率。结果显示，"道："在5部现代小说中共有994个，其中《呐喊》与《彷徨》中有47个；《家》147个；《子夜》374个；《丰乳肥臀》426个。按照百分比来看，鲁迅两部小说比例最低，《子夜》比例最高（见图2-5）。

| No. | Search Terms | Freq. | File Count | 1.丰乳肥臀 | 2.家 | 3.鲁迅小说 | 4.子夜 |
|---|---|---|---|---|---|---|---|
| | Size | 1089480 | 4 | 464970 | 229422 | 134207 | 260881 |
| | Tokens | 994 | 4 | 426 | 147 | 47 | 374 |
| | Types | 1 | 4 | 1 | 1 | 1 | 1 |
| 1 | 道： | 994 | 4 | 426 | 147 | 47 | 374 |

图2-5 "道："在几部现代小说中的字频分布统计

关于"道："左侧的词语，出现频率最高的是"问"，有132个，其统计分布情况如图2-6所示；其次是"说"，有117个，其统计分布情况如图2-7所示；再次是"骂"，有63个，其统计分布情况如图2-8所示；然后是"喊"，有59个，其统计分布情况如图2-9所示；最后是"笑"，有50个，其统计分布情况如图2-10所示。

| No. | Search Terms | Freq. | File Count | 1.丰乳肥臀 | 2.家 | 3.鲁迅小说 | 4.子夜 |
|---|---|---|---|---|---|---|---|
| | Size | 1089480 | 4 | 464970 | 229422 | 134207 | 260881 |
| | Tokens | 132 | 4 | 7 | 33 | 3 | 89 |
| | Types | 1 | 4 | 1 | 1 | 1 | 1 |
| 1 | 问道： | 132 | 4 | 7 | 33 | 3 | 89 |

图2-6 "问道："在几部现代小说中的词频分布统计

| No. | Search Terms | Freq. | File Count | 1. 丰乳肥臀 | 2. 家 | 3. 鲁迅小说 | 4. 子夜 |
|-----|-----|-----|-----|-----|-----|-----|-----|
| | Size | 1089480 | 4 | 464970 | 229422 | 134207 | 260881 |
| | Tokens | 117 | 3 | 0 | 5 | 14 | 98 |
| | Types | 1 | 3 | 0 | 1 | 1 | 1 |
| 1 | 说道: | 117 | 3 | | 5 | 14 | 98 |

图 2-7 "说道:"在几部现代小说中的词频分布统计

| No. | Search Terms | Freq. | File Count | 1. 丰乳肥臀 | 2. 家 | 3. 鲁迅小说 | 4. 子夜 |
|-----|-----|-----|-----|-----|-----|-----|-----|
| | Size | 1089480 | 4 | 464970 | 229422 | 134207 | 260881 |
| | Tokens | 63 | 3 | 47 | 3 | 0 | 13 |
| | Types | 1 | 3 | 1 | 1 | 0 | 1 |
| 1 | 骂道: | 63 | 3 | 47 | 3 | | 13 |

图 2-8 "骂道:"在几部现代小说中的词频分布统计

| No. | Search Terms | Freq. | File Count | 1. 丰乳肥臀 | 2. 家 | 3. 鲁迅小说 | 4. 子夜 |
|-----|-----|-----|-----|-----|-----|-----|-----|
| | Size | 1089480 | 4 | 464970 | 229422 | 134207 | 260881 |
| | Tokens | 59 | 3 | 9 | 0 | 2 | 48 |
| | Types | 1 | 3 | 1 | 0 | 1 | 1 |
| 1 | 喊道: | 59 | 3 | 9 | | 2 | 48 |

图 2-9 "喊道:"在几部现代小说中的词频分布统计

| No. | Search Terms | Freq. | File Count | 1. 丰乳肥臀 | 2. 家 | 3. 鲁迅小说 | 4. 子夜 |
|-----|-----|-----|-----|-----|-----|-----|-----|
| | Size | 1089480 | 4 | 464970 | 229422 | 134207 | 260881 |
| | Tokens | 50 | 3 | 35 | 13 | 0 | 2 |
| | Types | 1 | 3 | 1 | 1 | 0 | 1 |
| 1 | 笑道: | 50 | 3 | 35 | 13 | | 2 |

图 2-10 "笑道:"在几部现代小说中的词频分布统计

（三）关于"笑"字的研究

"笑"字在 5 部现代小说中总共有 2119 个，其中《子夜》中的比例最高，为 0.34%，《丰乳肥臀》中的比例最低，仅有 0.08%，与《红楼梦》会话引导语中的 2.98% 相差甚远。

"笑:"直接做会话引导语的情况共有 6 例，其中《丰乳肥臀》3 例、《子夜》3

例、《家》0 例、《呐喊》与《彷徨》0 例(见图 2－11):

| No. | Search Terms | Freq. | File Count | 1.丰乳肥臀 | 2.家 | 3.鲁迅小说 | 4.子夜 |
|---|---|---|---|---|---|---|---|
| | Size | 1089480 | 4 | 464970 | 229422 | 134207 | 260881 |
| | Tokens | 6 | 2 | 3 | 0 | 0 | 3 |
| | Types | 1 | 2 | 1 | 0 | 0 | 1 |
| 1 | 笑: | 6 | 2 | 3 | | | 3 |

图 2－11　"笑:"在几部现代小说中的字频分布统计

"笑道:"共有 50 例,其中《丰乳肥臀》35 例、《家》13 例、《子夜》2 例、《呐喊》和《彷徨》0 例(见图 2－12):

| No. | Search Terms | Freq. | File Count | 1.丰乳肥臀 | 2.家 | 3.鲁迅小说 | 4.子夜 |
|---|---|---|---|---|---|---|---|
| | Size | 1089480 | 4 | 464970 | 229422 | 134207 | 260881 |
| | Tokens | 50 | 3 | 35 | 13 | 0 | 2 |
| | Types | 1 | 3 | 1 | 1 | 0 | 1 |
| 1 | 笑道: | 50 | 3 | 35 | 13 | | 2 |

图 2－12　"笑道:"在几部现代小说中的词频分布统计

"笑说:"13 例,其中《家》7 例、《呐喊》和《彷徨》1 例、《子夜》5 例、《丰乳肥臀》0 例(见图 2－13):

| No. | Search Terms | Freq. | File Count | 1.丰乳肥臀 | 2.家 | 3.鲁迅小说 | 4.子夜 |
|---|---|---|---|---|---|---|---|
| | Size | 1089480 | 4 | 464970 | 229422 | 134207 | 260881 |
| | Tokens | 13 | 3 | 0 | 7 | | 5 |
| | Types | 1 | 3 | 0 | 1 | 1 | 1 |
| 1 | 笑说: | 13 | 3 | | 7 | 1 | 5 |

图 2－13　"笑说:"在几部现代小说中的词频分布统计

"笑着说:"32 例,其中《丰乳肥臀》15 例、《家》7 例、《呐喊》和《彷徨》1 例、《子夜》9 例(见图 2－14):

| No. | Search Terms | Freq. | File Count | 1.丰乳肥臀 | 2.家 | 3.鲁迅小说 | 4.子夜 |
|---|---|---|---|---|---|---|---|
| | Size | 1089480 | 4 | 464970 | 229422 | 134207 | 260881 |
| | Tokens | 32 | 4 | 15 | 7 | 1 | 9 |
| | Types | 1 | 4 | 1 | 1 | 1 | 1 |
| 1 | 笑着说: | 32 | 4 | 15 | 7 | | 9 |

图 2－14　"笑着说:"在几部现代小说中的词频分布统计

（四）关于"因"字的研究

在 5 部现代小说中，"因"字的比例也与《红楼梦》会话引导语有显著差异，且最多的搭配是"因为"（542 次）、"因此"（59 次）和"原因"（32 次），与《红楼梦》中的用法有很大的不同。其词频分布情况如图 2 - 15、图 2 - 16、图 2 - 17 所示。

| No. | Search Terms | Freq. | File Count | 1.丰乳肥臀 | 2.家 | 3.鲁迅小说 | 4.子夜 |
|-----|-------------|-------|-----------|-----------|------|-----------|--------|
|  | Size | 1089480 | 4 | 464970 | 229422 | 134207 | 260881 |
|  | Tokens | 542 | 4 | 144 | 147 | 175 | 76 |
|  | Types | 1 | 4 | 1 | 1 | 1 | 1 |
| 1 | 因为 | 542 | 4 | 144 | 147 | 175 | 76 |

图 2 - 15 "因为"在几部现代小说中的词频分布统计

| No. | Search Terms | Freq. | File Count | 1.丰乳肥臀 | 2.家 | 3.鲁迅小说 | 4.子夜 |
|-----|-------------|-------|-----------|-----------|------|-----------|--------|
|  | Size | 1089480 | 4 | 464970 | 229422 | 134207 | 260881 |
|  | Tokens | 59 | 4 | 7 | 16 | 20 | 16 |
|  | Types | 1 | 4 | 1 | 1 | 1 | 1 |
| 1 | 因此 | 59 | 4 | 7 | 16 | 20 | 16 |

图 2 - 16 "因此"在几部现代小说中的词频分布统计

| No. | Search Terms | Freq. | File Count | 1.丰乳肥臀 | 2.家 | 3.鲁迅小说 | 4.子夜 |
|-----|-------------|-------|-----------|-----------|------|-----------|--------|
|  | Size | 1089480 | 4 | 464970 | 229422 | 134207 | 260881 |
|  | Tokens | 32 | 4 | 10 | 5 | 6 | 11 |
|  | Types | 1 | 4 | 1 | 1 | 1 | 1 |
| 1 | 原因 | 32 | 4 | 10 | 5 | 6 | 11 |

图 2 - 17 "原因"在几部现代小说中的词频分布统计

# 第四节 《红楼梦》前八十回与后四十回会话引导语对比研究

曹雪芹的《红楼梦》保存下来的只有八十回。后世广为流传的一百二十回本《红楼梦》为高鹗续写而成。前八十回与后四十回在思想旨意、人物描写与艺术风格上均存在差异。本节将比较曹雪芹前八十回与高鹗后四十回在会话引导语使用方面的差异。

## 一、《红楼梦》前八十回与后四十回会话引导语高频字研究

笔者使用 WCONCORD 软件分别对《红楼梦》前八十回以及后四十回的会话引导语内容进行字频统计，字频位居前 50 位的字符分别如表 2 - 14、表 2 - 15 所示：

表 2 - 14  前八十回会话引导语字频前 50 位

| 前八十回 | 字符 | 字频 | 百分比 | 前八十回 | 字符 | 字频 | 百分比 |
|---|---|---|---|---|---|---|---|
| 1 | ： | 7832 | 12.011 | 26 | 黛 | 418 | 0.641 |
| 2 | 道 | 6067 | 9.304 | 27 | 钗 | 350 | 0.537 |
| 3 | 笑 | 2595 | 3.980 | 28 | 头 | 342 | 0.524 |
| 4 | 说 | 1984 | 3.043 | 29 | 回 | 325 | 0.498 |
| 5 | 玉 | 1545 | 2.369 | 30 | 袭 | 321 | 0.492 |
| 6 | 宝 | 1473 | 2.259 | 31 | 只 | 311 | 0.477 |
| 7 | 了 | 1139 | 1.747 | 32 | 老 | 289 | 0.443 |
| 8 | 人 | 1112 | 1.705 | 33 | 众 | 286 | 0.439 |
| 9 | 贾 | 1083 | 1.661 | 34 | 不 | 284 | 0.436 |
| 10 | 一 | 789 | 1.210 | 35 | 春 | 269 | 0.413 |
| 11 | 儿 | 718 | 1.101 | 36 | 都 | 266 | 0.408 |
| 12 | 又 | 718 | 1.101 | 37 | 夫 | 264 | 0.405 |
| 13 | 来 | 715 | 1.096 | 38 | 子 | 261 | 0.400 |
| 14 | 便 | 708 | 1.086 | 39 | 王 | 243 | 0.373 |
| 15 | 姐 | 696 | 1.067 | 40 | 向 | 240 | 0.368 |
| 16 | 忙 | 655 | 1.004 | 41 | 平 | 233 | 0.357 |
| 17 | 凤 | 629 | 0.965 | 42 | 湘 | 232 | 0.356 |
| 18 | 听 | 613 | 0.940 | 43 | 那 | 219 | 0.336 |
| 19 | 问 | 607 | 0.931 | 44 | 上 | 218 | 0.334 |
| 20 | 的 | 594 | 0.911 | 45 | 个 | 212 | 0.325 |
| 21 | 因 | 543 | 0.833 | 46 | 云 | 207 | 0.317 |
| 22 | 见 | 504 | 0.773 | 47 | 面 | 206 | 0.316 |
| 23 | 母 | 499 | 0.765 | 48 | 薛 | 205 | 0.314 |
| 24 | 着 | 491 | 0.753 | 49 | 家 | 196 | 0.301 |
| 25 | 他 | 440 | 0.675 | 50 | 想 | 192 | 0.294 |

表 2-15 后四十回会话引导语字频前 50 位

| 后四十回 | 字符 | 字频 | 百分比 | 后四十回 | 字符 | 字频 | 百分比 |
|---|---|---|---|---|---|---|---|
| 1 | ： | 3802 | 11.170 | 26 | 只 | 239 | 0.702 |
| 2 | 道 | 3049 | 8.958 | 27 | 头 | 224 | 0.658 |
| 3 | 说 | 1128 | 3.314 | 28 | 回 | 213 | 0.626 |
| 4 | 贾 | 835 | 2.453 | 29 | 凤 | 211 | 0.620 |
| 5 | 人 | 745 | 2.189 | 30 | 里 | 201 | 0.591 |
| 6 | 玉 | 672 | 1.974 | 31 | 不 | 197 | 0.579 |
| 7 | 宝 | 626 | 1.839 | 32 | 袭 | 189 | 0.555 |
| 8 | 了 | 553 | 1.625 | 33 | 想 | 182 | 0.535 |
| 9 | 便 | 552 | 1.622 | 34 | 黛 | 169 | 0.497 |
| 10 | 来 | 435 | 1.278 | 35 | 瑆 | 157 | 0.461 |
| 11 | 一 | 416 | 1.222 | 36 | 紫 | 147 | 0.432 |
| 12 | 着 | 390 | 1.146 | 37 | 因 | 146 | 0.429 |
| 13 | 的 | 380 | 1.116 | 38 | 心 | 139 | 0.408 |
| 14 | 笑 | 363 | 1.066 | 39 | 薛 | 138 | 0.405 |
| 15 | 见 | 358 | 1.052 | 40 | 叫 | 134 | 0.394 |
| 16 | 问 | 293 | 0.861 | 41 | 在 | 131 | 0.385 |
| 17 | 母 | 284 | 0.834 | 42 | 钗 | 127 | 0.373 |
| 18 | 又 | 272 | 0.799 | 43 | 他 | 127 | 0.373 |
| 19 | 听 | 269 | 0.790 | 44 | 进 | 123 | 0.361 |
| 20 | 王 | 261 | 0.767 | 45 | 子 | 123 | 0.361 |
| 21 | 儿 | 254 | 0.746 | 46 | 鹃 | 117 | 0.344 |
| 22 | 政 | 252 | 0.740 | 47 | 上 | 117 | 0.344 |
| 23 | 夫 | 249 | 0.732 | 48 | 是 | 117 | 0.344 |
| 24 | 那 | 249 | 0.732 | 49 | 起 | 115 | 0.338 |
| 25 | 姐 | 240 | 0.705 | 50 | 话 | 113 | 0.332 |

接下来是《红楼梦》会话引导语总文本前 50 个高频字在前八十回和后四十回中的字频和分布情况（见表 2-16）。

表 2-16 会话引导语总文本前 50 位高频字在前八十回及后四十回中的分布情况

| 排序 | 字符 | 会话引导语 | 百分比 | 前八十回 | 百分比 | 后四十回 | 百分比 |
|---|---|---|---|---|---|---|---|
| 1 | 道 | 9116 | 9.185 | 6067 | 9.304 | 3049 | 8.958 |
| 2 | 说 | 3112 | 3.136 | 1984 | 3.043 | 1128 | 3.314 |
| 3 | 笑 | 2958 | 2.98 | 2595 | 3.980 | 363 | 1.066 |
| 4 | 了 | 1692 | 1.705 | 1139 | 1.747 | 553 | 1.625 |
| 5 | 便 | 1260 | 1.27 | 708 | 1.086 | 552 | 1.622 |
| 6 | 一 | 1205 | 1.214 | 789 | 1.210 | 416 | 1.222 |
| 7 | 来 | 1150 | 1.159 | 715 | 1.096 | 435 | 1.278 |
| 8 | 又 | 990 | 0.998 | 718 | 1.101 | 272 | 0.799 |
| 9 | 的 | 974 | 0.981 | 594 | 0.911 | 380 | 1.116 |
| 10 | 问 | 900 | 0.907 | 607 | 0.931 | 293 | 0.861 |
| 11 | 听 | 882 | 0.889 | 613 | 0.940 | 269 | 0.790 |
| 12 | 着 | 881 | 0.888 | 491 | 0.753 | 390 | 1.146 |
| 13 | 见 | 862 | 0.869 | 504 | 0.773 | 358 | 1.052 |
| 14 | 忙 | 753 | 0.759 | 655 | 1.004 | 98 | 0.288 |
| 15 | 因 | 689 | 0.694 | 543 | 0.833 | 146 | 0.429 |
| 16 | 他 | 567 | 0.571 | 440 | 0.675 | 127 | 0.373 |
| 17 | 头 | 566 | 0.57 | 342 | 0.524 | 224 | 0.658 |
| 18 | 只 | 550 | 0.554 | 311 | 0.477 | 239 | 0.702 |
| 19 | 回 | 538 | 0.542 | 325 | 0.498 | 213 | 0.626 |
| 20 | 不 | 481 | 0.485 | 284 | 0.436 | 197 | 0.579 |
| 21 | 那 | 468 | 0.472 | 219 | 0.336 | 249 | 0.732 |
| 22 | 众 | 390 | 0.393 | 286 | 0.439 | 104 | 0.306 |
| 23 | 子 | 384 | 0.387 | 261 | 0.400 | 123 | 0.361 |
| 24 | 想 | 374 | 0.377 | 192 | 0.294 | 182 | 0.535 |
| 25 | 里 | 338 | 0.341 | 137 | 0.210 | 201 | 0.591 |
| 26 | 上 | 335 | 0.338 | 218 | 0.334 | 117 | 0.344 |
| 27 | 都 | 322 | 0.324 | 266 | 0.408 | 56 | 0.165 |

（续表）

| 排序 | 字符 | 会话引导语 | 百分比 | 前八十回 | 百分比 | 后四十回 | 百分比 |
|---|---|---|---|---|---|---|---|
| 28 | 个 | 321 | 0.323 | 212 | 0.325 | 109 | 0.320 |
| 29 | 起 | 303 | 0.305 | 188 | 0.288 | 115 | 0.338 |
| 30 | 在 | 303 | 0.305 | 172 | 0.264 | 131 | 0.385 |
| 31 | 向 | 298 | 0.3 | 240 | 0.368 | 58 | 0.170 |
| 32 | 面 | 286 | 0.288 | 206 | 0.316 | 80 | 0.235 |
| 33 | 家 | 282 | 0.284 | 196 | 0.301 | 86 | 0.253 |
| 34 | 也 | 280 | 0.282 | 182 | 0.279 | 98 | 0.288 |
| 35 | 这 | 273 | 0.275 | 166 | 0.255 | 107 | 0.314 |
| 36 | 叫 | 271 | 0.273 | 137 | 0.210 | 134 | 0.394 |
| 37 | 心 | 261 | 0.263 | 122 | 0.187 | 139 | 0.408 |
| 38 | 小 | 258 | 0.26 | 165 | 0.253 | 93 | 0.273 |
| 39 | 话 | 251 | 0.253 | 138 | 0.212 | 113 | 0.332 |
| 40 | 进 | 246 | 0.248 | 123 | 0.189 | 123 | 0.361 |
| 41 | 丫 | 245 | 0.247 | 164 | 0.251 | 81 | 0.238 |
| 42 | 看 | 236 | 0.238 | 133 | 0.204 | 103 | 0.303 |
| 43 | 下 | 227 | 0.229 | 153 | 0.235 | 74 | 0.217 |
| 44 | 正 | 225 | 0.227 | 120 | 0.184 | 105 | 0.308 |
| 45 | 出 | 217 | 0.219 | 130 | 0.199 | 87 | 0.256 |
| 46 | 是 | 217 | 0.219 | 100 | 0.153 | 117 | 0.344 |
| 47 | 手 | 209 | 0.211 | 152 | 0.233 | 57 | 0.167 |
| 48 | 得 | 204 | 0.206 | 108 | 0.166 | 96 | 0.282 |
| 49 | 去 | 191 | 0.192 | 123 | 0.189 | 68 | 0.200 |
| 50 | 走 | 190 | 0.191 | 116 | 0.178 | 74 | 0.217 |

　　通过上述统计我们可以发现，《红楼梦》原文前八十回和后四十回字频差异显著的有"笑""忙""因""都"等。

## 二、《红楼梦》前八十回与后四十回会话引导语特色字研究

我们使用 AntConc 软件检索前八十回会话引导语相对于后四十回的特色字,位居前 50 位的字为(阴影部分为后四十回会话引导语相对于前八十回的特色字前 50 位,见表 2－17):

表 2－17　《红楼梦》前八十回与后四十回会话引导语特色字统计

| 排序 | 字符 | 字频 | 关键度 | 排序 | 字符 | 字频 | 关键度 |
|---|---|---|---|---|---|---|---|
| 1 | 笑 | 2595 | 758.714 | 25 | 方 | 85 | 29.026 |
| 2 | 忙 | 655 | 178.752 | 26 | 香 | 72 | 28.312 |
| 3 | 嬷 | 116 | 97.717 | 27 | 官 | 86 | 27.346 |
| 4 | 雯 | 131 | 93.866 | 28 | 菱 | 61 | 26.651 |
| 5 | 晴 | 127 | 90.619 | 29 | 蓉 | 70 | 24.467 |
| 6 | 尤 | 163 | 85.905 | 30 | 老 | 289 | 23.273 |
| 7 | 氏 | 168 | 78.975 | 31 | 又 | 718 | 21.671 |
| 8 | 湘 | 232 | 75.280 | 32 | 钟 | 25 | 21.060 |
| 9 | 因 | 543 | 57.548 | 33 | 柳 | 33 | 20.912 |
| 10 | 云 | 207 | 52.663 | 34 | 身 | 131 | 20.839 |
| 11 | 妇 | 62 | 52.228 | 35 | 瑞 | 99 | 19.817 |
| 12 | 蟠 | 94 | 50.263 | 36 | 宝 | 1473 | 19.713 |
| 13 | 媳 | 58 | 48.858 | 37 | 燕 | 29 | 17.796 |
| 14 | 命 | 134 | 47.603 | 38 | 娘 | 71 | 16.849 |
| 15 | 都 | 266 | 46.126 | 39 | 玉 | 1545 | 16.554 |
| 16 | 莲 | 46 | 38.750 | 40 | 推 | 37 | 16.265 |
| 17 | 他 | 440 | 38.709 | 41 | 刘 | 121 | 15.436 |
| 18 | 冷 | 104 | 33.746 | 42 | 乃 | 18 | 15.163 |
| 19 | 凤 | 629 | 33.592 | 43 | 探 | 178 | 15.132 |
| 20 | 姐 | 696 | 33.213 | 44 | 珍 | 106 | 13.833 |
| 21 | 秦 | 39 | 32.853 | 45 | 琴 | 33 | 13.554 |
| 22 | 芳 | 48 | 32.807 | 46 | 钗 | 350 | 13.243 |
| 23 | 向 | 240 | 32.297 | 47 | 幻 | 15 | 12.636 |
| 24 | 儿 | 718 | 30.625 | 48 | 警 | 15 | 12.636 |

（续表）

| 排序 | 字符 | 字频 | 关键度 | 排序 | 字符 | 字频 | 关键度 |
|---|---|---|---|---|---|---|---|
| 49 | 如 | 56 | 12.388 | 25 | 甄 | 2 | 27.125 |
| 50 | 鬟 | 31 | 12.228 | 26 | 人 | 1112 | 26.535 |
| 1 | 政 | 154 | 128.993 | 27 | 叫 | 137 | 25.946 |
| 2 | 里 | 137 | 88.318 | 28 | 屋 | 11 | 25.652 |
| 3 | 紫 | 85 | 80.711 | 29 | 儒 | 3 | 25.581 |
| 4 | 那 | 219 | 69.425 | 30 | 代 | 5 | 25.324 |
| 5 | 贾 | 1083 | 68.906 | 31 | 进 | 123 | 25.283 |
| 6 | 王 | 243 | 64.083 | 32 | 好 | 39 | 24.902 |
| 7 | 鹃 | 68 | 63.836 | 33 | 冯 | 10 | 24.424 |
| 8 | 蟾 | 3 | 56.288 | 34 | 传 | 7 | 24.037 |
| 9 | 蝌 | 2 | 54.816 | 35 | 禀 | 2 | 23.299 |
| 10 | 到 | 54 | 52.025 | 36 | 包 | 9 | 23.208 |
| 11 | 轻 | 4 | 50.412 | 37 | 惜 | 29 | 22.589 |
| 12 | 便 | 708 | 47.981 | 38 | 桂 | 20 | 22.000 |
| 13 | 夫 | 264 | 43.463 | 39 | 书 | 10 | 21.413 |
| 14 | 心 | 122 | 38.927 | 40 | 急 | 39 | 20.648 |
| 15 | 着 | 491 | 36.836 | 41 | 英 | 14 | 19.464 |
| 16 | 微 | 9 | 36.077 | 42 | 嚷 | 15 | 19.422 |
| 17 | 是 | 100 | 34.630 | 43 | 只 | 311 | 19.419 |
| 18 | 琏 | 155 | 33.373 | 44 | 见 | 504 | 19.027 |
| 19 | 兰 | 3 | 33.053 | 45 | 尚 | 9 | 15.781 |
| 20 | 想 | 192 | 32.239 | 46 | 静 | 9 | 15.781 |
| 21 | 光 | 4 | 31.661 | 47 | 站 | 39 | 15.695 |
| 22 | 雁 | 13 | 31.142 | 48 | 大 | 98 | 15.158 |
| 23 | 呆 | 3 | 27.431 | 49 | 芸 | 36 | 15.147 |
| 24 | 雪 | 18 | 27.361 | 50 | 知 | 58 | 15.053 |

除了人名和地名用字，位居前八十回会话引导语特色字前列的有"笑""忙""嬷""因"等。

（一）关于"笑"字的研究

通过字频和特色字统计我们发现，"笑"是《红楼梦》前八十回会话引导语中第一特色字，关键度高达 758.714。"笑"字在前八十回的字频为 2595，占全文本的 3.98%，而在后四十回中仅有 363 个，比例仅为 1.066%。前八十回"笑"的字频是后四十回的 7 倍多，占总文本的比例也是后四十回的 4 倍左右。使用 AntConc 软件的 Concordance Plot 功能，我们可以清晰地看到"笑"字在《红楼梦》前八十回和后四十回会话引导语文本中的差异（见图 2-18）：

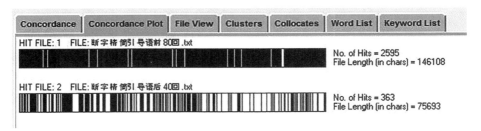

图 2-18　"笑"字在《红楼梦》前八十回和后四十回会话引导语中的分布情况

"笑"字在《红楼梦》原文前八十回和后四十回总文本中的差异也很明显（见图 2-19）：

图 2-19　"笑"字在《红楼梦》前八十回和后四十回全文中的分布情况

究其原因，或许是因为《红楼梦》演绎的是一出悲剧，后四十回的整体趋势是讲述封建大家族的衰败过程，因此"笑"的元素越来越少也是情理之中。此外，前八十回和后四十回出自不同作者之手，作者的风格差异也是重要原因之一。

（二）关于"忙"字的研究

"忙"字是《红楼梦》前八十回会话引导语相对于后四十回的第二大特色字，关键度为 178.752。"忙"字在前八十回中字频为 655，排名 16 位，而在后四十回中并未跻身前 50 位，仅出现过 98 次，还不到前八十回字频的六分之一。我们通过 AntConc 的统计可以清晰地看出"忙"字在两个文本中的分布情况（见

图 2‐20）：

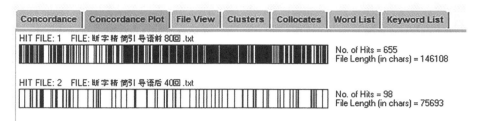

图 2‐20 "忙"字在前八十回和后四十回会话引导语中的分布情况

《红楼梦》汉语原文中，尤其是会话引导语中有大量的"忙××"结构，如"忙道""忙笑道""忙说"等。这一结构大多用于表达说话者对听话者的一种"尊敬"或"示好"，说话者的态度和姿态是比较谦卑的，因此"忙"字的用法可以显示出话语双方的身份与地位（至少在当时会话时的情景中）。

《新华字典》对于"忙"字的解释为：①〈形容词〉事情多，没空闲。如：田家少闲月，五月人倍忙。（白居易《观刈麦》）②〈动词〉赶快；赶紧；急于。如：胡屠户忙躲进女儿房里，不敢出来。（《儒林外史》）

《红楼梦》中"忙"与会话引导词搭配使用时，除了具有"赶快""赶紧"的动词意义外，还具有修饰会话引导词的副词功能，表示说话人的态度和姿态。

我们使用 PowerConc 软件检索"忙"字右侧一字（去除"："后的一字，以下同）搭配，频率位居前 5 位的分别为"道"（81 次）、"笑"（78 次）、"问"（76 次）、"说"（55 次）、"陪"（23 次）。"忙道"是出现次数最多的搭配，总共有 81 次，也是前八十回和后四十回差异最大的搭配，其中前八十回 80 次，后四十回仅有 1 次（说，心下着忙 道：）。以下是前八十回的用法：

| | | | | | | | | |
|---|---|---|---|---|---|---|---|---|
| 宝钗 | 忙 | 道：(2) | 凤姐 | 忙 | 道：(1) | 刘老老 | 忙 | 道：(3) |
| 宝琴也 | 忙 | 道：(1) | 凤姐儿 | 忙 | 道：(4) | 刘老老吓的忙 | | 道：(1) |
| 宝玉 | 忙 | 道：(13) | 贾琏 | 忙 | 道：(2) | 柳家的 | 忙 | 道：(2) |
| 宝玉听了， | 忙 | 道：(1) | 贾母 | 忙 | 道：(3) | 那太医 | 忙 | 道：(1) |
| 宝玉喜的 | 忙 | 道：(1) | 贾母听了， | 忙 | 道：(1) | 平儿 | 忙 | 道：(4) |
| 不容情，也 | 忙 | 道：(1) | 贾母听说， | 忙 | 道：(1) | 平儿袭人 | 忙 | 道：(1) |
| 吃去，宝玉 | 忙 | 道：(1) | 贾珍 | 忙 | 道：(1) | 如此说，便 | 忙 | 道：(1) |
| 黛玉 | 忙 | 道：(1) | 贾政 | 忙 | 道：(2) | 宋嬷嬷 | 忙 | 道：(1) |
| 黛玉又 | 忙 | 道：(1) | 见问得奇， | 忙 | 道：(1) | 探春 | 忙 | 道：(2) |
| 二字，众人 | 忙 | 道：(1) | 赖大家的 | 忙 | 道：(1) | 王夫人 | 忙 | 道：(2) |
| 芳官 | 忙 | 道：(1) | 赖嬷嬷 | 忙 | 道：(1) | 王夫人也 | 忙 | 道：(1) |

| | | | | | | | | |
|---|---|---|---|---|---|---|---|---|
| 王一贴又 | 忙 | 道:(1) | 薛蟠 | 忙 | 道:(2) | 尤二姐 | 忙 | 道:(1) |
| 袭人 | 忙 | 道:(2) | 薛姨妈 | 忙 | 道:(1) | 鸳鸯 | 忙 | 道:(1) |
| 袭人平儿 | 忙 | 道:(1) | 丫鬟们 | 忙 | 道:(1) | 这贾琏 | 忙 | 道:(1) |
| 湘云 | 忙 | 道:(2) | 莺儿 | 忙 | 道:(1) | 众人都 | 忙 | 道:(1) |
| 湘云又 | 忙 | 道:(2) | 迎春 | 忙 | 道:(1) | 紫鹃 | 忙 | 道:(1) |

我们再对"忙"字右侧的二字搭配进行检索,频率位居前5位的分别为"笑道"(63次)、"陪笑"(21次)、"问道"(17次)、"说道"(14次)、"起身"(13次)。其中"忙笑道"的用法最多,有63次,且前八十回与后四十回对比显著,前八十回有62次,后四十回仅1次(凤姐赶　忙　笑道:)。以下是前八十回的用法:

| | | | | | | | | |
|---|---|---|---|---|---|---|---|---|
| 贾政 | 忙 | 笑道: | 如此谦逊, | 忙 | 笑道: | 平儿 | 忙 | 笑道: |
| | 忙 | 笑道: | 黛玉 | 忙 | 笑道: | 宝玉 | 忙 | 笑道: |
| 宝玉 | 忙 | 笑道: | 凤姐 | 忙 | 笑道: | 宝钗 | 忙 | 笑道: |
| 媳妇秦氏便 | 忙 | 笑道: | 凤姐 | 忙 | 笑道: | 宝玉会意, | 忙 | 笑道: |
| | 忙 | 笑道: | 凤姐儿 | 忙 | 笑道: | 家的见了, | 忙 | 笑道: |
| 蟠听说,连 | 忙 | 笑道: | 黛玉 | 忙 | 笑道: | 宝玉 | 忙 | 笑道: |
| 凤姐 | 忙 | 笑道: | 凤姐听了, | 忙 | 笑道: | 便知其意, | 忙 | 笑道: |
| 姨妈听了, | 忙 | 笑道: | 平儿 | 忙 | 笑道: | 宝玉 | 忙 | 笑道: |
| 吓了一跳, | 忙 | 笑道: | 薛蟠 | 忙 | 笑道: | 宝玉听说, | 忙 | 笑道: |
| 凤姐 | 忙 | 笑道: | 如获奇珍, | 忙 | 笑道: | 喜出意外, | 忙 | 笑道: |
| 湘云 | 忙 | 笑道: | 宝玉 | 忙 | 笑道: | 湘莲 | 忙 | 笑道: |
| 雨村 | 忙 | 笑道: | 宝琴也 | 忙 | 笑道: | 老祝妈 | 忙 | 笑道: |
| 了刘老老, | 忙 | 笑道: | 黛玉 | 忙 | 笑道: | 平儿 | 忙 | 笑道: |
| 凤姐儿 | 忙 | 笑道: | 贾母喜的 | 忙 | 笑道: | 王家的 | 忙 | 笑道: |
| 刘老老 | 忙 | 笑道: | 凤姐儿 | 忙 | 笑道: | 尤氏 | 忙 | 笑道: |
| 王夫人 | 忙 | 笑道: | 宝玉 | 忙 | 笑道: | 宝玉 | 忙 | 笑道: |
| 如此说,便 | 忙 | 笑道: | 贾蓉也 | 忙 | 笑道: | 香菱 | 忙 | 笑道: |
| ,禁不起, | 忙 | 笑道: | 贾蓉等 | 忙 | 笑道: | 宝玉听了, | 忙 | 笑道: |
| 贾母 | 忙 | 笑道: | 那媳妇们 | 忙 | 笑道: | 宝玉 | 忙 | 笑道: |
| 刘老老 | 忙 | 笑道: | 宝玉听了, | 忙 | 笑道: | 黛玉 | 忙 | 笑道: |
| 刘老老 | 忙 | 笑道: | 李纨 | 忙 | 笑道: | | | |

### (三)关于"嬷"字的研究

"嬷"字是《红楼梦》前八十回会话引导语中的第三大特色字,关键度为97.717,字频116(见图2-21)。"嬷"字也是前八十回会话引导语中的独特字,在后四十回中一次都没有出现。

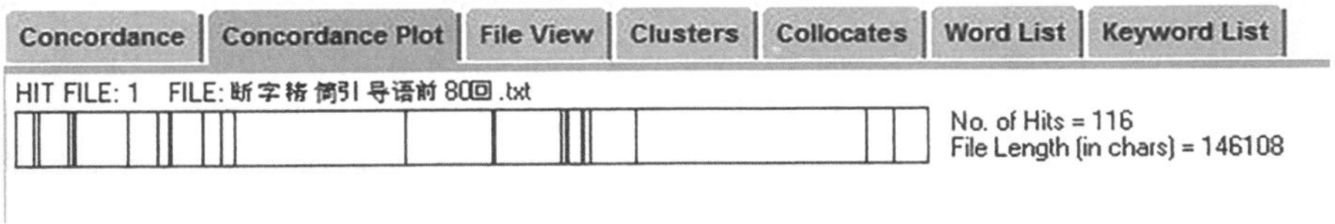

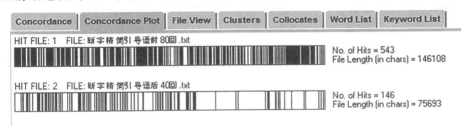

图 2－21 "嬷"字在《红楼梦》前八十回会话引导语中的分布情况

前文已经有关于"嬷"字的探讨,经检索核查后发现,"嬷"字最后的一次使用是在第七十七回中的"李嬷嬷指道:"。嬷嬷们在《红楼梦》的后三分之一部分(确切地说是在第七十七回以后)的话语权、角色身份等已经较之以前淡化了许多。这也符合《红楼梦》整个故事的发展脉络和趋势。

(四)关于"因"字的研究

"因"字是《红楼梦》前八十回会话引导语中去除人名之外的第四大特色字,关键度为 57.548。如图 2－22 所示,"因"字在前八十回会话引导语文本中的字频为 543,占总文本的 0.833%,位列第 21 位;在后四十回会话引导语文本中的字频为 146,占总文本的 0.429%,位列第 37 位。我们通过 AntConc 的统计可以清晰地看到"因"字在两个文本中的分布情况:

图 2－22 "因"字在前八十回和后四十回会话引导语中的分布情况

我们使用 PowerConc 软件检索"因"字右侧一字搭配,频率位居前 5 位的分别为"问"(75 次)、"说"(61 次)、"道"(11 次)、"想"(8 次)和"命"(3 次)。"因问"的用法最多,有 75 次,其中前八十回有 68 次,后四十回有 7 次;其次是"因说"61 次,其中前八十回有 54 次,后四十回有 7 次。

以下为前八十回的用法:

| 听了大喜, | 因 | 问: | 烟也笑了, | 因 | 问: | 当是真事, | 因 | 问: |
| --- | --- | --- | --- | --- | --- | --- | --- | --- |
| 贾妃 | 因 | 问: | 宝玉 | 因 | 问: | | 因 | 问: |
| 元妃 | 因 | 问: | 越发忙了, | 因 | 问: | | 因 | 问: |
| 宝玉 | 因 | 问: | 时解不来, | 因 | 问: | | 因 | 问: |

| | 因 | 问： | 王夫人 | 因 | 问： | 低头含笑， | 因 | 说： |
|---|---|---|---|---|---|---|---|---|
| 在台阶上， | 因 | 问： | 贾母 | 因 | 问： | 父亲,凤姐 | 因 | 说： |
| 宝玉 | 因 | 问： | 鸳鸯 | 因 | 问： | 的答应了， | 因 | 说： |
| 贾母 | 因 | 问： | | 因 | 问： | 来找宝玉， | 因 | 说： |
| 宝钗 | 因 | 问： | | 因 | 问： | 早写出来， | 因 | 说： |
| | 因 | 问： | 丫头媳妇们 | 因 | 问： | 李纨 | 因 | 说： |
| 宝玉 | 因 | 问： | | 因 | 问： | 周瑞家的 | 因 | 说： |
| 心下纳闷， | 因 | 问： | | 因 | 问： | 晴雯 | 因 | 说： |
| 贾母 | 因 | 问： | | 因 | 问： | 贾母 | 因 | 说： |
| 平儿 | 因 | 问： | 贾母 | 因 | 问： | 贾母 | 因 | 说： |
| 贾母 | 因 | 问： | | 因 | 问： | 家祖母 | 因 | 说： |
| 来请过安， | 因 | 问： | 人皆咤异， | 因 | 问： | 去住,贾母 | 因 | 说： |
| 众人不解， | 因 | 问： | 贾政 | 因 | 问： | 王夫人 | 因 | 说： |
| 贾母 | 因 | 问： | | 因 | 问： | 发倦,袭人 | 因 | 说： |
| 黛玉 | 因 | 问： | | 因 | 问： | 湘云 | 因 | 说： |
| | 因 | 问： | 姐儿坐下， | 因 | 问： | 晴雯 | 因 | 说： |
| | 因 | 问： | 雨村 | 因 | 问： | | 因 | 说： |
| 贾母 | 因 | 问： | | 因 | 问： | 他娘 | 因 | 说： |
| | 因 | 问： | 不足之症， | 因 | 问： | 不知何意， | 因 | 说： |
| 贾母 | 因 | 问： | | 因 | 问： | 宝玉点头， | 因 | 说： |
| 探春 | 因 | 问： | 贾政 | 因 | 问： | 宝玉 | 因 | 说： |
| 凤姐 | 因 | 问： | 王夫人 | 因 | 说： | 吃酒,鲍二 | 因 | 说： |
| 也着了忙， | 因 | 问： | 回去,贾母 | 因 | 说： | 二姐 | 因 | 说： |
| 说着， | 因 | 问： | 贾母 | 因 | 说： | 饭后,贾母 | 因 | 说： |
| 青的走来， | 因 | 问： | 零星绸缎， | 因 | 说： | 尤氏 | 因 | 说： |
| 方看真切， | 因 | 问： | | 因 | 说： | 在过不去， | 因 | 说： |
| 两钟新茶， | 因 | 问： | 贾母 | 因 | 说： | 贾琏 | 因 | 说： |
| 宝玉 | 因 | 问： | 宝钗 | 因 | 说： | 邢夫人 | 因 | 说： |
| 低头弄裙， | 因 | 问： | 榭去,黛玉 | 因 | 说： | | 因 | 说： |
| 嬷嬷叫住， | 因 | 问： | 贾母 | 因 | 说： | | 因 | 说： |
| 众人 | 因 | 问： | 刘老老 | 因 | 说： | | 因 | 说： |
| 宝玉 | 因 | 问： | 宝玉 | 因 | 说： | 人宽慰他， | 因 | 说： |
| 姨妈和宝钗 | 因 | 问： | 贾母 | 因 | 说： | | 因 | 说： |
| 纹在屋里， | 因 | 问： | | 因 | 说： | | 因 | 说： |
| | 因 | 问： | | 因 | 说： | | 因 | 说： |

| 王夫人 | 因 | 说： | | 因 | 说： | 只是纳闷， | 因 | 说： |
|---|---|---|---|---|---|---|---|---|
| | 因 | 说： | 把心放下， | 因 | 说： | 自己还笑， | 因 | 说： |
| 笑了一笑， | 因 | 说： | 了"是"， | 因 | 说： | 见他要去， | 因 | 说： |
| 说了一遍， | 因 | 说： | 放了心了， | 因 | 说： | | 因 | 说： |

以下为后四十回的用法：

| | 因 | 问： | 宝玉 | 因 | 问： | | 因 | 问： |
|---|---|---|---|---|---|---|---|---|
| 却是锄药， | 因 | 问： | | 因 | 问： | 见了宝玉， | 因 | 问： |
| 一面哭着， | 因 | 问： | | | | | | |

我们再对"因"字右侧的二字搭配进行检索，频率位居前 5 位的分别为"说道"(77 次)、"笑道"(63 次)、"问道"(21 次)、"问他"(7 次)、"叹道"(6 次)。"因说道"的用法最多，为 77 次，其中前八十回有 54 次，后四十回有 23 次。

以下为前八十回的用法：

| 士隐 | 因 | 说道： | 誊写出来， | 因 | 说道： | 越发骇异， | 因 | 说道： |
|---|---|---|---|---|---|---|---|---|
| 宝钗 | 因 | 说道： | 李纨等 | 因 | 说道： | 也不好任， | 因 | 说道： |
| 见是宝玉， | 因 | 说道： | | 因 | 说道： | 劝了一回， | 因 | 说道： |
| | 因 | 说道： | 却是黄酒， | 因 | 说道： | | 因 | 说道： |
| | 因 | 说道： | | 因 | 说道： | ，倒好笑， | 因 | 说道： |
| | 因 | 说道： | 看了一回， | 因 | 说道： | 气白了脸 | 因 | 说道： |
| 黛玉，迎春 | 因 | 说道： | 起一事来， | 因 | 说道： | | 因 | 说道： |
| 十分诧异， | 因 | 说道： | | 因 | 说道： | 毕，邢夫人 | 因 | 说道： |
| 探春 | 因 | 说道： | 上下不来， | 因 | 说道： | 绣橘 | 因 | 说道： |
| 了八九分， | 因 | 说道： | 赦恼起来， | 因 | 说道： | 又气又急 | 因 | 说道： |
| 日的事了， | 因 | 说道： | 嗽了两声， | 因 | 说道： | 贾政 | 因 | 说道： |
| | 因 | 说道： | | 因 | 说道： | ，说笑话， | 因 | 说道： |
| 黛玉 | 因 | 说道： | | 因 | 说道： | 自是喜悦 | 因 | 说道： |
| 浑身乱战， | 因 | 说道： | 踏上坐了， | 因 | 说道： | | 因 | 说道： |
| | 因 | 说道： | | 因 | 说道： | 太爷 | 因 | 说道： |
| 呼唤之事， | 因 | 说道： | 探春 | 因 | 说道： | 邢夫人等 | 因 | 说道： |
| | 因 | 说道： | 着一张纸， | 因 | 说道： | 的水灵了， | 因 | 说道： |
| | 因 | 说道： | 何事口角， | 因 | 说道： | | 因 | 说道： |

以下为后四十回的用法：

| | | | | | | | | |
|---|---|---|---|---|---|---|---|---|
| 也唬怔了， | 因 | 说道： | | 因 | 说道： | 钗的事来， | 因 | 说道： |
| 自是心烦， | 因 | 说道： | 要献勤儿， | 因 | 说道： | 王夫人 | 因 | 说道： |
| 不便追问， | 因 | 说道： | | 因 | 说道： | 想了一想， | 因 | 说道： |
| 贾母 | 因 | 说道： | | 因 | 说道： | 打量他冷， | 因 | 说道： |
| 人都笑了， | 因 | 说道： | 忘了神了， | 因 | 说道： | 住流下来， | 因 | 说道： |
| 点点头儿， | 因 | 说道： | 也是情理， | 因 | 说道： | | | |
| 贾母 | 因 | 说道： | 讪的起来， | 因 | 说道： | 平儿 | 因 | 说道： |
| | | | 脸飞红了， | 因 | 说道： | | | |

值得一提的是，63次"因笑道"的用法全部出现在前八十回，后四十回中一次都没有出现。

| | | | | | | | | |
|---|---|---|---|---|---|---|---|---|
| | 因 | 笑道： | | 因 | 笑道： | 宝钗 | 因 | 笑道： |
| | 因 | 笑道： | 张材两家的 | 因 | 笑道： | 四人乱滚， | 因 | 笑道： |
| | 因 | 笑道： | 不会说话， | 因 | 笑道： | 南安太妃 | 因 | 笑道： |
| 方听出来， | 因 | 笑道： | 老老口中， | 因 | 笑道： | 喜鸾 | 因 | 笑道： |
| | 因 | 笑道： | 不解何故， | 因 | 笑道： | 媳妇会意， | 因 | 笑道： |
| 装看不见， | 因 | 笑道： | 想毕， | 因 | 笑道： | 深知其意， | 因 | 笑道： |
| 事来解说， | 因 | 笑道： | 香菱 | 因 | 笑道： | 薛姨妈 | 因 | 笑道： |
| | 因 | 笑道： | 贾母 | 因 | 笑道： | | 因 | 笑道： |
| | 因 | 笑道： | 宝钗 | 因 | 笑道： | | | |
| | 因 | 笑道： | 湘云 | 因 | 笑道： | | 因 | 笑道： |
| 说话知趣， | 因 | 笑道： | 知有文章， | 因 | 笑道： | 贾母 | 因 | 笑道： |
| 宝钗 | 因 | 笑道： | 也笑起来， | 因 | 笑道： | 起的事来， | 因 | 笑道： |
| 想是宝玉， | 因 | 笑道： | 方知原故， | 因 | 笑道： | | | |
| 王夫人 | 因 | 笑道： | 贾母坐了， | 因 | 笑道： | | 因 | 笑道： |
| 感谢不尽， | 因 | 笑道： | 宝钗 | 因 | 笑道： | | | |
| | 因 | 笑道： | 镯子事发， | 因 | 笑道： | | | |
| 不便再问， | 因 | 笑道： | 了话答对， | 因 | 笑道： | 说上学去， | 因 | 笑道： |
| 想毕， | 因 | 笑道： | 也是喷香， | 因 | 笑道： | | | |
| 探春 | 因 | 笑道： | 柳家的 | 因 | 笑道： | 戴权会意， | 因 | 笑道： |
| | 因 | 笑道： | 喜欢起来， | 因 | 笑道： | 秦钟 | 因 | 笑道： |
| 只答应着， | 因 | 笑道： | 贾琏 | 因 | 笑道： | 佯作不知， | 因 | 笑道： |

根据"因"字的意义发展轨迹，从古代汉语中两个义项"因为""因此，于是"到现代汉语中仅有"因为"这一个义项，可以看出表示结果的那个义项是逐渐消

失的过程。然而语言的发展不是突变的,是有一个变化的过程,《红楼梦》所在的时期正是近代汉语向现代汉语过渡的转折期。"因 Y,因 G"这一特殊的因果类复句,仅在前八十回中有用例,后四十回中没有。在表达同一逻辑关系时,后四十回更多地使用的表达式是"因 Y,所以 G"。说明"因"标果的用例已经逐渐减少,同时标因标果的用法已经被取代,"因"仅保留标因功能,标果的功能分配给了"所以"。

本章对《红楼梦》原文中会话引导语的语言特点进行了分析和研究,分别从《红楼梦》原文会话引导语与非引导语对比、《红楼梦》与古典白话小说作品会话引导语对比、《红楼梦》与现代小说作品会话引导语对比、《红楼梦》前八十回与后四十回会话引导语对比等方面展开。通过多角度、多层次的深入分析,《红楼梦》原文会话引导语的语言特点和使用特色得到全方位的凸显,为我们在此基础上开展英译研究提供了非常重要的思路和前提。

# 第三章 《红楼梦》译文会话引导语研究

堪称中华民族传统文化总汇的《红楼梦》被翻译成多国文字流传海外。在众多的红楼译本中,两部全译本一直在翻译界享有盛誉:英国汉学家、翻译家大卫·霍克思与女婿约翰·闵福德共同翻译了一百二十回共五卷全译本《石头记》(*The Story of the Stone*),于1973—1986年间由企鹅出版集团(Penguin Group)陆续出版;1978—1980年,我国著名翻译家杨宪益与戴乃迭夫妇翻译的英文全译本《红楼梦》(*A Dream of Red Mansions*)由中国外文出版社分三卷出版发行(为方便起见,笔者将这两部全译本分别简称为霍译本和杨译本)。霍译本和杨译本是《红楼梦》英译史上真正的英文全译本,出版以来一直被公认为是优秀的翻译作品。霍克思和闵福德深厚的中文功底以及刻苦钻研的精神为翻译的成功奠定了基础,两人分别扮演了曹雪芹与高鹗的角色,创作出和谐优美的译文。杨宪益和戴乃迭的合作是中西文化的水乳交融,可以弥补双方在理解和表达上的不足。两个译本各自特点鲜明,它们的出版也在很大程度上引发了《红楼梦》英译研究的热潮。一般来说,大家普遍认为杨译本在语言上更贴近原著,霍译本则更趋自由,更能迎合英语读者的审美趣味。本章将分析《红楼梦》霍译本和杨译本这两部优秀译文中的会话引导语特色,为《红楼梦》会话引导语的英译提供必要的前提和基础。

## 第一节 《红楼梦》译文会话引导语与非引导语对比研究

为了凸显《红楼梦》译文中会话引导语的特色,本章首先采取将其中的会话引导语内容与非会话引导语内容作对比研究。会话引导语内容的筛选是基于笔者自行创建的"《红楼梦》汉英双语平行语料库",文本依据是上海外语教育出版社2012年出版发行的汉英对照版《红楼梦》。笔者在语料库中提取出《红楼梦》会话引导语语料的A版本(前文已有说明,在此不再赘述),该版本是原文—霍译本—杨译本对照的双语版本,并将对霍译本会话引导语和杨译本会话引导语分别进行研究。

## 一、《红楼梦》霍译本会话引导语与非引导语对比研究

本部分首先开展《红楼梦》霍译本中会话引导语与非引导语的对比分析,主要从高频词、特色词等角度进行研究。

### (一) 高频词对比研究

笔者对《红楼梦》霍译本中的会话引导语进行词频统计,得出数量位居前100位的高频词,随后列举这100个词在《红楼梦》霍译本总文本中的词频,由此得出其在非引导语中的词频,以供对比研究(见表3-1)。

表 3-1　霍译本会话引导语前 100 位高频词及其在霍译本非引导语和全文中的词频统计

| 排序 | 词语 | 引导语词频 | 百分比 | 非引导语词频 | 百分比 | 全文词频 | 百分比 |
|---|---|---|---|---|---|---|---|
| 1 | the | 6399 | 3.47 | 30 474 | 4.58 | 36 873 | 4.34 |
| 2 | to | 5591 | 3.03 | 23 196 | 3.48 | 28 787 | 3.39 |
| 3 | said | 4848 | 2.63 | 973 | 0.15 | 5821 | 0.68 |
| 4 | and | 3756 | 2.04 | 21 414 | 3.22 | 25 170 | 2.96 |
| 5 | you | 3571 | 1.94 | 10 019 | 1.51 | 13 590 | 1.60 |
| 6 | a | 3420 | 1.85 | 13 389 | 2.01 | 16 809 | 1.98 |
| 7 | of | 3109 | 1.69 | 16 581 | 2.49 | 19 690 | 2.32 |
| 8 | I | 2891 | 1.57 | 9138 | 1.37 | 12 029 | 1.42 |
| 9 | she | 2847 | 1.54 | 7545 | 1.13 | 10 392 | 1.22 |
| 10 | her | 2622 | 1.42 | 9082 | 1.36 | 11 704 | 1.38 |
| 11 | that | 2381 | 1.29 | 8256 | 1.24 | 10 637 | 1.25 |
| 12 | it | 2357 | 1.28 | 8362 | 1.26 | 10 719 | 1.26 |
| 13 | in | 2160 | 1.17 | 9570 | 1.44 | 11 730 | 1.38 |
| 14 | was | 1967 | 1.07 | 7499 | 1.13 | 9466 | 1.11 |
| 15 | he | 1799 | 0.98 | 5994 | 0.90 | 7793 | 0.92 |
| 16 | Jia | 1694 | 0.92 | 2882 | 0.43 | 4576 | 0.54 |
| 17 | with | 1442 | 0.78 | 5394 | 0.81 | 6836 | 0.80 |
| 18 | Bao-yu | 1389 | 0.75 | 2065 | 0.31 | 3454 | 0.41 |
| 19 | for | 1319 | 0.72 | 6353 | 0.95 | 7672 | 0.90 |
| 20 | what | 1106 | 0.60 | 2386 | 0.36 | 3492 | 0.41 |

（续表）

| 排序 | 词语 | 引导语词频 | 百分比 | 非引导语词频 | 百分比 | 全文词频 | 百分比 |
|---|---|---|---|---|---|---|---|
| 21 | on | 1099 | 0.60 | 4945 | 0.74 | 6044 | 0.71 |
| 22 | this | 1091 | 0.59 | 3580 | 0.54 | 4671 | 0.55 |
| 23 | had | 1075 | 0.58 | 5034 | 0.76 | 6109 | 0.72 |
| 24 | at | 999 | 0.54 | 3476 | 0.52 | 4475 | 0.53 |
| 25 | as | 976 | 0.53 | 4018 | 0.60 | 4994 | 0.59 |
| 26 | is | 971 | 0.53 | 3431 | 0.52 | 4402 | 0.52 |
| 27 | be | 951 | 0.52 | 4441 | 0.67 | 5392 | 0.63 |
| 28 | his | 951 | 0.52 | 4336 | 0.65 | 5287 | 0.62 |
| 29 | have | 934 | 0.51 | 3863 | 0.58 | 4797 | 0.56 |
| 30 | but | 908 | 0.49 | 3504 | 0.53 | 4412 | 0.52 |
| 31 | all | 900 | 0.49 | 3306 | 0.50 | 4206 | 0.49 |
| 32 | they | 866 | 0.47 | 3510 | 0.53 | 4376 | 0.51 |
| 33 | Xi-feng | 843 | 0.46 | 939 | 0.14 | 1782 | 0.21 |
| 34 | him | 839 | 0.46 | 2961 | 0.44 | 3800 | 0.45 |
| 35 | when | 750 | 0.41 | 2649 | 0.40 | 3399 | 0.40 |
| 36 | not | 725 | 0.39 | 2636 | 0.40 | 3361 | 0.40 |
| 37 | me | 723 | 0.39 | 2464 | 0.37 | 3187 | 0.37 |
| 38 | them | 711 | 0.39 | 2926 | 0.44 | 3637 | 0.43 |
| 39 | one | 703 | 0.38 | 2416 | 0.36 | 3119 | 0.37 |
| 40 | are | 688 | 0.37 | 1803 | 0.27 | 2491 | 0.29 |
| 41 | out | 679 | 0.37 | 2407 | 0.36 | 3086 | 0.36 |
| 42 | Grandmother | 672 | 0.36 | 1043 | 0.16 | 1715 | 0.20 |
| 43 | from | 656 | 0.36 | 2622 | 0.39 | 3278 | 0.39 |
| 44 | asked | 646 | 0.35 | 371 | 0.06 | 1017 | 0.12 |
| 45 | Lady | 642 | 0.35 | 1360 | 0.20 | 2002 | 0.24 |
| 46 | we | 642 | 0.35 | 2495 | 0.37 | 3137 | 0.37 |
| 47 | about | 632 | 0.34 | 2017 | 0.30 | 2649 | 0.31 |
| 48 | so | 628 | 0.34 | 2621 | 0.39 | 3249 | 0.38 |

（续表）

| 排序 | 词语 | 引导语词频 | 百分比 | 非引导语词频 | 百分比 | 全文词频 | 百分比 |
|---|---|---|---|---|---|---|---|
| 49 | your | 625 | 0.34 | 2040 | 0.31 | 2665 | 0.31 |
| 50 | there | 621 | 0.34 | 2397 | 0.36 | 3018 | 0.36 |
| 51 | no | 584 | 0.32 | 1743 | 0.26 | 2327 | 0.27 |
| 52 | now | 581 | 0.32 | 2173 | 0.33 | 2754 | 0.32 |
| 53 | up | 576 | 0.31 | 2158 | 0.32 | 2734 | 0.32 |
| 54 | do | 558 | 0.30 | 1654 | 0.25 | 2212 | 0.26 |
| 55 | if | 556 | 0.30 | 2915 | 0.44 | 3471 | 0.41 |
| 56 | Dai-yu | 552 | 0.30 | 748 | 0.11 | 1300 | 0.15 |
| 57 | Aroma | 531 | 0.29 | 589 | 0.09 | 1120 | 0.13 |
| 58 | been | 530 | 0.29 | 2152 | 0.32 | 2682 | 0.32 |
| 59 | who | 497 | 0.27 | 1457 | 0.22 | 1954 | 0.23 |
| 60 | Wang | 489 | 0.27 | 963 | 0.14 | 1452 | 0.17 |
| 61 | were | 488 | 0.26 | 2551 | 0.38 | 3039 | 0.36 |
| 62 | just | 481 | 0.26 | 1248 | 0.19 | 1729 | 0.20 |
| 63 | by | 480 | 0.26 | 2540 | 0.38 | 3020 | 0.36 |
| 64 | my | 478 | 0.26 | 1791 | 0.27 | 2269 | 0.27 |
| 65 | Bao-chai | 475 | 0.26 | 616 | 0.09 | 1091 | 0.13 |
| 66 | go | 452 | 0.25 | 1551 | 0.23 | 2003 | 0.24 |
| 67 | can | 444 | 0.24 | 1775 | 0.27 | 2219 | 0.26 |
| 68 | then | 441 | 0.24 | 1488 | 0.22 | 1929 | 0.23 |
| 69 | Zheng | 414 | 0.22 | 626 | 0.09 | 1040 | 0.12 |
| 70 | come | 409 | 0.22 | 1050 | 0.16 | 1459 | 0.17 |
| 71 | Lian | 404 | 0.22 | 772 | 0.12 | 1176 | 0.14 |
| 72 | old | 392 | 0.21 | 1068 | 0.16 | 1460 | 0.17 |
| 73 | very | 392 | 0.21 | 1053 | 0.16 | 1445 | 0.17 |
| 74 | came | 374 | 0.20 | 824 | 0.12 | 1198 | 0.14 |
| 75 | replied | 371 | 0.20 | 39 | 0.01 | 410 | 0.05 |
| 76 | well | 370 | 0.20 | 755 | 0.11 | 1125 | 0.13 |

（续表）

| 排序 | 词语 | 引导语词频 | 百分比 | 非引导语词频 | 百分比 | 全文词频 | 百分比 |
|---|---|---|---|---|---|---|---|
| 77 | Xue | 368 | 0.20 | 629 | 0.09 | 997 | 0.12 |
| 78 | like | 366 | 0.20 | 1386 | 0.21 | 1752 | 0.21 |
| 79 | after | 362 | 0.20 | 1348 | 0.20 | 1710 | 0.20 |
| 80 | see | 362 | 0.20 | 1170 | 0.18 | 1532 | 0.18 |
| 81 | know | 361 | 0.20 | 1003 | 0.15 | 1364 | 0.16 |
| 82 | here | 357 | 0.19 | 1031 | 0.15 | 1388 | 0.16 |
| 83 | Patience | 356 | 0.19 | 397 | 0.06 | 753 | 0.09 |
| 84 | some | 354 | 0.19 | 1521 | 0.23 | 1875 | 0.22 |
| 85 | back | 349 | 0.19 | 1464 | 0.22 | 1813 | 0.21 |
| 86 | could | 348 | 0.19 | 1403 | 0.21 | 1751 | 0.21 |
| 87 | how | 329 | 0.18 | 1015 | 0.15 | 1344 | 0.16 |
| 88 | good | 322 | 0.17 | 770 | 0.12 | 1092 | 0.13 |
| 89 | an | 321 | 0.17 | 1392 | 0.21 | 1713 | 0.20 |
| 90 | little | 314 | 0.17 | 1171 | 0.18 | 1485 | 0.17 |
| 91 | Aunt | 313 | 0.17 | 549 | 0.08 | 862 | 0.10 |
| 92 | would | 311 | 0.17 | 1843 | 0.28 | 2154 | 0.25 |
| 93 | time | 304 | 0.16 | 1329 | 0.20 | 1633 | 0.19 |
| 94 | laughed | 297 | 0.16 | 88 | 0.01 | 385 | 0.05 |
| 95 | two | 297 | 0.16 | 1371 | 0.21 | 1668 | 0.20 |
| 96 | Li | 283 | 0.15 | 402 | 0.06 | 685 | 0.08 |
| 97 | thought | 283 | 0.15 | 582 | 0.09 | 865 | 0.10 |
| 98 | why | 283 | 0.15 | 671 | 0.10 | 954 | 0.11 |
| 99 | oh | 282 | 0.15 | 157 | 0.02 | 439 | 0.05 |
| 100 | their | 279 | 0.15 | 1831 | 0.28 | 2110 | 0.25 |

通过表3-1我们可以看出,除了 the、to、and、a、of 这些无特定语义的冠词、介词、连词之外,在会话引导语文本中词频高居榜首的是 said,有4848个,占文本总量的2.63%,成为霍克思会话引导语译文中使用频率最高的词,而

said 在非引导语文本中仅有 973 个,只占文本总量的 0.15%。此外我们还发现,在会话引导语前 100 位高频词中,只有 4 个动词上榜,除了使用频率最高的 said 之外,其余几个动词为 asked(词频 646,占总文本的 0.35%),replied(词频 371,占总文本的 0.20%)和 laughed(词频 297,占总文本的 0.16%)。

对比分析上表中各个词语在会话引导语和非引导语中的百分比,笔者着重关注两者之间差距在 2 倍以上的词语(即会话引导语与非引导语百分比的比例 ≥2 或 ≤0.5),将比例差异显著的词语列举如下(以下均为引导语相对于非引导语的比例):

| | | |
|---|---|---|
| said(18:1) | Dai-yu(2.7:1) | Patience(3.2:1) |
| Jia(2.1:1) | Aroma(3.3:1) | Aunt(2.1:1) |
| Bao-yu(2.4:1) | Bao-chai(2.8:1) | laughed(12.2:1) |
| Xi-feng(3.2:1) | Zheng(2.4:1) | Li(2.5:1) |
| grandmother(2.3:1) | replied(34.3:1) | Oh(6.5:1) |
| asked(6.3:1) | Xue(2.1:1) | |

我们不难发现,在《红楼梦》霍译本会话引导语词频位居前 100 的词中,与非引导语差距达到 2 倍以上的有 17 个,其中有 12 个人名用词,分别为 Jia、Bao-yu、Xi-feng、grandmother、Dai-yu、Aroma、Bao-chai、Zheng、Xue、Patience、Aunt 和 Li;4 个动词,分别为 said、asked、replied 和 laughed;另外还有 1 个感叹词"Oh"。人名和动词在会话引导语译文中的优势恰与会话引导语的基本格式,即"人物+会话引导词"完全相符。几个人名用词代表的人物均属于《红楼梦》中非常重要和关键的人物,因此作为会话引导语的主语次数势必也是最多。几个动词应是对应原文中的会话引导语核心动词,在会话引导语和非引导语中的差别非常大。我们可以通过图 3-1 清晰地看出几个动词在会话引导语和非引导语中的差异。

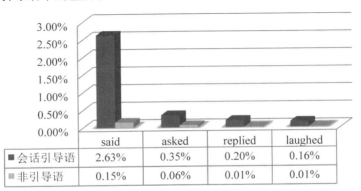

图 3-1　霍译本会话引导语与非引导语动词对比

（二）特色词对比研究

笔者使用文本分析软件 AntConc 对《红楼梦》霍译本中会话引导语文本与全文文本进行比较，提取霍译本中会话引导语相对于总文本的特色词。统计结果显示，霍译本中会话引导语文本相对于总文本共有 522 个特色词，限于篇幅，在此仅列举"关键度"≥50 的特色词（灰底部分为使用 negative keyword 功能提取的总文本相对于会话引导语文本的关键度≥50 的特色词，见表 3－2）：

**表 3－2　霍译本会话引导语相对于霍译本全文的特色词统计**

| 排序 | 词语 | 词频 | 关键度 |
|---|---|---|---|
| 1 | said | 4848 | 4280.407 |
| 2 | Bao | 2130 | 536.118 |
| 3 | yu | 1961 | 509.583 |
| 4 | asked | 646 | 402.941 |
| 5 | replied | 371 | 356.872 |
| 6 | Jia | 1694 | 319.743 |
| 7 | feng | 849 | 313.468 |
| 8 | Xi | 940 | 308.413 |
| 9 | laughed | 297 | 239.905 |
| 10 | smile | 237 | 208.004 |
| 11 | Aroma | 531 | 195.544 |
| 12 | oh | 279 | 186.691 |
| 13 | Parfum | 58 | 182.869 |
| 14 | what | 529 | 178.451 |
| 15 | smiled | 209 | 173.319 |
| 16 | Grandmother | 653 | 167.058 |
| 17 | Dai | 574 | 157.646 |
| 18 | chai | 488 | 152.511 |
| 19 | Patience | 353 | 129.954 |
| 20 | exclaimed | 127 | 124.591 |
| 21 | Xiang | 267 | 105.664 |
| 22 | you | 813 | 104.264 |
| 23 | she | 2179 | 104.021 |

（续表）

| 排序 | 词语 | 词频 | 关键度 |
|------|------|------|--------|
| 24 | yun | 228 | 97.976 |
| 25 | Zheng | 413 | 97.091 |
| 26 | smiling | 112 | 88.384 |
| 27 | yes | 164 | 84.827 |
| 28 | Tan | 252 | 81.527 |
| 29 | voice | 134 | 78.837 |
| 30 | cried | 102 | 77.46 |
| 31 | Grannie | 183 | 76.072 |
| 32 | Li | 283 | 75.138 |
| 33 | laughing | 141 | 74.618 |
| 34 | chun | 372 | 74.153 |
| 35 | lady | 550 | 71.559 |
| 36 | that | 316 | 70.764 |
| 37 | laugh | 121 | 69.939 |
| 38 | protested | 70 | 68.73 |
| 39 | Liu | 174 | 68.665 |
| 40 | Xue | 367 | 67.597 |
| 41 | right | 252 | 66.995 |
| 42 | Wang | 489 | 63.89 |
| 43 | well | 169 | 63.835 |
| 44 | Aunt | 294 | 61.613 |
| 45 | Wan | 199 | 60.917 |
| 46 | turned | 215 | 58.943 |
| 47 | Lian | 404 | 57.607 |
| 48 | sighed | 68 | 57.337 |
| 49 | shouted | 67 | 56.298 |
| 50 | where | 103 | 55.386 |
| 1 | and | 2407 | 390.263 |

（续表）

| 排序 | 词语 | 词频 | 关键度 |
|---|---|---|---|
| 2 | of | 1561 | 204.464 |
| 3 | the | 4253 | 137.361 |
| 4 | to | 3712 | 135.771 |
| 5 | had | 597 | 124.342 |
| 6 | their | 159 | 76.476 |
| 7 | as | 481 | 71.135 |
| 8 | or | 151 | 71.110 |
| 9 | for | 892 | 54.207 |

通过表 3-2 我们可以看到，said 是霍译本会话引导语的第一大特色词，关键度高达 4280.407。其他特色动词包括 asked（关键度 402.941）、replied（关键度 356.872）、laughed（关键度 239.905）等。

还有一些词频并未出现在前 100 位的动词，关键度却位居前列，说明尽管出现次数不是很多，却在会话引导语中的比例远超非引导语中的比例，这些动词包括：smiled（词频 209，关键度 173.319）、exclaimed（词频 127，关键度 124.591）、cried（词频 102，关键度 77.46）、protested（词频 70，关键度 68.73）、turned（词频 215，关键度 58.943）、sighed（词频 68，关键度 57.337）、shouted（词频 67，关键度 56.298）等（见图 3-2）。

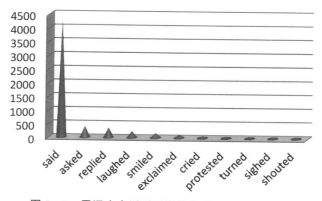

图 3-2　霍译本会话引导语特色动词的关键度

通过特色词列表里出现的人名用词我们可以大致推测作为会话引导语中最关键的几个人物，这些人物未必是产生会话最多的，却是相对于译文总文本来讲,作为会话主语的地位最为关键,这些人物如"宝玉""熙凤""贾母""贾政""黛玉""宝钗""袭人""芳官""王夫人""薛姨妈""平儿""刘老老"等。

此外,在特色词列表中,除了动词 laughed 和 smiled 等之外,还出现了它们的名词和现在分词形式,如 smile(词频 237,关键度 208.004)和 smiling(词频 112,关键度 88.384)、laugh(词频 121,关键度 69.939)和 laughing(词频 141,关键度 74.618)。

## 二、《红楼梦》杨译本会话引导语与非引导语对比

接下来笔者对《红楼梦》杨译本中会话引导语与非引导语进行对比分析,同样从高频词、特色词等角度进行研究。

### (一)高频词对比研究

笔者对《红楼梦》杨译本中的会话引导语进行词频统计,得出数量位居前 100 位的高频词,随后列举这 100 个词在《红楼梦》杨译本总文本中的词频以及由此计算出在非引导语中的词频,以供对比研究(见表 3-3)。

表 3-3 杨译本会话引导语前 100 位高频词及其在杨译本非引导语及全文中的词频统计

| 排序 | 词语 | 引导语词频 | 百分比 | 非引导语词频 | 百分比 | 全文词频 | 百分比 |
|---|---|---|---|---|---|---|---|
| 1 | the | 4882 | 3.53 | 21 956 | 4.34 | 26 838 | 4.17 |
| 2 | to | 3747 | 2.71 | 17 866 | 3.53 | 21 613 | 3.36 |
| 3 | you | 2913 | 2.11 | 7758 | 1.53 | 10 671 | 1.66 |
| 4 | she | 2516 | 1.82 | 6240 | 1.23 | 8756 | 1.36 |
| 5 | and | 2506 | 1.81 | 15 391 | 3.05 | 17 897 | 2.78 |
| 6 | a | 2346 | 1.70 | 9022 | 1.79 | 11 368 | 1.77 |
| 7 | I | 2053 | 1.48 | 6381 | 1.26 | 8434 | 1.31 |
| 8 | he | 1860 | 1.34 | 5052 | 1.00 | 6912 | 1.07 |
| 9 | her | 1793 | 1.30 | 6912 | 1.37 | 8705 | 1.35 |
| 10 | of | 1641 | 1.19 | 9180 | 1.82 | 10 821 | 1.68 |
| 11 | in | 1590 | 1.15 | 6536 | 1.29 | 8126 | 1.26 |
| 12 | that | 1559 | 1.13 | 5255 | 1.04 | 6814 | 1.06 |
| 13 | said | 1550 | 1.12 | 581 | 0.11 | 2131 | 0.33 |
| 14 | it | 1512 | 1.09 | 5103 | 1.01 | 6615 | 1.03 |
| 15 | was | 1132 | 0.82 | 4640 | 0.92 | 5772 | 0.90 |

（续表）

| 排序 | 词语 | 引导语词频 | 百分比 | 非引导语词频 | 百分比 | 全文词频 | 百分比 |
|---|---|---|---|---|---|---|---|
| 16 | this | 1126 | 0.81 | 3838 | 0.76 | 4964 | 0.77 |
| 17 | with | 1104 | 0.80 | 4040 | 0.80 | 5144 | 0.80 |
| 18 | lady | 1056 | 0.76 | 2167 | 0.43 | 3223 | 0.50 |
| 19 | Baoyu | 932 | 0.67 | 1858 | 0.37 | 2790 | 0.43 |
| 20 | asked | 919 | 0.66 | 465 | 0.09 | 1384 | 0.21 |
| 21 | for | 914 | 0.66 | 4697 | 0.93 | 5611 | 0.87 |
| 22 | Jia | 807 | 0.58 | 1855 | 0.37 | 2662 | 0.41 |
| 23 | what | 805 | 0.58 | 1559 | 0.31 | 2364 | 0.37 |
| 24 | on | 741 | 0.54 | 3642 | 0.72 | 4383 | 0.68 |
| 25 | they | 740 | 0.54 | 3042 | 0.60 | 3782 | 0.59 |
| 26 | his | 734 | 0.53 | 3350 | 0.66 | 4084 | 0.63 |
| 27 | him | 684 | 0.49 | 2378 | 0.47 | 3062 | 0.48 |
| 28 | is | 683 | 0.49 | 2160 | 0.43 | 2843 | 0.44 |
| 29 | Xifeng | 659 | 0.48 | 915 | 0.18 | 1574 | 0.24 |
| 30 | as | 655 | 0.47 | 3635 | 0.72 | 4290 | 0.67 |
| 31 | then | 642 | 0.46 | 1807 | 0.36 | 2449 | 0.38 |
| 32 | at | 639 | 0.46 | 2240 | 0.44 | 2879 | 0.45 |
| 33 | but | 624 | 0.45 | 3258 | 0.64 | 3882 | 0.60 |
| 34 | have | 624 | 0.45 | 2379 | 0.47 | 3003 | 0.47 |
| 35 | so | 605 | 0.44 | 2685 | 0.53 | 3290 | 0.51 |
| 36 | me | 601 | 0.43 | 2133 | 0.42 | 2734 | 0.42 |
| 37 | not | 601 | 0.43 | 2438 | 0.48 | 3039 | 0.47 |
| 38 | all | 598 | 0.43 | 2290 | 0.45 | 2888 | 0.45 |
| 39 | had | 597 | 0.43 | 3851 | 0.76 | 4448 | 0.69 |
| 40 | be | 591 | 0.43 | 2595 | 0.51 | 3186 | 0.49 |
| 41 | old | 590 | 0.43 | 1441 | 0.29 | 2031 | 0.32 |
| 42 | we | 590 | 0.43 | 2242 | 0.44 | 2832 | 0.44 |
| 43 | your | 541 | 0.39 | 1816 | 0.36 | 2357 | 0.37 |

（续表）

| 排序 | 词语 | 引导语词频 | 百分比 | 非引导语词频 | 百分比 | 全文词频 | 百分比 |
|---|---|---|---|---|---|---|---|
| 44 | out | 538 | 0.39 | 1949 | 0.39 | 2487 | 0.39 |
| 45 | when | 536 | 0.39 | 1991 | 0.39 | 2527 | 0.39 |
| 46 | just | 500 | 0.36 | 1308 | 0.26 | 1808 | 0.28 |
| 47 | up | 494 | 0.36 | 1831 | 0.36 | 2325 | 0.36 |
| 48 | told | 493 | 0.36 | 611 | 0.12 | 1104 | 0.17 |
| 49 | are | 490 | 0.35 | 1169 | 0.23 | 1659 | 0.26 |
| 50 | them | 489 | 0.35 | 1988 | 0.39 | 2477 | 0.38 |
| 51 | no | 464 | 0.34 | 1627 | 0.32 | 2091 | 0.32 |
| 52 | if | 459 | 0.33 | 2489 | 0.49 | 2948 | 0.46 |
| 53 | Baochai | 438 | 0.32 | 646 | 0.13 | 1084 | 0.17 |
| 54 | one | 437 | 0.32 | 1537 | 0.30 | 1974 | 0.31 |
| 55 | there | 430 | 0.31 | 1539 | 0.30 | 1969 | 0.31 |
| 56 | Daiyu | 422 | 0.31 | 731 | 0.14 | 1153 | 0.18 |
| 57 | how | 407 | 0.29 | 1170 | 0.23 | 1577 | 0.24 |
| 58 | go | 405 | 0.29 | 1193 | 0.24 | 1598 | 0.25 |
| 59 | who | 402 | 0.29 | 1372 | 0.27 | 1774 | 0.28 |
| 60 | can | 399 | 0.29 | 1655 | 0.33 | 2054 | 0.32 |
| 61 | now | 384 | 0.28 | 1706 | 0.34 | 2090 | 0.32 |
| 62 | smile | 379 | 0.27 | 81 | 0.02 | 460 | 0.07 |
| 63 | madam | 374 | 0.27 | 646 | 0.13 | 1020 | 0.16 |
| 64 | Wang | 372 | 0.27 | 778 | 0.15 | 1150 | 0.18 |
| 65 | my | 367 | 0.27 | 1505 | 0.30 | 1872 | 0.29 |
| 66 | why | 363 | 0.26 | 800 | 0.16 | 1163 | 0.18 |
| 67 | Xiren | 360 | 0.26 | 517 | 0.10 | 877 | 0.14 |
| 68 | do | 358 | 0.26 | 1025 | 0.20 | 1383 | 0.21 |
| 69 | too | 356 | 0.26 | 1390 | 0.28 | 1746 | 0.27 |
| 70 | by | 351 | 0.25 | 1919 | 0.38 | 2270 | 0.35 |
| 71 | from | 350 | 0.25 | 1561 | 0.31 | 1911 | 0.30 |

（续表）

| 排序 | 词语 | 引导语词频 | 百分比 | 非引导语词频 | 百分比 | 全文词频 | 百分比 |
|------|------|-----------|--------|-------------|--------|---------|--------|
| 72 | here | 348 | 0.25 | 961 | 0.19 | 1309 | 0.20 |
| 73 | good | 330 | 0.24 | 962 | 0.19 | 1292 | 0.20 |
| 74 | cried | 322 | 0.23 | 70 | 0.01 | 392 | 0.06 |
| 75 | back | 316 | 0.23 | 1283 | 0.25 | 1599 | 0.25 |
| 76 | after | 305 | 0.22 | 1370 | 0.27 | 1675 | 0.26 |
| 77 | some | 298 | 0.22 | 1381 | 0.27 | 1679 | 0.26 |
| 78 | were | 295 | 0.21 | 1731 | 0.34 | 2026 | 0.31 |
| 79 | know | 291 | 0.21 | 819 | 0.16 | 1110 | 0.17 |
| 80 | come | 288 | 0.21 | 944 | 0.19 | 1232 | 0.19 |
| 81 | about | 285 | 0.21 | 837 | 0.17 | 1122 | 0.17 |
| 82 | Xue | 282 | 0.20 | 544 | 0.11 | 826 | 0.13 |
| 83 | came | 273 | 0.20 | 631 | 0.12 | 904 | 0.14 |
| 84 | Pinger | 273 | 0.20 | 359 | 0.07 | 632 | 0.10 |
| 85 | Zheng | 273 | 0.20 | 405 | 0.08 | 678 | 0.11 |
| 86 | replied | 266 | 0.19 | 19 | 0.00 | 285 | 0.04 |
| 87 | been | 259 | 0.19 | 1165 | 0.23 | 1424 | 0.22 |
| 88 | Li | 256 | 0.19 | 357 | 0.07 | 613 | 0.10 |
| 89 | right | 252 | 0.18 | 362 | 0.07 | 614 | 0.10 |
| 90 | see | 250 | 0.18 | 776 | 0.15 | 1026 | 0.16 |
| 91 | Lian | 245 | 0.18 | 531 | 0.11 | 776 | 0.12 |
| 92 | well | 245 | 0.18 | 671 | 0.13 | 916 | 0.14 |
| 93 | over | 237 | 0.17 | 923 | 0.18 | 1160 | 0.18 |
| 94 | let | 233 | 0.17 | 831 | 0.16 | 1064 | 0.17 |
| 95 | put | 233 | 0.17 | 457 | 0.09 | 690 | 0.11 |
| 96 | like | 230 | 0.17 | 977 | 0.19 | 1207 | 0.19 |
| 97 | exclaimed | 227 | 0.16 | 30 | 0.01 | 257 | 0.04 |
| 98 | Aunt | 226 | 0.16 | 444 | 0.09 | 670 | 0.10 |
| 99 | Dowager | 226 | 0.16 | 425 | 0.08 | 651 | 0.10 |

（续表）

| 排序 | 词语 | 引导语词频 | 百分比 | 非引导语词频 | 百分比 | 全文词频 | 百分比 |
|------|------|-----------|--------|-------------|--------|---------|--------|
| 100 | two | 217 | 0.16 | 1048 | 0.21 | 1265 | 0.20 |

通过上表我们可以看到,在会话引导语文本中位居前100位的词中,除了冠词、介词和人称代词之外,词频最高的也是"said",词频为1550,占文本总量的1.12%;而在非引导语文本中,该词的词频仅为581,仅占文本总量的0.11%。因此"said"也是杨宪益会话引导语译文中使用频率最高的词。然而,相对于霍译本会话引导语前100名中仅有4个动词而言,杨译本会话引导语前100名中的动词种类略多,除了使用频率最高的"said"外,还有"asked"(词频919,占总文本的0.66%)、"told"(词频493,占总文本的0.36%)、"cried"(词频322,占总文本的0.23%)、"replied"(词频266,占总文本的0.19%)和"exclaimed"(词频227,占总文本的0.16%)。

与霍译本的研究方式相同,笔者在此也特别关注杨译本会话引导语文本与非引导语文本之间差距在2倍以上的词语(同样是筛选会话引导语与非引导语百分比的比例≥2或≤0.5的词语),将比例差异显著的词语列举如下(均为引导语相对于非引导语的比例):

said(9.7:1)

asked(7.2:1)

Xifeng(2.6:1)

told(2.9:1)

Baochai(2.5:1)

Daiyu(2.1:1)

smile(17.1:1)

Madam(2.1:1)

Xiren(2.5:1)

cried(16.8:1)

Pinger(2.8:1)

Zheng(2.5:1)

replied(51.2:1)

Li(2.6:1)

right(2.5:1)

exclaimed(27.7:1)

我们可以看到,在《红楼梦》杨译译本会话引导语词频位居前100的词中,与非引导语差距达到2倍以上的有16个,其中有8个人名用词,分别为Xifeng、Baochai、Daiyu、Madam、Xiren、Pinger、Zheng和Li;6个动词,分别为said、asked、told、cried、replied和exclaimed;另外还有1个名词"smile"和1个形容词"right"。除了人名用词代表了《红楼梦》中几位重要人物外,几个动词在会话引导语和非引导语中的差异非常显著。

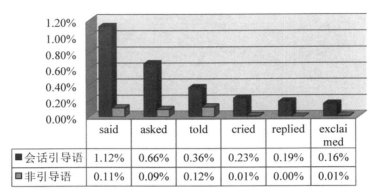

| | said | asked | told | cried | replied | exclaimed |
|---|---|---|---|---|---|---|
| ■会话引导语 | 1.12% | 0.66% | 0.36% | 0.23% | 0.19% | 0.16% |
| □非引导语 | 0.11% | 0.09% | 0.12% | 0.01% | 0.00% | 0.01% |

**图 3‑3　关键动词在杨译本会话引导语和非引导语中的词频对比**

## （二）特色词对比研究

笔者使用文本分析软件 AntConc 对《红楼梦》杨译本中会话引导语文本与全文文本进行比较，提取杨译本中会话引导语相对于总文本的特色词。统计结果显示，杨译本中会话引导语文本相对于总文本共有 487 个特色词，限于篇幅，在此仅列举"关键度"≥50 的特色词（阴影部分为使用"negative keyword"功能提取的总文本相对于会话引导语文本的关键度≥50 的特色词）：

**表 3‑4　杨译本会话引导语特色词**

| 排序 | 词语 | 词频 | 关键度 |
|---|---|---|---|
| 1 | said | 1550 | 1210.736 |
| 2 | asked | 905 | 626.956 |
| 3 | smile | 379 | 343.137 |
| 4 | cried | 322 | 289.872 |
| 5 | replied | 266 | 273.306 |
| 6 | exclaimed | 227 | 220.735 |
| 7 | what | 491 | 209.033 |
| 8 | answered | 208 | 197.465 |
| 9 | Xifeng | 658 | 191.731 |
| 10 | told | 492 | 170.068 |
| 11 | remarked | 169 | 170.016 |
| 12 | smiled | 187 | 166.441 |
| 13 | chuckled | 154 | 162.01 |

| 排序 | 词语 | 词频 | 关键度 |
|:---:|:---:|:---:|:---:|
| 14 | you | 752 | 160.306 |
| 15 | she | 1998 | 149.212 |
| 16 | that | 384 | 143.441 |
| 17 | retorted | 135 | 141.198 |
| 18 | Baoyu | 932 | 132.332 |
| 19 | laughed | 178 | 125.923 |
| 20 | announced | 148 | 121.691 |
| 21 | Baochai | 438 | 116.332 |
| 22 | protested | 108 | 108.855 |
| 23 | Xiren | 360 | 100.018 |
| 24 | demanded | 100 | 90.626 |
| 25 | Pinger | 273 | 86.346 |
| 26 | Daiyu | 422 | 83.553 |
| 27 | urged | 138 | 82.461 |
| 28 | Tanchun | 215 | 80.325 |
| 29 | lady | 610 | 79.915 |
| 30 | Li | 257 | 77.671 |
| 31 | sighed | 85 | 73.705 |
| 32 | Jia | 806 | 73.004 |
| 33 | Zheng | 272 | 71.306 |
| 34 | right | 248 | 69.556 |
| 35 | yes | 112 | 67.296 |
| 36 | he | 1506 | 66.481 |
| 37 | Wan | 181 | 64.938 |
| 38 | why | 271 | 64.727 |
| 39 | madam | 211 | 61.086 |
| 40 | scolded | 76 | 59.677 |
| 41 | no | 148 | 59.058 |

（续表）

| 排序 | 词语 | 词频 | 关键度 |
|:---:|:---:|:---:|:---:|
| 42 | lady | 447 | 58.461 |
| 43 | objected | 59 | 58.079 |
| 44 | observed | 69 | 56.669 |
| 45 | rejoined | 59 | 55.465 |
| 46 | granny | 116 | 55.343 |
| 47 | where | 102 | 55.104 |
| 48 | agreed | 123 | 54.817 |
| 49 | teased | 55 | 54.612 |
| 50 | it | 381 | 52.122 |
| 1 | and | 2407 | 390.263 |
| 2 | of | 1561 | 204.464 |
| 3 | the | 4253 | 137.361 |
| 4 | to | 3712 | 135.771 |
| 5 | had | 597 | 124.342 |
| 6 | their | 159 | 76.476 |
| 7 | as | 481 | 71.135 |
| 8 | or | 151 | 71.110 |
| 9 | for | 892 | 54.207 |

通过上表我们可以看到,"said"也是杨译本会话引导语的第一大特色词,关键度为1210.736。其他特色动词包括"asked"(关键度626.956)、"cried"(关键度289.872)、"replied"(关键度273.306)、"exclaimed"(关键度220.735)、"told"(关键度170.068)等。

还有一些特色动词,词频并未出现在前100位,关键度此次却跃居前列,这些动词多达17个,包括:"answered"(词频208,关键度197.465)、"remarked"(词频169,关键度170.016)、"smiled"(词频187,关键度166.441)、"chuckled"(词频154,关键度162.01)、"retorted"(词频135,关键度141.198)、"laughed"(词频178,关键度125.923)、"announced"(词频148,121.691)、"protested"(词频108,关键度108.855)、"demanded"(词频100,关键度90.626)、"urged"(词频138,关键度82.461)、"sighed"(词频85,关键度73.705)、"scolded"(词频76,

关键度 59.677）、"objected"（词频 59，关键度 58.079）、"observed"（词频 69，关键度 56.669）、"rejoined"（词频 59，关键度 55.465）、"agreed"（词频 123，关键度 54.817）、"teased"（词频 55，关键度 54.612）等（见图 3 - 4）。

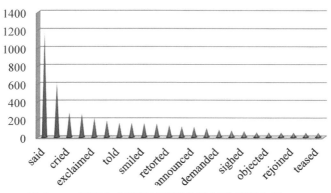

图 3 - 4 杨译本会话引导语特色动词关键度分析

与霍译本会话引导语文本中一些人名特色词一样，杨译本中的特色词同样清晰地反映了作为会话主语的一些主要人物，如"熙凤""宝玉""宝钗""袭人""黛玉""平儿""探春""贾政""刘老老"等。

此外，名词"smile"高居杨译本会话引导语特色词第三位（词频 379，关键度 343.137），仅次于"said"和"asked"。它也是关键度≥50 的特色字中唯一的名词（除了人名用字外），非常值得我们关注。

### 三、《红楼梦》霍、杨译本会话引导语与非引导语对比小结

通过对《红楼梦》霍译本和杨译本中的会话引导语文本与非引导语文本进行高频词、特色词等方面的对比研究，可初步得出以下结论：

（1）"said"是《红楼梦》霍译本和杨译本会话引导语译文中使用频率最高的词语，也是第一大特色词。

（2）会话引导语与非引导语的对比充分凸显《红楼梦》译文中作为会话引导语主语的关键人物。

（3）在高频动词和特色动词的统计中，霍译本和杨译本除了"said"外，还同时使用了其他多样化的动词，有些动词虽不是高频词，但确是非常重要的特色词。

## 第二节 《红楼梦》译文与英文小说会话引导语对比研究

将中文原著的英译文与英文原版著作进行语内对比，可以看出译文的遣词

造句是否正确、地道,表达方式是否符合英文表达习惯,这有着非常重要的意义。为了分析《红楼梦》英译文中会话引导语的特色,笔者引入了几部非常有名的英文原版小说——《飘》(*Gone with the Wind*)、《名利场》(*Vanity Fair:A Novel Without a Hero*)和《大卫·科波菲尔》(*David Copperfield*)。《飘》是美国女作家玛格丽特·米切尔十年磨一剑的唯一作品,出版于1936年,是美国史上最为畅销的小说之一;《名利场》是英国伟大现实主义作家和幽默大师萨克雷的代表作,于1847年出版;《大卫·科波菲尔》是19世纪英国批判现实主义作家查尔斯·狄更斯的重要作品,写于1848—1850年。

为便于对比,笔者分别将《红楼梦》霍译本和杨译本的会话引导语与三部英文原版小说做对比研究。研究将围绕高频词、独特词和特色词展开。

## 一、《红楼梦》霍译本与英文小说会话引导语对比研究

《红楼梦》霍译本是由以英语为母语的西方译者翻译的,人们普遍认为该译本更能迎合英语读者的审美趣味。下面笔者将对《红楼梦》霍译本中的会话引导语与三部英文原版小说进行对比研究。

（一）高频词对比研究

首先筛选出《红楼梦》霍译本会话引导语中词频位于前100位的高频词(人物、地点用词不计算在内),然后按顺序将这100个高频词在《红楼梦》(表中简称《红》)霍译本全文以及英文小说《飘》《名利场》和《大卫·科波菲尔》(表中简称《大卫》)中的词频及百分比列举对比如表3-5所示。

表3-5　霍译本会话引导语前100位高频词及其在霍译本全文和几部英文小说中的词频统计

| 排序 | 词语 | 《红》引导语词频 | 百分比 | 《红》全文词频 | 百分比 | 《飘》词频 | 百分比 | 《名利场》词频 | 百分比 | 《大卫》词频 | 百分比 |
|---|---|---|---|---|---|---|---|---|---|---|---|
| 1 | the | 6399 | 3.47 | 36 873 | 4.34 | 18 197 | 4.617 | 17 463 | 5.620 | 13 686 | 3.771 |
| 2 | to | 5591 | 3.03 | 28 787 | 3.39 | 9297 | 2.359 | 8094 | 2.606 | 10 406 | 2.867 |
| 3 | said | 4848 | 2.63 | 5821 | 0.68 | 1368 | 0.347 | 1347 | 0.433 | 2942 | 0.811 |
| 4 | and | 3756 | 2.04 | 25 170 | 2.96 | 14 947 | 3.792 | 12927 | 4.160 | 12 264 | 3.379 |
| 5 | you | 3571 | 1.94 | 13 590 | 1.60 | 4759 | 1.207 | 2143 | 0.690 | 3686 | 1.016 |
| 6 | a | 3420 | 1.85 | 16 809 | 1.98 | 7217 | 1.831 | 6763 | 2.176 | 7951 | 2.191 |
| 7 | of | 3109 | 1.69 | 19 690 | 2.32 | 8065 | 2.046 | 8545 | 2.750 | 8669 | 2.389 |
| 8 | I | 2891 | 1.57 | 12 029 | 1.42 | 4893 | 1.241 | 2562 | 0.824 | 13 419 | 3.698 |
| 9 | she | 2847 | 1.54 | 10 392 | 1.22 | 7600 | 1.928 | 3231 | 1.040 | 2760 | 0.761 |

（续表）

| 排序 | 词语 | 《红》引导语词频 | 百分比 | 《红》全文词频 | 百分比 | 《飘》词频 | 百分比 | 《名利场》词频 | 百分比 | 《大卫》词频 | 百分比 |
|---|---|---|---|---|---|---|---|---|---|---|---|
| 10 | her | 2622 | 1.42 | 11 704 | 1.38 | 7473 | 1.896 | 4613 | 1.484 | 3857 | 1.063 |
| 11 | that | 2381 | 1.29 | 10 637 | 1.25 | 4212 | 1.069 | 3349 | 1.078 | 5374 | 1.481 |
| 12 | it | 2357 | 1.28 | 10 719 | 1.26 | 4132 | 1.048 | 2399 | 0.772 | 5022 | 1.384 |
| 13 | in | 2160 | 1.17 | 11 730 | 1.38 | 5582 | 1.416 | 5472 | 1.761 | 6208 | 1.711 |
| 14 | was | 1967 | 1.07 | 9466 | 1.11 | 5524 | 1.402 | 4454 | 1.433 | 5301 | 1.461 |
| 15 | he | 1799 | 0.98 | 7793 | 0.92 | 4534 | 1.150 | 3906 | 1.257 | 3626 | 0.999 |
| 16 | with | 1442 | 0.78 | 6836 | 0.80 | 3092 | 0.785 | 3086 | 0.993 | 3359 | 0.926 |
| 17 | for | 1319 | 0.72 | 7672 | 0.90 | 3079 | 0.781 | 2272 | 0.731 | 2605 | 0.718 |
| 18 | what | 1106 | 0.60 | 3492 | 0.41 | 1210 | 0.307 | 668 | 0.215 | 1367 | 0.377 |
| 19 | on | 1099 | 0.60 | 6044 | 0.71 | 2219 | 0.563 | 1519 | 0.489 | 2371 | 0.653 |
| 20 | this | 1091 | 0.59 | 4671 | 0.55 | 1092 | 0.277 | 1036 | 0.333 | 1398 | 0.385 |
| 21 | had | 1075 | 0.58 | 6109 | 0.72 | 4118 | 1.045 | 2753 | 0.886 | 3055 | 0.842 |
| 22 | at | 999 | 0.54 | 4475 | 0.53 | 2240 | 0.568 | 2451 | 0.789 | 2656 | 0.732 |
| 23 | as | 976 | 0.53 | 4994 | 0.59 | 2755 | 0.699 | 2563 | 0.825 | 3191 | 0.879 |
| 24 | is | 971 | 0.53 | 4402 | 0.52 | 877 | 0.223 | 1426 | 0.459 | 1744 | 0.481 |
| 25 | be | 951 | 0.52 | 5392 | 0.63 | 1924 | 0.488 | 1342 | 0.432 | 2020 | 0.557 |
| 26 | his | 951 | 0.52 | 5287 | 0.62 | 2855 | 0.724 | 4045 | 1.302 | 2938 | 0.810 |
| 27 | have | 934 | 0.51 | 4797 | 0.56 | 1514 | 0.384 | 1216 | 0.391 | 2380 | 0.656 |
| 28 | but | 908 | 0.49 | 4412 | 0.52 | 2810 | 0.713 | 1237 | 0.398 | 2203 | 0.607 |
| 29 | all | 900 | 0.49 | 4206 | 0.49 | 1582 | 0.401 | 1101 | 0.354 | 1520 | 0.419 |
| 30 | they | 866 | 0.47 | 4376 | 0.51 | 2284 | 0.580 | 922 | 0.297 | 772 | 0.213 |
| 31 | him | 839 | 0.46 | 3800 | 0.45 | 1909 | 0.484 | 1659 | 0.534 | 1709 | 0.471 |
| 32 | when | 750 | 0.41 | 3399 | 0.40 | 1391 | 0.353 | 1134 | 0.365 | 1660 | 0.457 |
| 33 | not | 725 | 0.39 | 3361 | 0.40 | 2158 | 0.548 | 1651 | 0.531 | 2014 | 0.555 |
| 34 | me | 723 | 0.39 | 3187 | 0.37 | 1336 | 0.339 | 653 | 0.210 | 3607 | 0.994 |
| 35 | them | 711 | 0.39 | 3637 | 0.43 | 1344 | 0.341 | 572 | 0.184 | 637 | 0.176 |
| 36 | one | 703 | 0.38 | 3119 | 0.37 | 872 | 0.221 | 736 | 0.237 | 913 | 0.252 |

| 排序 | 词语 | 《红》引导语词频 | 百分比 | 《红》全文词频 | 百分比 | 《飘》词频 | 百分比 | 《名利场》词频 | 百分比 | 《大卫》词频 | 百分比 |
|------|------|------|------|------|------|------|------|------|------|------|------|
| 37 | are | 688 | 0.37 | 2491 | 0.29 | 810 | 0.206 | 645 | 0.208 | 714 | 0.197 |
| 38 | out | 679 | 0.37 | 3086 | 0.36 | 1050 | 0.266 | 874 | 0.281 | 1117 | 0.308 |
| 39 | from | 656 | 0.36 | 3278 | 0.39 | 1536 | 0.390 | 1096 | 0.353 | 1064 | 0.293 |
| 40 | asked | 646 | 0.35 | 1017 | 0.12 | 96 | 0.024 | 166 | 0.053 | 201 | 0.055 |
| 41 | we | 642 | 0.35 | 3137 | 0.37 | 689 | 0.175 | 600 | 0.193 | 1505 | 0.415 |
| 42 | about | 632 | 0.34 | 2649 | 0.31 | 1274 | 0.323 | 651 | 0.209 | 658 | 0.181 |
| 43 | so | 628 | 0.34 | 3249 | 0.38 | 1807 | 0.458 | 989 | 0.318 | 1710 | 0.471 |
| 44 | your | 625 | 0.34 | 2665 | 0.31 | 771 | 0.196 | 479 | 0.154 | 578 | 0.159 |
| 45 | there | 621 | 0.34 | 3018 | 0.36 | 1378 | 0.350 | 816 | 0.263 | 1208 | 0.333 |
| 46 | no | 584 | 0.32 | 2327 | 0.27 | 1400 | 0.355 | 688 | 0.221 | 1236 | 0.341 |
| 47 | now | 581 | 0.32 | 2754 | 0.32 | 1000 | 0.254 | 373 | 0.120 | 742 | 0.204 |
| 48 | up | 576 | 0.31 | 2734 | 0.32 | 1074 | 0.273 | 730 | 0.235 | 897 | 0.247 |
| 49 | do | 558 | 0.30 | 2212 | 0.26 | 925 | 0.235 | 370 | 0.119 | 902 | 0.249 |
| 50 | if | 556 | 0.30 | 3471 | 0.41 | 1540 | 0.391 | 620 | 0.200 | 1556 | 0.429 |
| 51 | been | 530 | 0.29 | 2682 | 0.32 | 1089 | 0.276 | 751 | 0.242 | 1113 | 0.307 |
| 52 | who | 497 | 0.27 | 1954 | 0.23 | 964 | 0.245 | 1366 | 0.440 | 683 | 0.188 |
| 53 | were | 488 | 0.26 | 3039 | 0.36 | 1944 | 0.493 | 1066 | 0.343 | 1253 | 0.345 |
| 54 | just | 481 | 0.26 | 1729 | 0.20 | 687 | 0.174 | 151 | 0.049 | 146 | 0.040 |
| 55 | by | 480 | 0.26 | 3020 | 0.36 | 961 | 0.244 | 1244 | 0.400 | 1423 | 0.392 |
| 56 | my | 478 | 0.26 | 2269 | 0.27 | 816 | 0.207 | 1007 | 0.324 | 5180 | 1.427 |
| 57 | go | 452 | 0.25 | 2003 | 0.24 | 580 | 0.147 | 359 | 0.116 | 414 | 0.114 |
| 58 | can | 444 | 0.24 | 2219 | 0.26 | 736 | 0.187 | 267 | 0.086 | 472 | 0.130 |
| 59 | then | 441 | 0.24 | 1929 | 0.23 | 547 | 0.139 | 304 | 0.098 | 624 | 0.172 |
| 60 | come | 409 | 0.22 | 1459 | 0.17 | 502 | 0.127 | 43 | 0.014 | 571 | 0.157 |
| 61 | old | 392 | 0.21 | 1460 | 0.17 | 668 | 0.169 | 914 | 0.294 | 636 | 0.175 |
| 62 | very | 392 | 0.21 | 1445 | 0.17 | 360 | 0.091 | 880 | 0.283 | 1002 | 0.276 |
| 63 | came | 374 | 0.20 | 1198 | 0.14 | 525 | 0.133 | 413 | 0.133 | 460 | 0.127 |

（续表）

| 排序 | 词语 | 《红》引导语词频 | 百分比 | 《红》全文词频 | 百分比 | 《飘》词频 | 百分比 | 《名利场》词频 | 百分比 | 《大卫》词频 | 百分比 |
|---|---|---|---|---|---|---|---|---|---|---|---|
| 64 | replied | 371 | 0.20 | 410 | 0.05 | 20 | 0.005 | 67 | 0.022 | 208 | 0.057 |
| 65 | well | 370 | 0.20 | 1125 | 0.13 | 685 | 0.174 | 312 | 0.100 | 546 | 0.150 |
| 66 | like | 366 | 0.20 | 1752 | 0.21 | 1019 | 0.259 | 360 | 0.116 | 639 | 0.176 |
| 67 | after | 362 | 0.20 | 1710 | 0.20 | 480 | 0.122 | 500 | 0.161 | 448 | 0.123 |
| 68 | see | 362 | 0.20 | 1532 | 0.18 | 463 | 0.117 | 389 | 0.125 | 562 | 0.155 |
| 69 | know | 361 | 0.20 | 1364 | 0.16 | 766 | 0.194 | 346 | 0.111 | 821 | 0.226 |
| 70 | here | 357 | 0.19 | 1388 | 0.16 | 378 | 0.096 | 250 | 0.080 | 434 | 0.120 |
| 71 | some | 354 | 0.19 | 1875 | 0.22 | 447 | 0.113 | 450 | 0.145 | 661 | 0.182 |
| 72 | back | 349 | 0.19 | 1813 | 0.21 | 731 | 0.185 | 282 | 0.091 | 402 | 0.111 |
| 73 | could | 348 | 0.19 | 1751 | 0.21 | 1386 | 0.352 | 497 | 0.160 | 860 | 0.237 |
| 74 | how | 329 | 0.18 | 1344 | 0.16 | 806 | 0.205 | 656 | 0.211 | 618 | 0.170 |
| 75 | good | 322 | 0.17 | 1092 | 0.13 | 473 | 0.120 | 629 | 0.202 | 579 | 0.160 |
| 76 | an | 321 | 0.17 | 1713 | 0.20 | 1007 | 0.256 | 770 | 0.248 | 965 | 0.266 |
| 77 | little | 314 | 0.17 | 1485 | 0.17 | 593 | 0.150 | 1122 | 0.361 | 1087 | 0.300 |
| 78 | would | 311 | 0.17 | 2154 | 0.25 | 1533 | 0.389 | 916 | 0.295 | 1007 | 0.277 |
| 79 | time | 304 | 0.16 | 1633 | 0.19 | 519 | 0.132 | 341 | 0.110 | 671 | 0.185 |
| 80 | laughed | 297 | 0.16 | 385 | 0.05 | 128 | 0.032 | 81 | 0.026 | 65 | 0.018 |
| 81 | two | 297 | 0.16 | 1668 | 0.20 | 360 | 0.091 | 357 | 0.115 | 323 | 0.089 |
| 82 | thought | 283 | 0.15 | 865 | 0.10 | 811 | 0.206 | 377 | 0.121 | 448 | 0.123 |
| 83 | why | 283 | 0.15 | 954 | 0.11 | 516 | 0.131 | 156 | 0.050 | 234 | 0.064 |
| 84 | oh | 282 | 0.15 | 439 | 0.05 | 672 | 0.171 | 86 | 0.028 | 373 | 0.103 |
| 85 | their | 279 | 0.15 | 2110 | 0.25 | 1136 | 0.288 | 745 | 0.240 | 324 | 0.089 |
| 86 | say | 276 | 0.15 | 1062 | 0.12 | 393 | 0.100 | 356 | 0.115 | 611 | 0.168 |
| 87 | think | 272 | 0.15 | 1180 | 0.14 | 503 | 0.128 | 221 | 0.071 | 590 | 0.163 |
| 88 | get | 266 | 0.14 | 1364 | 0.16 | 574 | 0.146 | 148 | 0.048 | 143 | 0.039 |
| 89 | right | 264 | 0.14 | 610 | 0.07 | 274 | 0.070 | 87 | 0.028 | 192 | 0.053 |
| 90 | got | 263 | 0.14 | 1134 | 0.13 | 401 | 0.102 | 164 | 0.053 | 296 | 0.082 |

（续表）

| 排序 | 词语 | 《红》引导语词频 | 百分比 | 《红》全文词频 | 百分比 | 《飘》词频 | 百分比 | 《名利场》词频 | 百分比 | 《大卫》词频 | 百分比 |
|---|---|---|---|---|---|---|---|---|---|---|---|
| 91 | more | 257 | 0.14 | 1643 | 0.19 | 688 | 0.175 | 494 | 0.159 | 782 | 0.251 |
| 92 | tell | 257 | 0.14 | 1085 | 0.13 | 430 | 0.109 | 147 | 0.047 | 222 | 0.061 |
| 93 | too | 257 | 0.14 | 1289 | 0.15 | 692 | 0.176 | 375 | 0.121 | 413 | 0.114 |
| 94 | told | 256 | 0.14 | 893 | 0.11 | 235 | 0.060 | 182 | 0.059 | 248 | 0.068 |
| 95 | only | 252 | 0.14 | 1699 | 0.20 | 693 | 0.176 | 389 | 0.125 | 352 | 0.097 |
| 96 | over | 249 | 0.14 | 1354 | 0.16 | 657 | 0.167 | 470 | 0.151 | 435 | 0.120 |
| 97 | again | 247 | 0.13 | 1036 | 0.12 | 491 | 0.125 | 159 | 0.051 | 505 | 0.139 |
| 98 | did | 246 | 0.13 | 984 | 0.12 | 1041 | 0.264 | 493 | 0.159 | 470 | 0.130 |
| 99 | down | 242 | 0.13 | 1164 | 0.14 | 729 | 0.185 | 424 | 0.136 | 618 | 0.170 |
| 100 | smile | 236 | 0.13 | 285 | 0.03 | 127 | 0.032 | 58 | 0.019 | 84 | 0.023 |

从《红楼梦》霍译本会话引导语前100位高频词与《红楼梦》霍译本全文、《飘》《名利场》和《大卫·科波菲尔》的对比中我们可以发现，绝大部分高频词在《红楼梦》霍译本全文的百分比基本和《飘》《名利场》及《大卫·科波菲尔》中的百分比达成一致，相差幅度非常小，最多的也没有超过2倍。《红楼梦》霍译本中关键动词"said"的高频率（0.68%）得到了三部英文小说的支持，比例分别为0.347%、0.433%和0.811%（见图3-5）。

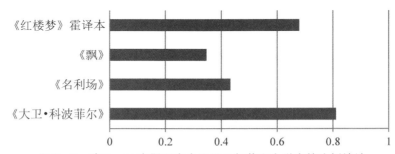

图3-5 动词 said 在霍译本全文及几部英文小说中的比例统计

只有一个动词"asked"比较特殊，它的比例在《红楼梦》霍译本中和几部英文小说中差异较大。"asked"在《红楼梦》霍译本会话引导语中的比例高达0.35%，在《红楼梦》霍译本全文中占0.12%，但在几部英文原版小说中的比例很低,分别为:《飘》0.024%,为霍译本全文比例的1/5;《名利场》0.053%,不到霍译本全文比例的1/2;《大卫·科波菲尔》0.055%,也不到霍译本全文比例的1/2。

此外,动词"replied"在《红楼梦》霍译本全文中的比例为0.05%,虽然与《大卫·科波菲尔》中0.057%的比例基本相当,但却是《飘》(0.005%)的10倍,是《名利场》(0.022%)的2.3倍。还有动词"told"在《红楼梦》霍译本全文中的比例为0.11%,比《飘》(0.060%)、《名利场》(0.059%)和《大卫·科波菲尔》(0.068%)中的比例也高出约1倍。以上这两个动词同样值得我们关注(见图3-6)。

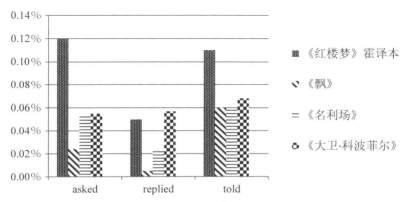

**图3-6 asked、replied 和 told 在霍译本全文及几部英文小说中的比例统计**

(二)独特词、特色词对比研究

随即笔者考察了《红楼梦》霍译本会话引导语相对于三部英文小说的独特词和特色词。方法是使用 AntConc 里的 wordlist 和 keyword list 功能,将《飘》《名利场》和《大卫·科波菲尔》三部著作合并成一个文本进行分析比较。

《红楼梦》霍译本中的会话引导语相对于三部英文小说来讲,独特词多达2400个,且多为人名、地名用词。在筛除人名、地名用词后,词频在5次以上的词语有55个:

| | | | |
|---|---|---|---|
| monk(41) | Buddha(15) | incense(11) | nannies(9) |
| taels(38) | couplet(13) | kotow(11) | nuns(9) |
| Taoist(36) | Aiyo(12) | ladyships(11) | rhyme(9) |
| kang(35) | jokingly(12) | calligraphy(10) | tael(9) |
| coz(24) | kotowed(12) | concubine(9) | troupe(9) |
| eunuch(19) | preceptor(12) | gauze(9) | fetch(8) |

| landscape(8) | threshold(7) | orchid(6) | hmn(5) |
| rhymes(8) | Buddhist(6) | phoenix(6) | inkstone(5) |
| sis(8) | chided(6) | snowing(6) | inside(5) |
| yamen(8) | gateman(6) | carry(5) | inspected(5) |
| enquired(7) | janitors(6) | cassia(5) | plasters(5) |
| genially(7) | karma(6) | congee(5) | spice(5) |
| kowtowed(7) | kylin(6) | edict(5) | willow(5) |
| sympathetically(7) | missus(6) | exasperatedly(5) | |

　　《红楼梦》霍译本中的会话引导语相对于三部英文小说来讲,特色词有138个,筛除人名、地名用词后共有22个(见表3-6):

表3-6　霍译本会话引导语相对于几部英文小说的特色词

| 排序 | 词语 | 词频 | 关键度 |
|:---:|:---:|:---:|:---:|
| 1 | taels | 38 | 302.075 |
| 2 | Taoist | 36 | 286.177 |
| 3 | kang | 35 | 278.227 |
| 4 | coz | 24 | 190.784 |
| 5 | eunuch | 19 | 151.038 |
| 6 | Buddha | 15 | 119.24 |
| 7 | couplet | 13 | 103.342 |
| 8 | Aiyo | 12 | 95.392 |
| 9 | jokingly | 12 | 95.392 |
| 10 | kotowed | 12 | 95.392 |
| 11 | Preceptor | 12 | 95.392 |
| 12 | incense | 11 | 87.443 |
| 13 | kotow | 11 | 87.443 |
| 14 | Ladyships | 11 | 87.443 |
| 15 | calligraphy | 10 | 79.493 |
| 16 | gauze | 9 | 71.544 |
| 17 | lotus | 9 | 71.544 |
| 18 | nannies | 9 | 71.544 |
| 19 | nuns | 9 | 71.544 |

（续表）

| 排序 | 词语 | 词频 | 关键度 |
|------|------|------|--------|
| 20 | rhyme | 9 | 71.544 |
| 21 | tael | 9 | 71.544 |
| 22 | troupe | 9 | 71.544 |

在《红楼梦》霍译本会话引导语的独特词和特色词中，相当一部分词的出现主要是与原著的创作主题和时代背景相关，如宗教信仰方面的 monk、Taoist、Buddha、incense、nuns 等，历史时代方面的 taels、tael、kang、eunuch、couplet、gauze、calligraphy 等，年龄地位方面的 kotow、kotowed、preceptor、ladyships、nannies 等。对此笔者不多做研究。

有几个口语的缩写体，如 coz（cousin）、sis（sister）和 missus（对"夫人""太太"的口语化称呼）等，用于对人物的称呼，使得译文非常亲切、地道和真实，这可以反映霍克思译文的特点。

此外还有几个以-ly 形式结尾的副词，如 jokingly、genially、sympathetically 和 exasperatedly 也是霍译本会话引导语中的独特词。其中 jokingly 既是独特词也是特色词，词频为 12，关键度为 95.392。

我们先来看几部权威词典对于副词 jokingly 的释义：

（1）《牛津高阶英语词典》（第 6 版）（Oxford Advanced Learner's Dictionary）：in a way that is intended to be amusing and not serious。

（2）《柯林斯高阶英语词典》（Collins COBUILD Advanced Learner's English Dictionary）：If you say or do something jokingly，you say or do it with the intention of amusing someone，rather than with any serious meaning or intention.

由此我们可以推断出 jokingly 在译文中是用来表达"开玩笑地、戏谑地"之意。该词在《红楼梦》霍译本会话引导语文本中出现的上下文为：

| | | |
|---|---|---|
| myself，' he said | **jokingly** | . |
| maid called ' Prettikins ' | **jokingly** | accused Bao-chai of having hid |
| together ? ' he whispered | **jokingly** | . |
| , he said to her | **jokingly** | : |
| Bao-yu commented | **jokingly** | on the choice ：' |
| , ' said Aunt Xue | **jokingly** | . |

| | | | |
|---|---|---|---|
| and when Tan-chun | **jokingly** | called to her through the |
| possessions，' Xi-feng expostulated | **jokingly** | . |
| ？' she asked him | **jokingly** | . |
| taste！' said Parfumée | **jokingly** | . |
| did observe，half- | **jokingly** | ，When she had looked |
| said Jia Rong half- | **jokingly** | 'No，I think |

## 二、《红楼梦》杨译本与英文小说会话引导语对比研究

《红楼梦》杨译本是由汉语为母语的中国译者杨宪益携手英国夫人戴乃迭共同翻译的，人们普遍认为该译本在语言上更贴近原著，下面笔者将对《红楼梦》杨译本中的会话引导语与三部英文原版小说进行对比研究。

### （一）高频词对比研究

与上述霍译本与英文小说的对比方法同样，笔者首先筛选出《红楼梦》杨译本会话引导语中词频位于前100位的高频词（人名、地名用词不计算在内），将这100个高频词在《红楼梦》（表中简称《红》）杨译本全文以及英文小说《飘》《名利场》和《大卫·科波菲尔》（表中简称《大卫》）中的词频及百分比列举对比如表3-7所示。

表3-7　杨译本会话引导语前100位高频词及其在杨译本全文及几部英文小说中的词频统计

| 排序 | 词语 | 《红》引导语词频 | 百分比 | 《红》全文词频 | 百分比 | 《飘》词频 | 百分比 | 《名利场》词频 | 百分比 | 《大卫》词频 | 百分比 |
|---|---|---|---|---|---|---|---|---|---|---|---|
| 1 | the | 4882 | 3.53 | 26 838 | 4.17 | 18 197 | 4.617 | 17 463 | 5.620 | 13 686 | 3.771 |
| 2 | to | 3747 | 2.71 | 21 613 | 3.36 | 9297 | 2.359 | 8094 | 2.606 | 10 406 | 2.867 |
| 3 | you | 2913 | 2.11 | 10 671 | 1.66 | 4759 | 1.207 | 2143 | 0.690 | 3686 | 1.016 |
| 4 | she | 2516 | 1.82 | 8756 | 1.36 | 7600 | 1.928 | 3231 | 1.040 | 2760 | 0.761 |
| 5 | and | 2506 | 1.81 | 17 897 | 2.78 | 14 947 | 3.792 | 12 927 | 4.160 | 12 264 | 3.379 |
| 6 | a | 2346 | 1.70 | 11 368 | 1.77 | 7217 | 1.831 | 6763 | 2.176 | 7951 | 2.191 |
| 7 | I | 2053 | 1.48 | 8434 | 1.31 | 4893 | 1.241 | 2562 | 0.824 | 13 419 | 3.698 |
| 8 | he | 1860 | 1.34 | 6912 | 1.07 | 4534 | 1.150 | 3906 | 1.257 | 3626 | 0.999 |
| 9 | her | 1793 | 1.30 | 8705 | 1.35 | 7473 | 1.896 | 4613 | 1.484 | 3857 | 1.063 |

（续表）

| 排序 | 词语 | 《红》引导语词频 | 百分比 | 《红》全文词频 | 百分比 | 《飘》词频 | 百分比 | 《名利场》词频 | 百分比 | 《大卫》词频 | 百分比 |
|---|---|---|---|---|---|---|---|---|---|---|---|
| 10 | of | 1641 | 1.19 | 10821 | 1.68 | 8065 | 2.046 | 8545 | 2.750 | 8669 | 2.389 |
| 11 | in | 1590 | 1.15 | 8126 | 1.26 | 5582 | 1.416 | 5472 | 1.761 | 6208 | 1.711 |
| 12 | that | 1559 | 1.13 | 6814 | 1.06 | 4212 | 1.069 | 3349 | 1.078 | 5374 | 1.481 |
| 13 | said | 1550 | 1.12 | 2131 | 0.33 | 1368 | 0.347 | 1347 | 0.433 | 2942 | 0.811 |
| 14 | it | 1512 | 1.09 | 6615 | 1.03 | 4132 | 1.048 | 2399 | 0.772 | 5022 | 1.384 |
| 15 | was | 1132 | 0.82 | 5772 | 0.90 | 5524 | 1.402 | 4454 | 1.433 | 5301 | 1.461 |
| 16 | this | 1126 | 0.81 | 4964 | 0.77 | 1092 | 0.277 | 1036 | 0.333 | 1398 | 0.385 |
| 17 | with | 1104 | 0.80 | 5144 | 0.80 | 3092 | 0.785 | 3086 | 0.993 | 3359 | 0.926 |
| 18 | asked | 919 | 0.66 | 1384 | 0.21 | 96 | 0.024 | 166 | 0.053 | 201 | 0.055 |
| 19 | for | 914 | 0.66 | 5611 | 0.87 | 3079 | 0.781 | 2272 | 0.731 | 2605 | 0.718 |
| 20 | what | 805 | 0.58 | 2364 | 0.37 | 1210 | 0.307 | 668 | 0.215 | 1367 | 0.377 |
| 21 | on | 741 | 0.54 | 4383 | 0.68 | 2219 | 0.563 | 1519 | 0.489 | 2371 | 0.653 |
| 22 | they | 740 | 0.54 | 3782 | 0.59 | 2284 | 0.580 | 922 | 0.297 | 772 | 0.213 |
| 23 | his | 734 | 0.53 | 4084 | 0.63 | 2855 | 0.724 | 4045 | 1.302 | 2938 | 0.810 |
| 24 | him | 684 | 0.49 | 3062 | 0.48 | 1909 | 0.484 | 1659 | 0.534 | 1709 | 0.471 |
| 25 | is | 683 | 0.49 | 2843 | 0.44 | 877 | 0.223 | 1426 | 0.459 | 1744 | 0.481 |
| 26 | as | 655 | 0.47 | 4290 | 0.67 | 2755 | 0.699 | 2563 | 0.825 | 3191 | 0.879 |
| 27 | then | 642 | 0.46 | 2449 | 0.38 | 547 | 0.139 | 304 | 0.098 | 624 | 0.172 |
| 28 | at | 639 | 0.46 | 2879 | 0.45 | 2240 | 0.568 | 2451 | 0.789 | 2656 | 0.732 |
| 29 | but | 624 | 0.45 | 3882 | 0.60 | 2810 | 0.713 | 1237 | 0.398 | 2203 | 0.607 |
| 30 | have | 624 | 0.45 | 3003 | 0.47 | 1514 | 0.384 | 1216 | 0.391 | 2380 | 0.656 |
| 31 | so | 605 | 0.44 | 3290 | 0.51 | 1807 | 0.458 | 989 | 0.318 | 1710 | 0.471 |
| 32 | me | 601 | 0.43 | 2734 | 0.42 | 1336 | 0.339 | 653 | 0.210 | 3607 | 0.994 |
| 33 | not | 601 | 0.43 | 3039 | 0.47 | 2158 | 0.548 | 1651 | 0.531 | 2014 | 0.555 |
| 34 | all | 598 | 0.43 | 2888 | 0.45 | 1582 | 0.401 | 1101 | 0.354 | 1520 | 0.419 |
| 35 | had | 597 | 0.43 | 4448 | 0.69 | 4118 | 1.045 | 2753 | 0.886 | 3055 | 0.842 |
| 36 | be | 591 | 0.43 | 3186 | 0.49 | 1924 | 0.488 | 1342 | 0.432 | 2020 | 0.557 |

| 排序 | 词语 | 《红》引导语词频 | 百分比 | 《红》全文词频 | 百分比 | 《飘》词频 | 百分比 | 《名利场》词频 | 百分比 | 《大卫》词频 | 百分比 |
|---|---|---|---|---|---|---|---|---|---|---|---|
| 37 | old | 590 | 0.43 | 2031 | 0.32 | 668 | 0.169 | 914 | 0.294 | 636 | 0.175 |
| 38 | we | 590 | 0.43 | 2832 | 0.44 | 689 | 0.175 | 600 | 0.193 | 1505 | 0.415 |
| 39 | your | 541 | 0.39 | 2357 | 0.37 | 771 | 0.196 | 479 | 0.154 | 578 | 0.159 |
| 40 | out | 538 | 0.39 | 2487 | 0.39 | 1050 | 0.266 | 874 | 0.281 | 1117 | 0.308 |
| 41 | when | 536 | 0.39 | 2527 | 0.39 | 1391 | 0.353 | 1134 | 0.365 | 1660 | 0.457 |
| 42 | just | 500 | 0.36 | 1808 | 0.28 | 687 | 0.174 | 151 | 0.049 | 146 | 0.040 |
| 43 | up | 494 | 0.36 | 2325 | 0.36 | 1074 | 0.273 | 730 | 0.235 | 897 | 0.247 |
| 44 | told | 493 | 0.36 | 1104 | 0.17 | 235 | 0.060 | 182 | 0.059 | 248 | 0.068 |
| 45 | are | 490 | 0.35 | 1659 | 0.26 | 810 | 0.206 | 645 | 0.208 | 714 | 0.197 |
| 46 | them | 489 | 0.35 | 2477 | 0.38 | 1344 | 0.341 | 572 | 0.184 | 637 | 0.176 |
| 47 | no | 464 | 0.34 | 2091 | 0.32 | 1400 | 0.355 | 688 | 0.221 | 1236 | 0.341 |
| 48 | if | 459 | 0.33 | 2948 | 0.46 | 1540 | 0.391 | 620 | 0.200 | 1556 | 0.429 |
| 49 | one | 437 | 0.32 | 1974 | 0.31 | 872 | 0.221 | 736 | 0.237 | 913 | 0.252 |
| 50 | there | 430 | 0.31 | 1969 | 0.31 | 1378 | 0.350 | 816 | 0.263 | 1208 | 0.333 |
| 51 | how | 407 | 0.29 | 1577 | 0.24 | 806 | 0.205 | 656 | 0.211 | 618 | 0.170 |
| 52 | go | 405 | 0.29 | 1598 | 0.25 | 580 | 0.147 | 359 | 0.116 | 414 | 0.114 |
| 53 | who | 402 | 0.29 | 1774 | 0.28 | 964 | 0.245 | 1366 | 0.440 | 683 | 0.188 |
| 54 | can | 399 | 0.29 | 2054 | 0.32 | 736 | 0.187 | 267 | 0.086 | 472 | 0.130 |
| 55 | now | 384 | 0.28 | 2090 | 0.32 | 1000 | 0.254 | 373 | 0.120 | 742 | 0.204 |
| 56 | smile | 379 | 0.27 | 460 | 0.07 | 127 | 0.032 | 58 | 0.019 | 84 | 0.023 |
| 57 | my | 367 | 0.27 | 1872 | 0.29 | 816 | 0.207 | 1007 | 0.324 | 5180 | 1.427 |
| 58 | why | 363 | 0.26 | 1163 | 0.18 | 516 | 0.131 | 156 | 0.050 | 234 | 0.064 |
| 59 | do | 358 | 0.26 | 1383 | 0.21 | 925 | 0.235 | 370 | 0.119 | 902 | 0.249 |
| 60 | too | 356 | 0.26 | 1746 | 0.27 | 692 | 0.176 | 375 | 0.121 | 413 | 0.114 |
| 61 | by | 351 | 0.25 | 2270 | 0.35 | 961 | 0.244 | 1244 | 0.400 | 1423 | 0.392 |
| 62 | from | 350 | 0.25 | 1911 | 0.30 | 1536 | 0.390 | 1096 | 0.363 | 1064 | 0.293 |
| 63 | here | 348 | 0.25 | 1309 | 0.20 | 378 | 0.096 | 250 | 0.080 | 434 | 0.120 |

（续表）

| 排序 | 词语 | 《红》引导语词频 | 百分比 | 《红》全文词频 | 百分比 | 《飘》词频 | 百分比 | 《名利场》词频 | 百分比 | 《大卫》词频 | 百分比 |
|---|---|---|---|---|---|---|---|---|---|---|---|
| 64 | good | 330 | 0.24 | 1292 | 0.20 | 473 | 0.120 | 629 | 0.202 | 579 | 0.160 |
| 65 | cried | 322 | 0.23 | 392 | 0.06 | 263 | 0.067 | 133 | 0.043 | 187 | 0.052 |
| 66 | back | 316 | 0.23 | 1599 | 0.25 | 731 | 0.185 | 282 | 0.091 | 402 | 0.111 |
| 67 | after | 305 | 0.22 | 1675 | 0.26 | 480 | 0.122 | 500 | 0.161 | 448 | 0.123 |
| 68 | some | 298 | 0.22 | 1679 | 0.26 | 447 | 0.113 | 450 | 0.145 | 661 | 0.182 |
| 69 | were | 295 | 0.21 | 2026 | 0.31 | 1944 | 0.493 | 1066 | 0.343 | 1253 | 0.345 |
| 70 | know | 291 | 0.21 | 1110 | 0.17 | 766 | 0.194 | 346 | 0.111 | 821 | 0.226 |
| 71 | come | 288 | 0.21 | 1232 | 0.19 | 502 | 0.127 | 43 | 0.014 | 571 | 0.157 |
| 72 | about | 285 | 0.21 | 1122 | 0.17 | 1274 | 0.323 | 651 | 0.209 | 658 | 0.181 |
| 73 | came | 273 | 0.20 | 904 | 0.14 | 525 | 0.133 | 413 | 0.133 | 460 | 0.127 |
| 74 | replied | 266 | 0.19 | 285 | 0.04 | 20 | 0.005 | 67 | 0.022 | 208 | 0.057 |
| 75 | been | 259 | 0.19 | 1424 | 0.22 | 1089 | 0.276 | 751 | 0.242 | 1113 | 0.307 |
| 76 | right | 252 | 0.18 | 614 | 0.10 | 274 | 0.070 | 87 | 0.028 | 192 | 0.053 |
| 77 | see | 250 | 0.18 | 1026 | 0.16 | 463 | 0.117 | 389 | 0.125 | 562 | 0.155 |
| 78 | well | 245 | 0.18 | 916 | 0.14 | 685 | 0.174 | 312 | 0.100 | 546 | 0.150 |
| 79 | over | 237 | 0.17 | 1160 | 0.18 | 657 | 0.167 | 470 | 0.151 | 435 | 0.120 |
| 80 | let | 233 | 0.17 | 1064 | 0.17 | 329 | 0.083 | 174 | 0.056 | 203 | 0.056 |
| 81 | put | 233 | 0.17 | 690 | 0.11 | 249 | 0.063 | 197 | 0.063 | 322 | 0.089 |
| 82 | like | 230 | 0.17 | 1207 | 0.19 | 1019 | 0.259 | 360 | 0.116 | 639 | 0.176 |
| 83 | exclaimed | 227 | 0.16 | 257 | 0.04 | 0 | 0 | 0 | 0 | 63 | 0.017 |
| 84 | two | 217 | 0.16 | 1265 | 0.20 | 360 | 0.091 | 357 | 0.115 | 323 | 0.089 |
| 85 | did | 215 | 0.16 | 829 | 0.13 | 1041 | 0.264 | 493 | 0.159 | 470 | 0.130 |
| 86 | answered | 208 | 0.15 | 241 | 0.04 | 63 | 0.016 | 68 | 0.022 | 102 | 0.028 |
| 87 | our | 207 | 0.15 | 1131 | 0.18 | 225 | 0.057 | 318 | 0.102 | 593 | 0.163 |
| 88 | young | 206 | 0.15 | 981 | 0.15 | 200 | 0.051 | 554 | 0.178 | 286 | 0.079 |
| 89 | could | 203 | 0.15 | 1129 | 0.18 | 1386 | 0.352 | 497 | 0.160 | 860 | 0.237 |
| 90 | other | 202 | 0.15 | 1233 | 0.19 | 403 | 0.102 | 402 | 0.129 | 386 | 0.106 |

（续表）

| 排序 | 词语 | 《红》引导语词频 | 百分比 | 《红》全文词频 | 百分比 | 《飘》词频 | 百分比 | 《名利场》词频 | 百分比 | 《大卫》词频 | 百分比 |
|---|---|---|---|---|---|---|---|---|---|---|---|
| 91 | again | 197 | 0.14 | 809 | 0.13 | 491 | 0.125 | 159 | 0.051 | 505 | 0.139 |
| 92 | more | 196 | 0.14 | 1148 | 0.18 | 688 | 0.175 | 494 | 0.159 | 782 | 0.215 |
| 93 | has | 193 | 0.14 | 895 | 0.14 | 173 | 0.044 | 429 | 0.138 | 428 | 0.118 |
| 94 | where | 193 | 0.14 | 640 | 0.10 | 379 | 0.096 | 360 | 0.116 | 404 | 0.111 |
| 95 | time | 192 | 0.14 | 1122 | 0.17 | 519 | 0.132 | 341 | 0.110 | 139 | 0.038 |
| 96 | called | 191 | 0.14 | 503 | 0.08 | 118 | 0.030 | 114 | 0.037 | 124 | 0.034 |
| 97 | others | 190 | 0.14 | 723 | 0.11 | 93 | 0.024 | 41 | 0.013 | 33 | 0.009 |
| 98 | must | 189 | 0.14 | 973 | 0.15 | 359 | 0.091 | 329 | 0.106 | 359 | 0.099 |
| 99 | smiled | 187 | 0.14 | 230 | 0.04 | 95 | 0.024 | 15 | 0.005 | 20 | 0.006 |
| 100 | thought | 187 | 0.14 | 485 | 0.08 | 811 | 0.206 | 377 | 0.121 | 448 | 0.123 |

在将《红楼梦》杨译本会话引导语前100位高频词与《红楼梦》杨译本全文、《飘》《名利场》和《大卫·科波菲尔》的对比过程中，有几个关键词值得我们关注：

高频动词 said（1.12%）在《红楼梦》杨译本全文中所占的比例（0.33%）统统小于其他三部英文原版小说（比例分别为 0.347%、0.433% 和 0.811%）。而其他几个动词的比例统统高于其他三部英文原版小说。

动词"asked"（会话引导语中比例为 0.66%）在《红楼梦》杨译本原文中比例为 0.21%，分别为《飘》中百分比（0.024%）的 8.75 倍，《名利场》中百分比（0.053%）的 3.96 倍，《大卫·科波菲尔》中百分比（0.055%）的 3.8 倍。我们尤其要关注动词 exclaimed，它在《红楼梦》杨译本会话引导语中的比例为 0.16%，在杨译本全文中比例为 0.04%，在《大卫·科波菲尔》中比例为 0.017%，还不到杨译本全文的 1/2，而在《飘》和《名利场》中的比例为 0，一次都没有被使用。

名词 smile（杨译本会话引导语文本中比例 0.27%）在《红楼梦》杨译本全文中的比例为 0.07%，分别为《飘》中百分比（0.032%）的 2.2 倍，《名利场》中百分比（0.019%）的 3.68 倍，《大卫·科波菲尔》中百分比（0.023%）的 3.0 倍（见图 3-7）。

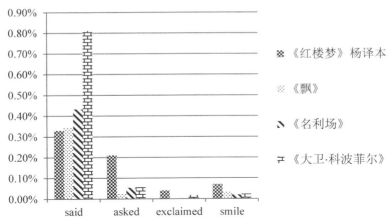

**图 3 - 7  动词 said、asked、exclaimed 与名词 smile 在杨译本全文及几部英文小说中的比例统计**

（二）独特词、特色词对比研究

随即笔者考察了《红楼梦》杨译本会话引导语相对于三部英文小说的独特词和特色词，同样是使用 AntConc 里的 wordlist 和 keyword list 功能。

《红楼梦》杨译本中的会话引导语相对于三部英文小说来讲，独特词多达 1588 个，且多为人名、地名用词。在筛除人名、地名用词后，词频在 5 次以上的词语有 60 个：

| | | | |
|---|---|---|---|
| concubine(54) | secretaries(16) | rhyme(9) | versifying(6) |
| Buddha(48) | granny(15) | actresses(8) | aunty(5) |
| monk(39) | gauze(14) | congee(8) | eunuchs(5) |
| taels(32) | incense(14) | nuns(8) | gaffe(5) |
| Taoist(30) | quipped(13) | fetch(7) | inkstone(5) |
| kang(29) | stewards(12) | tael(7) | judging(5) |
| concubine(24) | Aiya(11) | yamen(7) | kowtow(5) |
| scoffed(23) | jokingly(11) | buddhist(6) | lotus(5) |
| eunuch(19) | lotus(11) | orchid(6) | lute(5) |
| Amida(18) | abbess(10) | osmanthus(6) | nunnery(5) |
| kowtowed(18) | pointing(10) | ounces(6) | phoenix(5) |
| ladyships(18) | rhymes(10) | priestess(6) | plaster(5) |
| chortled(17) | declaimed(9) | sniggered(6) | prevaricated(5) |
| gateman(17) | nannies(9) | tellers(6) | reliable(5) |
| nanny(16) | portiere(9) | unicorn(6) | suppressing(5) |

　　《红楼梦》杨译本中的会话引导语相对于三部英文小说来讲,特色词有 138 个,筛除人名、地名用词后共有 33 个(见表 3 - 8)。

表 3 - 8　杨译本会话引导语相对于几部英文小说的特色词

| 排序 | 词语 | 词频 | 关键度 |
|------|------|------|--------|
| 1 | Buddha | 48 | 436.622 |
| 2 | monk | 39 | 354.755 |
| 3 | taels | 32 | 291.081 |
| 4 | concubine | 30 | 272.889 |
| 5 | Taoist | 30 | 272.889 |
| 6 | kang | 29 | 263.792 |
| 7 | scoffed | 23 | 209.215 |
| 8 | eunuch | 19 | 172.83 |
| 9 | Amida | 18 | 163.733 |
| 10 | kowtowed | 18 | 163.733 |
| 11 | ladyships | 18 | 163.733 |
| 12 | chortled | 17 | 154.637 |
| 13 | gateman | 17 | 154.637 |
| 14 | nanny | 16 | 145.541 |
| 15 | secretaries | 16 | 145.541 |
| 16 | granny | 15 | 136.444 |
| 17 | gauze | 14 | 127.348 |
| 18 | incense | 14 | 127.348 |
| 19 | quipped | 13 | 118.252 |
| 20 | stewards | 12 | 109.155 |
| 21 | Aiya | 11 | 100.059 |
| 22 | jokingly | 11 | 100.059 |
| 23 | lotus | 11 | 100.059 |
| 24 | abbess | 10 | 90.963 |
| 25 | pointing | 10 | 90.963 |
| 26 | rhymes | 10 | 90.963 |
| 27 | declaimed | 9 | 81.867 |

（续表）

| 排序 | 词语 | 词频 | 关键度 |
|------|------|------|--------|
| 28 | nannies | 9 | 81.867 |
| 29 | portiere | 9 | 81.867 |
| 30 | rhyme | 9 | 81.867 |
| 31 | actresses | 8 | 72.77 |
| 32 | congee | 8 | 72.77 |
| 33 | nuns | 8 | 72.77 |

与霍译本一样，《红楼梦》杨译本会话引导语中的一部分独特词和特色词是源于故事主题与创作背景的，如与时代背景相关的 taels、kang、eunuch、portiere、yamen、portiere 等；与宗教信仰相关的 Buddha、monk、Taoist、Amida、Buddhist、nun、nunnery、priestess 等；与身份地位相关的 concubine、nanny、secretary、gateman、steward、actress、aunty、granny 等。对此笔者不多做研究。

《红楼梦》杨译本会话引导语中的一些独特动词值得我们关注，如 scoffed（23 次）、chortled（17 次）、quipped（13 次）、declaimed（9 次）、sniggered（6 次）、prevaricated（5 次）。其中 scoffed、chortled、quipped 和 declaimed 还是《红楼梦》杨译本会话引导语中的特色词，且关键度均较高，分别为 209.215、154.637、118.252 和 81.867。

接下来笔者将对几个既是杨译本会话引导语独特动词、又是特色动词的 scoffed、chortled、quipped 和 declaimed 分别进行研究。

**1. 动词 scoffed**

我们先来看几部权威词典对于 scoff 的定义，此处只考察译文中 scoff 作为动词的意义：

（1）《牛津高阶英语词典》（第 6 版）（*Oxford Advanced Learner's Dictionary*）：~（at sb/sth）*to talk about sb/sth in a way that makes it clear that you think they are stupid or ridiculous*.

（2）《朗文当代英语词典》（第 4 版）（*Longman Dictionary of Contemporary English*）：*to laugh at a person or idea，and talk about them in a way that shows you think they are stupid*.

（3）《柯林斯高阶英语词典》（*Collins COBUILD Advanced Learner's English Dictionary*）：*If you scoff at something，you speak about it in a way that shows you think it is ridiculous or inadequate*.

（4）《美国传统词典》（双解）（*E-C American Heritage Dictionary*）：vt.（及物动词）*to mock at or treat with derision* 嘲笑或嘲弄　vi.（不及物动词）*to treat or express derisively*；*mock* 嘲弄；嘲弄地对待或表达；嘲笑。

（5）《牛津高阶英汉双解词典》（*Oxford Advanced Learner's English-Chinese Dictionary*）：～（*at sb/sth*）*speak contemptuously*（*about or to sb/sth*）；*jeer or mock* 嘲弄；嘲笑。

通过以上几部词典的定义，我们可以推断 scoff 一词表达的是"轻蔑地嘲弄、嘲笑"之意。接下来列举《红楼梦》杨译文会话引导语文本中的上下文：

| | | |
|---|---|---|
| to handle him，" | **scoffed** | Xifeng. |
| taste of swan，" | **scoffed** | Pinger. " The beast |
| young fellow，" they | **scoffed** | . |
| even less sense，" | **scoffed** | his father. |
| What nonsense，" she | **scoffed** | . " Why make such |
| can lay eggs，" | **scoffed** | his mother. |
| re easily pleased，" | **scoffed** | Qingwen. |
| that a poem，" | **scoffed** | Daiyu，" I can |
| ，young master，' | **scoffed** | Qingwen from her pillow. |
| last few days？' | **scoffed** | Daiyu. |
| re crazy！" she | **scoffed** | . |
| two different households，" | **scoffed** | Jia Rong. " We |
| stop dilly-dallying，" they | **scoffed** | . |
| ，Master Bao！" | **scoffed** | Xiren from inside. |
| gateman called Li Shier， | **scoffed** | ， |
| that soft-hearted act，" | **scoffed** | Xifeng. |
| fine garden？" he | **scoffed** | . |
| great to-do！" they | **scoffed** | . |
| Yucun from his chair | **scoffed** | ， |
| 't count，" | **scoffed** | ha Lian. |
| " What nonsense！" | **scoffed** | Jia Zheng. |
| " Oh！" | **scoffed** | Baochai. " What nonsense |
| be a nun！" | **scoffed** | Madam You. |

**2. 动词 chortled**

我们来看几部权威词典对于 chortle 的定义,同样只考察 chortle 的动词意义:

（1）《牛津高阶英语词典》（第 6 版）（Oxford Advanced Learner's Dictionary）: to laugh loudly with pleasure or amusement。

（2）《朗文当代英语词典》（第 4 版）（Longman Dictionary of Contemporary English）: to laugh because you are amused or pleased about something。

（3）《柯林斯高阶英语词典》（Collins COBUILD Advanced Learner's English Dictionary）: to chortle means to laugh in a way that shows you are very pleased。

（4）《美国传统词典》（双解）（E-C American Heritage Dictionary）: to utter or express with a snorting，joyful laugh or chuckle 大笑;发出哈哈大笑或用哈哈大笑来表达。

（5）《牛津高阶英汉双解词典》（Oxford Advanced Learner's English-Chinese Dictionary）: utter a loud chuckle of pleasure or amusement 哈哈大笑;咯咯笑。

通过以上几部词典的释义,我们可以推断 chortle 一词在文中表达的是"哈哈大笑、咯咯笑"之意。接下来列举《红楼梦》杨译文会话引导语文本中的上下文:

| | | |
|---|---|---|
| general laugh. Nanny Zhao | **chortled** | as if she would never |
| with it，" he | **chortled** | . |
| shame！" Jia Lian | **chortled** | . |
| either，" Granny Liu | **chortled** | . " That ' s |
| The others | **chortled** | ，" That ' s |
| ? ' the old lady | **chortled** | |
| ，brother ? ' he | **chortled** | ，staggering forward to catch |
| your word，' he | **chortled** | |
| " Aiyaya！" | **chortled** | the boy. |
| it suits me！" | **chortled** | Xiangyun. |
| right time，" they | **chortled** | . " We couldn ' |
| a fine couple，" | **chortled** | Xinger. |
| The old lady | **chortled** | ，" As the proverb |
| be praised！" they | **chortled** | . |

| | | |
|---|---|---|
| to shout，"she | **chortled** | . "All right — |
| The old lady | **chortled** | ，"Quite right and |
| Only one page | **chortled** | ， |

### 3. 动词 quipped

我们先来考察几部权威词典对于 quip 作为动词的释义：

（1）《牛津高阶英语词典》（第 6 版）（*Oxford Advanced Learner's Dictionary*）：*to make a quick and clever remark*。

（2）《朗文当代英语词典》（第 4 版）（*Longman Dictionary of Contemporary English*）：*to say something clever and amusing*。

（3）《柯林斯高阶英语词典》（*Collins COBUILD Advanced Learner's English Dictionary*）：*to quip means to say something that is intended to be amusing or clever*。

（4）《美国传统词典》（双解）（*E-C American Heritage Dictionary*）：*to make a clever，witty remark often prompted by the occasion* 说妙语，说俏皮话（经常是即兴说出的机智风趣的话语）。

（5）《牛津高阶英汉双解词典》（*Oxford Advanced Learner's English-Chinese Dictionary*）：*make a witty or sarcastic remark* 说风趣的或讽刺的话。

通过以上几部词典的释义，我们可以推断 quip 一词在文中表达的是"说俏皮话；口出妙语"之意。接下来列举《红楼梦》杨译文会话引导语文本中的上下文：

| | | |
|---|---|---|
| on me！"Xifeng | **quipped** | . |
| anyone else could comment Xifeng | **quipped** | ，"If you hadn |
| beasts started dancing，" | **quipped** | Daiyu. |
| teaching others，" | **quipped** | Daiyu.'Since she |
| that venison！'they | **quipped** | . |
| The Magic Box，' | **quipped** | Qiuwen.'So where |
| doctor，"he | **quipped** | . |
| for Xiuyan the old lady | **quipped** | ， |
| Baoqin | **quipped** | ，"Please get into |
| is uncertain，"Baoyu | **quipped** | |
| of all times，" | **quipped** | Madam You. |
| heard that outside."| **quipped** | Xifeng，"you should |

is Cousin Bao，" **quipped** Xiangyun. " So why

### 4. 动词 declaimed

几部权威词典对于 declaim 作为动词的释义为：

（1）《牛津高阶英语词典》（第 6 版）（*Oxford Advanced Learner's Dictionary*）：（*formal*）*to say sth loudly*；*to speak loudly and forcefully about sth you feel strongly about*，*especially in public*。

（2）《朗文当代英语词典》（第 4 版）（*Longman Dictionary of Contemporary English*）：*to speak loudly*，*sometimes with actions*，*so that people notice you*。

（3）《柯林斯高阶英语词典》（*Collins COBUILD Advanced Learner's English Dictionary*）：*If you declaim*，*you speak dramatically*，*as if you were acting in a theatre.*

（4）《美国传统词典（双解）》（*E-C American Heritage Dictionary*）：*vi.*（不及物动词） *a. to deliver a formal recitation*，*especially as an exercise in rhetoric or elocution* 朗诵：正式地朗诵,尤指为练习口才或演讲。*b. to speak loudly and vehemently*；*inveigh* 慷慨陈词；猛烈抨击。*vt.*（及物动词）*to utter or recite with rhetorical effect* 慷慨激昂地演说或朗诵。

（5）《牛津高阶英汉双解词典》（*Oxford Advanced Learner's English-Chinese Dictionary*）：*speak*（*sth*）*as if addressing an audience*（像演讲般）说（话）。

通过以上几部词典的释义,我们可以推断 declaim 一词表达的是"慷慨陈词;高声朗诵"之意。接下来列举《红楼梦》杨译文会话引导语文本中的上下文：

| | | |
|---|---|---|
| of laughter. He then | **declaimed** | : |
| Shiyin then | **declaimed** | |
| Baochai | **declaimed** | : |
| Liu stood up then and | **declaimed** | at the top of her |
| now she straightened up and | **declaimed** | : |
| Then Xiangyun | **declaimed** | |
| Baoyu had just | **declaimed** | this when he heard a |
| tossed off a cup and | **declaimed** | : |
| Without further argument Baoyu | **declaimed** | : |

鉴于 declaimed 一词在《红楼梦》杨译本会话引导语中的比例与三部英文

原版小说中的比例差异巨大,笔者决定借助英国国家语料库来检索 declaimed 一词的使用频率。BNC 是目前网络可直接使用的最大语料库之一,也是目前世界上最具代表性的当代英语语料库之一,非常具有权威性。笔者在 BNC 里检索 declaimed 一词,共得到 33 条反馈结果,其中小说体裁中有 17 条结果(见图 3-8),其具体例句如表 3-9 所示。

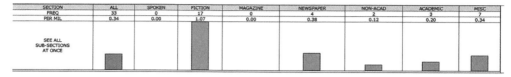

**图 3 - 8  declaimed 一词在英语国家语料库中检索分布情况**

**表 3 - 9  动词 declaimed 经检索后在小说体裁中的具体使用情况**

| 序号 | 例句 |
| --- | --- |
| 1 | 'I have never known you be so patient, Miss Jay Goodtime! ' **declaimed** Jamie, gluing centipede eyelashes into unlikely pools of stage make-up.' Shall I |
| 2 | have a friend without being labelled queer.' He stared aggressively at Burden and **declaimed** loudly and meaningfully,' O brave new world, that has such people in |
| 3 | snapped the Junior Minister of Trade.' Thank God for that,' Mark **declaimed**.' Your views are too simplistic for me,' said the young politician |
| 4 | 'Those who can not hear must feel the rod of correction,' she **declaimed**, raising the stick as she advanced, Martha let out a shriek, leaped |
| 5 | at moments when her difficulties seemed overwhelming, Constance would remember her father's words **declaimed** into the vast skies of Northumberland:' Never be afraid, Constance. You |
| 6 | Emperor in the wake of that direst of victories against the renegade Horus,' **declaimed** moon-faced combat-Chaplain Lo Chang in chapel;' and after he had overseen the construction |
| 7 | course you don't, I will perforce have to demonstrate.' As he **declaimed** we were weaving our way through the late-afternoon shoppers who thronged the centre of the |
| 8 | what I have to do, as they say in Western films,' he **declaimed**, ogling my ear.' Bulgarians are masterly. In Bulgaria the woman is |
| 9 | I think so,' Jacob replied and then, in a fruity voice, **declaimed**:♯' There is a green island in lone Gougane Barra ♯ Where an |

（续表）

| 序号 | 例句 |
|---|---|
| 10 | if in greeting. Tristan immediately threw out a band in a dramatic gesture and **declaimed**："Speak on, sweet lips that never told a lie! " That |
| 11 | . " It is the East, and Juliet is the sun," Miles **declaimed**, waving toast and marmalade in the air. " Wrong play, " said |
| 12 | , accumulate! This is Moses and the prophets to the capitalists! ' he **declaimed** to his fellow students in the college library. Unlike Ellen, though, he |
| 13 | right occasion.' He pulled a piece of paper out of his pocket and **declaimed**：♯' Love a woman? You're an ass! ♯' T |
| 14 | . The lame walked. The deaf heard. The dumb spoke. Childless women **declaimed** prayers to the Virgin in Latin while tears rolled down their faces; and the |
| 15 | songs of the season emerged at full volume, the tough, shallow lyrics gloatingly **declaimed** by a star of the mid-sixties who had traded in her artless looks and girlish |
| 16 | shine. Momentarily his jaw tightened, then, twirling an imaginary moustache, he **declaimed**,' So, my proud beauty! I've got you where I want |
| 17 | was a parrot on her shoulder. Striking an attitude, she scowled ferociously and **declaimed**,' Aha, Jim lad! ' The sudden laughter startled her. Michele |

# 第三节 《红楼梦》霍译本与杨译本会话引导语对比研究

"不同的文化决定着不同的思维模式，不同的思维模式决定着不同的语言表达方式，不同的语言表达方式又决定着原作与译作的遣词用句。"（冯庆华，2012）《红楼梦》的杨译本和霍译本是其迄今为止最为权威和优秀的翻译巨作，两个译本本身就具有极高的文学价值和艺术价值。霍译的译者有着更多的西方文化因素，杨译的译者有着更多的中国文化因素。接下来将从细微之处着眼，对《红楼梦》霍译本与杨译本中的会话引导语进行分析和对比。

## 一、高频词对比研究

本书使用 PowerConc 软件对霍译本和杨译本中的会话引导语文本进行词频统计，将两个文本词频位于前 100 位的高频词列举如表 3-10 所示。

表 3-10　霍译本和杨译本会话引导语前 100 位高频词

| 排序 | 霍译会话引导语 | 词频 | 百分比 | 排序 | 杨译会话引导语 | 词频 | 百分比 |
|---|---|---|---|---|---|---|---|
| 1 | the | 6399 | 3.47 | 1 | the | 4882 | 3.53 |
| 2 | to | 5591 | 3.03 | 2 | to | 3747 | 2.71 |
| 3 | said | 4848 | 2.63 | 3 | you | 2913 | 2.11 |
| 4 | and | 3756 | 2.04 | 4 | she | 2516 | 1.82 |
| 5 | you | 3571 | 1.94 | 5 | and | 2506 | 1.81 |
| 6 | a | 3420 | 1.85 | 6 | a | 2346 | 1.70 |
| 7 | of | 3109 | 1.69 | 7 | I | 2053 | 1.48 |
| 8 | I | 2891 | 1.57 | 8 | he | 1860 | 1.34 |
| 9 | she | 2847 | 1.54 | 9 | her | 1793 | 1.30 |
| 10 | her | 2622 | 1.42 | 10 | of | 1641 | 1.19 |
| 11 | that | 2381 | 1.29 | 11 | in | 1590 | 1.15 |
| 12 | it | 2357 | 1.28 | 12 | that | 1559 | 1.13 |
| 13 | in | 2160 | 1.17 | 13 | said | 1550 | 1.12 |
| 14 | was | 1967 | 1.07 | 14 | it | 1512 | 1.09 |
| 15 | he | 1799 | 0.98 | 15 | was | 1132 | 0.82 |
| 16 | Jia | 1694 | 0.92 | 16 | this | 1126 | 0.81 |
| 17 | with | 1442 | 0.78 | 17 | with | 1104 | 0.80 |
| 18 | Bao-yu | 1389 | 0.75 | 18 | lady | 1056 | 0.76 |
| 19 | for | 1319 | 0.72 | 19 | Baoyu | 932 | 0.67 |
| 20 | what | 1106 | 0.60 | 20 | asked | 919 | 0.66 |
| 21 | on | 1099 | 0.60 | 21 | for | 914 | 0.66 |
| 22 | this | 1091 | 0.59 | 22 | Jia | 807 | 0.58 |
| 23 | had | 1075 | 0.58 | 23 | what | 805 | 0.58 |
| 24 | at | 999 | 0.54 | 24 | on | 741 | 0.54 |
| 25 | as | 976 | 0.53 | 25 | they | 740 | 0.54 |
| 26 | is | 971 | 0.53 | 26 | his | 734 | 0.53 |
| 27 | be | 951 | 0.52 | 27 | him | 684 | 0.49 |

（续表）

| 排序 | 霍译<br>会话引导语 | 词频 | 百分比 | 排序 | 杨译<br>会话引导语 | 词频 | 百分比 |
|---|---|---|---|---|---|---|---|
| 28 | his | 951 | 0.52 | 28 | is | 683 | 0.49 |
| 29 | have | 934 | 0.51 | 29 | Xifeng | 659 | 0.48 |
| 30 | but | 908 | 0.49 | 30 | as | 655 | 0.47 |
| 31 | all | 900 | 0.49 | 31 | then | 642 | 0.46 |
| 32 | they | 866 | 0.47 | 32 | at | 639 | 0.46 |
| 33 | Xi-feng | 843 | 0.46 | 33 | but | 624 | 0.45 |
| 34 | him | 839 | 0.46 | 34 | have | 624 | 0.45 |
| 35 | when | 750 | 0.41 | 35 | so | 605 | 0.44 |
| 36 | not | 725 | 0.39 | 36 | me | 601 | 0.43 |
| 37 | me | 723 | 0.39 | 37 | not | 601 | 0.43 |
| 38 | them | 711 | 0.39 | 38 | all | 598 | 0.43 |
| 39 | one | 703 | 0.38 | 39 | had | 597 | 0.43 |
| 40 | are | 688 | 0.37 | 40 | be | 591 | 0.43 |
| 41 | out | 679 | 0.37 | 41 | old | 590 | 0.43 |
| 42 | Grandmother | 672 | 0.36 | 42 | we | 590 | 0.43 |
| 43 | from | 656 | 0.36 | 43 | your | 541 | 0.39 |
| 44 | asked | 646 | 0.35 | 44 | out | 538 | 0.39 |
| 45 | lady | 642 | 0.35 | 45 | when | 536 | 0.39 |
| 46 | we | 642 | 0.35 | 46 | just | 500 | 0.36 |
| 47 | about | 632 | 0.34 | 47 | up | 494 | 0.36 |
| 48 | so | 628 | 0.34 | 48 | told | 493 | 0.36 |
| 49 | your | 625 | 0.34 | 49 | are | 490 | 0.35 |
| 50 | there | 621 | 0.34 | 50 | them | 489 | 0.35 |
| 51 | no | 584 | 0.32 | 51 | no | 464 | 0.34 |
| 52 | now | 581 | 0.32 | 52 | if | 459 | 0.33 |
| 53 | up | 576 | 0.31 | 53 | Baochai | 438 | 0.32 |
| 54 | do | 558 | 0.30 | 54 | one | 437 | 0.32 |
| 55 | if | 556 | 0.30 | 55 | there | 430 | 0.31 |

（续表）

| 排序 | 霍译会话引导语 | 词频 | 百分比 | 排序 | 杨译会话引导语 | 词频 | 百分比 |
|---|---|---|---|---|---|---|---|
| 56 | Dai-yu | 552 | 0.30 | 56 | Daiyu | 422 | 0.31 |
| 57 | Aroma | 531 | 0.29 | 57 | how | 407 | 0.29 |
| 58 | been | 530 | 0.29 | 58 | go | 405 | 0.29 |
| 59 | who | 497 | 0.27 | 59 | who | 402 | 0.29 |
| 60 | Wang | 489 | 0.27 | 60 | can | 399 | 0.29 |
| 61 | were | 488 | 0.26 | 61 | now | 384 | 0.28 |
| 62 | just | 481 | 0.26 | 62 | smile | 379 | 0.27 |
| 63 | by | 480 | 0.26 | 63 | madam | 374 | 0.27 |
| 64 | my | 478 | 0.26 | 64 | Wang | 372 | 0.27 |
| 65 | Bao-chai | 475 | 0.26 | 65 | my | 367 | 0.27 |
| 66 | go | 452 | 0.25 | 66 | why | 363 | 0.26 |
| 67 | can | 444 | 0.24 | 67 | Xiren | 360 | 0.26 |
| 68 | then | 441 | 0.24 | 68 | do | 358 | 0.26 |
| 69 | Zheng | 414 | 0.22 | 69 | too | 356 | 0.26 |
| 70 | come | 409 | 0.22 | 70 | by | 351 | 0.25 |
| 71 | Lian | 404 | 0.22 | 71 | from | 350 | 0.25 |
| 72 | old | 392 | 0.21 | 72 | here | 348 | 0.25 |
| 73 | very | 392 | 0.21 | 73 | good | 330 | 0.24 |
| 74 | came | 374 | 0.20 | 74 | cried | 322 | 0.23 |
| 75 | replied | 371 | 0.20 | 75 | back | 316 | 0.23 |
| 76 | well | 370 | 0.20 | 76 | after | 305 | 0.22 |
| 77 | Xue | 368 | 0.20 | 77 | some | 298 | 0.22 |
| 78 | like | 366 | 0.20 | 78 | were | 295 | 0.21 |
| 79 | after | 362 | 0.20 | 79 | know | 291 | 0.21 |
| 80 | see | 362 | 0.20 | 80 | come | 288 | 0.21 |
| 81 | know | 361 | 0.20 | 81 | about | 285 | 0.21 |
| 82 | here | 357 | 0.19 | 82 | Xue | 282 | 0.20 |
| 83 | Patience | 356 | 0.19 | 83 | came | 273 | 0.20 |

（续表）

| 排序 | 霍译<br>会话引导语 | 词频 | 百分比 | 排序 | 杨译<br>会话引导语 | 词频 | 百分比 |
|---|---|---|---|---|---|---|---|
| 84 | some | 354 | 0.19 | 84 | Pinger | 273 | 0.20 |
| 85 | back | 349 | 0.19 | 85 | Zheng | 273 | 0.20 |
| 86 | could | 348 | 0.19 | 86 | replied | 266 | 0.19 |
| 87 | how | 329 | 0.18 | 87 | been | 259 | 0.19 |
| 88 | good | 322 | 0.17 | 88 | Li | 256 | 0.19 |
| 89 | an | 321 | 0.17 | 89 | right | 252 | 0.18 |
| 90 | little | 314 | 0.17 | 90 | see | 250 | 0.18 |
| 91 | aunt | 313 | 0.17 | 91 | Lian | 245 | 0.18 |
| 92 | would | 311 | 0.17 | 92 | well | 245 | 0.18 |
| 93 | time | 304 | 0.16 | 93 | over | 237 | 0.17 |
| 94 | laughed | 297 | 0.16 | 94 | let | 233 | 0.17 |
| 95 | two | 297 | 0.16 | 95 | put | 233 | 0.17 |
| 96 | Li | 283 | 0.15 | 96 | like | 230 | 0.17 |
| 97 | thought | 283 | 0.15 | 97 | exclaimed | 227 | 0.16 |
| 98 | why | 283 | 0.15 | 98 | aunt | 226 | 0.16 |
| 99 | oh | 282 | 0.15 | 99 | Dowager | 226 | 0.16 |
| 100 | their | 279 | 0.15 | 100 | two | 217 | 0.16 |

霍译本和杨译本中 said 都是使用最多的动词,但两个文本中 said 的词频和比例差异显著:霍译本中 said 有 4848 个,占文本总量的 2.63%;杨译文本中 said 仅 1550 个,占文本总量的 1.12%,比例还不到霍译文本的 1/2。

## 二、独特词对比研究

霍译本会话引导语相对于杨译本会话引导语的独特词有 5015 个,其中词频在 2 次以上的有 1497 个。笔者将人名、地名用词筛除,仅选取词频≥5 的独特词,共 182 个:

| | | |
|---|---|---|
| junior(45) | moments(29) | coz(24) |
| smilingly(38) | father(26) | tone(24) |

perhaps(23)

particularly(20)

almost(19)

behalf(19)

advanced(16)

name(16)

bless(15)

evidently(14)

various(14)

affected(13)

brief(13)

nasty(13)

aiyo(12)

drily(12)

kotowed(12)

preceptor(12)

shock(12)

chanced(11)

kotow(11)

shortly(11)

attempted(10)

completed(10)

contemptuously(10)

convey(10)

material(10)

otherwise(10)

purpose(10)

shortly(10)

south(10)

bidding(9)

contrary(9)

definitely(9)

effect(9)

feigned(9)

honestly(9)

oz(9)

pondered(9)

altogether(8)

bothering(8)

deeply(8)

deprecatingly(8)

ease(8)

finally(8)

firmly(8)

grace(8)

graciously(8)

humouredly(8)

landscape(8)

leaped(8)

midst(8)

opposite(8)

rapid(8)

reference(8)

sis(8)

struggling(8)

uttered(8)

attitude(7)

big(7)

chorus(7)

deemed(7)

enquired(7)

enthusiastically(7)

fiercely(7)

genially(7)

gentle(7)

including(7)

nervously(7)

picture(7)

reassuringly(7)

relations(7)

responsibility(7)

responsible(7)

sickness(7)

slightest(7)

sniffed(7)

solution(7)

sympathetically(7)

uneasy(7)

visiting(7)

apprehensive(6)

college(6)

considerable(6)

consoled(6)

facts(6)

han(6)

heavily(6)

ho(6)

hysterically(6)

imploringly(6)

impulsively(6)

intendant(6)

intending(6)

janitors(6)

karma(6)

kylin(6)

lend(6)

missus(6)

momentarily(6)

mysterious(6)

nevertheless(6)

occasions(6)

onto(6)

ruefully(6)

sadly(6)

service(6)

silently(6)

simple(6)

struggled(6)

uncomfortable(6)

undertone(6)

unfortunate(6)

vexation(6)

welcomed(6)

wrath(6)

youth(6)

aghast(5)

audience(5)

awoke(5)

ballad(5)

begun(5)

bitterness(5)

boy(5)

branch(5)

carry(5)

cassia(5)

caution(5)

chamberlain(5)

commanded(5)

conceal(5)

contained(5)

curiously(5)

deceive(5)

delighted(5)

edict(5)

elsewhere(5)

enthusiastic(5)

entire(5)

exasperatedly(5)

excuses(5)

faced(5)

fastened(5)

fierce(5)

forwards(5)

hmn(5)

hold(5)

horrible(5)

huh(5)

ignored(5)

inside(5)

insistent(5)

ladies(5)

malice(5)

overhear(5)

papa(5)

peered(5)

penny(5)

perfecta(5)

perfume(5)

pious(5)

players(5)

poster(5)

precisely(5)

principal(5)

proffered(5)

reaction(5)

rejected(5)

roused(5)

sensed(5)

senses(5)

ship(5)

sickly(5)

spice(5)

surprising(5)

tearful(5)

time(5)

topic(5)

《红楼梦》霍译本引导语文本相对于杨译本会话引导语文本的独特词中，以-ly 结尾的副词较多，如 smilingly、particularly、evidently、contemptuously、definitely、honestly、deprecatingly 等,这些副词在杨译本引导语文本中一次都没有出现过,其中又以 smilingly 出现次数最多,有 38 次。

笔者在几部权威词典里找到了关于 smilingly 的定义：

（1）《牛津高阶英语词典》（第 6 版）（*Oxford Advanced Learner's Dictionary*）：*with a smile or smiles*。

（2）《朗文当代英语词典》（第 4 版）（*Longman Dictionary of Contemporary English*）：*done or said with a smile*。

（3）《柯林斯高阶英语词典》（*Collins COBUILD Advanced Learner's English Dictionary*）：*If someone does something smilingly，they smile as they do it.*

综合以上几部词典对于 smilingly 的释义，我们可以推断出 smilingly 的意思为"微笑着；微笑地；带着微笑地"，在句中作伴随状语。《红楼梦》霍译本引导语文本中 smilingly 使用的上下文为：

| | | |
|---:|:---:|:---|
| she went，but Dai-yu | **smilingly** | replied that though it was |
| wife of Jia Rong， | **smilingly** | proposed an alternative. |
| of withdrawing when Aunt Xue | **smilingly** | enjoined her to stay. |
| yours，' she said | **smilingly** | ，' but I have |
| ，' he said， | **smilingly** | and softly，' I |
| her hair into place， | **smilingly** | com？placently： |
| on them and reproved them | **smilingly** | for abandoning her：' |
| going back again when Aroma | **smilingly** | detained her： |
| ？' she asked him | **smilingly** | . |
| time ripe to entreat her | **smilingly** | for his lunch.' |
| was done，Xi-feng turned | **smilingly** | to Silver and congratulated her |
| She turned， | **smilingly** | ，to Bao-yu and pointed |
| Grandmother Jia | **smilingly** | pointed a finger in Xi-chun |
| ！' said Aunt Xue | **smilingly** | when all were seated once |
| Lian had gone，she | **smilingly** | inquired after her injuries. |
| Xi-feng | **smilingly** | inquired of Lai Da ' |
| club，' said Tan-chun | **smilingly** | . |
| this request，nevertheless she | **smilingly** | promised that she would do |
| over its disappearance when Xi-feng | **smilingly** | put an end to the |
| Li Qi acknowledged | **smilingly** | that this was correct. |
| They protested | **smilingly** | and begged him to go |
| front of him，peered | **smilingly** | into his face.' |
| with these？' Oriole | **smilingly** | asked her companion. |
| daughter Swallow walked up and | **smilingly** | asked her what she was |
| You-shi and Li Wan | **smilingly** | confirmed the invitation. |
| ，she pressed it， | **smilingly** | ，into Cook Liu ' |
| said Bao-yu. He pointed | **smilingly** | at Aroma：' She |
| me，' said Dai-yu | **smilingly** | .' I can ' |

| | | | | |
|---|---|---|---|---|
| say to him，turned | **smilingly** | towards her，holding up | | |
| senior of the servants now | **smilingly** | addressed Xi-feng on her mistress | | |
| Jia Lian looked down | **smilingly** | and reflected，then clapped | | |
| stupid，'she said | **smilingly** | . | | |
| that？'she asked | **smilingly** | . | | |
| Huan as a reward and | **smilingly** | patted him on the head | | |
| sitting in the room， | **smilingly** | intervened. | | |
| 'said the literary gentlemen | **smilingly** | . | | |
| Bao-chai | **smilingly** | expostulated.'People like | | |
| seemed unperturbed，and announced | **smilingly** | ：'Gentlemen，please | | |

smilingly 一词在英文原版小说《飘》《名利场》和《大卫·科波菲尔》中共出现了 3 次,其中《名利场》中 2 次、《大卫·科波菲尔》中 1 次、《飘》中 0 次(见图 3-9)。

| No. | Search Terms | Freq. | File Count | 1. 飘 | 2. 大卫科波菲尔 | 3. 名利场 |
|---|---|---|---|---|---|---|
| | **Size** | 1294946 | 3 | 497333 | 443731 | 353882 |
| | **Tokens** | 3 | 2 | 0 | 1 | 2 |
| | **Types** | 1 | 2 | 0 | 1 | 1 |
| 1 | smilingly | 3 | 2 | | 1 | 2 |

图 3-9　smilingly 在几部英文小说中的词频统计

《大卫·科波菲尔》中的例句为：

| | | |
|---|---|---|
| The Doctor stopped， | **smilingly** | clapped me on the shoulder |

《名利场》中的例句为：

| | | |
|---|---|---|
| carriage，and rebuked him | **smilingly** | for not having taken any |
| wiped them away，and | **smilingly** | kissed him，and tied |

笔者在英国国家语料库中也检索到了 40 次 smilingly 的用法,其中有 31 次用于小说体裁(见图 3-10),其具体使用例句如表 3-11 所示：

| SECTION | ALL | SPOKEN | FICTION | MAGAZINE | NEWSPAPER | NON-ACAD | ACADEMIC | MISC |
|---|---|---|---|---|---|---|---|---|
| FREQ | 40 | 0 | 31 | 2 | 2 | 2 | 0 | 4 |
| PER MIL | 0.42 | 0.00 | 1.95 | 0.14 | 0.19 | 0.12 | 0.00 | 0.19 |

SEE ALL SUB-SECTIONS AT ONCE

图 3-10 smilingly 在英国国家语料库中不同体裁的使用情况

表 3-11 smilingly 一词经检索后具体使用例句

| 序号 | 例　句 |
|---|---|
| 1 | attempts to draw M. Dupont aside for some private conversation，only for Mr Lewis **smilingly** to impose himself upon them with some remark like：' Pardon me，gentlemen |
| 2 | with the version of events contained in this last sentence by ignoring it and saying **smilingly**，' You no pay here，baby. Manager is friend of mine. |
| 3 | the edge of the bed where Kate lies fenced in by bolsters and proffers it **smilingly**. The coffee is strong and sweet with a glass of tea accompanying it to |
| 4 | . Prince Richard approached then and invited her to dance with him，and she **smilingly** accepted，feeling like one in a dream. Prince Richard was struck by her |
| 5 | sight of the young king. As the cavalcade proceeded through the city，Edward **smilingly** acknowledged the acclamations and Richard of Gloucester — well aware that it was the very |
| 6 | ? We receive no news. " In rude health —' Joan said **smilingly**，echoing his own words' — though anxious needless to say for the welfare |
| 7 | . " I want to go to Greece，' said Mary，but **smilingly** and rather sleepily.' No， you don't，my sweetheart. You |
| 8 | the faintest idea what she was saying，but had learned by rote，she **smilingly** asked me' Saywhenpleasesir? ' She must have thought she was using some magic |
| 9 | . It had looked more suitable for a West End hairdressing salon. He was **smilingly** recognized at the reception desk，but his credentials were still carefully scrutinized and he |
| 10 | must in all honesty say says Howard very quickly，jutting his chin out and **smilingly** blinking his eyes，' that I still think there are a number of things |

（续表）

| 序号 | 例　句 |
|------|--------|
| 11 | relieved that in some ways Xanthe could still be her age. She countered，**smilingly** behind the menu：' The French have a different attitude to rape：resistance |
| 12 | to have enough strength to carry on. And at last，Rosalba sighed，**smilingly**，as she dipped and looped and drew out the thread herself，there was |
| 13 | ' Gina is anxious to return to bed, I think,' Lotta taunted **smilingly**, lifting her glass towards him.' Skl! " Skl! ' |
| 14 | back from her cruise.' He took a sip of wine, studying Merrill **smilingly**.' I reckon you'd like Heather. Everyone does. Luke thinks there |
| 15 | breath of fresh air，Mrs Alderley！" Call me Rose,' **smilingly** requested the lady.' And I won't forget my promise，Theodosia， |
| 16 | inside the old building she had found the staff reassuringly up to date，and **smilingly** efficient. They had provided her with a local map，pin-pointing the exact location |
| 17 | ' Is he on th'level? ' he asked weakly. Springfield and Pam both **smilingly** nodded their confirmation，knowing how pleased he would be at learning the news that |
| 18 | like a child until awoken，long after dawn，by my master. He **smilingly** proffered me a cup of watered wine in one of the goblets I had hidden |
| 19 | .' I imagine so... I suspect I do...' They're as **smilingly** elusive as his expression in the photograph on the boxes opposite me，as charmingly |
| 20 | , for some anyway，must be the holiday of a lifetime,' Lindsey **smilingly** agreed. She rose to her feet，reaching for the white coat that hung |
| 21 | — Lindsey Blake. Lindsey，this is Jesus，pronounced Hayzoos,' Niall **smilingly** enunciated for her benefit.' Jesus and I have got to know each other |
| 22 | 'm sure you don't need to worry.' Having seen the reassured mother **smilingly** on her way，Lindsey switched off the computer and set about clearing her desk |
| 23 | like some time on your own with Laura，wouldn't you? ' Carole **smilingly** asked the tall Englishman. Ross's smooth reply,' Yes，indeed. |
| 24 | She pulled up outside a large Victorian house，collected her case，and walked **smilingly** up the steps to the front door. Once the budgies and the two cats |

（续表）

| 序号 | 例　　句 |
|------|---------|
| 25 | blaze of fury in Sophie's eyes, but, ignoring it, he added **smilingly**,' Fate seems to have taken a hand in our affairs.' She |
| 26 | you allow me to take you to lunch,' he followed up, and **smilingly** waited. What should she do? Fabia wondered. He was transparent, but |
| 27 | would have to eat something, she looked hopelessly at the menu again, and **smilingly** suggested,' Perhaps you wouldn't mind ordering for me.' Her order |
| 28 | and, Azor wanting to be away,' See you! ' she added **smilingly**, and, unleashing the dog, set off. Azor had been well trained |
| 29 | feeling dreadful on a couple more counts.' Of course,' she replied **smilingly**, and didn't need him to wait with her by the lift or to |
| 30 | , winked at the girl and held out the goblet to be refilled. Philippa **smilingly** obliged and Athelstan groaned. He didn't know what was worse, Cranston sulking |
| 31 | the street in a mirror ♯ and the street itself as my enemy ♯ comes **smilingly** towards me ♯ from two directions. I could gulp my beer ♯ and vanish |

　　杨译本会话引导语相对于霍译本会话引导语的独特词有 2482 个,其中词频在 2 次以上的有 691 个。限于篇幅,本书将人名、地名用词筛除,然后仅选取词频≥5 的独特词共 59 个,列举如下:

| | | | |
|---|---|---|---|
| approved(39) | granny(15) | verdict(8) | unicorn(6) |
| nanny(31) | fine(13) | faltered(7) | versifying(6) |
| ancestress(30) | smart(12) | messengers(7) | whom(6) |
| fumed(27) | abbess(10) | sacrifice(7) | aunty(5) |
| scoffed(23) | consort(10) | described(6) | bah(5) |
| mansion(21) | unwell(10) | holding(6) | blushing(5) |
| priest(19) | coaxed(9) | jar(6) | blustered(5) |
| third(19) | east(9) | osmanthus(6) | cane(5) |
| amida(18) | lodge(9) | ounces(6) | charged(5) |
| chortled(17) | portiere(9) | priestess(6) | dense(5) |
| lordship(17) | joked(8) | sniggered(6) | feasting(5) |
| secretaries(16) | operas(8) | spluttered(6) | flour(5) |
| sternly(16) | standing(8) | spoilt(6) | gaffe(5) |

| juice(5) | muddle(5) | prevaricated(5) | talks(5) |
| marvelled(5) | nunnery(5) | respectfully(5) | |

《红楼梦》杨译本会话引导语相对于霍译本会话引导语而言,独特词以动词居多,如 approved、fumed、scoffed、chortled、joked、coaxed 等。其中 scoffed、chortled、sniggered 和 prevaricated 也是杨译本会话引导语与三部英文原版小说对照时的独特动词,这几个动词在霍译本中也一次都没有出现过(见图 3‑11)。

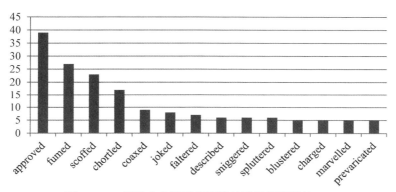

图 3‑11　杨译本会话引导语独特动词词频统计

## 三、特色词对比研究

霍译本会话引导语相对于杨译本会话引导语的特色词有 731 个。将人名、地名用词筛除后,发现关键度≥50 的特色词仅有 8 个(见表 3‑12)。

表 3‑12　霍译本会话引导语相对于杨译本会话引导语的特色词

| 排序 | 词语 | 词频 | 关键度 |
|---|---|---|---|
| 1 | said | 4848 | 892.567 |
| 2 | oh | 279 | 178.425 |
| 3 | of | 3033 | 126.191 |
| 4 | very | 345 | 107.373 |
| 5 | began | 157 | 95.559 |
| 6 | little | 296 | 62.186 |
| 7 | moment | 155 | 55.309 |
| 8 | got | 263 | 50.763 |

杨译本会话引导语相对于霍译本会话引导语的特色词有 677 个，限于篇幅，本书同样将人名、地名用词筛除，关键度≥50 的特色词有 40 个（见表 3－13）。

**表 3－13 杨译本会话引导语相对于霍译本会话引导语的特色词**

| 排序 | 词语 | 词频 | 关键度 |
|:---:|:---:|:---:|:---:|
| 1 | chuckled | 154 | 233.743 |
| 2 | answered | 208 | 209.617 |
| 3 | cried | 322 | 201.111 |
| 4 | remarked | 169 | 197.478 |
| 5 | told | 492 | 170.313 |
| 6 | asked | 919 | 165.839 |
| 7 | demanded | 100 | 155.667 |
| 8 | old | 549 | 155.570 |
| 9 | retorted | 135 | 142.598 |
| 10 | urged | 138 | 129.268 |
| 11 | he | 1506 | 124.802 |
| 12 | scolded | 76 | 109.376 |
| 13 | then | 230 | 109.286 |
| 14 | second | 70 | 105.126 |
| 15 | so | 162 | 99.986 |
| 16 | sister | 97 | 96.146 |
| 17 | smile | 379 | 94.158 |
| 18 | teased | 55 | 86.303 |
| 19 | rejoined | 59 | 76.743 |
| 20 | hastily | 83 | 76.225 |
| 21 | ordered | 131 | 74.259 |
| 22 | swore | 53 | 71.660 |
| 23 | sister | 130 | 71.555 |
| 24 | exclaimed | 227 | 69.651 |
| 25 | announced | 148 | 69.142 |
| 26 | agreed | 123 | 68.438 |
| 27 | put | 230 | 68.373 |

| 排序 | 词语 | 词频 | 关键度 |
|------|------|------|--------|
| 28 | approved | 39 | 67.537 |
| 29 | countered | 49 | 63.579 |
| 30 | too | 345 | 61.434 |
| 31 | declared | 47 | 57.716 |
| 32 | warned | 47 | 57.716 |
| 33 | she | 1998 | 56.374 |
| 34 | why | 271 | 56.167 |
| 35 | how | 244 | 55.527 |
| 36 | assured | 48 | 55.460 |
| 37 | nanny | 31 | 53.683 |
| 38 | ancestress | 30 | 51.951 |
| 39 | lady | 610 | 51.860 |
| 40 | master | 73 | 51.425 |

said 是《红楼梦》会话引导语霍译本相对于杨译本的第一大特色词，关键度高达 892.567，说明在霍译本会话引导语文本中 said 的使用远远超过杨译本的会话引导语文本。而在杨译本的会话引导语文本中，相对于霍译本会话引导语文本的特色词有很多，尤其是关键度在 50 以上的动词竟多达 22 个，这实在是一个惊人的数字。我们完全可以判断，很多时候在霍克思使用单纯的 said 来翻译会话引导语时，杨译却采用了其他多种不同的动词来翻译。

汪维辉（2003）曾指出动词语义场中有上位词和下位词之分。上位词是只有核心义素而无限定义素的词，如"说"的义素可以分析为："使用＋言语＋表达＋意义"；下位词则是在核心义素的基础上加上各种各样限定义素的词，如"骂"的义素为："使用＋（粗野/恶意的）言语＋表达＋（侮辱/斥责等）意思"。

霍译本会话引导语文本中的特色词 said 便属于上义词的范畴，而笔者推测杨译本中可能更多地使用了 said 的下义词来强调更加具体的内容。事实上，said 这一上义词可以添加各种不同的义素来构成几百个的下义词，如：

| | | | |
|------|------|------|------|
| accused | acquired | admonished | alleged |
| acknowledged | added | advised | allowed |
| acquiesced | admitted | agreed | alluded |

| | | | |
|---|---|---|---|
| announced | challenged | crooned | feared |
| answered | changed | cross-examined | frowned |
| apologized | charged | cursed | fumed |
| appeased | chatted | cussed | gagged |
| approved | cheered | debated | gasped |
| argued | chided | decided | gibbered |
| articulated | chipped in | declared | giggled |
| asked | choked | declined | gloated |
| assented | chortled | defended | goaded |
| asserted | chuckled | demanded | grinned |
| assured | churned | denied | groaned |
| attributed | cited | described | growled |
| babbled | claimed | determined | grumbled |
| baited | clamored | interrogated | grunted |
| barked | coaxed | dictated | guessed |
| bawled | comforted | discussed | guffawed |
| began | commented | drawled | gulped |
| begged | complained | droned | gurgled |
| believed | conceded | echoed | gushed |
| bellowed | concluded | edited | hastened |
| beseeched | concurred | ejaculated | hesitated |
| besought | confessed | elaborated | hinted |
| bleated | confirmed | emphasized | hissed |
| blubbered | consented | ended | hollered |
| boasted | consoled | entreated | hooted |
| bragged | contended | enumerated | horned in |
| breathed | contested | enunciated | howled |
| broke in | continued | exaggerated | imitated |
| cackled | contributed | exclaimed | implied |
| cajoled | cooed | exhorted | implored |
| calculated | coughed | explained | informed |
| called | countered | exploded | inquired |
| cannonaded | cried | expostulated | insinuated |
| caroled | criticized | extolled | insisted |
| cautioned | croaked | faltered | interjected |

| | | | |
|---|---|---|---|
| interposed | perceived | recommended | sighed |
| interpreted | persisted | regretted | sizzled |
| interrupted | persuaded | reiterated | slurred |
| intimidated | pestered | rejoined | smiled |
| intoned | piped up | remained | smoldered |
| jabbered | pleaded | remembered | snapped |
| jeered | pointed | reminded | snarled |
| jested | pondered | remonstrated | sneered |
| joked | pouted | renounced | snickered |
| lambasted | praised | repeated | snorted |
| lamented | preached | replied | sobbed |
| laughed | predicted | reported | soliloquied |
| lectured | prevaricated | reprehended | soothed |
| lied | proceeded | reprimanded | specified |
| listed | proclaimed | requested | spelled |
| made known | prodded | resolved | spoke |
| maligned | profaned | responded | spurted |
| marveled | professed | resumed | sputtered |
| mentioned | promised | retorted | squawked |
| mimicked | prompted | revealed | squeaked |
| moaned | prophesied | roared | squealed |
| mocked | proposed | rumbled | stammered |
| mourned | protested | sang | stated |
| mumbled | purred | sang out | stormed |
| murmured | pursuedput in | scoffed | stressed |
| mused | quavered | scolded | struggled |
| muttered | queried | scorned | stuttered |
| nagged | questioned | screamed | submitted |
| nodded | quibbled | screeched | suggested |
| noted | quipped | sermonized | surmised |
| objected | quoted | shifted | swore |
| observed | railed | shouted | sympathized |
| offered | raved | shrieked | tantalized |
| ordered | recalled | shrilled | tattled |
| panted | recited | shrugged | taunted |

| teased | uttered | want to know | worried |
|---|---|---|---|
| testified | vaunted | warned | yearned |
| thought | ventured | wavered | yelled |
| threatened | voiced | whispered | yelped |
| told | volunteered | wondered | yowled |
| urged | wailed | wore on | |

下面笔者将对《红楼梦》会话引导语霍译本和杨译本中的几个重要的特色词进行分析,首先将这些特色词的对比数据列举如表3-14所示。

表3-14　霍译本会话引导语及杨译本会话引导语特色词对比分析

| 序号 | 词语 | 霍译引导语词频 | 百分比 | 杨译引导语词频 | 百分比 | 关键度 |
|---|---|---|---|---|---|---|
| 1 | said | 4848 | 2.63 | 1550 | 1.12 | 892.567 |
| 2 | chuckled | 4 | 0.00 | 154 | 0.11 | 233.743 |
| 3 | answered | 31 | 0.02 | 208 | 0.15 | 209.617 |
| 4 | cried | 102 | 0.06 | 322 | 0.23 | 201.111 |
| 5 | remarked | 17 | 0.01 | 169 | 0.12 | 197.478 |
| 6 | told | 256 | 0.14 | 492 | 0.36 | 170.313 |
| 7 | asked | 646 | 0.35 | 919 | 0.66 | 165.839 |
| 8 | demanded | 2 | 0.00 | 100 | 0.07 | 155.667 |
| 9 | retorted | 18 | 0.01 | 135 | 0.10 | 142.598 |
| 10 | urged | 24 | 0.01 | 138 | 0.10 | 129.268 |
| 11 | scolded | 3 | 0.00 | 76 | 0.05 | 109.376 |
| 12 | teased | 1 | 0.00 | 55 | 0.04 | 86.303 |
| 13 | rejoined | 4 | 0.00 | 59 | 0.04 | 76.743 |
| 14 | ordered | 46 | 0.02 | 131 | 0.09 | 74.259 |
| 15 | swore | 3 | 0.00 | 53 | 0.04 | 71.66 |
| 16 | exclaimed | 127 | 0.07 | 227 | 0.16 | 69.651 |
| 17 | announced | 62 | 0.03 | 148 | 0.11 | 69.142 |
| 18 | agreed | 45 | 0.02 | 123 | 0.09 | 68.438 |
| 19 | approved | 0 | 0.00 | 39 | 0.03 | 67.537 |
| 20 | countered | 3 | 0.00 | 49 | 0.03 | 63.579 |

（续表）

| 序号 | 词语 | 霍译引导语词频 | 百分比 | 杨译引导语词频 | 百分比 | 关键度 |
|---|---|---|---|---|---|---|
| 21 | declared | 4 | 0.00 | 47 | 0.03 | 57.716 |
| 22 | warned | 4 | 0.00 | 47 | 0.03 | 57.716 |
| 23 | assured | 5 | 0.00 | 48 | 0.03 | 55.46 |

  笔者将上表中的 23 个特色动词放在一个.txt 文档里，使用 PowerConc 软件中的 Batch Search 功能，检索这 23 个动词在三部英文原版小说《飘》《名利场》和《大卫·科波菲尔》（表中简称《大卫》）中的使用情况，将检索结果汇总如表 3-15 所示：

表 3-15   霍译本会话引导语及杨译本会话引导语特色词在英文小说中的词频统计

| 序号 | 词语 | 霍译本 | 百分比 | 杨译本 | 百分比 | 《飘》 | 《名利场》 | 《大卫》 | 英文小说总百分比 |
|---|---|---|---|---|---|---|---|---|---|
| 词数 | | 850 001 | | 643 727 | | | | | 1 097 602 |
| 1 | said | 5821 | 0.68 | 2131 | 0.33 | 1494 | 1330 | 2942 | 0.53 |
| 2 | chuckled | 4 | 0.00 | 161 | 0.03 | 1 | 2 | 5 | 0.00 |
| 3 | answered | 51 | 0.01 | 241 | 0.04 | 68 | 68 | 102 | 0.02 |
| 4 | cried | 139 | 0.02 | 392 | 0.06 | 294 | 132 | 187 | 0.06 |
| 5 | remarked | 21 | 0.00 | 185 | 0.03 | 7 | 54 | 24 | 0.01 |
| 6 | told | 893 | 0.11 | 1104 | 0.17 | 251 | 180 | 248 | 0.06 |
| 7 | asked | 1017 | 0.12 | 1384 | 0.21 | 109 | 165 | 201 | 0.04 |
| 8 | demanded | 14 | 0.00 | 121 | 0.02 | 7 | 1 | 5 | 0.00 |
| 9 | retorted | 18 | 0.00 | 142 | 0.02 | 8 | 0 | 21 | 0.00 |
| 10 | urged | 45 | 0.01 | 230 | 0.04 | 4 | 6 | 9 | 0.00 |
| 11 | scolded | 9 | 0.00 | 105 | 0.02 | 7 | 2 | 1 | 0.00 |
| 12 | teased | 5 | 0.00 | 61 | 0.01 | 9 | 0 | 1 | 0.00 |
| 13 | rejoined | 10 | 0.00 | 69 | 0.01 | 2 | 2 | 31 | 0.00 |
| 14 | ordered | 181 | 0.02 | 335 | 0.05 | 24 | 51 | 17 | 0.01 |
| 15 | swore | 9 | 0.00 | 76 | 0.01 | 7 | 23 | 6 | 0.00 |
| 16 | exclaimed | 137 | 0.02 | 257 | 0.04 | 3 | 11 | 63 | 0.01 |

（续表）

| 序号 | 词语 | 霍译本 | 百分比 | 杨译本 | 百分比 | 《飘》 | 《名利场》 | 《大卫》 | 英文小说总百分比 |
|---|---|---|---|---|---|---|---|---|---|
| 17 | announced | 93 | 0.01 | 195 | 0.03 | 18 | 25 | 10 | 0.00 |
| 18 | agreed | 113 | 0.01 | 245 | 0.04 | 17 | 42 | 12 | 0.01 |
| 19 | approved | 10 | 0.00 | 52 | 0.01 | 6 | 5 | 10 | 0.00 |
| 20 | countered | 5 | 0.00 | 52 | 0.01 | 2 | 0 | 0 | 0.00 |
| 21 | declared | 13 | 0.00 | 59 | 0.01 | 23 | 37 | 8 | 0.01 |
| 22 | warned | 15 | 0.00 | 67 | 0.01 | 5 | 10 | 6 | 0.00 |
| 23 | assured | 19 | 0.00 | 63 | 0.01 | 12 | 4 | 9 | 0.00 |

通过上表我们可以发现，said 在霍译本和杨译本会话引导语中的高比例得到了三部英文原版小说的支持。在《飘》中 said 有 1494 个，约占总文本0.35%；《名利场》中 said 有1330 个，约占总文本 0.43%；《大卫·科波菲尔》中 said 有 2942 个，约占总文本 0.82%。

下面是小说《飘》中使用 said 的 50 个例子：

| | | |
|---:|:---:|:---|
| or Tom either ，she | **said** | . But what about Boyd |
| to be any war ， | **said** | Scarlett ，bored. It |
| to be a war ， | **said** | Stuart. The Yankees may |
| She meant what she | **said** | ，for she could never |
| Well ， | **said** | Stuart ，she hasn ' |
| when she saw us she | **said** | : ' In Heaven ' |
| snorting and rearing and she | **said** | : ' Get out of |
| runt of the litter ， | **said** | Stuart ，proud of his |
| t let her. They | **said** | they were going to have |
| ' t rain tomorrow ， | **said** | Scarlett. It ' s |
| and hot as June ， | **said** | Stuart. Look at that |
| Scarlett. About tomorrow ， | **said** | Brent. Just because we |
| fortunes. You know she | **said** | I was going to marry |
| tell you a secret ， | **said** | Stuart. |
| I know about that ， | **said** | Scarlett in disappointment. That |
| going to be announced ， | **said** | Stuart triumphantly. It ' |

| | | |
|---:|:---:|:---|
| course I will，Scarlett | said | automatically. |
| ' em be mad， | said | Brent. We two can |
| little attention to what they | said | ，although she made the |
| Look，he | said | . Don ' t it |
| I thought she would， | said | Stuart. I kept waiting |
| . Do you suppose we | said | something that made her mad |
| was something we did or | said | that made her shut up |
| ' t see why， | said | Stuart. My Lord ！ |
| do you suppose，he | said | ，that maybe Ashley hadn |
| Well，look， | said | Brent. Let ' s |
| I forgot about that， | said | Brent hastily. No， |
| one of you，she | said | . Or maybe she ' |
| and have supper. Scarlett | said | Cathleen was home from Charleston |
| t have done it， | said | Stuart. And Cade never |
| Yankee stepmother who squalled and | said | I was a wild barbarian |
| Tony ' s aim. | Said | she guessed licker was spoiling |
| ' s a card ！ | said | Brent with loving approval. |
| we get home tonight， | said | Stuart gloomily. Look， |
| Europe. You know Mother | said | if we got expelled from |
| Ashley Wilkes | said | they had an awful lot |
| gwine git much supper， | said | JeeMs Dey cook done died |
| the three of us， | said | Stuart. Come on， |
| catchin ' a cole， | said | Mammy suspiciously. |
| I ' m not， | said | Scarlett impatiently. You fetch |
| shining silver. And he | said | ，So you ' ve |
| In a neighborhood where everyone | said | exactly what he thought as |
| from Fairhill，he had | said | ；Scarlett，I have |
| come. Then he had | said | ：Not now ！ We |
| Well，Missy，he | said | ，pinching her cheek， |
| very presentable now，she | said | ，and I don ' |
| her arm through his and | said | ：I was waiting for |
| never will I have it | said | that Gerald O ' Hara |

| | | |
|---:|:---:|:---|
| Still she | **said** | nothing，wishing that it |
| did his sisters，and | **said** | they hoped nothing would keep |

下面是小说《名利场》中使用 said 的 50 个例子：

| | | |
|---:|:---:|:---|
| friend｜s hand and | **said** | ，looking up in her |
| Miss Pinkerton，Becky！ | **said** | Miss Jemima to a young |
| I suppose I must， | **said** | Miss Sharp calmly，and |
| very unconcerned manner，and | **said** | in French，and with |
| solemn turban），she | **said** | ，Miss Sharp，I |
| you，my child， | **said** | she，embracing Amelia， |
| Come away，Becky， | **said** | Miss Jemima，pulling the |
| sandwiches，my dear， | **said** | she to Amelia. You |
| . Well，I never— | **said** | she—what an audacious—Emotion prevented her |
| gentleman of sixty-eight，who | **said** | to me one morning at |
| and eight，and had | **said** | in awful voice，Boy |
| Rebecca？at last she | **said** | ，after a pause. |
| back to the black-hole？ | **said** | Rebecca，laughing. |
| world used her ill， | **said** | this young misanthropist，and |
| been a girl，she | **said** | ；she had been a |
| ｜s grand-daughter，she | **said** | of one. How they |
| with the children，Rebecca | **said** | abruptly，not to teach |
| For five-and-thirty years，she | **said** | ，and with great justice |
| A viper—a fiddlestick， | **said** | Miss Sharp to the old |
| a sum of money， | **said** | the girl，and get |
| cannot，certainly，she | **said** | ，find fault with Miss |
| Amelia｜s behaviour， | **said** | Minerva，which has not |
| was riding by，and | **said** | ，A dem fine gal |
| to his sister，she | **said** | ，with perfect truth， |
| Not alone， | **said** | Amelia；you know， |
| t he very rich？ | **said** | Rebecca. They say all |
| Joseph is not married， | **said** | Amelia，laughing again. |
| she was sure Amelia had | **said** | he was，and she |

| | | |
|---:|:---:|:---|
| of them at Chiswick， | **said** | Amelia，rather wondering at |
| it beats，dear！ | **said** | she to her friend. |
| it doesn't， | **said** | Amelia. Come in， |
| your sister，Joseph， | **said** | Amelia，laughing and shaking |
| ，upon my word， | **said** | the head under the neckcloth |
| Do you think so？ | **said** | the latter. I' |
| ！not for worlds， | **said** | Miss Sharp，starting back |
| beautiful shawls，brother， | **said** | Amelia to the fire poker |
| O heavenly！ | **said** | Miss Sharp，and her |
| is a one-horse palanquin， | **said** | the old gentleman，who |
| our service，sir， | **said** | Joseph，to dine with |
| these two young women， | **said** | the father，and he |
| . What is it？ | **said** | she，turning an appealing |
| Capital， | **said** | he. His mouth was |
| is an Indian dish， | **said** | Miss Rebecca. I am |
| curry，my dear， | **said** | Mr Sedley，laughing. |
| everything else from India？ | **said** | Mr Sedley. |
| Oh，excellent！ | **said** | Rebecca，who was suffering |
| it，Miss Sharp， | **said** | Joseph，really interested. |
| A chili， | **said** | Rebecca，gasping. Oh |
| green they look，she | **said** | ，and put one into |
| ，I assure you， | **said** | he. Sambo，give |

下面是小说《大卫·科波菲尔》中使用 said 的 50 个例子：

| | | |
|---:|:---:|:---|
| and，as I have | **said** | ，six months before I |
| ，I think，' | **said** | Miss Betsey；the emphasis |
| 'Yes，' | **said** | my mother，faintly. |
| 'Miss Trotwood，' | **said** | the visitor. 'You |
| you see her，' | **said** | Miss Betsey. My mother |
| seated，and Miss Betsey | **said** | nothing，my mother， |
| tut，tut！' | **said** | Miss Betsey，in a |
| cap，child，' | **said** | Miss Betsey，'and |
| ，poor thing，and | **said** | ，sobbing，that indeed |

| | | |
|---|---|---|
| name of Heaven，' | said | Miss Betsey，suddenly， |
| ' Why Rookery？' | said | Miss Betsey. ' Cookery |
| have lived here，' | said | my mother. ' We |
| ' Well？' | said | Miss Betsey，coming back |
| no，no，' | said | Miss Betsey. ' Have |
| course it will，' | said | Miss Betsey. ' It |
| ma ' am，' | said | my mother innocently. |
| ' Peggotty，' | said | my mother. |
| s her surname，' | said | my mother，faintly. |
| being a girl，' | said | Miss Betsey. ' I |
| were very happy，' | said | my mother. ' Mr |
| ' t cry！' | said | Miss Betsey. ' You |
| we were married，' | said | my mother simply. |
| ，for instance，' | said | Miss Betsey. |
| it himself！' ) | said | Miss Betsey in a parenthesis |
| Well，well！' | said | Miss Betsey. |
| Well，well！' | said | Miss Betsey. ' Don |
| make yourself ill，' | said | Miss Betsey，' and |
| ，I know，' | said | she，by and by |
| ' Mr Copperfield，' | said | my mother，answering with |
| pounds a year，' | said | my mother. |
| have done worse，' | said | my aunt. |
| her a little bow， | said | ，in allusion to the |
| ' Well？' | said | my aunt，taking the |
| ' Ba—a—ah！' | said | my aunt，with a |
| ' Well？' | said | my aunt，taking out |
| ' Ya—a—ah！' | said | my aunt. With such |
| break his spirit，he | said | afterwards. He preferred to |
| was at liberty，and | said | to my aunt in his |
| ' What upon？' | said | my aunt，sharply. |
| ma ' am，' | said | Mr Chillip，in his |
| How is she？' | said | my aunt，folding her |

| | | |
|---|---|---|
| How is SHE？ ⌐ | **said** | my aunt，sharply. |
| ⌐ The baby，⌐ | **said** | my aunt. ⌐ How |
| My aunt | **said** | never a word，but |
| may with greater propriety be | **said** | not to have lost the |
| handsome，Davy！⌐ | **said** | Peggotty. ⌐ Lawk， |
| opinion，Peggotty？⌐ | **said** | I. |
| My opinion is，⌐ | **said** | Peggotty，taking her eyes |
| ，are you？⌐ | **said** | I，after sitting quiet |
| about the Crorkindills，⌐ | **said** | Peggotty，who was not |

　　而杨译本会话引导语相对于霍译本会话引导语的特色动词绝大多数未得到英文原版小说的支持。许多杨译本特色词在霍译本和三部英文原版小说中百分比均为 0,这些动词如表 3－16 所示。

表 3－16　杨译本会话引导语特色词在霍译本及几部英文小说中的比例

| 序号 | 词语 | 杨译本会话引导语 | 霍译本会话引导语 | 英文原版小说合集 |
|---|---|---|---|---|
| 1 | chuckled | 0.11 | 0.00 | 0.00 |
| 2 | demanded | 0.07 | 0.00 | 0.00 |
| 3 | scolded | 0.05 | 0.00 | 0.00 |
| 4 | teased | 0.04 | 0.00 | 0.00 |
| 5 | rejoined | 0.04 | 0.00 | 0.00 |
| 6 | swore | 0.04 | 0.00 | 0.00 |
| 7 | approved | 0.03 | 0.00 | 0.00 |
| 8 | countered | 0.03 | 0.00 | 0.00 |
| 9 | warned | 0.03 | 0.00 | 0.00 |
| 10 | assured | 0.03 | 0.00 | 0.00 |

　　chuckled 是杨译本会话引导语相对于霍译本会话引导语的第一特色词,我们首先来看一下 chuckle 作为动词使用时的释义:

　　(1)《牛津高阶英语词典》(第 6 版)(*Oxford Advanced Learner's Dictionary*):~ (*at ∕ about sth*) *to laugh quietly*。

　　(2)《朗文当代英语词典》(第 4 版)(*Longman Dictionary of Contemporary English*):*to laugh quietly*。

（3）《柯林斯高阶英语词典》（*Collins COBUILD Advanced Learner's English Dictionary*）：*When you chuckle，you laugh quietly*.

（4）《美国传统词典》（双解）（*E-C American Heritage Dictionary*）：① *to laugh quietly or to oneself* 轻笑或自笑；② *to cluck or chuck，as a hen* 像母鸡一样略略笑。

（5）《牛津高阶英汉双解词典》（*Oxford Advanced Learner's English-Chinese Dictionary*）：*laugh quietly or to oneself* 轻声地笑；暗自笑。

根据以上几部词典的定义，我们可以推断 chuckle 的意思应为"轻声地笑；略略笑"。该词在杨译本的会话引导语中出现频率较高，有 154 次，现仅列举前50 个例子：

| | | |
|---|---|---|
| very smart. " Zixing | **chuckled** | . |
| . " The Lady Dowager | **chuckled** | . |
| ! " Mrs. Zhou | **chuckled** | . " How terribly chancy |
| disobey ? " Jia Rong | **chuckled** | . |
| me again. " Baoyu | **chuckled** | . |
| gentlemen ? " Jia Zheng | **chuckled** | . |
| of me ! " he | **chuckled** | . |
| Mingyan | **chuckled** | . " But what if |
| Baoyu | **chuckled** | . " If you stay |
| caught her meaning then and | **chuckled** | . " You were begging |
| Baoyu | **chuckled** | . |
| ! " The old lady | **chuckled** | . |
| The old lady | **chuckled** | . " None of them |
| right then , " he | **chuckled** | . |
| right , " Ni Er | **chuckled** | . |
| t you ? " She | **chuckled** | . |
| Xifeng | **chuckled** | . |
| did I ? " Baoyu | **chuckled** | . |
| " Fine ! " Feng | **chuckled** | . |
| Xifeng | **chuckled** | . |
| Tanchun | **chuckled** | . " These last few |
| Baoyu | **chuckled** | . " It ' s |
| are. " Feng Ziying | **chuckled** | . |

| | | |
|---|---|---|
| Zhang the Taoist | **chuckled** | . " I brought the |
| ' s observant ，" | **chuckled** | Tanchun. " She never |
| too seriously. " He | **chuckled** | . |
| Baoyu | **chuckled** | . |
| bring it. " Baoyu | **chuckled** | . |
| Baoyu | **chuckled** | . " I always say |
| Xiangyun | **chuckled** | . " In that case |
| Baoyu | **chuckled** | . |
| you are ！" Baochai | **chuckled** | . |
| s become ！" he | **chuckled** | . |
| got one. " Baochai | **chuckled** | . " Much Ado About |
| . " The old lady | **chuckled** | . |
| for a day ，" | **chuckled** | Granny Liu. |
| fond of flowers ，" | **chuckled** | Granny Liu. |
| me for boasting ，" | **chuckled** | Granny Liu as she scrambled |
| ，" the Lady Dowager | **chuckled** | . |
| games，madam ，" | **chuckled** | Aunt Xue. " But |
| ' t do ，" | **chuckled** | the others. |
| just have one ，" | **chuckled** | Xifeng. " None of |
| d forgotten them ，" | **chuckled** | the Lady Dowager. |
| of that. " Baoyu | **chuckled** | . " So I ' |
| Of course ，" he | **chuckled** | . |
| of the world ，" | **chuckled** | Granny Liu. |
| we were strangers ，' | **chuckled** | Pinger. |
| t talk rubbish ，' | **chuckled** | Xifeng. |
| make her drink ，' | **chuckled** | the old lady ，' |
| come in force ，' | **chuckled** | Xifeng. |

霍译本会话引导语中 chuckled 仅出现了 4 次：

| | | |
|---|---|---|
| addressing ？' The Taoist | **chuckled** | . ' I don ' |
| She | **chuckled** | . ' Holy Name ！ |
| his dream，and he | **chuckled** | aloud with satisfaction： |
| so you should ！' | **chuckled** | the monk. |

在三部英文原版小说《飘》《名利场》和《大卫·科波菲尔》中,chuckled 总共被使用了 8 次,其中《飘》1 次、《名利场》2 次、《大卫·科波菲尔》5 次。

《飘》中的例句为:

He stopped and   **chuckled**   as he tugged at his

《名利场》中的例句为:

old Sir Pitt,who   **chuckled**   at her airs and graces

not follow it. He   **chuckled**   and swore to himself behind

《大卫·科波菲尔》中的例句为:

indeed,that he sometimes   **chuckled**   audibly over this reflection,

inventing conversation. He manifestly   **chuckled**   over it for some time

' and he sat and   **chuckled**   at her for some time

the word Murphy,and   **chuckled**   . Glass tinkled tremulously.

them softly,and softly   **chuckled**   ; looking as like a

笔者检索了英国国家语料库中 chuckled 的使用情况,共搜寻到 411 条结果,其中小说体裁有 378 条反馈(见图 3-12),占比为每百万词 23.76。限于篇幅,在此仅截取 50 条例句(见表 3-17)。

| SECTION | ALL | SPOKEN | FICTION | MAGAZINE | NEWSPAPER | NON-ACAD | ACADEMIC | MISC |
|---|---|---|---|---|---|---|---|---|
| FREQ | 411 | 2 | 378 | 9 | 10 | 1 | 1 | 10 |
| PER MIL | 4.27 | 0.20 | 23.76 | 1.24 | 0.96 | 0.06 | 0.07 | 0.48 |
| SEE ALL SUB-SECTIONS AT ONCE | | | | | | | | |

图 3-12　chuckled 在英国国家语料库中不同体裁的使用情况

表 3-17　chuckled 一词经检索后具体使用例句

| 序号 | 例　句 |
|---|---|
| 1 | with the herds of others,their oats still standing in November... Old Donald **chuckled** in himself as the scene in the road came over him again. The horse |
| 2 | properly grateful to the fathers had been put for centuries. But even as she **chuckled**,Phoebe knew now that this was not fair. There had been a time |
| 3 | her,and licked her toes with such a gathered pure tenderness,such a **chuckled** tickliness,that it was heartbreaking. Fenna came offering now only love,huge |
| 4 | . Now when I was down by the river at half seven...' He **chuckled**. Clytemnestra whimpered. Wexford went to the door and the dog screamed for joy |

（续表）

| 序号 | 例　句 |
|---|---|
| 5 | its father's athletic limbs. Vigo lifted the boy high，laughing as he **chuckled**，and there came into his face an intense besotted adoration.' Meet my |
| 6 | 'll reimburse you out of petty cash.' The doctor went unwillingly. Wexford **chuckled** to himself in the car. Crocker's cautious approach to the electricity showroom， |
| 7 | need to. You've been mooning about for a few weeks,' she **chuckled**, ruefully.' I'm not blind，you know. " It |
| 8 | ' They'll call again，anyway. Bet your boots on it. Omi **chuckled**.' Ah，Liebchen，you do my heart good. She peered over |
| 9 | ear with the paper.' Well，stone me，wack,' he **chuckled**.' The bastard's even against that. " He's against every |
| 10 | . Gina had ditched her performing side.' Too old,' Nigel had **chuckled**. But now，much worse than that，she was taking up writing. |
| 11 | .' Tug pushed his head deeper into the soft，musty cushions. Doyle **chuckled**.' Scared? ' Defiantly Tug raised his head.' Of course I |
| 12 | ' She broke off.' That person I was living with,' she **chuckled**,' she thought a lot of you when you came to see us. |
| 13 | illuminated booth. His yellow' KISS ME SLOWLY' hat bobbed about as Tony **chuckled** to himself over his comic.' Cor! A bank account! ' Gazzer |
| 14 | 're forgetting is that you were an actor in civiLian life.' The CO **chuckled** with unashamed glee at the little joke he was about to make at Charles's |
| 15 | 's ask the Adjutant if he's yet appointed an Entertainments Officer. ' He **chuckled** even more when the Adjutant confessed he hadn't.' Well，we have |
| 16 | He made Bumface grovel.... This time Charles couldn't resist the intervention. He **chuckled**.' Good show! " And to some purpose. You're to |
| 17 | . He looked sweet. " Solid wood，you mean.' He **chuckled** and started coughing.' I'll say this for old Wix,' he |
| 18 | the glory.' You're threatening me. " Me? ' He **chuckled**.' That's a good one. Just trying to help，Mrs Redburn |
| 19 | Molland.' It is time for you to serve me.' Leo had **chuckled** when Barbara told him the story of Hubert's conversion. They were in the |

（续表）

| 序号 | 例 句 |
|---|---|
| 20 | said Sergeant Joe.' And Shelley. And their ladies.' Mr Singleton **chuckled**.' All sailing on a sea of ItaLian misadventures. " End of |
| 21 | mischief，I'll tell you. Little tinkers，we were.' She **chuckled** at the memory. As she cleared away the tray，Stanley picked up a |
| 22 | along the embankment，late，fresh from her lover's embraces.' He **chuckled**. The latecomers ordered breakfast. Rozanov removed his parka then hid his face behind |
| 23 | I fuck you still,' murmured Masha，misquoting Pushkin. Rozanov and I **chuckled**.' Didn't you also fuck Thatcher，Victor，when she was in |
| 24 | of Marie Grubbe，if I'm not mistaken! ' And the old woman **chuckled**.' I wonder，sometimes，what it is about that woman that haunts |
| 25 | " I've never met one yet that couldn't be broken,' **chuckled** Tiptoe.' No，listen to me.' Biff held up a finger |
| 26 | hat on the hall table. " That old felt one? ' Jackie **chuckled**，his good humour restored.' The one he wears for visiting? ' |
| 27 | swaying unsteadily，as if the metal floor were running in wavelets. The wino **chuckled** silently. She realised that the strange thing about him was that he was not |
| 28 | hairy hands.' Rich pickins' tonight，me' andsomes,' he **chuckled**.' I knew we was onto a good' un when we comes to |
| 29 | she puts the stone back. " You're right，Tom,' **chuckled** his aunt,' none of' em's ready for buryin' yet. |
| 30 | Enjoy the girl's company. I should be so lucky.' Stuart Baxter **chuckled**，and put down the phone. ♯' Well — what did you make |
| 31 | forward to stand beside Martha. Mrs Joyce turned them back-to-back and the smaller children **chuckled** and somersaulted in their amusement to see the two girls were the same height. |
| 32 | good. " You have to keep people on their toes.' Morgan **chuckled**，a wheezing sound.' Management must manage.' Evans got his blow |
| 33 | monster's going away now,' said Nellie. In the bed，Kevin **chuckled**.' I never had no trouble startin' up old Random，God Bless |

（续表）

| 序号 | 例　句 |
|------|--------|
| 34 | offered a cigarette. Kevin hesitated.' Don't ye smoke?' Kevin **chuckled** as he took the cigarette.' I don't know. " Try |
| 35 | ,' said the police-sergeant. Mary stared. The keeper saw her look and **chuckled**.' He's Sir Benson Craig, the new owner of Enderley,' |
| 36 | he sniggered,' Luke won't be long after him.' Bull O'Malley **chuckled** and drained his glass.' Indeed and I think ye may be right, |
| 37 | , but remembered Selwyn asleep upstairs.' Don't be daft,' he **chuckled**,' just think, I will be able to take you to dances at |
| 38 | he's only laughed once, hysterically, underneath the cliff. He's never **chuckled**, or giggled, or even smiled. This laugh now's a bit hysterical |
| 39 | it was a place for the aged and moribund — St Cemetery's-on-Sea!' He **chuckled** at his grim little joke.' What's your name?' he rapped |
| 40 | all, when you want to ask people like Chignell to tea.' Breeze **chuckled**, as she unwrapped a piece of nut-milk chocolate for her sister.' All |
| 41 | that? " Lor bless' ee, missie! Whatever next?' **chuckled** the gnome-like Grimble.' I'd like to see any sperrit hidin' there |
| 42 | eating sandwiches — postingthem, Breeze, like letters in a pillar-box!' Breeze **chuckled**. That was the final insult, then; Tony, after hearing Felicity's |
| 43 | found you'd cut loose the horses. " You saw?' he **chuckled**.' I saw you lying in front of that bush. It was your |
| 44 | be, her allowance a pittance. Half stale buns and mouldy meat. She **chuckled** to herself; Rab not so smart, the mouldy meat. The butcher had |
| 45 | Parker approved enough to remember the name. He would buy some more. He **chuckled**. They should have named it resurrection. The frightened nervous wretch he'd been |
| 46 | as that of the King when the royal cohort arrived from the palace. Astorre **chuckled**.' So it was like that!' said the captain.' Well |
| 47 | .' Kelly made her way through the hall towards the front door. Short **chuckled** randily.' Who's talking about horses?' he called out as she |
| 48 | there,' I asked,' a telephone on the train?' He **chuckled**.' You bet your life. But it's a radio phone, eh |

（续表）

| 序号 | 例　句 |
|---|---|
| 49 | be told that she should let me in whenever I asked，eh? George **chuckled** his way out of the horse car and we meandered back down the train together |
| 50 | the horse car belongs to Canadian pacific.' I looked even blanker. He **chuckled**.' The Canadian Pacific and VIA Rail，who work so closely together， |

　　再来看 countered 这一动词，在杨译本会话引导语中出现了 49 次，在霍译本会话引导语中仅有 3 次，《飘》中使用了 2 次，《名利场》和《大卫·科波菲尔》中均为 0 次。

　　几部权威词典关于 counter 作为动词使用时的释义为：

　　（1）《牛津高阶英语词典》（第 6 版）（*Oxford Advanced Learner's Dictionary*）：～（*sb*/*sth*）（*with sth*）*to reply to sb by trying to prove that what they said is not true*。

　　（2）《朗文当代英语词典》（第 4 版）（*Longman Dictionary of Contemporary English*）：*to say something in order to try to prove that what someone said was not true or as a reply to something*。

　　（3）《柯林斯高阶英语词典》（*Collins COBUILD Advanced Learner's English Dictionary*）：*If you counter something that someone has said，you say something which shows that you disagree with them or which proves that they are wrong*.

　　（4）《美国传统词典》（双解）（*E-C American Heritage Dictionary*）：*to offer in response* 反驳，回答。

　　（5）《牛津高阶英汉双解词典》（*Oxford Advanced Learner's English-Chinese Dictionary*）：～ *with sth*；～ *sb*/*sth*（*with sth*）*respond to*（*sb*/*sth*）*with an opposing view，a return attack，etc* 反对，反击（某人/某事物）。

　　根据以上几部词典的定义，我们可以推断出 counter 用来表达"反驳，驳斥"之意。在杨译本会话引导语中使用的上下文为：

| | | |
|---|---|---|
| " Surely，" | **countered** | Yucun in surprise，" |
| dear cousin，" he | **countered** | coaxingly. |
| you enlighten me ?" | **countered** | the doctor. |
| ，sir，" they | **countered** | . |
| s well done，" | **countered** | the others. " Even |
| fun of you ?" | **countered** | Baoyu. |

| | | |
|---|---|---|
| What an idea ! " | countered | Xiaohong. |
| , cousin , " he | countered | . |
| on either side , " | countered | Xifeng. |
| no harm , " she | countered | . |
| hands to yourself , " | countered | Qingwen. |
| s all right , " | countered | Xifeng quickly amid general laughter |
| say that auntie , " | countered | Xifeng. |
| ' s necessary , " | countered | Xiren. |
| , who is ? " | countered | Yingchun with a smile. |
| only white begonia , " | countered | Baochai. |
| Baochai | countered | , " Just now the |
| is even better , " | countered | Li Wan. |
| been for that ? " | countered | Baochai with a smile. |
| the old lady , ' | countered | Tanchun. |
| a fair proposal , ' | countered | Baochai. ' Listen , |
| ' Nonsense ! ' | Countered | Xifeng softly. |
| , dear sister , ' | countered | Xifeng. |
| and aunt ? ' he | countered | . |
| it for fun ? ' | countered | Tanchun and Daiyu. |
| eating it raw , ' | countered | Baoyu. |
| sense of duty , ' | countered | Xifeng laughingly. |
| graveyard trees ? ' Sheyue | countered | . |
| on medicine , ' she | countered | . |
| all move inside ? ' | countered | the old lady. |
| the different apartments , ' | countered | Tanchun. |
| s my way , ' | countered | Pinger. |
| as you are , ' | countered | Tanchun , ' haven ' |
| want with me ? ' | countered | Baoyu as soon as he |
| else is there ? ' | countered | Cuimo. |
| yourself over this ? " | countered | Pinger. |
| smooth and wide , " | countered | the old lady. |
| Madam You | countered | gaily , " I ' |

| turned up，" she | **countered** | . |
| from school，" he | **countered** | quickly，" Li Gui |
| aunt was here？" | **countered** | the old lady，laughing |
| crazy talk，" Sheyue | **countered** | . |
| 't matter，" | **countered** | Xiren. " We ' |
| 't do，" | **countered** | Tanchun. |
| . Stepping over quickly he | **countered** | with a smile， |
| 't matter，" | **countered** | Baochan. |
| charge outside？" they | **countered** | . |
| a child，" she | **countered** | ，" the sages of |
| Xichun，however， | **countered** | ， |

霍译本会话引导语中 countered 仅出现了 3 次：

| grudge against me，' | **countered** | Xi-feng with a smile. |
| be easily explained，' | **countered** | another. |
| s not recklessness，' | **countered** | Xiang-yun. ' It ' |

在三部英文原版小说《飘》《名利场》和《大卫·科波菲尔》中，countered 只在《飘》中出现了 2 次、《名利场》和《大卫·科波菲尔》中一次都没有使用。

以下是《飘》中的例句：

| lady and she eats， | **countered** | Scarlett. |
| needer hyah no dar， | **countered** | Mammy，girding herself for |

笔者检索了英国国家语料库中 countered 的使用情况，共搜寻到 417 条结果，其中小说体裁有 154 条反馈，占比为每百万词 9.68。限于篇幅，在此仅截取 50 条例句。

| SECTION | ALL | SPOKEN | FICTION | MAGAZINE | NEWSPAPER | NON-ACAD | ACADEMIC | MISC |
|---|---|---|---|---|---|---|---|---|
| FREQ | 417 | 0 | 154 | 22 | 55 | 64 | 52 | 70 |
| PER MIL | 4.33 | 0.00 | 9.68 | 3.03 | 5.25 | 3.88 | 3.39 | 3.36 |
| SEE ALL SUB-SECTIONS AT ONCE | | | | | | | | |

图 3‑13　countered 在英国国家语料库中不同体裁的使用情况

表 3 - 18 countered 一词经检索后具体使用例句

| 序号 | 例 句 |
|---|---|
| 1 | Maybe we are not always that good ourselves if we look closer,' Rose **countered** quickly. Michael looked up from where he knelt on the floor in front of |
| 2 | brightly, which observation — if it brought forth a reply at all — was **countered** by a snapped:' I didn't buy it as an investment'. |
| 3 | Managing Director and Treasurer, was manned throughout by Irish men and women, they **countered** with,' Ah yes, but it's the Trade unions, you see |
| 4 | about. " Yes, I know that, Mark,' the American **countered**.' But Nate has specifically said that you are the man he wants to |
| 5 | ' But you never give the planning presentations. That s my bailiwick,' **countered** the Englishman, with growing resentment in his voice and manner.' Yes, |
| 6 | reassurance with younger girls', it said. Nigel was not amused. He **countered** by leaving other articles around on pre-menstrual tension. She couldn't have it both |
| 7 | hedged at every new question. When the doctor opened a large book, he **countered**,' I bet you're going to show me some bloody ink blots. |
| 8 | Excellent. I can tell them you're experienced.' He thanked her but **countered** cunningly with a query about who her friends might be. She resisted the trap |
| 9 | suggested that they had met before, I had thought that the other man had **countered** with a faintly wary look. And Ewen himself, for all his outgoing charm |
| 10 | ' What's all that offal and stuff in your dustbin then? ' Jeremiah **countered**.' Refuse collectors reported it. " Well, you don't think |
| 11 | saddened.' I'm surprised you don't know, personally,' George **countered**,' very surprised. You're a man who keeps his eyes open, |
| 12 | Kathleen. Bones, the look said.' They were fillets,' Kathleen **countered**.' So I am imagining a bone? " I didn't say |
| 13 | it's true. " Oh, in a philosophical sense,' Rozanov **countered**,' we are all capable of everything. But most of us don't |
| 14 | ' she declared.' It's my place to do so,' he **countered**.' I'm going,' she repeated with determination.' Then we |
| 15 | , right? " An Englishman might not agree with that,' she **countered**.' But basically it's true,' he persisted. Basically,' |

（续表）

| 序号 | 例　句 |
|---|---|
| 16 | ' Attlee might be，but Bevin and Dalton are for it，' Nevil **countered**.' The unions are against it,' Mr Sanderson said.' Oh |
| 17 | ,' Bragg said amiably.' I know nothing about that,' Peace **countered** sharply.' Mr Livesey always kept that — and his father before him. |
| 18 | " Why would he do that at this time of night？' Newman **countered**. That was when Howard，Director of the Secret Service，appeared framed in |
| 19 | asked him.' I'm paying you，aren't I？' he **countered** angrily. He thrust the money at her.' You ought to be in |
| 20 | boy at home？' asked the policeman lightly.' Which one？' **countered** Nessie with a smile.' The one that's not making a fortune in |
| 21 | gaze on him.' It's nothing like that Tom Hook,' she **countered**，going red in the face. Sticking her nose in the air she hurried |
| 22 | plenty of liquor to swill out your guts. " What guts？' **countered** Knocker,' this stuff must have burned out your guts years ago.' |
| 23 | ' Well，for Pete's sake，let's go somewhere,' Sheila **countered**.' Where？" I du n no.' Sheila puckered her |
| 24 | finding it pretty dull around here after the States. " No,' **countered** Barney,' she seems as happy as a pig in poop. She told |
| 25 | ' What did we talk about when we were in Three A？' she **countered**，and all three racked their brains in vain.' It's like one |
| 26 | ？' The weird，ill-formed mouth moved again，and ignoring her question，**countered** with its own.' I... do... not... know... you. |
| 27 | blocking the hand chop，attacking again，gouging at Delaney's eyes. Delaney **countered**，smothering the Russian's arms as he came in close，face inches from |
| 28 | of personal curiosity，or does it represent an official line of enquiry？' **countered** Toby，crossing his skeletal ankles.' The latter. " Ah. |
| 29 | lions took on the Christians. The Maggot，faced with these scathing judgments，**countered** by asserting that Ellen's education had ruined what might otherwise have been a useful |
| 30 | round here. " The first thing they'd look at,' Billy **countered**,' is a woman drivin' my auld rattlebones of a car! Have |

| 序号 | 例 句 |
|---|---|
| 31 | it,' she said.' So's the rain,' Michael Harvey **countered**.' Reminds me of Rademon on a Sunday. All the pubs shut and |
| 32 | conscience ever since. " It's no good blaming yourself,' he **countered**.' It was a hopeless misalLiance. Most people would have reacted as you |
| 33 | you on a busy shopping morning and ask you to sign petitions? ' Markby **countered** craftily.' That's unfair! ' Meredith said indignantly.' All right |
| 34 | " It flamin' isn't, and I should know,' Vi **countered**.' I'm a Catholic. " The old religion, Vi, |
| 35 | ' Ludo grinned sheepishly.' But you have been in Monte-catini,' he **countered**.' You couldn't have come in any case. I know how you |
| 36 | White Lions protected him from many assassination attempts and his personal retinue of Sapherian wizards **countered** all death-spells. Finally at the field of Maledor at the very entrance to the |
| 37 | asked him. That was a sensitive question.' Do you? ' Sharpe **countered**.' He's a drunk.' Paulette did not bother with tact, |
| 38 | looked at him derisively.' What're you up to then? ' he **countered**.' It's gone wrong,' Freddie replied. " E was |
| 39 | " Madame simply took me out shopping and to have lunch,' Ellie **countered**.' What could she possibly be having a hand in? Please may I |
| 40 | at least one bodyguard in the room with you at all times,' Whitlock **countered**.' Even when I'm sleeping? " Even when you're sleeping |
| 41 | fail to point out that the school would have helped upon request. Mrs Maugham **countered** this with contemptuous remarks about charity, and about the dignity of the family, |
| 42 | Winchester. Indeed, she was rather proud of the magnificent logic with which she **countered** his Winchester admission. " Ah, then, " she said, sucking on |
| 43 | build another four ketches and run a fleet, come to that, " Gristy **countered**. " There's good steady trade in pilchards. Settle down and marry, |
| 44 | it comes from. " Yes, you do, Mat,' Violette **countered** her.' Apart from the tiny genetic component, it has everything to do |

(续表)

| 序号 | 例　句 |
|------|--------|
| 45 | trigonometry，but what the girls get up to is something else，'Violette **countered** mysteriously. What the girls got up to was something Katherine was to learn only |
| 46 | to you. " The trouble with you，Portia Gaitskell，'Katherine **countered**，'is that you're too good for any man. And don't |
| 47 | squirmed.'I'm nobody's mistress，you daft beggar，'she **countered**，beating him with mock ferocity about the head，cheeks burning with delight. |
| 48 | Father? " Do you have any objection to my presence here? '**countered** the old man.'No，not exactly，but there's nothing for |
| 49 | much? 'he said at length. The Factor named a price，Antinou **countered** and so it went on for quite a while. The Fat Controller and I |
| 50 | probably trying to get money out of you. " No，'Eloise **countered**.' She said herself she could lose her job. I believe her， |

## 第四节　《红楼梦》霍译本前八十回与后四十回会话引导语对比研究

迄今最为流行和权威的两部《红楼梦》英文全译本皆是合作翻译的结果。1973 至 1986 年，大卫·霍克思与女婿约翰·闵福德合译的全译本《红楼梦》陆续出版，共五卷，英文名为 *The Story of the Stone*。1978 至 1980 年，杨宪益与戴乃迭夫妇合译的《红楼梦》，英文名为 *A Dream of Red Mansions*，分三卷出版发行。在 2003 年曹雪芹逝世二百四十周年纪念大会上，杨宪益和夫人戴乃迭、大卫·霍克思和女婿闵福德因出色的合作而荣获"《红楼梦》翻译贡献奖"。

杨宪益和戴乃迭是一对夫妻翻译家，他们的合作被誉为是珠联璧合，中西文化的水乳交融，具有得天独厚的优势。他们有着独特的合作方式：在翻译中国文学作品时，大多数时候是杨宪益翻译粗稿，戴乃迭再对其进行润色和加工。而霍克思与闵福德的合作方式不同：霍克思是当代研究中国文学的巨擘、翻译界的泰斗，十分热爱中国文化，十五年如一日潜心翻译《红楼梦》；闵福德是著名的汉学家也是翻译家，少年时就向往中国文化，曾翻译过许多中国经典名作，如《易经》《孙子兵法》《聊斋志异》等，投身霍克思门下后更表现出对《红楼梦》的浓厚兴趣。霍克思在翻译《红楼梦》时，考虑到既然前八十回和后四十回是两位作者所作，那么为了最大程度地再现原著的形式，翻译也理应由两位译者来完成。

霍克思毅然邀请了对《红楼梦》翻译同样有极大兴趣的学生闵福德来翻译后四十回,于是才有了如今的恢宏译作,使得我们有幸领略到异域的"曹雪芹"和"高鹗"。

众所周知,曹雪芹与高鹗在原文中的写作风格存在一定差异,同样地,译者霍克思和闵福德的英译也势必有各自的特色。本小节笔者将从细节入手,对《红楼梦》前八十回霍克思译本与后四十回闵福德译本中的会话引导语进行对比分析。

## 一、高频词对比研究

笔者首先将《红楼梦》前八十回霍克思译本与后四十回闵福德译本中的会话引导语进行词频统计,将位列前 100 位的高频词进行对比分析(见表 3-19)。

表 3-19　霍译本前八十回与后四十回会话引导语前 100 位高频词统计

| 霍译前 80 回 | 词语 | 词频 | 百分比 | 闵译后 40 回 | 字符 | 词频 | 百分比 |
|---|---|---|---|---|---|---|---|
| 1 | the | 4446 | 3.44 | 1 | the | 1953 | 3.54 |
| 2 | said | 4150 | 3.21 | 2 | to | 1765 | 3.20 |
| 3 | to | 3826 | 2.96 | 3 | and | 1384 | 2.51 |
| 4 | you | 2643 | 2.05 | 4 | a | 1090 | 1.97 |
| 5 | and | 2372 | 1.84 | 5 | of | 971 | 1.76 |
| 6 | a | 2330 | 1.80 | 6 | you | 928 | 1.68 |
| 7 | of | 2138 | 1.66 | 7 | I | 792 | 1.43 |
| 8 | I | 2099 | 1.62 | 8 | she | 759 | 1.37 |
| 9 | she | 2088 | 1.62 | 9 | Jia | 755 | 1.37 |
| 10 | her | 1954 | 1.51 | 10 | In | 723 | 1.31 |
| 11 | that | 1807 | 1.40 | 11 | said | 698 | 1.26 |
| 12 | it | 1766 | 1.37 | 12 | her | 668 | 1.21 |
| 13 | in | 1437 | 1.11 | 13 | was | 635 | 1.15 |
| 14 | was | 1332 | 1.03 | 14 | he | 634 | 1.15 |
| 15 | he | 1165 | 0.90 | 15 | it | 591 | 1.07 |
| 16 | Bao-yu | 992 | 0.77 | 16 | that | 574 | 1.04 |
| 17 | with | 981 | 0.76 | 17 | with | 461 | 0.83 |
| 18 | for | 965 | 0.75 | 18 | Bao-yu | 397 | 0.72 |
| 19 | Jia | 939 | 0.73 | 19 | his | 369 | 0.67 |

（续表）

| 霍译<br>前80回 | 词语 | 词频 | 百分比 | 闵译<br>后40回 | 字符 | 词频 | 百分比 |
|---|---|---|---|---|---|---|---|
| 20 | what | 797 | 0.62 | 20 | for | 354 | 0.64 |
| 21 | had | 787 | 0.61 | 21 | replied | 338 | 0.61 |
| 22 | on | 778 | 0.60 | 22 | on | 321 | 0.58 |
| 23 | this | 776 | 0.60 | 23 | this | 315 | 0.57 |
| 24 | at | 711 | 0.55 | 24 | is | 309 | 0.56 |
| 25 | be | 691 | 0.53 | 25 | what | 309 | 0.56 |
| 26 | as | 681 | 0.53 | 26 | as | 295 | 0.53 |
| 27 | all | 665 | 0.51 | 27 | asked | 291 | 0.53 |
| 28 | have | 662 | 0.51 | 28 | lady | 291 | 0.53 |
| 29 | is | 662 | 0.51 | 29 | at | 288 | 0.52 |
| 30 | they | 646 | 0.50 | 30 | had | 288 | 0.52 |
| 31 | but | 639 | 0.49 | 31 | have | 272 | 0.49 |
| 32 | Xi-feng | 624 | 0.48 | 32 | but | 269 | 0.49 |
| 33 | him | 593 | 0.46 | 33 | be | 260 | 0.47 |
| 34 | his | 582 | 0.45 | 34 | Zheng | 258 | 0.47 |
| 35 | them | 533 | 0.41 | 35 | him | 246 | 0.45 |
| 36 | are | 532 | 0.41 | 36 | not | 244 | 0.44 |
| 37 | me | 528 | 0.41 | 37 | all | 235 | 0.43 |
| 38 | when | 526 | 0.41 | 38 | Grandmother | 235 | 0.43 |
| 39 | about | 496 | 0.38 | 39 | Wang | 231 | 0.42 |
| 40 | one | 484 | 0.37 | 40 | when | 224 | 0.41 |
| 41 | not | 481 | 0.37 | 41 | they | 220 | 0.40 |
| 42 | so | 476 | 0.37 | 42 | one | 219 | 0.40 |
| 43 | out | 463 | 0.36 | 43 | Xi-feng | 219 | 0.40 |
| 44 | there | 458 | 0.35 | 44 | out | 216 | 0.39 |
| 45 | now | 448 | 0.35 | 45 | from | 212 | 0.38 |
| 46 | from | 444 | 0.34 | 46 | we | 208 | 0.38 |
| 47 | Grandmother | 437 | 0.34 | 47 | me | 195 | 0.35 |

（续表）

| 霍译前80回 | 词语 | 词频 | 百分比 | 闵译后40回 | 字符 | 词频 | 百分比 |
|---|---|---|---|---|---|---|---|
| 48 | we | 434 | 0.34 | 48 | your | 193 | 0.35 |
| 49 | your | 432 | 0.33 | 49 | Lian | 185 | 0.34 |
| 50 | if | 429 | 0.33 | 50 | came | 178 | 0.32 |
| 51 | no | 423 | 0.33 | 51 | them | 178 | 0.32 |
| 52 | do | 420 | 0.33 | 52 | Aroma | 174 | 0.32 |
| 53 | up | 414 | 0.32 | 53 | been | 174 | 0.32 |
| 54 | Dai-yu | 404 | 0.31 | 54 | my | 166 | 0.30 |
| 55 | just | 372 | 0.29 | 55 | there | 163 | 0.30 |
| 56 | were | 358 | 0.28 | 56 | up | 162 | 0.29 |
| 57 | Aroma | 357 | 0.28 | 57 | no | 161 | 0.29 |
| 58 | been | 356 | 0.28 | 58 | then | 161 | 0.29 |
| 59 | asked | 355 | 0.27 | 59 | by | 157 | 0.28 |
| 60 | Lady | 351 | 0.27 | 60 | are | 156 | 0.28 |
| 61 | Bao-chai | 349 | 0.27 | 61 | so | 152 | 0.28 |
| 62 | who | 349 | 0.27 | 62 | Dai-yu | 148 | 0.27 |
| 63 | can | 342 | 0.26 | 63 | who | 148 | 0.27 |
| 64 | go | 324 | 0.25 | 64 | Xue | 143 | 0.26 |
| 65 | by | 323 | 0.25 | 65 | do | 138 | 0.25 |
| 66 | my | 312 | 0.24 | 66 | about | 136 | 0.25 |
| 67 | very | 308 | 0.24 | 67 | come | 133 | 0.24 |
| 68 | some | 286 | 0.22 | 68 | now | 133 | 0.24 |
| 69 | back | 281 | 0.22 | 69 | were | 130 | 0.24 |
| 70 | like | 280 | 0.22 | 70 | go | 128 | 0.23 |
| 71 | Then | 280 | 0.22 | 71 | if | 127 | 0.23 |
| 72 | come | 276 | 0.21 | 72 | Bao-chai | 126 | 0.23 |
| 73 | good | 272 | 0.21 | 73 | heard | 123 | 0.22 |
| 74 | old | 269 | 0.21 | 74 | old | 123 | 0.22 |
| 75 | Patience | 267 | 0.21 | 75 | could | 122 | 0.22 |

| 霍译<br>前80回 | 词语 | 词频 | 百分比 | 闵译<br>后40回 | 字符 | 词频 | 百分比 |
|---|---|---|---|---|---|---|---|
| 76 | here | 263 | 0.20 | 76 | how | 118 | 0.21 |
| 77 | Wang | 258 | 0.20 | 77 | after | 117 | 0.21 |
| 78 | well | 258 | 0.20 | 78 | thought | 116 | 0.21 |
| 79 | know | 251 | 0.19 | 79 | An | 115 | 0.21 |
| 80 | see | 250 | 0.19 | 80 | exclaimed | 114 | 0.21 |
| 81 | after | 245 | 0.19 | 81 | Aunt | 112 | 0.20 |
| 82 | laughed | 240 | 0.19 | 82 | see | 112 | 0.20 |
| 83 | get | 237 | 0.18 | 83 | well | 112 | 0.20 |
| 84 | little | 237 | 0.18 | 84 | know | 110 | 0.20 |
| 85 | got | 236 | 0.18 | 85 | just | 109 | 0.20 |
| 86 | would | 236 | 0.18 | 86 | smile | 106 | 0.19 |
| 87 | time | 232 | 0.18 | 87 | can | 102 | 0.18 |
| 88 | could | 226 | 0.17 | 88 | Nightingale | 102 | 0.18 |
| 89 | Xue | 225 | 0.17 | 89 | Bao | 99 | 0.18 |
| 90 | two | 221 | 0.17 | 90 | sir | 98 | 0.18 |
| 91 | cousin | 220 | 0.17 | 91 | their | 97 | 0.18 |
| 92 | Lian | 219 | 0.17 | 92 | here | 94 | 0.17 |
| 93 | oh | 214 | 0.17 | 93 | has | 92 | 0.17 |
| 94 | right | 212 | 0.16 | 94 | went | 90 | 0.16 |
| 95 | how | 211 | 0.16 | 95 | Patience | 89 | 0.16 |
| 96 | an | 206 | 0.16 | 96 | say | 88 | 0.16 |
| 97 | think | 205 | 0.16 | 97 | Li | 87 | 0.16 |
| 98 | why | 202 | 0.16 | 98 | again | 86 | 0.16 |
| 99 | Aunt | 201 | 0.16 | 99 | did | 86 | 0.16 |
| 100 | came | 196 | 0.15 | 100 | like | 86 | 0.16 |

　　从上表我们可以看到,前八十回霍克思译本和后四十回闵福德译本中的会话引导语前 100 位高频词差别还是比较明显的。其中有几点差异值得我们关

注和探讨：

霍克思译本会话引导语中的核心动词 said 高居第 2 名，词频为 4150，占总文本的 3.21%；而在闵福德译本会话引导语中 said 仅排在第 11 位，词频 698，仅占总文本的 1.26%。也就是说，闵福德在后四十回的英译中使用了其他方式来代替霍克思青睐的动词 said。我们在闵福德译本会话引导语前 100 位高频词中找到了 replied（词频 338，占总文本的 0.61%）、asked（词频 291，占总文本的 0.53%，是霍译前八十回中比例 0.27%的近 2 倍）、exclaimed（词频 114，占总文本的 0.21%）等动词。

笔者在阅读《红楼梦》后四十回闵福德译文的过程中发现，闵译文还有一大特点，就是直接使用"："来替代会话引导语动词，这一现象可以通过数据来印证。笔者使用 PowerConc 软件搜寻了"："在前八十回霍克思译本和后四十回闵福德译本中的数量，发现差别迥异（见图 3－14）。

| No. | Search Terms | Freq. | File Count | 1.后四十回闵译引导语 | 2.前八十回霍译引导语 |
|---|---|---|---|---|---|
| | Size | 240443 | 2 | 71711 | 168732 |
| | Tokens | 1892 | 2 | 1136 | 756 |
| | Types | 1 | 2 | 1 | 1 |
| 1 | : | 1892 | 2 | 1136 | 756 |

图 3－14 "："在霍译本前八十回和后四十回中使用情况统计

前八十回霍克思译本会话引导语文本总字数为 129 174，其中"："仅出现了 756 次，比例大约为 0.59%；而后四十回闵福德译本会话引导语文本总字数只有 55 221，其中"："却高达 1136 次，比例约为 2.1%，为霍译文比例的 3.6 倍。现列举一些闵译文中使用"："来代替动词的例子：

| | |
|---|---|
| Turning to Bao-yu | : ' Off with you ! |
| Aroma seized her opportunity | : ' Caltrop，did I |
| . She rose to leave | : |
| Dai-yu opened her eyes feebly | : |
| Then she turned to Xi-feng | : |
| Grandmother Jia asked Aunt Xue | : |
| this，Bao-yu chirped up | : |
| . She turned to Xi-feng | : |
| She turned to Lady Wang | : |

| | | |
|---|---|---|
| Jia turned to Lady Wang | : | |
| Xue went up to Dai-yu | : | |
| rapidly kotowed to the bench | : | |
| judge turned to Mrs Zhang | : | ' What further need have |
| Bao-yu was completely carried away | : | ' Oh coz！How |
| Adamantina turned her head | : | ' Who ' s that |
| . Then aloud to Crimson | : | ' You ' d better |
| Bao-yu | : | ' I won ' t |
| Aroma | : | ' Well，you might |
| Bao-yu | : | ' I want to keep |
| Aroma | : | ' It ' s not |

这种非常简洁的会话引导语表达方式是闵译文的重要特色之一。

## 二、独特词对比研究

前八十回霍克思译本会话引导语相对于后四十回闵福德译本中会话引导语的独特词多达 4628 个。笔者筛除了人名、地名用词,将词频在 5 次以上的独特词列举如下,共 220 个:

delightedly(22)
waited(17)
clung(15)
knowing(15)
shout(14)
boys(13)
enjoying(13)
lately(13)
promised(13)
box(12)
coldly(12)
guess(12)
plays(12)
arm(11)
bright(11)
chanced(11)

floor(11)
ha(11)
phoenix(11)
calligraphy(10)
fixed(10)
horse(10)
indoors(10)
jokingly(10)
latter(10)
lots(10)
nine(10)
theme(10)
admiringly(9)
below(9)
detained(9)
draw(9)

gently(9)
giggle(9)
heat(9)
hit(9)
nannies(9)
oz(9)
paused(9)
refuse(9)
shut(9)
sky(9)
understanding(9)
welcome(9)
beaten(8)
bothering(8)
card(8)
chap(8)

coloured(8)

consequence(8)

crab(8)

deprecatingly(8)

ended(8)

everybody(8)

gauze(8)

gentleman(8)

glancing(8)

intervened(8)

leaped(8)

midst(8)

nevertheless(8)

offended(8)

prevented(8)

push(8)

rain(8)

rapid(8)

rhymes(8)

slip(8)

sun(8)

treat(8)

trees(8)

warmly(8)

accepted(7)

apart(7)

approvingly(7)

bamboo(7)

beauty(7)

crabs(7)

genially(7)

hid(7)

horrible(7)

inclined(7)

invitation(7)

jealous(7)

kite(7)

lightning(7)

loss(7)

mistake(7)

mock(7)

mockingly(7)

nicely(7)

obvious(7)

pushed(7)

reassuringly(7)

remembering(7)

sending(7)

share(7)

splendid(7)

string(7)

sympathetically(7)

tear(7)

unfair(7)

venison(7)

basket(6)

blossom(6)

bosom(6)

clumsy(6)

crossly(6)

cure(6)

fan(6)

fly(6)

force(6)

forth(6)

good-humouredly(6)

grandfather(6)

ho(6)

hurt(6)

imploringly(6)

intended(6)

intending(6)

kill(6)

kylin(6)

north(6)

perfect(6)

pills(6)

pinch(6)

planning(6)

poured(6)

rhyme(6)

rocks(6)

ruefully(6)

saucer(6)

scrambled(6)

slap(6)

tael(6)

unfortunately(6)

useless(6)

visitor(6)

wash(6)

whoever(6)

accordingly(5)

alarmed(5)

all-spice(5)

appealed(5)

apricot(5)

assured(5)

astonishment(5)

bearers(5)

believed(5)

blossoms(5)

bottom(5)

boxes(5)

chrysanthemums(5)

collected(5)     huh(5)     pushing(5)

continuing(5)     imagined(5)     raw(5)

creatures(5)     inkstone(5)     remind(5)

dance(5)     innocent(5)     riddles(5)

deceive(5)     insistent(5)     roses(5)

declined(5)     inspected(5)     scrutiny(5)

drenched(5)     lanterns(5)     ship(5)

elsewhere(5)     lively(5)     shoulders(5)

enthusiastic(5)     lower(5)     sickness(5)

examining(5)     malice(5)     sing(5)

exasperatedly(5)     meat(5)     smell(5)

excuses(5)     mistaken(5)     snorted(5)

fastened(5)     nurses(5)     stories(5)

feels(5)     ornaments(5)     surprising(5)

forwards(5)     performance(5)     thinks(5)

frantic(5)     perfume(5)     tiny(5)

glared(5)     plantains(5)     vain(5)

god(5)     plasters(5)     verandah(5)

guest(5)     poetic(5)     weight(5)

halted(5)     practically(5)     winning(5)

happening(5)     principal(5)     wished(5)

happily(5)     protesting(5)

hmn(5)     purse(5)

后四十回闵福德译本中会话引导语相对于前八十回霍克思译本会话引导语的独特词有1742个。笔者筛除了人名、地名用词,词频在5次以上的独特词仅有20个:

Preceptor(12)     bedside(6)     annoyed(5)

clerk(7)     curtly(6)     congee(5)

enquired(7)     gateman(6)     congratulate(5)

excitement(7)     Intendant(6)     farewell(5)

kowtowed(7)     night-duty(6)     poster(5)

mused(7)     whispering(6)     sufficiently(5)

slightest(7)     acknowledgement(5)

我们可以发现在前八十回霍克思译本会话引导语的独特词中包含很多以 -ly 结尾的副词形式，如 delightedly、lately、coldly、jokingly、admiringly、gently、 deprecatingly、 warmly、 approvingly、 genially、 mockingly、reassuringly、 sympathetically、 crossly、 good-humouredly、 imploringly、unfortunately、accordingly、exasperatedly、practically 等。这些副词在闵译本会话引导语中一次都没有出现过。"v＋ing＋ly"形式的副词是霍译本中的特色之一。

## 三、特色词对比研究

前八十回霍克思译本会话引导语相对于后四十回闵福德译本中会话引导语的特色词多达 1196 个。笔者筛除了人名、地名用词，将关键度在 10 以上的特色词列举如下，共 62 个（见表 3 - 20）。

表 3 - 20　霍译本会话引导语相对于闵译本会话引导语的特色词

| 排序 | 词语 | 词频 | 关键度 | 排序 | 词语 | 词频 | 关键度 |
|---|---|---|---|---|---|---|---|
| 1 | said | 4150 | 636.116 | 19 | ought | 73 | 23.843 |
| 2 | got | 236 | 58.688 | 20 | you | 632 | 23.782 |
| 3 | get | 219 | 50.438 | 21 | literary | 42 | 22.726 |
| 4 | laughing | 131 | 44.941 | 22 | pointed | 42 | 22.726 |
| 5 | good | 246 | 38.258 | 23 | gentlemen | 55 | 22.671 |
| 6 | hurriedly | 51 | 36.196 | 24 | woman | 157 | 21.819 |
| 7 | it | 1328 | 34.743 | 25 | about | 493 | 21.755 |
| 8 | that | 1565 | 33.301 | 26 | you | 2147 | 21.432 |
| 9 | smiling | 103 | 32.209 | 27 | some | 284 | 21.236 |
| 10 | her | 1860 | 28.382 | 28 | shouted | 62 | 20.515 |
| 11 | but | 500 | 27.557 | 29 | smilingly | 37 | 19.427 |
| 12 | she | 1638 | 27.433 | 30 | back | 276 | 18.991 |
| 13 | now | 129 | 25.747 | 31 | really | 148 | 18.467 |
| 14 | much | 188 | 25.492 | 32 | Just | 103 | 17.81 |
| 15 | ah | 46 | 25.385 | 33 | laughed | 240 | 17.607 |
| 16 | others | 179 | 24.773 | 34 | give | 89 | 16.75 |
| 17 | wife | 178 | 24.393 | 35 | very | 275 | 16.291 |
| 18 | are | 509 | 24.054 | 36 | people | 90 | 15.531 |

（续表）

| 排序 | 词语 | 词频 | 关键度 | 排序 | 词语 | 词频 | 关键度 |
|---|---|---|---|---|---|---|---|
| 37 | madam | 31 | 15.518 | 50 | person | 54 | 11.766 |
| 38 | delightedly | 21 | 14.904 | 51 | angry | 36 | 11.646 |
| 39 | poem | 41 | 14.444 | 52 | girls | 73 | 11.601 |
| 40 | poetry | 35 | 14.112 | 53 | er | 87 | 11.445 |
| 41 | nice | 34 | 13.515 | 54 | waited | 16 | 11.355 |
| 42 | bit | 109 | 13.129 | 55 | right | 200 | 11.023 |
| 43 | because | 76 | 12.834 | 56 | clung | 15 | 10.646 |
| 44 | girl | 107 | 12.421 | 57 | pleasure | 15 | 10.646 |
| 45 | cousins | 26 | 12.315 | 58 | answer | 34 | 10.556 |
| 46 | so | 441 | 11.931 | 59 | cousin | 34 | 10.556 |
| 47 | doing | 81 | 11.875 | 60 | telling | 34 | 10.556 |
| 48 | they | 531 | 11.86 | 61 | all | 81 | 10.521 |
| 49 | look | 135 | 11.839 | 62 | finger | 23 | 10.426 |

后四十回闵福德译本中会话引导语相对于前八十回霍克思译本会话引导语的特色词有 833 个。笔者筛除了人名、地名用词,将关键度在 10 以上的特色词列举如下,共 100 个(见表 3 - 21)。

表 3 - 21　闵译本会话引导语相对于霍译本会话引导语的特色词

| 排序 | 词语 | 词频 | 关键度 | 排序 | 词语 | 词频 | 关键度 |
|---|---|---|---|---|---|---|---|
| 1 | replied | 338 | 617.506 | 11 | himself | 84 | 41.322 |
| 2 | exclaimed | 114 | 200.82 | 12 | news | 31 | 34.413 |
| 3 | sir | 74 | 95.703 | 13 | continued | 55 | 34.074 |
| 4 | and | 1337 | 76.98 | 14 | apartment | 34 | 32.441 |
| 5 | cried | 72 | 71.693 | 15 | commented | 29 | 30.83 |
| 6 | asked | 291 | 65.941 | 16 | reply | 46 | 30.483 |
| 7 | protested | 52 | 58.624 | 17 | letter | 17 | 29.712 |
| 8 | heard | 123 | 56.255 | 18 | Preceptor | 12 | 28.997 |
| 9 | came | 178 | 51.625 | 19 | retorted | 16 | 27.525 |
| 10 | but | 139 | 49.147 | 20 | family | 60 | 27.199 |

（续表）

| 排序 | 词语 | 词频 | 关键度 | 排序 | 词语 | 词频 | 关键度 |
|---|---|---|---|---|---|---|---|
| 21 | then | 52 | 25.329 | 49 | speaking | 31 | 14.783 |
| 22 | his | 335 | 24.786 | 50 | previous | 10 | 14.77 |
| 23 | he | 178 | 24.258 | 51 | bedside | 6 | 14.499 |
| 24 | returned | 46 | 24.253 | 52 | curtly | 6 | 14.499 |
| 25 | prince | 21 | 24.223 | 53 | gateman | 6 | 14.499 |
| 26 | smile | 106 | 23.207 | 54 | intendant | 6 | 14.499 |
| 27 | informed | 20 | 22.394 | 55 | turning | 6 | 14.499 |
| 28 | school | 21 | 22.261 | 56 | whispering | 6 | 14.499 |
| 29 | honestly | 9 | 21.748 | 57 | promptly | 11 | 14.162 |
| 30 | serving | 16 | 21.486 | 58 | prince | 17 | 13.925 |
| 31 | aloud | 11 | 20.407 | 59 | cases | 8 | 13.762 |
| 32 | deep | 11 | 20.407 | 60 | off | 8 | 13.762 |
| 33 | sobbed | 11 | 20.407 | 61 | hardly | 20 | 13.304 |
| 34 | home | 55 | 18.779 | 62 | most | 39 | 13.126 |
| 35 | judge | 13 | 18.1 | 63 | whispered | 22 | 12.789 |
| 36 | inner | 26 | 17.18 | 64 | seemed | 39 | 12.486 |
| 37 | enquired | 7 | 16.915 | 65 | sobbing | 10 | 12.248 |
| 38 | excitement | 7 | 16.915 | 66 | finally | 20 | 12.195 |
| 39 | kowtowed | 7 | 16.915 | 67 | as | 69 | 12.132 |
| 40 | mused | 7 | 16.915 | 68 | maid | 69 | 12.132 |
| 41 | slightest | 7 | 16.915 | 69 | monk | 23 | 12.126 |
| 42 | such | 68 | 16.898 | 70 | acknowledgement | 5 | 12.082 |
| 43 | inform | 11 | 16.838 | 71 | annoyed | 5 | 12.082 |
| 44 | his | 34 | 16.663 | 72 | clerk | 5 | 12.082 |
| 45 | sister | 12 | 16.114 | 73 | congee | 5 | 12.082 |
| 46 | tears | 34 | 15.802 | 74 | congratulate | 5 | 12.082 |
| 47 | thought | 116 | 15.751 | 75 | farewell | 5 | 12.082 |
| 48 | please | 29 | 15.007 | 76 | ladies | 5 | 12.082 |

(续表)

| 排序 | 词语 | 词频 | 关键度 | 排序 | 词语 | 词频 | 关键度 |
|---|---|---|---|---|---|---|---|
| 77 | poster | 5 | 12.082 | 89 | went | 90 | 11.073 |
| 78 | sufficiently | 5 | 12.082 | 90 | understand | 25 | 11.061 |
| 79 | in | 700 | 12.064 | 91 | tone | 15 | 10.879 |
| 80 | goodness | 11 | 12.022 | 92 | ahead | 19 | 10.861 |
| 81 | spirits | 11 | 12.022 | 93 | staff | 8 | 10.743 |
| 82 | house | 19 | 11.909 | 94 | man | 39 | 10.708 |
| 83 | respects | 18 | 11.632 | 95 | stood | 32 | 10.653 |
| 84 | landscape | 7 | 11.597 | 96 | of | 37 | 10.581 |
| 85 | witness | 7 | 11.597 | 97 | began | 66 | 10.419 |
| 86 | yamen | 7 | 11.597 | 98 | paid | 9 | 10.381 |
| 87 | saying | 44 | 11.338 | 99 | mentioned | 11 | 10.255 |
| 88 | report | 30 | 11.301 | 100 | state | 20 | 10.223 |

said 是前八十回霍克思译本会话引导语相对于后四十回闵福德译本中会话引导语的第一大特色词,关键度高达 636.116,这说明在后四十回闵福德译本中会话引导语中使用了许多其他动词来代替 said。这些动词首推 replied,它是后四十回闵福德译本中会话引导语相对于前八十回霍克思译本会话引导语的第一大特色词,关键度高达 617.506,前八十回霍译本会话引导语中也有 replied 的用法,不过仅有 33 个。

以下是前八十回霍译本使用 replied 的例句:

| | | |
|---:|:---:|:---|
| Do not ask , ' | **replied** | the monk with a laugh |
| worry about him ! ' | **replied** | the monk with a laugh |
| " done", ' | **replied** | the Taoist with a smile |
| went , but Dai-yu smilingly | **replied** | that though it was very |
| deceive Your Honour , ' | **replied** | the usher with a grin |
| , ' the fairy woman | **replied** | . ' I live beyond |
| to see you , ' | **replied** | Grannie Liu mendaciously , ' |
| ' My dear , ' | **replied** | Grannie Liu with a laugh |
| four of them , ' | **replied** | Lady Wang. |
| one of the women attendants | **replied** | for her : |

| The women | **replied** | that it was waiting， |
| very indifferent scholar，' | **replied** | Dr Zhang，' and |
| wife，' Jia Rong | **replied** | . |
| ，' the old woman | **replied** | . |
| puzzling illness，' You-shi | **replied** | . |
| ，' the old woman | **replied** | . |
| they come，' Xi-feng | **replied** | ，' you are still |
| ' too，but Bao-yu | **replied** | that they did not. |
| Jia Lian | **replied** | in the same vein： |
| ，' the literary gentlemen | **replied** | . |
| ornaments，' Cousin Zhen | **replied** | ，' we have already |
| ，Father，' Bao-yu | **replied** | promptly，' but then |
| little nuns，and he | **replied** | as Xi-feng had instructed him |
| She | **replied** | with some bitterness： |
| you are，' she | **replied** | bad-temperedly. |
| The voice in which he | **replied** | to her was broken with |
| Oriole | **replied** | without raising her head from |
| Tell her，' Bao-yu | **replied** | politely，' that as |
| Why not？' she | **replied** | ，a trifle sharply. |
| a somewhat dazed expression and | **replied** | that ' " day" |
| the youth on the bed | **replied** | ： |
| Ladyship，' Jia Bin | **replied** | ，' so she sent |
| was crying weakly as she | **replied** | . |

以下是后四十回闵译本使用 replied 的 50 个例句：

| thought of something，' | **replied** | Bao-yu somewhat unexpectedly.' |
| like that！' he | **replied** | at last，with a |
| Miss Ying，' Dai-yu | **replied** | .' I ' m |
| It was Tan-chun who | **replied** | ： |
| must go first，' | **replied** | Bao-yu.' I insist |
| ' t know，' | **replied** | Musk. |
| ' Tell me，' | **replied** | Grandmother Jia，' can |
| was a voice，' | **replied** | Xi-feng，' that seemed |

| | | |
|---|---|---|
| Ask your aunt，' | **replied** | Grandmother Jia. |
| she was here，' | **replied** | Lady Wang. ' She |
| ' t forget，' | **replied** | Lady Wang. ' We |
| to read Octopartites，' | **replied** | Dai-yu. ' But when |
| ' Go on，' | **replied** | Nightingale. ' Let him |
| ，nothing much，' | **replied** | Aroma pointedly. |
| ' I know，' | **replied** | Bao-yu. ' But I |
| ' Not really，' | **replied** | Dai-yu. ' I suppose |
| s at school，' | **replied** | Aroma，' it ' |
| for Miss Bao-chai，' | **replied** | the woman. ' Something |
| ，Miss Lin，' | **replied** | the old woman，her |
| ，nanny dear，' | **replied** | Aroma. ' And how |
| advantages，' Grandmother Jia | **replied** | . |
| are wrong，' he | **replied** | . ' But if you |
| stay here，' he | **replied** | calmly. |
| want to sleep，' | **replied** | Dai-yu. ' But what |
| ' Sleep ? ' | **replied** | Nightingale cheerfully. ' It |
| you two arrived，' | **replied** | Snowgoose. |
| It was Ebony who | **replied** | : |
| night，Miss，' | **replied** | Kingfisher，' and was |
| ' Quite sure，' | **replied** | Kingfisher. |
| Why not ? ' ? | **replied** | Dai-yu. ' Stop behaving |
| must be thinking，' | **replied** | Doctor Wang with a knowledgeable |
| for a moment，then | **replied** | : |
| the ? Temple，' | **replied** | Mrs Zhou. |
| it particularly funny，' | **replied** | Xi-feng. ' It ' |
| ' None，' | **replied** | Lian. |
| to the College，' | **replied** | Lian，' to see |
| ' Very well，' | **replied** | Grandmother Jia. ' You |
| shakily to her feet and | **replied** | : |
| Your Grace，' she | **replied** | ，and sat down. |
| more seriously now，' | **replied** | Lady Jia. |

| the least idea，ˈ | **replied** | Moonbeam coolly．ˈ If |
| ma ˈ am，ˈ | **replied** | the maid．ˈ Her |
| ˈ Her solicitude，ˈ | **replied** | Jia Zheng with a sarcastic |
| me，Mother，ˈ | **replied** | Jia Zheng rather stiffly． |
| your decision！ˈ she | **replied** | testily，ˈ and that |
| have，sir，ˈ | **replied** | Bao-yu．ˈ I have |
| ，Book Two，ˈ | **replied** | Bao-yu．ˈ " Annos |
| ˈ s application，ˈ | **replied** | Bao-yu，ˈ is a |
| ˈ Good，ˈ | **replied** | Jia Zheng．ˈ I |
| is all right，ˈ | **replied** | Grandmother Jia．ˈ She |

后四十回闵福德译本中会话引导语相对于前八十回霍克思译本会话引导语的第二大特色词是 exclaimed，关键度为 200.82。该词在前八十回霍译本会话引导语中仅有 13 个。我们先来查阅几部权威词典对于 exclaim 的解释：

（1）《牛津高阶英语词典》（第 6 版）（*Oxford Advanced Learnerˈs Dictionary*）：（*written*）*to say sth suddenly and loudly，especially because of strong emotion or pain*。

（2）《朗文当代英语词典》（第 4 版）（*Longman Dictionary of Contemporary English*）：*to say something suddenly and loudly because you are surprised，angry，or excited*。

（3）《柯林斯高阶英语词典》（*Collins COBUILD Advanced Learnerˈs English Dictionary*）：*Writers sometimes use exclaim to show that someone is speaking suddenly，loudly，or emphatically，often because they are excited，shocked，or angry*.

（4）《美国传统词典》（双解）（*E-C American Heritage Dictionary*）：① *vi*. 不及物动词：*to cry out suddenly or vehemently，as from surprise or emotion*：喊叫：由于惊奇或激动而突然或强烈地喊叫。*vt*. 及物动词：*to express or utter（something）suddenly or vehemently*：大声地说出：突然或强烈地表达或说出。

（5）《牛津高阶英汉双解词典》（*Oxford Advanced Learnerˈs English-Chinese Dictionary*）：*cry out suddenly and loudly from pain，anger，surprise，etc*（因疼痛、愤怒、惊奇等）惊叫，呼喊。

通过以上几部权威词典的释义，我们可以推断 exclaim 表达的是"（由于激动、震惊、愤怒等）突然呼喊，惊叫，大声喊"之意。下面笔者就该词在前八十回霍克思译本会话引导语和后四十回闵福德译本中会话引导语中的用法各举几个例子。

以下为前八十回霍译本的例句,共 13 个:

| ˈ No wonder！ˈ | **exclaimed** | Xi-feng when she had heard |
|---|---|---|
| Zhou Rui ˈ s wife | **exclaimed** | . |
| for you ！" he | **exclaimed** | , enfolding his beloved in |
| ！ˈ the literary gentlemen | **exclaimed** | . |
| ！ˈ the literary gentlemen | **exclaimed** | . |
| What magnificent blossom ！ˈ | **exclaimed** | the literary gentle ? men |
| ˈ Well ！ˈ | **exclaimed** | the literary gentlemen. |
| how beautiful ！ˈ she | **exclaimed** | . |
| Lord Buddha ！ˈ she | **exclaimed** | . |
| ˈ Shocking ！ˈ | **exclaimed** | the others. |
| bed yet ? ˈ she | **exclaimed** | , stepping nimbly into the |
| gracious me ！ˈ she | **exclaimed** | sarcastically. ˈ What swooning |
| ˈ How priceless ！ˈ | **exclaimed** | the literary gentlemen rapturously |

以下为后四十回闵译本中的 50 个例句:

| My dear child ！ˈ | **exclaimed** | Lady Wang , her voice |
|---|---|---|
| ˈ You see ！ˈ | **exclaimed** | Grandmother Jia , turning to |
| That settles it ！ˈ | **exclaimed** | the old lady. |
| definitely her doing ！ˈ | **exclaimed** | Xi-feng. |
| " Goodness ！ˈ | **exclaimed** | Bao-yu. ˈ I can |
| of your senses ? ˈ | **exclaimed** | Tan-chun severely. |
| wonder ！ˈ ? she | **exclaimed** | . ˈ Kingfisher said something |
| of the question ！ˈ | **exclaimed** | Grandmother Jia. |
| dare come home ！ˈ | **exclaimed** | the maid. |
| You silly boy ！ˈ | **exclaimed** | Grandmother Jia. |
| ˈ Honestly ！ˈ | **exclaimed** | Aroma. ˈ The pair |
| ˈ Hear that ！ˈ | **exclaimed** | Jia Yun. ˈ Now |
| ˈ Of course ！ˈ | **exclaimed** | Lady Wang. ˈ It |
| ˈ Really ? ˈ | **exclaimed** | Aunt Xue , rising to |
| ˈ Foolish woman ！ˈ | **exclaimed** | the judge. |
| hardly finished when Xue Ke | **exclaimed** | : |
| ˈ Goodness ！ˈ | **exclaimed** | Bao-yu , aroused by the |

| | | |
|---|---|---|
| of me！'he | **exclaimed** | with a laugh.' |
| 'Aiyo！' | **exclaimed** | Xi-chun.' You had |
| saying a word？' | **exclaimed** | Xi-chun. |
| 'Of course！' | **exclaimed** | one of the others， |
| 's sake！' | **exclaimed** | Grandmother Jia. |
| bit of fruit！' | **exclaimed** | Cousin Zhen.' It |
| is the limit！' | **exclaimed** | Cousin Zhen. |
| 'Of course！' | **exclaimed** | Bao-yu. |
| for nothing！'she | **exclaimed** | . |
| 'sake！'she | **exclaimed** | . |
| and Snowgoose | **exclaimed** | : |
| ，coz！'he | **exclaimed** | ， |
| Of course！'he | **exclaimed** | with a laugh.' |
| What a story！' | **exclaimed** | Xi-feng，aghast at this |
| 'Amazing！' | **exclaimed** | Zhan Guang. |
| state of affairs！' | **exclaimed** | Jia Lian. |
| Lian read the poster and | **exclaimed** | : |
| a disgraceful business！' | **exclaimed** | Lady Wang in horror. |
| complete surprise to Faithful who | **exclaimed** | :'That's |
| 'Aiyo！'she | **exclaimed** | . |
| sounds pretty good！' | **exclaimed** | Li Wan. |
| 'Merciful Buddha！' | **exclaimed** | Grandmother Jia. |
| My dear boy！' | **exclaimed** | Grandmother Jia.' I |
| 'No！' | **exclaimed** | Lady Wang，aghast. |
| ，you two！' | **exclaimed** | Grandmother Jia.' Let |
| 'Of course！' | **exclaimed** | Dai-yu. |
| were nearly there，Nightingale | **exclaimed** | :'Lord Buddha be |
| a terrible thing！' | **exclaimed** | Grandmother Jia，aghast. |
| How odd！'he | **exclaimed** | . |
| 'You monkey！' | **exclaimed** | Grandmother Jia. |
| 'Good heavens！' | **exclaimed** | Jia Zheng in some alarm |
| listen to that！' | **exclaimed** | Xi-feng. |
| for a moment，then | **exclaimed** | : |

185

## 四、与 smile 和 laugh 相关搭配对比

笔者将 laughing、smiling、with a smile、with a laugh 和 smilingly 放在同一个文本中,在前八十回霍克思译本会话引导语和后四十回闵福德译本中会话引导语中进行 batch search,得到如图 3－15 所示结果:

| No. | Search Terms | Freq. | File Count | 1. 后四十回闵译引导语 | 2. 前八十回霍译引导语 |
|---|---|---|---|---|---|
| | Size | 240443 | 2 | 71711 | 168732 |
| | Tokens | 412 | 2 | 61 | 351 |
| | Types | 5 | 2 | 5 | 5 |
| 1 | laughing | 139 | 2 | 8 | 131 |
| 2 | smiling | 112 | 2 | 9 | 103 |
| 3 | with a smile | 83 | 2 | 36 | 47 |
| 4 | with a laugh | 40 | 2 | 7 | 33 |
| 5 | smilingly | 38 | 2 | 1 | 37 |

图 3－15 laughing 等词在霍译本会话引导语及闵译本会话引导语中的词频统计

我们可以看到,smilingly 一词在霍译引导语文本和闵译引导语文本中的差异最为显著:闵译文本中仅出现了 1 次,而霍译文本中有 37 次,是闵译文本的 37 倍。

以下是闵译本中的 1 个例句:

seemed unperturbed，and announced **smilingly** ：'Gentlemen，please

以下是霍译本中的例句:

| | | |
|---|---|---|
| she went，but Dai-yu | **smilingly** | replied that though it was |
| wife of Jia Rong， | **smilingly** | proposed an alternative. |
| of withdrawing when Aunt Xue | **smilingly** | enjoined her to stay. |
| yours，'she said | **smilingly** | ，'but I have |
| ，'he said， | **smilingly** | and softly，'I |
| her hair into place， | **smilingly** | complacently ： |
| on them and reproved them | **smilingly** | for abandoning her：' |
| going back again when Aroma | **smilingly** | detained her： |
| ?'she asked him | **smilingly** | . |
| time ripe to entreat her | **smilingly** | for his lunch.' |
| was done，Xi-feng turned | **smilingly** | to Silver and congratulated her |

|  |  |  |
|---|---|---|
| She turned， | **smilingly** | ，to Bao-yu and pointed |
| Grandmother Jia | **smilingly** | pointed a finger in Xi-chun |
| ！'said Aunt Xue | **smilingly** | when all were seated once |
| Lian had gone，she | **smilingly** | inquired after her injuries. |
| Xi-feng | **smilingly** | inquired of Lai Da ' |
| club，'said Tan-chun | **smilingly** | . |
| this request，nevertheless she | **smilingly** | promised that she would do |
| over its disappearance when Xi-feng | **smilingly** | put an end to the |
| Li Qi acknowledged | **smilingly** | that this was correct. |
| They protested | **smilingly** | and begged him to go |
| front of him，peered | **smilingly** | into his face. ' |
| with these ? 'Oriole | **smilingly** | asked her companion. |
| daughter Swallow walked up and | **smilingly** | asked her what she was |
| You-shi and Li Wan | **smilingly** | confirmed the invitation. |
| ，she pressed it， | **smilingly** | ，into Cook Liu ' |
| said Bao-yu. He pointed | **smilingly** | at Aroma：' She |
| me，'said Dai-yu | **smilingly** | . ' I can ' |
| say to him，turned | **smilingly** | towards her，holding up |
| senior of the servants now | **smilingly** | addressed Xi-feng on her mistress |
| Jia Lian looked down | **smilingly** | and reflected，then clapped |
| stupid，'she said | **smilingly** | . |
| that ? 'she asked | **smilingly** | . |
| Huan as a reward and | **smilingly** | patted him on the head |
| sitting in the room， | **smilingly** | intervened. |
| 'said the literary gentlemen | **smilingly** | . |
| Bao-chai | **smilingly** | expostulated. ' People like |

其次两个文本中数量差别最大的当属 laughing,闵译文本中只有 8 个,而霍译文本中多达 131 个,数量是闵译文本的 16 倍多。现举例如下：

闵译文本中的 8 个例句为：

|  |  |  |
|---|---|---|
| great joke，and started | **laughing** | and calling Grandmother Jia a |
| queer effect on you， | **laughing** | one minute，crying your |
| This had everyone | **laughing** | ，and it was proposed |

| | | |
|---:|:---:|:---|
| Then suddenly he burst out | **laughing** | and cried： |
| Tealeaf started | **laughing** | and clapping his hands. |
| ' said Aunt Xue， | **laughing** | in spite of herself， |
| ？' said Grannie Liu | **laughing** | . |
| ' they all cried， | **laughing** | nervously. |

以下是霍译文本中的例句：

| | | |
|---:|:---:|:---|
| stood on their desks， | **laughing** | and clapping their hands and |
| ，' said Dai-yu， | **laughing** | weakly，' I promise |
| Dai-yu burst out | **laughing** | ：' Lisping doesn ' |
| they all instantaneously burst out | **laughing** | ，so striking was the |
| talk！' said Bao-yu | **laughing** | .' Listen to you |
| ！' said Jia Lian | **laughing** | . |
| A | **laughing** | voice addressed him from behind |
| ' I wasn ' t | **laughing** | because of that，madam |
| want，' said Bao-yu | **laughing** | ，' it ' s |
| ' What are you | **laughing** | at ？' said Xue |
| he caught sight of Xi-feng | **laughing** | at him mockingly. ' |
| ' said Abbot Zhang， | **laughing** | ，' but it wasn |
| Xiang-yun was unable to avoid | **laughing** | at the girl ' s |
| ？' they said， | **laughing** | . |
| ' she asked her， | **laughing** | . |
| Grannie！' said Xi-feng | **laughing** | . |
| them got up，still | **laughing** | ，when they saw Silver |
| ' Flowers ' Aroma， | **laughing** | in spite of herself， |
| ！' said Xiang-yun， | **laughing** | .' You should be |
| so that I am always | **laughing** | ，' said Grandmother Jia |
| ，' said Amber， | **laughing** | ，' I wouldn ' |
| ' she said，both | **laughing** | and indignant. ' I |
| ，' said Patience， | **laughing** | .' She ' s |
| ，' said Patience， | **laughing** | ，' and what will |
| ' said Grandmother Jia， | **laughing** | in spite of herself. |
| up unaided，and was | **laughing** | herself. ' It serves |

| | | |
|---|---|---|
| for her niece，while | **laughing** | with the rest at her |
| ＇said Lady Wang， | **laughing** | . |
| unfair！＇said Tan-chun | **laughing** | . |
| ！＇said Xi-feng， | **laughing** | ， |
| ＇said Aunt Xue， | **laughing** | . |
| ＇said the others， | **laughing** | . |
| ＇said the others， | **laughing** | . |
| Yes，＇they said | **laughing** | .＇And it＇ |
| The others，still | **laughing** | ，shouted at her to |
| ！＇she said， | **laughing** | .＇The girl＇ |
| The others，still | **laughing** | ，assured Bao-chai that she |
| Dai-yu continued， | **laughing** | so much herself that she |
| ！＇they said， | **laughing** | .＇How pitifully she |
| Dai-yu rose to her feet | **laughing** | .＇That＇s |
| ＇said Grandmother Jia， | **laughing** | herself.＇Then what |
| ，＇said Bao-yu， | **laughing** | . |
| ＇said Grandmother Jia， | **laughing** | . |
| ＇said Jia Lian， | **laughing** | himself. |
| ＇said Li Wan， | **laughing** | . |
| ＇said the others， | **laughing** | .＇The very thing |
| Da＇s wife， | **laughing** | . |
| you，＇said Dai-yu | **laughing** | . |
| Aroma emerged， | **laughing** | ，as they did so |
| ＇said Grandmother Jia， | **laughing** | .＇So it＇ |

  smiling 一词差异也很大,闵译文本中只有 9 个,而霍译文本中有 103 个,数量是闵译文本的 11 倍多。

  闵译文本中的 9 个例句为:

| | | |
|---|---|---|
| Aroma could not help | **smiling** | :＇Musky dear， |
| ，＇said Dai-yu， | **smiling** | .＇Talking about music |
| ，＇confessed Bao-yu， | **smiling** | rather sheepishly.＇Please |
| Still | **smiling** | she said :＇Four |

|  | | |
|---|---|---|
| ，'replied Nightingale， | **smiling** | anxiously. |
| Still | **smiling** | ，Dai-yu allowed herself to |
| ?'said Xi-feng， | **smiling** | uneasily. |
| protested，blushing again and | **smiling** | coyly.'How can |
| Women（ | **smiling** | obsequiously now and pleading） |

以下是霍译文本中的例句：

|  | | |
|---|---|---|
| ，'said Yu-cun， | smiling | at the recollection，' |
| feet and came forward with | smiling | faces to welcome them. |
| finish her tea，a | smiling | maid came in wearing a |
| off to begin school was | smiling | but perfunctory：'Good |
| ，'said Xi-feng， | smiling | delightedly.'You really |
| ，and admonished her with | smiling | briskness：'Now， |
| behind her shoulder — the | smiling | peacemaker： |
| you?'said Aroma | smiling | . |
| ，'said Xi-feng， | smiling | rather spite?fully. |
| She tried again， | smiling | breezily： |
| to enjoy themselves and， | smiling | forcedly，appealed against his |
| ，'said Bao-yu， | smiling | at her.'Here |
| ?'said Dai-yu， | smiling | up at Bao-yu as she |
| up to her with a | smiling | face：'What can |
| A | smiling | Bao-yu appeared in the gateway |
| ，'said Bao-yu， | smiling | at her concern.' |
| ，'she said， | smiling | pleasantly，'there' |
| next morning to find Bao-yu | smiling | down at her： |
| But now here was Bao-yu | smiling | at her with sudden interest |
| Zhang at his elbow， | smiling | somewhat unnaturally.'Perhaps |
| He was followed by the | smiling | figure of the abbot， |
| hands in his own， | smiling | at her gently.' |
| The | smiling | answer she gave to Dai-yu |
| but Aroma， | smiling | through her tears，caught |
| back on the bed， | smiling | complacently.'I' |
| 'said Aunt Xue， | smiling | back，whereupon Xi-feng proceeded |

| | | |
|---:|:---:|:---|
| rolling her sleeves back and | **smiling** | at no one in particular |
| ！' he said， | **smiling** | broadly at her. |
| ' said Jia Qiang， | **smiling** | proudly. ' It can |
| me，' said Aroma | **smiling** | . ' I wouldn ' |
| ，' said Xiang-yun， | **smiling** | mis ? chievously，' |
| ，' said Tealeaf， | **smiling** | broadly，' but you |
| ！' said Xi-feng， | **smiling** | . ' These cups have |
| said Grandmother Jia，in | **smiling** | approval of what she saw |
| ，' he said， | **smiling** | demurely，but still not |
| ，' said Tealeaf， | **smiling** | at the na ? veté |
| Patience ' s face was | **smiling** | as she thanked her， |
| Bao-yu，who stood by | **smiling** | while she washed，now |
| ，' said Bao-chai， | **smiling** | . |
| ，' said Dai-yu， | **smiling** | . ' I should have |
| Jia Lian walked | **smiling** | into the room. ' |
| ，lurched towards him， | **smiling** | happily，and gripped him |
| ，she came forward， | **smiling** | herself，and handed the |
| words been uttered when a | **smiling** | Tan-chun came in looking for |
| ' said Li Wan， | **smiling** | ，' but we can |
| ，' said Musk， | **smiling** | . |
| ，' said Xi-feng， | **smiling** | . ' Surely you can |
| ，' she said， | **smiling** | gratefully. |
| said the blind woman， | **smiling** | . |
| Lady Wang rose， | **smiling** | ，to her feet ： |

with a smile 的使用数量在闵译文本和霍译文本中差异不大，分别是 36 和 47，但如果按照文本容量来算，则该短语在闵译文本中的百分比更高。

以下是闵译本中的例句：

| | | |
|---:|:---:|:---|
| you ? ' said Nightingale | **with a smile** | . ' All I meant |
| and her face lit up | **with a smile** | . |
| ，' said Grandmother Jia | **with a smile** | . |
| ，' said Aunt Xue | **with a smile** | ，' perhaps I shouldn |
| flowers，and greeted her | **with a smile** | ： |

| | | |
|---|---|---|
| , where Dai-ru greeted him | **with a smile** | : ' I have just |
| , halting by his side | **with a smile** | . ' I was on |
| . He turned to Dai-yu | **with a smile** | and said : ' Are |
| account , ' murmured Dai-yu | **with a smile** | . |
| in the room , inquired | **with a smile** | : ' To what are |
| right , ' she said | **with a smile** | . |
| Sister ! ' he said | **with a smile** | . ' Wherefore this rare |
| too ? ' asked Xi-chun | **with a smile** | . |
| | **With a smile** | Jia Yun advanced with her |
| Patience came in and said | **with a smile** | : |
| Yes , ' replied Aroma | **with a smile** | . ' I thought that |
| Bao , ' she said | **with a smile** | . |
| coz ? ' he inquired | **with a smile** | . |
| me , ' he replied | **with a smile** | . |
| Grandmother Jia said to Xi-feng | **with a smile** | : ' You shouldn ' |
| importance , ' replied Xiu-yan | **with a smile** | . ' Just an old |
| He turned | **with a smile** | to Grandmother Jia. |
| Jia Zheng ( | **with a smile** | ) : ' If that |
| right , ' she said | **with a smile** | . |
| change tack , and said | **with a smile** | : |
| Grandmother Jia finally said | **with a smile** | : ' Why not ? |
| Oh ! ' said Dai-yu | **with a smile** | . ' I thought you |
| home ? ' asked Dai-yu | **with a smile** | . |
| this moment , and inquired | **with a smile** | . |
| me , ' countered Xi-feng | **with a smile** | . ' It was Bao-yu |
| Li ( | **with a smile** | ) : ' That ' |
| rose and said to Bao-chai | **with a smile** | : |
| ' s side and added | **with a smile** | . |
| t ! ' said Aroma | **with a smile** | . |
| to her next and asked | **with a smile** | : |
| ! ' Bao-chai chided him | **with a smile** | . |

以下是霍译本中的例句：

| | | |
|---:|:---:|:---|
| his hand and addressed it | **with a smile** | : |
| , ' replied the Taoist | **with a smile** | , ' you may be |
| , ' said the usher | **with a smile** | . |
| hurried forward and saluted her | **with a smile** | . ' Madam Fairy , |
| province , ' said Disenchantment | **with a smile** | , |
| said Grannie Liu , advancing | **with a smile** | . |
| down , ' said Xi-feng | **with a smile** | . ' I have something |
| brush , turned towards her | **with a smile** | , |
| Zhou Rui ' s wife | **with a smile** | , ' Mrs Xue asked |
| along ! ' said Bao-yu | **with a smile** | , |
| Bao ! ' said Bao-chai | **with a smile** | . |
| feel , she answered him | **with a smile** | . ' I can see |
| one of the old women | **with a smile** | , when they caught sight |
| pair ! ' said You-shi | **with a smile** | . ' Once the two |
| ! ' said Lady Xing | **with a smile** | , |
| Cousin Zhen turned to her | **with a smile** | . ' Actually there isn |
| necessary , ' said Xi-feng | **with a smile** | . |
| now , ' said Xi-feng | **with a smile** | . ' I thought you |
| Xi-feng turned to Bao-yu | **with a smile** | : |
| , ' said Jia Zheng | **with a smile** | . ' But just imagine |
| He turned to Cousin Zhen | **with a smile** | : |
| There ! ' she said | **with a smile** | to the girls. ' |
| ' she said to Bao-yu | **with a smile** | . ' we can ' |
| either , ' said Bao-yu | **with a smile** | . ' I ' ve |
| something when Aroma cut in | **with a smile** | : |
| Glancing up | **with a smile** | from his peeling he said |
| for ? ' she said | **with a smile** | . |
| , he thanked Ni Er | **with a smile** | : |
| Yun hurried up to her | **with a smile** | of greeting : |
| She handed him his tea | **with a smile** | : |
| Li Wan observed to Bao-chai | **with a smile** | : |
| , and masked her emotion | **with a smile** | : ' That ' s |

| | | |
|---|---|---|
| up in front of her | **with a smile** | ：'I'll |
| , turning back to her | **with a smile** | . |
| he tossed them towards her | **with a smile** | . |
| Aunt Xue greeted her daughter | **with a smile** | of surprise.'You |
| girl ,'said Xi-feng | **with a smile** | . |
| Grandmother Jia now turned | **with a smile** | to Aunt Xue. |
| t ,'said Adanantina | **with a smile** | . |
| advice ,'he said | **with a smile** | . |
| Li Wan greeted them | **with a smile** | . |
| ,'said Lady Wang | **with a smile** | . |
| looked up at Grandmother Jia | **with a smile** | . |
| past ,'said Bao-chai | **with a smile** | ,'but you haven |
| yourself ,'he said | **with a smile** | to Skybright as he came |
| and two aunts before turning | **with a smile** | to Jia Lian ：' |
| dread , she masked it | **with a smile** | and nodded approvingly at his |

with a laugh 在闵译文本和霍译文本中均使用得不多,但两者差异较大,闵译文本中仅有 7 个,而霍译文本中有 33 个,是闵译文本的将近 5 倍。

闵译文本中的 7 个例句为:

| | | |
|---|---|---|
| !'Bao-yu chided them | **with a laugh** | .'Stop being so |
| me !'he exclaimed | **with a laugh** | .'I was so |
| course !'he exclaimed | **with a laugh** | .'That's |
| idea ,'said Zhan | **with a laugh** | |
| course ,'said Xi-feng | **with a laugh** | |
| game ,'she replied | **with a laugh** | ,'we'll |
| !'cried the messenger | **with a laugh** | , and rushed out to |

以下是霍译文本中的例句:

| | | |
|---|---|---|
| ,'replied the monk | **with a laugh** | . |
| !'replied the monk | **with a laugh** | . |
| Yu-cun clapped his hands | **with a laugh** | . |
| you ,'said Qin-shi | **with a laugh** | ,'where are we |
| album shut , she said | **with a laugh** | , |
| ,'replied Grannie Liu | **with a laugh** | , |

| | | |
|---|---|---|
| no ！' said Bao-chai | with a laugh | . |
| ' she said to Bao-yu | with a laugh | , nudging him playfully. |
| Pill ？' said Bao-yu | with a laugh | . ' Won ' t |
| ！' said Aunt Xue | with a laugh | . ' Have a drink |
| that ！' said Bao-yu | with a laugh | . |
| not ！' said Aroma | with a laugh | . |
| are ，' said You-shi | with a laugh | . |
| food ？' said Xi-feng | with a laugh | . （ She was halfway |
| ！' said Cousin Zhen | with a laugh | . ' Let me show |
| dear ！' he said | with a laugh | . ' Have mercy on |
| bit ？' said Bao-yu | with a laugh | . ' For eight bearers |
| season ？' said Dai-yu | with a laugh | . ' I ' m |
| accepted Dai-yu ' s condition | with a laugh | : |
| liar ！' said Xi-feng | with a laugh | . |
| Silly ！' said Aroma | with a laugh | . ' Don ' t |
| turned over and sat up | with a laugh | : |
| when Li Wan interrupted her | with a laugh | : ' What an extraordinary |
| ？' said Feng Zi-ying | with a laugh | . |
| attempted to pass it off | with a laugh | . ' I ' ll |
| treasure ，' she said | with a laugh | . ' I won ' |
| chrysanthemums ，' said Bao-chai | with a laugh | . |
| Faithful took up the cards | with a laugh | . |
| She shut the box hurriedly | with a laugh | . ' Goodness ，how |
| Zhen turned to Jia Rong | with a laugh | . ' You heard that |
| breaking away from the others | with a laugh | and hurrying after her. |
| Patience remembered | with a laugh | . ' Oh ，that |
| ，but presently gave up | with a laugh | . ' It ' s |

　　基于"《红楼梦》汉英双语平行语料库"中提取的会话引导语语料 A 版本，本章节主要对霍译本和杨译本这两部优秀全译本中的会话引导语进行数据统计和特色分析，研究层面包括：将两部译本的会话引导语文本分别与其非会话引导语文本进行对比、将两部译本的会话引导语文本分别与原版英文小说中的

会话引导语进行对比、将两部译本的会话引导语进行详细对比、将霍译本中前八十回与后四十回会话引导语进行对比等。

笔者在本章的对比研究中发现，不仅杨译本和霍译本这两部分别由中西方译者创作的译本语言风格差异显著，就连霍译本中两位西方译者的风格也不尽相同、各具特色，这源于不同的译者文化身份以及译者主体性的发挥。在整个翻译过程中，译者处于核心地位，译者主体性体现在翻译过程的各个阶段，从对原文的解读，到使用译文对原文进行阐释和再创造。译者的意识形态、时代背景、社会文化、翻译思想、审美取向、语言风格等多个方面贯穿翻译过程始终。由于译者所处的国家、文化、民族的不同，译者对社会意识形态和价值理念的不同理解、对翻译思想的不同领悟、对翻译策略的不同选择，以及对原语和译入语的不同掌握，使得译者风格表现出显著的差异。

至此，笔者完成了对于《红楼梦》会话引导语原文及译文的解读和分析。在接下来的研究中，笔者将把这两方面的研究结果有机结合起来，进行有关《红楼梦》会话引导语翻译问题的探讨。

# 第四章 《红楼梦》会话引导语翻译研究

自 20 世纪 70 年代《红楼梦》霍、杨两部译本先后推出以来，国内外许多学者从不同层面、多个学科视角对这两个英译本展开了研究，形成了一股不亚于"红学"研究的英译研究热潮。40 余年来，译界对两部译本的评价似乎也趋于共识，学者们普遍认为杨译本更加忠实于原文文本，多采用异化的翻译策略，更加完整地保留了中国文化的信息，而霍译本更多地忠实于译文读者，多采用归化的翻译策略，为便于以英语为母语的读者理解译文对许多中国文化进行了改写，在语言及艺术上的再创造方面更胜一筹。

本章笔者将在前期对于《红楼梦》原文以及译文中会话引导语研究的基础上，着重分析研究《红楼梦》会话引导语的翻译问题。为便于研究的开展，笔者先将《红楼梦》会话引导语划分为几个大的类别分别进行分析。《红楼梦》会话引导语的数量众多、形式复杂，仅以"道："结尾的会话引导语就能分出 75 个以上条目，如：

| | | |
|---|---|---|
| 道：(9198) | 劝道：(48) | 喜道：(4) |
| 笑道：(2407) | 都道：(52) | 央道：(4) |
| 冷笑道：(110) | 答道：(31) | 止道：(3) |
| 说道：(970) | 叫道：(36) | 求道：(4) |
| 问道：(301) | 啐道：(35) | 赞道：(4) |
| 回道：(126) | 嚷道：(24) | 乃道：(1) |
| 便道：(109) | 应道：(22) | 也道：(6) |
| 又道：(101) | 喝道：(15) | 启道：(7) |
| 忙道：(82) | 禀道：(10) | 奏道：(4) |
| 叹道：(77) | 喊道：(8) | 怒道：(4) |
| 想道：(68) | 思道：(5) | 恨道：(5) |
| 哭道：(50) | 因道：(11) | 点头道：(30) |
| 骂道：(48) | 泣道：(2) | 诧异道：(19) |

| | | |
|---|---|---|
| 吩咐道：(13) | 吃惊道：(4) | XX 道（纯粹）(3287) |
| 听了道：(19) | 商议道：(4) | 向/对 XX 道：(167) |
| 起来道：(14) | 嘱咐道：(7) | 问 XX 道：(73) |
| 拍手道：(11) | 抱怨道：(4) | 回 XX 道：(20) |
| 接口道：(12) | 拦住道：(9) | 回头……道：(16) |
| 央告道：(7) | 起身道：(5) | 嘱咐/吩咐 XX 道：(16) |
| 笑着道：(13) | 跺脚道：(4) | 拉 XX 道：(29) |
| 喜欢道：(7) | 叹口气道：(7) | 推 XX 道：(11) |
| 摇头道：(8) | 悄悄的道：(8) | 告诉 XX 道：(18) |
| 着急道：(7) | 叹了一口气道：(15) | 报道：(4) |
| 回头道：(5) | 接口道：(12) | 叫 XX 道：(9) |
| 正色道：(6) | 啐了一口道：(5) | 谢道：(6) |

鉴于篇幅有限，也考虑到研究的精确度，笔者在参考前期关于《红楼梦》原文及译文中会话引导语的高频字、常用搭配、独特字和特色字分析的基础上，将《红楼梦》会话引导语的翻译研究锁定在以下几个大的类别进行："说道"类、"笑道"类、"哭道"类、"骂道"类和"啐道"类。这几个类别都是《红楼梦》会话引导语中所占比例最高、最具典型和代表性的。

## 第一节　"说道"类会话引导语翻译研究

"说道"类会话引导语研究主要包括三大类别："XX 道：""XX 说："和"说道："。这三大类引导语表达的意思一致，无论是以单字还是双字形式出现，都只表达单纯的"说"之意。

### 一、《红楼梦》原文中的"说道"类会话引导语

笔者在第三章《红楼梦》原文会话引导语研究中曾统计过，会话引导语"道："作为一级检索时的数量是非常多的，有 9198 个。为了确保研究的精确度，笔者经过层层筛选、逐个排查，最终得到了一个纯粹的会话引导语"XX 道："文本，数量为 3287 个。该文本以纯粹的"人名（或代词）＋道："的形式出现，中间无任何标点或修饰成分。

同样地，会话引导语"说："作为一级检索时的数量也很多，有 1769 个。笔者最终筛选出了一个纯粹的会话引导语"XX 说："文本，数量为 181 个。该文本以纯粹的"人名（或代词）＋说："的形式出现，中间无任何标点或修饰成分，其中包括"有的说："，但是筛除了引经据典里的"说："，如"《古今人物通考》上说："

"古诗上说:"等形式。

"说道:"虽是二字词语,却表达的仅仅是"说:"或者"道:"之意。笔者将"说道:"作为一级检索时得到了960个结果,筛除"笑说道:"等形式后得到了921个纯粹的"说道:"形式。

因此,"说道"类会话引导语主要考察的种类和数量如表4-1所示。

表4-1 "说道"类会话引导语种类、数量统计

| 序号 | 种类 | 数量 |
|---|---|---|
| 1 | XX道: | 3287 |
| 2 | XX说: | 181 |
| 3 | 说道: | 921 |

笔者将"XX道:""XX说:"和"说道:"三个会话引导语文本合并成一个总的"说道"类文本(总数量为4389)统一进行研究。这个总的文本同时包括原文和译文的内容,是一个"原文—霍译—杨译"的"说道"类会话引导语平行语料库。笔者在此语料库的基础上分别整理出"说道"类会话引导语的原文、霍译本、杨译本文档,以供研究之用。其中"说道"类会话引导语的霍译本(或简称霍译文本)容量为61 551,"说道"类会话引导语的杨译本(或简称杨译文本)容量为46 786。

## 二、《红楼梦》译文中的"说道"类会话引导语

笔者将对《红楼梦》"说道"类会话引导语的霍译本和杨译本进行高频词、独特词以及特色词等方面的分析研究。

### (一)霍译本与杨译本高频词研究

笔者通过分别对《红楼梦》"说道"类会话引导语的霍译本和杨译本进行词频分析,将位列前100位的高频词列举如表4-2所示。

表4-2 "说道"类会话引导语霍译本和杨译本高频词对比

| 霍译 | 词语 | 词频 | 百分比 | 杨译 | 词语 | 词频 | 百分比 |
|---|---|---|---|---|---|---|---|
| 1 | said | 2288 | 3.72 | 1 | the | 1598 | 3.42 |
| 2 | the | 2046 | 3.32 | 2 | to | 1135 | 2.43 |
| 3 | to | 1663 | 2.70 | 3 | you | 1112 | 2.38 |
| 4 | you | 1411 | 2.29 | 4 | I | 998 | 2.13 |
| 5 | I | 1392 | 2.26 | 5 | said | 739 | 1.58 |

（续表）

| 霍译 | 词语 | 词频 | 百分比 | 杨译 | 词语 | 词频 | 百分比 |
|---|---|---|---|---|---|---|---|
| 6 | and | 1033 | 1.68 | 6 | and | 699 | 1.49 |
| 7 | a | 1012 | 1.64 | 7 | she | 663 | 1.42 |
| 8 | of | 999 | 1.62 | 8 | a | 659 | 1.41 |
| 9 | it | 936 | 1.52 | 9 | it | 646 | 1.38 |
| 10 | that | 855 | 1.39 | 10 | that | 623 | 1.33 |
| 11 | she | 703 | 1.14 | 11 | of | 561 | 1.20 |
| 12 | in | 649 | 1.05 | 12 | in | 523 | 1.12 |
| 13 | Jia | 626 | 1.02 | 13 | he | 520 | 1.11 |
| 14 | her | 623 | 1.01 | 14 | her | 474 | 1.01 |
| 15 | was | 504 | 0.82 | 15 | was | 353 | 0.75 |
| 16 | he | 467 | 0.76 | 16 | for | 337 | 0.72 |
| 17 | Bao-yu | 458 | 0.74 | 17 | lady | 326 | 0.70 |
| 18 | for | 440 | 0.71 | 18 | this | 315 | 0.67 |
| 19 | is | 430 | 0.70 | 19 | have | 288 | 0.62 |
| 20 | have | 387 | 0.63 | 20 | what | 273 | 0.58 |
| 21 | what | 375 | 0.61 | 21 | is | 266 | 0.57 |
| 22 | be | 362 | 0.59 | 22 | not | 266 | 0.57 |
| 23 | on | 359 | 0.58 | 23 | we | 266 | 0.57 |
| 24 | with | 356 | 0.58 | 24 | Jia | 263 | 0.56 |
| 25 | but | 355 | 0.58 | 25 | but | 260 | 0.56 |
| 26 | all | 352 | 0.57 | 26 | be | 254 | 0.54 |
| 27 | this | 340 | 0.55 | 27 | on | 247 | 0.53 |
| 28 | not | 316 | 0.51 | 28 | all | 243 | 0.52 |
| 29 | as | 311 | 0.51 | 29 | me | 234 | 0.50 |
| 30 | we | 294 | 0.48 | 30 | with | 233 | 0.50 |
| 31 | me | 291 | 0.47 | 31 | Baoyu | 231 | 0.49 |
| 32 | replied | 276 | 0.45 | 32 | so | 212 | 0.45 |
| 33 | at | 275 | 0.45 | 33 | they | 204 | 0.44 |

（续表）

| 霍译 | 词语 | 词频 | 百分比 | 杨译 | 词语 | 词频 | 百分比 |
|---|---|---|---|---|---|---|---|
| 34 | are | 271 | 0.44 | 34 | if | 202 | 0.43 |
| 35 | Xi-feng | 267 | 0.43 | 35 | no | 202 | 0.43 |
| 36 | no | 265 | 0.43 | 36 | as | 201 | 0.43 |
| 37 | your | 249 | 0.40 | 37 | your | 201 | 0.43 |
| 38 | one | 247 | 0.40 | 38 | old | 198 | 0.42 |
| 39 | his | 242 | 0.39 | 39 | asked | 197 | 0.42 |
| 40 | they | 242 | 0.39 | 40 | his | 189 | 0.40 |
| 41 | there | 241 | 0.39 | 41 | him | 187 | 0.40 |
| 42 | them | 239 | 0.39 | 42 | Just | 187 | 0.40 |
| 43 | had | 234 | 0.38 | 43 | can | 181 | 0.39 |
| 44 | if | 234 | 0.38 | 44 | Xifeng | 181 | 0.39 |
| 45 | lady | 229 | 0.37 | 45 | there | 178 | 0.38 |
| 46 | do | 226 | 0.37 | 46 | are | 176 | 0.38 |
| 47 | so | 225 | 0.37 | 47 | one | 172 | 0.37 |
| 48 | about | 223 | 0.36 | 48 | go | 171 | 0.37 |
| 49 | Grandmother | 215 | 0.35 | 49 | out | 168 | 0.36 |
| 50 | him | 209 | 0.34 | 50 | then | 165 | 0.35 |
| 51 | now | 209 | 0.34 | 51 | too | 158 | 0.34 |
| 52 | been | 204 | 0.33 | 52 | at | 157 | 0.34 |
| 53 | when | 198 | 0.32 | 53 | my | 153 | 0.33 |
| 54 | my | 197 | 0.32 | 54 | them | 152 | 0.32 |
| 55 | can | 189 | 0.31 | 55 | how | 150 | 0.32 |
| 56 | go | 187 | 0.30 | 56 | told | 150 | 0.32 |
| 57 | out | 185 | 0.30 | 57 | up | 149 | 0.32 |
| 58 | well | 185 | 0.30 | 58 | know | 147 | 0.31 |
| 59 | Aroma | 182 | 0.30 | 59 | do | 146 | 0.31 |
| 60 | Dai-yu | 180 | 0.29 | 60 | Why | 145 | 0.31 |
| 61 | Wang | 178 | 0.29 | 61 | when | 144 | 0.31 |

（续表）

| 霍译 | 词语 | 词频 | 百分比 | 杨译 | 词语 | 词频 | 百分比 |
|---|---|---|---|---|---|---|---|
| 62 | from | 173 | 0.28 | 62 | madam | 142 | 0.30 |
| 63 | Zheng | 173 | 0.28 | 63 | Baochai | 133 | 0.28 |
| 64 | just | 170 | 0.28 | 64 | now | 126 | 0.27 |
| 65 | know | 169 | 0.27 | 65 | good | 125 | 0.27 |
| 66 | Bao-chai | 165 | 0.27 | 66 | had | 122 | 0.26 |
| 67 | up | 161 | 0.26 | 67 | here | 120 | 0.26 |
| 68 | very | 160 | 0.26 | 68 | right | 116 | 0.25 |
| 69 | asked | 155 | 0.25 | 69 | who | 114 | 0.24 |
| 70 | come | 153 | 0.25 | 70 | about | 113 | 0.24 |
| 71 | then | 153 | 0.25 | 71 | Daiyu | 113 | 0.24 |
| 72 | by | 149 | 0.24 | 72 | replied | 113 | 0.24 |
| 73 | Lian | 149 | 0.24 | 73 | well | 113 | 0.24 |
| 74 | old | 145 | 0.24 | 74 | been | 109 | 0.23 |
| 75 | here | 131 | 0.21 | 75 | Wang | 109 | 0.23 |
| 76 | like | 130 | 0.21 | 76 | Xiren | 104 | 0.22 |
| 77 | were | 129 | 0.21 | 77 | by | 103 | 0.22 |
| 78 | will | 125 | 0.20 | 78 | cried | 103 | 0.22 |
| 79 | see | 124 | 0.20 | 79 | from | 103 | 0.22 |
| 80 | Xue | 122 | 0.20 | 80 | master | 102 | 0.22 |
| 81 | who | 119 | 0.19 | 81 | our | 102 | 0.22 |
| 82 | oh | 118 | 0.19 | 82 | back | 98 | 0.21 |
| 83 | how | 116 | 0.19 | 83 | come | 98 | 0.21 |
| 84 | right | 116 | 0.19 | 84 | some | 98 | 0.21 |
| 85 | why | 115 | 0.19 | 85 | like | 95 | 0.20 |
| 86 | would | 112 | 0.18 | 86 | answered | 91 | 0.19 |
| 87 | could | 108 | 0.18 | 87 | Li | 89 | 0.19 |
| 88 | good | 108 | 0.18 | 88 | let | 87 | 0.19 |
| 89 | too | 108 | 0.18 | 89 | Zheng | 87 | 0.19 |

（续表）

| 霍译 | 词语 | 词频 | 百分比 | 杨译 | 词语 | 词频 | 百分比 |
|---|---|---|---|---|---|---|---|
| 90 | Patience | 105 | 0.17 | 90 | after | 86 | 0.18 |
| 91 | tell | 105 | 0.17 | 91 | put | 84 | 0.18 |
| 92 | think | 105 | 0.17 | 92 | must | 83 | 0.18 |
| 93 | say | 104 | 0.17 | 93 | other | 82 | 0.18 |
| 94 | after | 101 | 0.16 | 94 | Xue | 81 | 0.17 |
| 95 | has | 101 | 0.16 | 95 | has | 80 | 0.17 |
| 96 | let | 101 | 0.16 | 96 | tell | 80 | 0.17 |
| 97 | Li | 101 | 0.16 | 97 | an | 78 | 0.17 |
| 98 | should | 98 | 0.16 | 98 | say | 78 | 0.17 |
| 99 | some | 98 | 0.16 | 99 | or | 77 | 0.16 |
| 100 | an | 97 | 0.16 | 100 | see | 77 | 0.16 |

通过列举《红楼梦》"说道"类会话引导语的霍译本和杨译本中的前 100 位高频词我们可以发现，在霍译本和杨译本中均出现了 said、replied 和 asked 这三个动词，但在两个译本中的数量和比例差异显著。在霍译本中，said 是排名第 1 位的词，有 2288 个，占总文本的 3.72%；而在杨译本中 said 虽也是排名第 1 位的动词，但数量只有 739 个，占总文本的 1.58%。在霍译本中，replied 的数量和比例高于 asked，排名第 32 位，有 276 个，比例 0.45%；asked 排名第 69位，数量为 155，比例为 0.25%。在杨译本中，asked 的数量和比例高于 replied，排名第 39 位，有 197 个，占文本总量的 0.42%；replied 排名 72 位，数量为 113，比例为 0.24%。图 4-1 可以清晰显示这三个动词在两个译本中的差异。

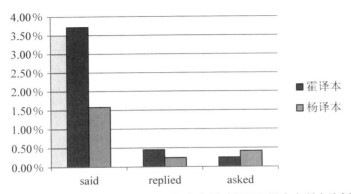

图 4-1 said、replied 和 asked 在"说道"类会话引导语两译本中所占比例对比

此外,杨译本前 100 位高频词中还有两个动词 cried 和 answered,其中 cried 有 103 个,比例为 0.22%;answered 有 91 个,比例为 0.19%。

（二）霍译本与杨译本独特词研究

《红楼梦》里"说道"类会话引导语的霍译本相对于杨译本的独特词有 2690 个,将人名、地名用词筛除后,词频在 5 次以上的有 54 个:

| | | |
|---|---|---|
| somewhat(18) | coz(6) | brief(5) |
| bother(13) | during(6) | carried(5) |
| bless(9) | glanced(6) | dreadful(5) |
| oz(9) | indignantly(6) | impatiently(5) |
| particularly(9) | listening(6) | intendant(5) |
| junior(8) | nasty(6) | lose(5) |
| merely(8) | pair(6) | manner(5) |
| preceptor(8) | pointing(6) | mentioned(5) |
| aiyo(7) | spare(6) | plays(5) |
| almost(7) | surprised(6) | polite(5) |
| direction(7) | wiped(6) | presented(5) |
| entirely(7) | younger(6) | realize(5) |
| greeted(7) | absolutely(5) | responsibility(5) |
| moments(7) | agitation(5) | shortly(5) |
| stared(7) | attitude(5) | silent(5) |
| tone(7) | beautiful(5) | unfair(5) |
| altogether(6) | board(5) | walk(5) |
| breath(6) | bothering(5) | wretched(5) |

杨译本相对于霍译本的独特词有 1571 个,将人名、地名用词筛除后,词频在 5 次以上的有 24 个:

| | | |
|---|---|---|
| demurred(15) | chuckled(7) | scoffed(6) |
| approved(14) | teacher(7) | smart(6) |
| fumed(12) | ancestress(6) | unwell(6) |
| swore(12) | confirmed(6) | chimed(5) |
| abbess(9) | honourable(6) | compare(5) |
| Amida(9) | Lordship(6) | declaimed(5) |
| joined(9) | relatives(6) | ounces(5) |

priest(5) | responded(5) | wits(5)

在以上杨译本相对于霍译本的独特词中出现了几个独特动词,被用来替代 said 来翻译"说道"之意,它们是 demurred、approved、fumed、swore、joined、chuckled、confirmed、scoffed、declaimed 和 responded。杨宪益在翻译过程中,根据上下文,将单纯的"说道"的意思显化,扩展成了"反对""赞成""发怒""咒骂""插嘴""轻笑""确认""嘲笑""抨击""回答"等意义。

贝克最初对于显化作了这样的论述:"相对于特定源语文本以及原创文本总体而言,翻译文本显化程度显著提高"(Baker,1993)。随后贝克又指出,"在翻译中,(译者)总体上往往会将各种情况加以详细说明而不是将含糊不清的地方保留下来"(Baker,1996)。塞盖诺特(Candace Seguinot)认为,显化不仅仅指原作中不存在而译作中添加的表述,也包括原文中所暗示或只有通过预设才能认识到的信息在译文中加以明示,还包括原文中的某些成分在译文中通过凸显、强调或措辞等手段而加以突出的现象(Klaudy,1996)。

(三)霍译本与杨译本特色词研究

《红楼梦》"说道"类会话引导语的霍译本相对于杨译本的特色词有 409 个将人名、地名用词筛除后,关键度在 5 以上的特色词有 117 个(见表 4-3)。

表 4-3 "说道"类会话引导语霍译本特色词

| 排序 | 词语 | 关键度 | 排序 | 词语 | 关键度 |
|---|---|---|---|---|---|
| 1 | said | 421.825 | 14 | minute | 13.664 |
| 2 | oh | 72.479 | 15 | bother | 13.185 |
| 3 | of | 33.24 | 16 | ought | 12.865 |
| 4 | replied | 29.051 | 17 | voice | 12.71 |
| 5 | very | 29.011 | 18 | think | 12.551 |
| 6 | moment | 24.538 | 19 | perhaps | 12.086 |
| 7 | began | 23.682 | 20 | himself | 11.896 |
| 8 | somewhat | 19.777 | 21 | ladyship | 11.311 |
| 9 | got | 19.435 | 22 | father | 10.987 |
| 10 | come | 17.034 | 23 | goodness | 10.987 |
| 11 | holy | 16.481 | 24 | name | 10.987 |
| 12 | will | 13.926 | 25 | about | 10.985 |
| 13 | dear | 13.874 | 26 | grand | 10.722 |

| 排序 | 词语 | 关键度 | 排序 | 词语 | 关键度 |
|------|------|--------|------|------|--------|
| 27 | that | 10.548 | 55 | bit | 7.291 |
| 28 | would | 10.473 | 56 | been | 7.251 |
| 29 | sure | 10.033 | 57 | afterwards | 6.924 |
| 30 | oz | 9.889 | 58 | perfectly | 6.924 |
| 31 | particularly | 9.889 | 59 | state | 6.924 |
| 32 | woman | 9.64 | 60 | visit | 6.924 |
| 33 | cousin | 9.561 | 61 | myself | 6.757 |
| 34 | had | 9.539 | 62 | breath | 6.592 |
| 35 | at | 9.113 | 63 | coz | 6.592 |
| 36 | old | 8.905 | 64 | glanced | 6.592 |
| 37 | junior | 8.79 | 65 | indignantly | 6.592 |
| 38 | merely | 8.79 | 66 | listening | 6.592 |
| 39 | preceptor | 8.79 | 67 | nasty | 6.592 |
| 40 | tone | 8.79 | 68 | pair | 6.592 |
| 41 | a | 8.637 | 69 | south | 6.592 |
| 42 | yes | 8.517 | 70 | stone | 6.592 |
| 43 | own | 7.969 | 71 | surprised | 6.592 |
| 44 | literary | 7.856 | 72 | wiped | 6.592 |
| 45 | shall | 7.797 | 73 | little | 6.402 |
| 46 | aiyo | 7.691 | 74 | seem | 6.228 |
| 47 | almost | 7.691 | 75 | certain | 6.008 |
| 48 | bless | 7.691 | 76 | following | 6.008 |
| 49 | direction | 7.691 | 77 | her | 5.84 |
| 50 | entirely | 7.691 | 78 | seemed | 5.804 |
| 51 | greeted | 7.691 | 79 | rather | 5.763 |
| 52 | honestly | 7.691 | 80 | is | 5.715 |
| 53 | moments | 7.691 | 81 | going | 5.702 |
| 54 | stared | 7.691 | 82 | into | 5.694 |

（续表）

| 排序 | 词语 | 关键度 | 排序 | 词语 | 关键度 |
|---|---|---|---|---|---|
| 83 | absolutely | 5.494 | 101 | polite | 5.494 |
| 84 | agitation | 5.494 | 102 | presented | 5.494 |
| 85 | altogether | 5.494 | 103 | realize | 5.494 |
| 86 | attack | 5.494 | 104 | responsibility | 5.494 |
| 87 | attitude | 5.494 | 105 | shortly | 5.494 |
| 88 | beautiful | 5.494 | 106 | silent | 5.494 |
| 89 | body | 5.494 | 107 | spare | 5.494 |
| 90 | bothering | 5.494 | 108 | unfair | 5.494 |
| 91 | brief | 5.494 | 109 | walking | 5.494 |
| 92 | dreadful | 5.494 | 110 | wretched | 5.494 |
| 93 | during | 5.494 | 111 | younger | 5.494 |
| 94 | impatiently | 5.494 | 112 | words | 5.409 |
| 95 | intendant | 5.494 | 113 | do | 5.343 |
| 96 | lose | 5.494 | 114 | lot | 5.307 |
| 97 | manner | 5.494 | 115 | surely | 5.146 |
| 98 | mentioned | 5.494 | 116 | able | 5.117 |
| 99 | plays | 5.494 | 117 | supposed | 5.109 |
| 100 | pointing | 5.494 | | | |

杨译本相对于霍译本的特色词有 642 个，将人名、地名用词筛除后，关键度在 5 以上的特色词有 216 个（见表 4 - 4）。

表 4 - 4 "说道"类会话引导语杨译本特色词

| 排序 | 词语 | 关键度 | 排序 | 词语 | 关键度 |
|---|---|---|---|---|---|
| 1 | answered | 99.048 | 7 | old | 50.255 |
| 2 | cried | 59.555 | 8 | told | 45.11 |
| 3 | demanded | 58.915 | 9 | urged | 44.216 |
| 4 | remarked | 58.7 | 10 | assured | 40.622 |
| 5 | he | 53.514 | 11 | agreed | 37.659 |
| 6 | retorted | 52.526 | 12 | that | 32.424 |

（续表）

| 排序 | 词语 | 关键度 | 排序 | 词语 | 关键度 |
|------|------|--------|------|------|--------|
| 13 | too | 30.896 | 41 | bad | 15.657 |
| 14 | so | 30.771 | 42 | abbess | 15.5 |
| 15 | scolded | 27.871 | 43 | amida | 15.5 |
| 16 | our | 26.537 | 44 | joined | 15.5 |
| 17 | demurred | 25.834 | 45 | the | 15.264 |
| 18 | then | 25.695 | 46 | buddha | 14.919 |
| 19 | countered | 24.775 | 47 | insisted | 14.919 |
| 20 | asked | 24.427 | 48 | ordered | 14.707 |
| 21 | objected | 24.325 | 49 | mistress | 12.857 |
| 22 | approved | 24.112 | 50 | hastily | 12.807 |
| 23 | second | 24.112 | 51 | good | 12.239 |
| 24 | put | 23.548 | 52 | observed | 12.165 |
| 25 | how | 23.269 | 53 | chuckled | 12.056 |
| 26 | answer | 22.169 | 54 | teacher | 12.056 |
| 27 | why | 22.027 | 55 | such | 11.85 |
| 28 | fumed | 20.667 | 56 | uncle | 11.761 |
| 29 | swore | 20.667 | 57 | we | 11.63 |
| 30 | declared | 20.195 | 58 | use | 11.286 |
| 31 | just | 19.473 | 59 | pay | 11.233 |
| 32 | warned | 18.689 | 60 | explained | 11.061 |
| 33 | she | 18.561 | 61 | you | 10.578 |
| 34 | brother | 17.223 | 62 | confirmed | 10.334 |
| 35 | till | 17.127 | 63 | honourable | 10.334 |
| 36 | if | 16.946 | 64 | lordship | 10.334 |
| 37 | sister | 16.383 | 65 | relatives | 10.334 |
| 38 | father | 16.341 | 66 | scoffed | 10.334 |
| 39 | interposed | 15.666 | 67 | smart | 10.334 |
| 40 | rejoined | 15.666 | 68 | unwell | 10.334 |

（续表）

| 排序 | 词语 | 关键度 | 排序 | 词语 | 关键度 |
|------|------|--------|------|------|--------|
| 69 | in | 9.992 | 97 | when | 7.512 |
| 70 | suggested | 9.615 | 98 | right | 7.453 |
| 71 | outside | 9.431 | 99 | have | 7.409 |
| 72 | wondered | 8.951 | 100 | apartments | 7.267 |
| 73 | quite | 8.697 | 101 | elder | 7.126 |
| 74 | ancestress | 8.611 | 102 | leave | 7.012 |
| 75 | chimed | 8.611 | 103 | asked | 6.889 |
| 76 | compare | 8.611 | 104 | behaved | 6.889 |
| 77 | declaimed | 8.611 | 105 | connection | 6.889 |
| 78 | exactly | 8.611 | 106 | consort | 6.889 |
| 79 | fine | 8.611 | 107 | creatures | 6.889 |
| 80 | mansion | 8.611 | 108 | depend | 6.889 |
| 81 | nanny | 8.611 | 109 | destroy | 6.889 |
| 82 | ounces | 8.611 | 110 | engaged | 6.889 |
| 83 | priest | 8.611 | 111 | essays | 6.889 |
| 84 | proposal | 8.611 | 112 | female | 6.889 |
| 85 | responded | 8.611 | 113 | fifth | 6.889 |
| 86 | wits | 8.611 | 114 | gifts | 6.889 |
| 87 | charge | 8.598 | 115 | guessed | 6.889 |
| 88 | announced | 8.41 | 116 | ha | 6.889 |
| 89 | cousin | 8.41 | 117 | loudly | 6.889 |
| 90 | proposed | 8.367 | 118 | matrons | 6.889 |
| 91 | imperial | 7.995 | 119 | messenger | 6.889 |
| 92 | never | 7.793 | 120 | once | 6.889 |
| 93 | back | 7.721 | 121 | painting | 6.889 |
| 94 | added | 7.705 | 122 | prevaricated | 6.889 |
| 95 | even | 7.694 | 123 | priestess | 6.889 |
| 96 | plenty | 7.693 | 124 | provincial | 6.889 |

（续表）

| 排序 | 词语 | 关键度 | 排序 | 词语 | 关键度 |
|------|------|--------|------|------|--------|
| 125 | shows | 6.889 | 153 | sobbed | 5.968 |
| 126 | silk | 6.889 | 154 | ten | 5.942 |
| 127 | situation | 6.889 | 155 | although | 5.691 |
| 128 | slightly | 6.889 | 156 | teased | 5.691 |
| 129 | some | 6.889 | 157 | today | 5.691 |
| 130 | sprang | 6.889 | 158 | keep | 5.615 |
| 131 | teach | 6.889 | 159 | sir | 5.591 |
| 132 | tutor | 6.889 | 160 | instead | 5.564 |
| 133 | whom | 6.889 | 161 | mind | 5.451 |
| 134 | worked | 6.889 | 162 | health | 5.301 |
| 135 | young | 6.659 | 163 | reported | 5.301 |
| 136 | official | 6.613 | 164 | snapped | 5.301 |
| 137 | search | 6.474 | 165 | our | 5.29 |
| 138 | stepped | 6.474 | 166 | can | 5.279 |
| 139 | exclaimed | 6.382 | 167 | actresses | 5.167 |
| 140 | lost | 6.348 | 168 | aiya | 5.167 |
| 141 | do | 6.311 | 169 | although | 5.167 |
| 142 | girls | 6.311 | 170 | apart | 5.167 |
| 143 | of | 6.277 | 171 | assented | 5.167 |
| 144 | respects | 6.27 | 172 | aunty | 5.167 |
| 145 | sight | 6.27 | 173 | auspicious | 5.167 |
| 146 | wait | 6.27 | 174 | bearing | 5.167 |
| 147 | after | 6.254 | 175 | begonia | 5.167 |
| 148 | sent | 6.245 | 176 | bird | 5.167 |
| 149 | let | 6.244 | 177 | bringing | 5.167 |
| 150 | this | 6.092 | 178 | capped | 5.167 |
| 151 | concubine | 5.968 | 179 | clouded | 5.167 |
| 152 | raise | 5.968 | 180 | copied | 5.167 |

（续表）

| 排序 | 词语 | 关键度 | 排序 | 词语 | 关键度 |
|------|------|--------|------|------|--------|
| 181 | cost | 5.167 | 199 | operas | 5.167 |
| 182 | deaconess | 5.167 | 200 | otherwise | 5.167 |
| 183 | deeds | 5.167 | 201 | outrageous | 5.167 |
| 184 | deliberately | 5.167 | 202 | passage | 5.167 |
| 185 | deny | 5.167 | 203 | plate | 5.167 |
| 186 | exploded | 5.167 | 204 | quilt | 5.167 |
| 187 | faltered | 5.167 | 205 | rowdy | 5.167 |
| 188 | feather | 5.167 | 206 | season | 5.167 |
| 189 | fooling | 5.167 | 207 | seats | 5.167 |
| 190 | handle | 5.167 | 208 | sly | 5.167 |
| 191 | hills | 5.167 | 209 | stormed | 5.167 |
| 192 | indigestion | 5.167 | 210 | surname | 5.167 |
| 193 | joked | 5.167 | 211 | thunderbolt | 5.167 |
| 194 | knowing | 5.167 | 212 | tossed | 5.167 |
| 195 | lodge | 5.167 | 213 | valuables | 5.167 |
| 196 | mama | 5.167 | 214 | warning | 5.167 |
| 197 | nowadays | 5.167 | 215 | send | 5.03 |
| 198 | nudged | 5.167 | 216 | go | 5.022 |

　　从上述《红楼梦》"说道"类会话引导语的霍译本、杨译本特色词的分析中可以看出，霍译本中"说道"类会话引导语的翻译较为单纯，特色词主要有 said 和 replied。而杨译本中对于"说道"类会话引导语的翻译处理非常多样化，特色词也非常多，其中关键度较高的有：answered、cried、demanded、remarked、retorted、told、urged、agreed、scolded、demurred、countered、asked、objected、approved、fumed、swore、declared、warned、interposed、rejoined、joined、insisted、ordered、observed、chuckled、explained、confirmed、scoffed 等。

　　（四）霍译本与杨译本二词以上搭配

　　以上笔者分析的都是使用单个动词来翻译《红楼梦》"说道"类会话引导语的情况。经过进一步检索（使用次数在 2 次以上），笔者发现还有一些二词以上的短语或其他表达形式，如：blurted out、chimed in、called out、turned to、went on、put in、was the answer、was the reply、with a smile、smiled and nodded 等。这些用法在霍译本和杨译本中的分布如下(左侧数字为霍译本数量,右侧数字为杨译本数量):

| | | |
|---|---|---|
| put in(16—49) | with a smile(3—12) | chimed in(0—5) |
| went on(16—16) | was the answer(0—13) | smiled and nodded(1—1) |
| turned to(13—10) | was the reply(2—10) | |
| called out(10—5) | blurted out(2—5) | |

从上表中我们可以看到,was the answer 和 chimed in 是杨译本的独特用法;put in、with a smile、was the reply、blurted out 是杨译本的特色用法;called out 是霍译本的特色用法。

## 三、《红楼梦》"说道"类会话引导语英译案例研究

以上笔者对《红楼梦》原文以及译文中的"说道"类会话引导语进行了分析统计,在此基础上开展《红楼梦》"说道"类会话引导语英译的案例研究。笔者选取在霍译本和杨译本中均遥遥领先的 said 以及词频均位列前 100 位的动词 replied 和 asked、杨译本独特词 demurred、杨译本关键度最高的特色词 answered,以及霍译本和杨译本中数量最多的动词短语 put in 来进行案例分析。

(一)"说道"类英译之 said

无论是原文中的"道:""说:"还是"说道:",英文中的 said 都是最直接的目的语对等词。在翻译《红楼梦》"说道"类会话引导语时,霍克思和杨宪益也都把 said 一词作为首选,该词在所有的翻译词中都遥遥领先,只不过霍克思使用 said 的次数比杨宪益更加频繁。以下为霍译和杨译均使用 said 的典型例子:

1.【原文】道人道:"既如此,便随你去来。"(第一回)

   【霍译】'Very good,I will go with you then,'**said** the Taoist.

   【杨译】"In that case I'm ready to go with you,"**said** the Taoist.

2.【原文】王夫人道:"有没有,什么要紧。"(第三回)

   【霍译】'Oh well,if you can't find it,it doesn't really matter,'**said** Lady Wang.

   【杨译】"It doesn't matter if there's none of that sort,"**said** Lady Wang.

3.【原文】平儿回了,凤姐道:"我这里陪客呢,晚上再来回。"(第六回)

   【霍译】'I am entertaining a guest,'**said** Xi-feng to Patience when she came in to announce their arrival. 'Let them leave it until this evening.'

【杨译】"I have a guest. They can come back this evening，" **said** Xifeng.

4.【原文】尤氏道:"这里也是才吃完了饭,就要过去了。"(第十一回)

【霍译】'Yes，we've finished too，' **said** You-shi. 'We were about to come over when you arrived.'

【杨译】"We've just finished our meal too，" **said** Madam You. "We're coming over."

5.【原文】凤姐道:"可是,别误了正事。"(第十六回)

【霍译】'Ah yes，' **said** Xi-feng. 'We mustn't make you late for that.

【杨译】"Yes，we mustn't delay you，" **said** his wife.

6.【原文】贾政道:"你且把园门关上,我们先瞧外面,再进去。"(第十七回)

【霍译】'I want you to close the gate，' **said** Jia Zheng, 'so that we can see what it looks like from outside before we go in.'

【杨译】"Close the gate，" **said** Jia Zheng. "Let us see what it looks like from outside before we go in."

7.【原文】宝玉道:"有我呢!"(第十九回)

【霍译】'I'll see you don't get into trouble，' **said** Bao-yu.

【杨译】"Leave it to me，" **said** Baoyu.

8.【原文】薛蟠道:"可是呢,你明儿来拜寿,打算送什么新鲜物儿?"(第二十六回)

【霍译】'Yes，' **said** Xue Pan. 'What are you planning to give me for my birthday next month? Something new and out of the ordinary，I hope.'

【杨译】"That's right，" **said** Xue Pan. "What are you planning to send me?"

9.【原文】湘云道:"花草也是和人一样,气脉充足,长的就好。"(第三十一回)

【霍译】'Plants are the same as people，' **said** Xiang-yun. 'The healthier their constitution is，the better they grow.'

【杨译】"Plants are like human beings，" **said** Xiangyun. "When they're filled with vital force they grow well."

10.【原文】探春道:"这个封号极好。"(第三十七回)

【霍译】'I think the title becomes her very well，' **said** Tan-chun.

【杨译】"An excellent title," **said** Tanchun.

11. 【原文】黛玉道:"咱们到了那里就知道了。"(第四十二回)

【霍译】'We shall soon find out if we go,' **said** Dai-yu.

【杨译】'We'll know when we get there,' **said** Daiyu.

12. 【原文】婆子答应了,方要走时,鸳鸯道:"我说去罢。他们那里听他的话?"(第七十一回)

【霍译】'Better let me go,' **said** Faithful, before the woman had time to get away. 'They'll never listen to her.'

【杨译】The woman assented and was about to leave when Yuanyang **said**, "I'll go. The people there wouldn't pay any attention to her."

13. 【原文】众人道:"二爷细心镂刻,定又是风流悲感,不同此等的了。"(第七十八回)

【霍译】'After all this careful chiseling, Mr Bao's poem is sure to be something of quite a different order from these two we have just heard,' **said** the literary gentlemen '—one, no doubt, in which the romantic and tragic aspects of the theme will both be fully exploited.'

【杨译】His protégés **said**, "The Second Young Master is composing his carefully. It's bound to be more stylish and poignant than the others."

14. 【原文】惜春道:"姐姐们先去,我回来再过去。"(第八十二回)

【霍译】Xi-chun **said** she would follow later.

【杨译】"The two of you go on ahead," **said** Xichun. "I'll go over later on."

15. 【原文】宝玉道:"不妨,把火盆挪过去就是了。"(第八十九回)

【霍译】'That doesn't matter,' **said** Bao-yu. 'Have the charcoal brazier moved in there.'

【杨译】"That's all right," he **said**. "Just put a brazier in there."

(二)"说道"类英译之 replied

replied 一词表"答复,回答"之意,在使用该词前一定有另外一段会话,且很有可能是询问性质的。replied 在霍译本《红楼梦》"说道"类会话引导语中出现了 276 次,占文本总量的 0.45%;在杨译本《红楼梦》"说道"类会话引导语中有 113 次,占文本总量的 0.24%。replied 还是霍译文本相对于杨译文本的第二大特色词,关键度为 29.051。以下为霍译本《红楼梦》中"说道"类会话引导语中使用 replied 的例子,杨译文本中有时也同样使用 replied,有时则使用其他动词。

1. 【原文】那仙姑道:"吾居离恨天之上,灌愁海之中,乃放春山遣香洞太虚幻境警幻仙姑是也。"(第五回)

   【霍译】'I am the fairy Disenchantment,' the fairy woman **replied**. 'I live beyond the Realm of Separation, in the Sea of Sadness. There is a Mountain of Spring Awakening which rises from the midst of that sea, and on that mountain is the Paradise of the Full-blown Flower, and in that paradise is the Land of Illusion, which is my home.

   【杨译】"My home is above the Sphere of Parting Sorrow in the Sea of Brimming Grief," she answered with a smile. "I am the Goddess of Disenchantment from the Grotto of Emanating Fragrance on the Mountain of Expanding Spring in the Illusory Land of Great Void.

2. 【原文】王夫人道:"你瞧谁闲着,叫四个女人去就完了;又来问我!"(第七回)

   【霍译】'Just see which women are free and send four of them,' **replied** Lady Wang. 'You don't have to ask me about things like that!'

   【杨译】"Any four women you see are free. Why consult me about such trifles?"

3. 【原文】贾蓉道:"正是。"(第十回)

   【霍译】'Yes, this is my wife,' Jia Rong **replied**.

   【杨译】"Yes, sir," said Jia Rong.

4. 【原文】张先生道:"晚生粗鄙下士,知识浅陋。"(第十回)

   【霍译】'I am only a very indifferent scholar,' **replied** Dr Zhang, 'and my knowledge is really extremely superficial.

   【杨译】"I am simply an ignorant layman," **replied** Dr. Zhang.

5. 【原文】尤氏道:"他这个病得的也奇。"(第十一回)

   【霍译】'It's a very puzzling illness,' You-shi **replied**.

   【杨译】"It's a very puzzling illness," **replied** Madam You.

6. 【原文】凤姐道:"他们来领的时候,你还做梦呢。(第十四回)

   【霍译】'At the time when they come,' Xi-feng **replied**, 'you are still fast asleep in bed.

【杨译】"When they came you were still fast asleep."

7.【原文】众清客道："这也无妨。"(第十七回)

【霍译】'That doesn't matter,' the literary gentlemen **replied**.

【杨译】"Have no fears about that," his secretaries assured him.

8.【原文】问他换不换,宝玉道："不换。"(第十五回)

【霍译】She asked them if they wanted to 'change' too, but Bao-yu **replied** that they did not.

【杨译】She urged the two boys to change, but Baoyu declined.

9.【原文】黛玉道："他为他二姐姐伤心;我是刚才眼睛发痒,揉的,并不为什么。"(第八十一回)

【霍译】'Oh, he's upset about Miss Ying,' Dai-yu **replied**. 'I'm all right. My eyes have been itching and I've been rubbing them, that's all.'

【杨译】"He was upset on account of Cousin Yingchun," Daiyu answered. "I was rubbing my eyes because they itched — that's all."

10.【原文】宝玉道："索性三妹妹合邢妹妹钓了我再钓。"(第八十一回)

【霍译】'Qi and Xiu-yan must go first,' **replied** Bao-yu. 'I insist.'

【杨译】"Let the other two girls try first," he urged.

11.【原文】麝月道："我也不知道。(第八十一回)

【霍译】'I don't know,' **replied** Musk.

【杨译】"I don't know," the maid answered.

12.【原文】凤姐道："好的时候好象空中有人说了几句话似的,却不记得说什么来着。"(第八十一回)

【霍译】'There was a voice,' **replied** Xi-feng, 'that seemed to speak to me from nowhere. But what it said I honestly can't remember.'

【杨译】"I thought I heard a voice in the air — just what it said I can't remember."

13.【原文】贾母道："你问你太太去,我懒怠说。"(第八十一回)

【霍译】'Ask your aunt,' **replied** Grandmother Jia. 'I've done enough of the talking.'

【杨译】"Ask your aunt. I'm too tired to tell you." Then Lady Wang explained.

14.【原文】雪雁道："我这里才要去,你们就来了。"(第八十二回)

【霍译】'I was on my way when you two arrived,' **replied** Snowgoose.

【杨译】"I was on my way there when you turned up," she countered.

15.【原文】凤姐儿**道**："你在外头听见，你来告诉我们，你这会子问谁呢?"（第八十五回）

　　【霍译】It was Xi-feng who **replied**: 'You're the one who's heard. Why ask us?'

　　【杨译】"If you heard that outside." quipped Xifeng, "you should come and tell us，not ask us about it."

　　笔者在归纳总结霍译本《红楼梦》"说道"类会话引导语中 replied 的用法时还发现一个现象：在霍译文本的 276 个 replied 中，前八十回中只有 14 个，分布于从第五回至第十九回之间；其余的 262 个统统出现在后四十回中，也就是说闵福德比霍克思更倾向于使用 replied 一词。

　　（三）"说道"类英译之 asked

　　《牛津高阶英语词典》（第 6 版）（*Oxford Advanced Learner's Dictionary*）对 asked 给出的定义是：①~（*sb*）（*about sb/sth*）*to say or write sth in the form of a question，in order to get information*；② *to tell sb that you would like them to do sth or that you would like sth to happen*。《柯林斯高阶英语词典》（*Collins COBUILD Advanced Learner's English Dictionary*）的定义为：① *if you ask someone something，you say something to them in the form of a question because you want to know the answer*；② *if you ask someone to do something，you tell them that you want them to do it*。由此我们可以推断出，asked 可以表达"询问，提问"或"要求，请求"之意。

　　asked 在《红楼梦》"说道"类会话引导语霍译本和杨译本中均属于高频词。该词在霍译文本中名列第 69 位，有 155 个，占文本总量的 0.25%；在杨译文本中名列第 39 位，有 197 个，占文本总量的 0.42%。绝大多数使用 asked 时，"说道"类引导语介导的是一个问句，以问号结尾。

　　以下为在杨译本《红楼梦》"说道"类会话引导语中使用 asked 的例子，霍译文本中有时也同样使用 asked，有时则使用 said 或其他动词代替。

1.【原文】他母亲**道**："何必如此招摇!"（第四回）

　　【杨译】"Why go to such trouble?" she **asked**.

　　【霍译】'Why ever should we go to any such trouble?' said his mother.

2.【原文】贾政**道**："诸公题以何名?"（第十七回）

　　【杨译】Jia Zheng **asked** them to suggest another inscription.

　　【霍译】'Very well，gentlemen. What are you going to call it?' said

Jia Zheng.

3. 【原文】平儿道:"屋里一个人没有,我在他跟前作什么?"(第二十一回)

【杨译】"Why should I stay there alone with him?" **asked** Pinger.

【霍译】'He's in there on his own,' said Patience. 'What should I be doing in there with him?'

4. 【原文】惜春道:"宝姐姐笑什么?"(第二十五回)

【杨译】This passed unnoticed by all but Xichun. "What are you laughing at,Cousin Baochai?" she **asked**.

【霍译】'Why do you laugh,Cousin Bao?' Xi-chun **asked** her.

5. 【原文】宝玉道:"几时的话?"(第二十六回)

【杨译】"When was that?" **asked** Baoyu.

【霍译】'When was this?' Bao-yu **asked** him.

6. 【原文】宝钗道:"你又禁不得风吹,怎么又站在那风口里?"(第二十八回)

【杨译】"Why are you standing there in a draught?" **asked** Baochai. "You know how easily you catch cold."

【霍译】'I thought you were so delicate,' said Bao-chai. 'What are you standing there in the draught for?'

7. 【原文】翠缕道:"这荷花怎么还不开?"(第三十一回)

【杨译】"Why isn't the lotus in bloom yet?" **asked** Cuilu.

【霍译】'Why aren't these water-lilies out yet?' said Kingfisher.

8. 【原文】贾母道:"老亲家,你今年多大年纪了?"(第三十九回)

【杨译】"How old are you,venerable kinswoman?" **asked** the Lady Dowager.

【霍译】'Now,old kinswoman,' said Grandmother Jia,'and what would your age be?'

9. 【原文】宝钗道:"何苦自寻烦恼?(第四十八回)

【杨译】'Why torture yourself?' **asked** Baochai.

【霍译】'Why give yourself so much trouble when you don't have to?' Bao-chai **asked** her.

10. 【原文】湘云道:"什么是'当票子'?"(第五十七回)

【杨译】'A pawn ticket? What's that?' **asked** Xiangyun.

【霍译】'What's a pawn ticket?' Xiang-yun **asked** her.

11. 【原文】探春道:"怎么不回大奶奶?"(第六十二回)

【杨译】"Why no report this to Madam Zhu?" **asked** Tanchun.

【霍译】'Why didn't you see Mrs Zhu about this?' said Tan-chun.

12.【原文】众人道:"那时难道你知道了也没找寻他去?"(第六十七回)

【杨译】"But when you heard about it,didn't you go to make a search?" they **asked**.

【霍译】'But didn't you look for Mr Liu yourself when you heard about this?' his guests **asked** him.

13.【原文】黛玉道:"你不睡了么?"(第八十二回)

【杨译】"Are you getting up?"Daiyu **asked**.

【霍译】'Haven't you gone to sleep?' **asked** Dai-yu.

14.【原文】贾母道:"怎么'掉包儿'?"(第九十六回)

【杨译】"Palm off what dummy?" the old lady **asked**.

【霍译】'Substitution? What do you mean?' **asked** Grandmother Jia.

15.【原文】那和尚道:"你到这里,曾偷看什么东西没有?"(第一百十六回)

【杨译】"Did you pry into any secrets here?" **asked** the monk.

【霍译】'When you first entered this place,' said the monk,'did you steal a look at anything in particular?'

(四)"说道"类英译之 demurred

demurred 一词是《红楼梦》"说道"类会话引导语杨译文本中的独特词,有 15 个,霍译文本中一次都没有出现过。我们先来看几部权威词典对于 demur 一词的定义:

(1)《牛津高阶英语词典》(第 6 版)(*Oxford Advanced Learner's Dictionary*): (*formal*) *to say that you do not agree with sth or that you refuse to do sth*。

(2)《朗文当代英语词典》(第 4 版)(*Longman Dictionary of Contemporary English*): *to express doubt about or opposition to a plan or suggestion*。

(3)《柯林斯高阶英语词典》(*Collins COBUILD Advanced Learner's English Dictionary*): *If you demur*,*you say that you do not agree with something or will not do something that you have been asked to do.* (*FORMAL*)。

(4)《美国传统词典》(双解)(*E-C American Heritage Dictionary*): *to voice opposition*;*object*:持反面观点;反对。

(5)《牛津高阶英汉双解词典》(*Oxford Advanced Learner's English-Chinese Dictionary*):~(*at sth*)(*fml* 文) *express a doubt*(*about sth*)*or an objection*(*to sth*):(对某事物)表示怀疑或反对。

通过以上几部词典的释义,我们可以推断 demur 一词是比较正式的,用于 "表示异议"或"反对",用法比较书面化。笔者考察了杨译文本中使用

demurred 的案例,同时对比霍译的英译情况。

1.【原文】凤姐儿说:"太太们在这里,我怎么敢点。"(第十一回)

【杨译】"How can I presume when Their Ladyships are present?" **demurred** Xifeng.

【霍译】'It's not for me to choose when Mother and Aunt Wang are here,' said Xi-feng.

2.【原文】北静王道:"逝者已登仙界,非你我碌碌尘寰中人。……"(第十五回)

【杨译】but he **demurred**:"The deceased has become an immortal and left our dusty world."

【霍译】'The Departed is now in paradise,' said the prince.

3.【原文】宝玉道:"老太太叫我呢,有话等回来罢!"(第二十八回)

【杨译】"The old lady is waiting for me," he **demurred**. "You can tell me when I come back."

【霍译】'I've got to see Grandma now,' said Bao-yu. 'If you've got anything else to say, you can tell me on my way back.'

4.【原文】迎春道:"依我说,也不必随一人出题限韵,竟是拈阄儿公道。"(第三十七回)

【杨译】"I don't think the subject and rhymes should be decided by one person," Yingchun **demurred**. "Drawing lots would be fairer."

【霍译】'If you ask me,' said Ying-chun, 'I think that rather than always have the same two people to choose the titles and set the rhymes, it would be better to draw lots.'

5.【原文】袭人道:"一件就当不起了。"(第五十一回)

【杨译】'One is already too much,' Xiren **demurred**.

【霍译】Aroma protested. 'I can't possibly take both of these,' she said. 'Even one of these would seem a bit on the grand side for me.'

6.【原文】王夫人道:"恐里头坐不下。"(第五十四回)

【杨译】'There may not be room for us all,' **demurred** Lady Wang.

【霍译】'I doubt there's room for us all,' said Lady Wang.

7.【原文】王夫人等道:"夜已深了,风露也大,请老太太安歇罢了,明日再赏;十六月色也好。"(第七十六回)

【杨译】Lady Wang **demurred**,"It's already the fourth watch,

madam，windy and with heavy dew. Won't you go and rest? You can enjoy the moon again tomorrow；it's still bright on the sixteenth."

【霍译】'It's very late，' said Lady Wang. 'The air is cold tonight and there is a lot of dew. Won't you go home and rest now，Mother？ We can have another moon-party tomorrow night，if you feel like it. The moon on the sixteenth is still well worth watching.'

8.【原文】贾政道："休谬加奖誉，且看转的如何。"（第七十八回）

【杨译】"Don't overdo your praise." **demurred** Jia Zheng. "Let's see how he turns the subject."

【霍译】'You shouldn't praise the boy so，' said Jia Zheng. 'You will turn his head. Let's see how he manages to develop this in his second stanza.'

9.【原文】只见李绮道："宝哥哥先钓罢。"（第八十一回）

【杨译】but Li Qi **demurred**. "No，Cousin Bao，you try first."

【霍译】'You go first，Cousin Bao，' protested Qi.

10.【原文】詹光道："这是老世翁过谦的话。不但王大兄这般说，就是我们看，宝二爷必定要高发的。"（第八十四回）

【杨译】Zhan Guang **demurred**，"You are too modest，sir. This is the opinion of us all，not only Mr. Wang. Master Bao is sure to distinguish himself in the examinations."

【霍译】'Come come，Sir Zheng！' said Zhan Guang. 'You are being too modest. Friend Wang's opinion is one we all share. Master Bao will surely go far.'

11.【原文】邢王二夫人道："老太太虽疼他，他那里耽的住？"（第八十四回）

【杨译】"We know how fond you are of her，but you shouldn't trouble，madam，" they **demurred**.

【霍译】The two ladies thanked Grandmother Jia for the kind thought，but begged her not to trouble herself for Qiao-jie's sake.

12.【原文】贾政道："这也不见得。"（第九十二回）

【杨译】"That's not necessarily so，" Jia Zheng **demurred**.

【霍译】'Oh come，I am sure you will find someone，' Jia Zheng consoled him.

13.【原文】袭人道:"不是'好些'。"(第九十六回)

【杨译】"Not just 'slightly fonder,'" Xiren **demurred**,

【霍译】'More than a little!' protested Aroma.

14.【原文】王夫人道:"放着他亲祖母在那里,托我做什么?"(第一百十七回)

【杨译】"The child has her grandmother here," **demurred** Lady Wang. "Why should you entrust her to me?"

【霍译】'With her own grandmother so close at hand, what need is there for you to entrust her to me?' asked Lady Wang.

15.【原文】平儿道:"太太该叫他进来,他是姐儿的干妈,也得告诉告诉他。"(第一百十九回)

【杨译】But Pinger **demurred**, "Better invite her in, madam. As Qiaojie's godmother she should be told about this."

【霍译】'Perhaps you should ask her in, ma'am,' said Patience. 'After all she is Qiao-jie's godmother. We should tell her what is happening.'

以上 15 个杨译文本中使用了 demurred 的例子,霍译文本中用了 9 个 said、2 个 protested、1 个 asked、1 个 consoled、1 个 protested 和 said、1 个 thanked 和 begged。霍译文本中 said 的使用率达到了 67%。

(五)"说道"类英译之 answered

answered 是《红楼梦》"说道"类会话引导语的杨译本相对于霍译本的第一大特色词,关键度为 99.048。answered 和 replied 是同义词,也是"回答,答复"之意,两者在很多情况下可以互换,《牛津高阶英汉双解词典》《朗文当代英语词典》《美国传统词典(双解)》等许多词典甚至直接用 reply 来解释 answer 的意思。replied 同为霍译文本和杨译文本的高频词,且还是霍译文本相对于杨译文本的第二大特色词。而 answered 在杨译文本中的特色更为突出。笔者之前对 replied 进行分析时已经发现,在霍译使用 replied 时,杨译有时更喜欢使用 answered。

下面笔者将考察杨译文本中使用 answered 的案例,同时对比霍译的英译情况。answered 在"说道"类会话引导语的杨译文本中使用了 91 次,现仅选取 15 例进行分析,其中霍译文本中有时同样使用了 answered,有时则以其他动词代替。

1.【原文】坠儿道:"何曾见林姑娘了?"(第二十七回)

【杨译】"Miss Lin? We haven't seen her," Zhuier **answered**.

【霍译】'I haven't seen Miss Lin,' said Trinket.

2.【原文】黛玉道："你别管我。"（第三十七回）

【杨译】"Don't worry about me," she **answered**.

【霍译】'Kindly mind your own business, would you?' said Dai-yu.

3.【原文】平儿道："也没打重。"（第四十四回）

【杨译】'It's nothing,' Pinger **answered**. 'You didn't hit hard.'

【霍译】'You didn't hit me very hard,' said Patience.

4.【原文】宝玉听说，就命麝月去取银子。麝月道："花大姐姐还不知搁在那里呢？"（第五十一回）

【杨译】Baoyu then ordered Sheyue to fetch some silver. 'I don't know where our Mistress Xiren keeps it,' she **answered** laughingly.

【霍译】Bao-yu ordered Musk to fetch a tael for him, but Musk said that she didn't know where Aroma kept her money.

5.【原文】晴雯道："这劳什子又不知怎么了，又得去收拾！"（第五十八回）

【杨译】'Something's wrong with that silly clock, it needs mending again,' **answered** Qingwen.

【霍译】'It didn't,' said Skybright. 'The wretched thing needs repairing again, I don't know why.'

6.【原文】二姐儿道："我虽标致，却没品行，看来倒是不标致的好。"（第六十五回）

【杨译】"I may have good looks but I've got a bad name," she **answered**. "So it seems not to be good-looking would be better."

【霍译】'I may have looks, but I've got no class,' said Er-jie. 'Without class, one might just as well not be good-looking.'

7.【原文】宝玉道："你原是个精细人，如何既许了定礼又疑惑起来？"（第六十六回）

【杨译】"You're a smart fellow," **answered** Baoyu. "Once you've given your pledge how can you start having second thoughts?"

【霍译】'For a person so intelligent you have left it a bit late to start feeling dubious now that you have promised to marry the girl and already given them your pledge,' said Bao-yu.

8.【原文】凤姐道："很不必，我没处使。"（第七十四回）

【杨译】"No, I don't need any," she **answered**.

【霍译】'I don't see that at all,' said Xi-feng. 'We don't really need two hundred taels ourselves.'

9. 【原文】麝月**道**："大白日里,还怕什么? ——还怕丢了你不成?"(第七十八回)

   【杨译】"What are you afraid of in broad daylight?" Sheyue **answered**. "You can't get lost."

   【霍译】'That's all right,' said Musk. 'We're not going to lose you in broad daylight!'

10. 【原文】宝蟾**道**："我那里知道? 他在奶奶跟前还不说,谁知道他那些事?"(第八十三回)

    【杨译】"How should I?" **answered** Baochan. "If he wouldn't tell even you,madam,who can possibly know what he's up to?"

    【霍译】'I've not the least idea,' replied Moonbeam coolly. 'If he wouldn't tell you, Mrs Pan, no one else is likely to know.'

11. 【原文】贾环**道**："今日太爷有事,说是放一天学,明儿再去呢。"(第八十七回)

    【杨译】Huan **answered**,"The tutor has some business today,so he's given us one day's holiday. We're to go back tomorrow."

    【霍译】'The Preceptor is busy today,' replied Huan, 'and says we can all have the day off. We're to attend as usual tomorrow.'

12. 【原文】宝玉**道**："我不吃了,心里不舒服。你们吃去罢。"(第八十九回)

    【杨译】"I don't want any,I'm not feeling well," he **answered**. "You go ahead and have yours."

    【霍译】Bao-yu:'I won't have anything to eat. I'm not feeling well. You just have yours.'

13. 【原文】那人**道**："我自南边甄府中来的。"(第九十三回)

    【杨译】"From the Zhen family in the south," he **answered**.

    【霍译】'From the Zhen family in the South,' was his reply.

14. 【原文】彩屏**道**："不用提了。姑娘这几天饭都没吃,只是歪着。"(第一百十五回)

    【杨译】"You may well ask," Caiping **answered**. "These days she won't eat a thing, just curls up on the kang."

    【霍译】'My mistress hasn't eaten for days,' exclaimed Landscape, 'and now she won't even get up from her bed.'

15. 【原文】宝玉**道**："太太不放心,便叫个人瞧瞧,我就吃药。"(第一百十五回)

【杨译】"If you're worried，madam，you can send for a doctor and I'll take some medicine，" he **answered**.

【霍译】'If you're still worried，Mother，' said Bao-yu，'then by all means send for a doctor and I'll take some medicine.'

（六）"说道"类英译之 put in

霍译本和杨译本在处理"说道"类会话引导语的英译时,除了采用单个动词,还采用了一些动词短语形式,其中两者用得最多的均为 put in,霍译文本中有 16 次,杨译文本中 49 次。

《柯林斯高阶英语词典》(*Collins COBUILD Advanced Learner's English Dictionary*)对 put in 的解释为：*if you put in a remark，you interrupt someone or add to what they have said with the remark*.《朗文当代英语词典》(*Longman Dictionary of Contemporary English*)的解释为：*to interrupt someone in order to say something*。因此我们可以推断 put in 表达的是"插话;补充说"之意。

下面笔者将考察霍译文本和杨译文本中使用 put in 的案例：

1.【原文】贾蓉道："他这病也不用别的,只吃得下些饭食就不怕了。"（第十一回）

【杨译】"She'd be all right if only she'd eat，" **put in** Jia Rong.

【霍译】'If only she could get a bit of food inside her. ' said Jia Rong. 'That's her real trouble：she won't eat anything.'

2.【原文】一句话尚未说完,只见他娘子**说道**："你又糊涂了!"（第二十四回）

【杨译】"Are you crazy?" **put in** his wife before he had half finished.

【霍译】'Are you crazy?' his wife's voice cut in from the kitchen.

3.【原文】宝玉道："押韵就好。"（第二十八回）

【杨译】Baoyu **put in**，"As long as he rhymes it，that's good enough."

【霍译】But Bao-yu allowed the line. 'As long as it rhymes，' he said，'we'll let it pass.'

4.【原文】宝玉道："太太屋里的彩云,是个老实人。"（第三十九回）

【杨译】"Caixia in my mother's apartments is an honest girl too，" **put in** Baoyu.

【霍译】'Mother's Suncloud is a good，honest soul，' said Bao-yu.

5.【原文】凤姐道："他早吃了饭了,不用给他。"（第四十回）

【杨译】"She's eaten already，" **put in** Xifeng. "There's no need."

【霍译】'No need，' said Xi-feng. 'She's had her lunch already.'

6. 【原文】秋纹道："不管你是谁的！你不给我,管把老太太的茶吊子倒了洗手!"（第五十四回）

　　【杨译】'Never mind who it's for,' **put in** Qiuwen. 'If you won't give us any,I'll pour water from the old lady's teapot to wash in.

　　【霍译】'I don't care who it's for,' said Ripple,'but if you won't pour that water out for her,I shall come and do it my-self.'

7. 【原文】探春见湘云冒失,连忙解**说道**："这不过是肺火上炎,带出一半点来,也是常事。"（第八十二回）

　　【杨译】To cover up Xiangyun's tactlessness,Tanchun hastily **put in**,"This is nothing out of the usual;it's just that a hot humour in the lungs made her bring up a drop or two."

　　【霍译】Tan-chun tried to cover up for Xiang-yun:'That only means you've got some inflammation on your lungs,and have brought a little up. It's quite common.'

8. 【原文】贾母**道**："你不懂得。"（第八十五回）

　　【杨译】"You wouldn't understand," said his grandmother.

　　【霍译】'Nothing you would understand,' **put in** Grandmother Jia promptly.

9. 【原文】贾琏**道**："听得内阁里人说起,雨村又要升了。"（第九十二回）

　　【杨译】Jia Lian changed the subject by saying,"I've heard from someone in the cabinet that Yucun is to be promoted again."

　　【霍译】'I heard from someone at the Grand Secretariat that Yu-cun is to be promoted again,' **put in** Jia Lian.

10. 【原文】宝玉恐袭人直告诉出来,便**说道**："太太,这事不与袭人相干,是我前日到临安伯府里听戏在路上丢了。"（第九十四回）

　　【杨译】For fear she might tell the truth Baoyu **put in**. "This has nothing to do with Xiren,madam. I lost it on the road the other day when I went to the duke's mansion to see the opera."

　　【霍译】Bao-yu finally spoke up,fearful that she might blurt out the truth. 'Mother,this has nothing to do with Aroma. I lost it the other day on my way back from seeing the plays at the Earl of Lin-an's.'

11. 【原文】平儿**道**："奶奶这么早起来做什么？何苦来呢!"（第一百一回）

　　【杨译】"Why get up so early,madam?" asked Pinger.

【霍译】'Why are you getting up，ma'am？' **put in** Patience.

12.【原文】贾母道："既这么着，索性等到后日初一，你再去求。"（第一百一回）

【杨译】"Better wait till the day after that — the first of the month，" said the old lady.

【霍译】'Why not wait until the day after？' **put in** Grandmother Jia. 'That will be the first of the month. Better to try then.'

13.【原文】雨村道："如今老先生仍是工部，想来京官是没有事的。"（第一百四回）

【杨译】"You are still in the Ministry of Works，sir，" pointed out Yucun. "A metropolitan post should be quite safe."

【霍译】'Now that you are reinstated at the Board of Works，sir，' **put in** Jia Yu-cun，'I think you will find life a great deal less fraught with difficulty.'

14.【原文】周瑞家的道："亲家太太别这么说。"（第一百三回）

【杨译】"Don't say that，madam，" **put in** Mrs. Zhou.

【霍译】'Come，ma'am，' **put in** Zhou Rui's wife，'that's hardly a very sensible question.'

15.【原文】凤姐道："不然，你带了他去罢。"（第一百十三回）

【杨译】Xifeng suggested，"Well，take her back with you."

【霍译】'In that case，' **put in** Xi-feng，'why not take her home with you for a visit？'

霍译文本和杨译文本只有一处是同时使用了 put in（例14），其他几处翻译方式均不相同。

## 第二节 "笑道"类会话引导语翻译研究

"笑道"类会话引导语研究主要包括五大类别："笑道：""笑说道：""笑着道：""笑说："和"笑着说："。"笑道"类会话引导语兼备"笑"和"道"双重形式和含义。

笔者将在本节最后把"冷笑道："作为"笑道"类会话引导语的一个特别分支单独进行分析研究，因为它无论在形式上还是在内涵上都与其他"笑道"类会话引导语有很大不同。

### 一、《红楼梦》原文中的"笑道"类会话引导语

"笑道"在《红楼梦》原文中可谓成千上万，俯拾即是，它的广泛使用也成为

《红楼梦》语言的一大特点。"笑道"的使用不仅推动了小说情节的发展，也在一定程度上反映了人物的性格特征。

会话引导语"笑道："作为一级检索时的数量非常多，有2407个。因其中包括105个"冷笑道："，所以真正纳入笔者"笑道："文本容量的有2302个。此外，还有"笑说道："49个、"笑着道："13个。

以"说："结尾的"笑道"类会话引导语有98个"笑说："（无"冷笑说："的用法）和4个"笑着说："。

因此，本节主要考察的"笑道"类会话引导语种类和数量分别如表4-5所示。

表4-5 "笑道"类会话引导语杨译本特色词

| 序号 | 分类 | 数量 |
|------|------|------|
| 1 | 笑道： | 2302 |
| 2 | 笑说道： | 49 |
| 3 | 笑着道： | 13 |
| 4 | 笑说： | 98 |
| 5 | 笑着说： | 4 |

笔者将以上5个文本合并成一个总的"笑道"类会话引导语文本（总数量为2466）统一进行研究，整理出一个"原文—霍译—杨译"的"笑道"类会话引导语语料库，在此语料库的基础上分别整理出"笑道"类会话引导语的原文、霍译本、杨译本文档，以供研究之用。其中"笑道"类会话引导语的霍译本（或称霍译文本）容量为39 345，"笑道"类会话引导语的杨译本（或称杨译文本）容量为30 527。

## 二、《红楼梦》译文中的"笑道"类会话引导语

笔者将对《红楼梦》"笑道"类会话引导语的霍译本和杨译本进行高频词、独特词以及特色词等方面的分析研究。

### （一）霍译本与杨译本高频词研究

笔者通过分别对《红楼梦》"笑道"类会话引导语的霍译本和杨译本进行词频分析，将位列前100位的高频词列举如表4-6所示。

表4-6 "笑道"类会话引导语霍译本和杨译本高频词

| 霍译 | 字符 | 字频 | 百分比 | 杨译 | 字符 | 字频 | 百分比 |
|------|------|------|--------|------|------|------|--------|
| 1 | said | 1403 | 3.57 | 1 | the | 922 | 3.02 |

（续表）

| 霍译 | 字符 | 字频 | 百分比 | 杨译 | 字符 | 字频 | 百分比 |
|---|---|---|---|---|---|---|---|
| 2 | the | 1150 | 2.92 | 2 | you | 839 | 2.75 |
| 3 | you | 1046 | 2.66 | 3 | a | 747 | 2.45 |
| 4 | to | 966 | 2.46 | 4 | to | 691 | 2.26 |
| 5 | a | 880 | 2.24 | 5 | I | 553 | 1.81 |
| 6 | I | 826 | 2.10 | 6 | and | 490 | 1.61 |
| 7 | and | 656 | 1.67 | 7 | she | 488 | 1.60 |
| 8 | of | 618 | 1.57 | 8 | with | 438 | 1.43 |
| 9 | it | 563 | 1.43 | 9 | of | 395 | 1.29 |
| 10 | that | 532 | 1.35 | 10 | said | 374 | 1.23 |
| 11 | she | 530 | 1.35 | 11 | that | 367 | 1.20 |
| 12 | her | 492 | 1.25 | 12 | it | 341 | 1.12 |
| 13 | with | 403 | 1.02 | 13 | her | 328 | 1.07 |
| 14 | in | 392 | 1.00 | 14 | he | 325 | 1.06 |
| 15 | Bao-yu | 354 | 0.90 | 15 | in | 291 | 0.95 |
| 16 | was | 304 | 0.77 | 16 | smile | 280 | 0.92 |
| 17 | Jia | 286 | 0.73 | 17 | Baoyu | 230 | 0.75 |
| 18 | he | 281 | 0.71 | 18 | this | 225 | 0.74 |
| 19 | laughed | 264 | 0.67 | 19 | Xifeng | 208 | 0.68 |
| 20 | for | 262 | 0.67 | 20 | lady | 199 | 0.65 |
| 21 | at | 245 | 0.62 | 21 | so | 185 | 0.61 |
| 22 | be | 235 | 0.60 | 22 | me | 180 | 0.59 |
| 23 | all | 230 | 0.58 | 23 | for | 175 | 0.57 |
| 24 | Xi-feng | 229 | 0.58 | 24 | what | 168 | 0.55 |
| 25 | what | 221 | 0.56 | 25 | we | 165 | 0.54 |
| 26 | have | 217 | 0.55 | 26 | was | 158 | 0.52 |
| 27 | on | 217 | 0.55 | 27 | laughed | 153 | 0.50 |
| 28 | is | 205 | 0.52 | 28 | your | 147 | 0.48 |
| 29 | me | 202 | 0.51 | 29 | Baochai | 145 | 0.47 |

（续表）

| 霍译 | 字符 | 字频 | 百分比 | 杨译 | 字符 | 字频 | 百分比 |
|------|------|------|--------|------|------|------|--------|
| 30 | this | 199 | 0.51 | 30 | they | 145 | 0.47 |
| 31 | are | 198 | 0.50 | 31 | old | 143 | 0.47 |
| 32 | as | 190 | 0.48 | 32 | chuckled | 142 | 0.47 |
| 33 | but | 185 | 0.47 | 33 | is | 142 | 0.47 |
| 34 | had | 180 | 0.46 | 34 | smiled | 140 | 0.46 |
| 35 | they | 179 | 0.45 | 35 | on | 139 | 0.46 |
| 36 | we | 168 | 0.43 | 36 | are | 134 | 0.44 |
| 37 | so | 167 | 0.42 | 37 | all | 133 | 0.44 |
| 38 | smile | 166 | 0.42 | 38 | as | 132 | 0.43 |
| 39 | your | 166 | 0.42 | 39 | be | 132 | 0.43 |
| 40 | smiled | 165 | 0.42 | 40 | at | 126 | 0.41 |
| 41 | Bao-chai | 157 | 0.40 | 41 | if | 125 | 0.41 |
| 42 | Dai-yu | 156 | 0.40 | 42 | have | 122 | 0.40 |
| 43 | grandmother | 155 | 0.39 | 43 | not | 122 | 0.40 |
| 44 | not | 152 | 0.39 | 44 | but | 120 | 0.39 |
| 45 | his | 146 | 0.37 | 45 | Daiyu | 120 | 0.39 |
| 46 | when | 146 | 0.37 | 46 | up | 114 | 0.37 |
| 47 | if | 145 | 0.37 | 47 | him | 113 | 0.37 |
| 48 | him | 142 | 0.36 | 48 | just | 112 | 0.37 |
| 49 | now | 137 | 0.35 | 49 | can | 109 | 0.36 |
| 50 | about | 136 | 0.35 | 50 | Jia | 106 | 0.35 |
| 51 | them | 132 | 0.34 | 51 | good | 105 | 0.34 |
| 52 | one | 131 | 0.33 | 52 | cried | 103 | 0.34 |
| 53 | there | 129 | 0.33 | 53 | them | 103 | 0.34 |
| 54 | can | 126 | 0.32 | 54 | his | 102 | 0.33 |
| 55 | my | 126 | 0.32 | 55 | madam | 101 | 0.33 |
| 56 | just | 125 | 0.32 | 56 | out | 100 | 0.33 |
| 57 | up | 123 | 0.31 | 57 | asked | 99 | 0.32 |

（续表）

| 霍译 | 字符 | 字频 | 百分比 | 杨译 | 字符 | 字频 | 百分比 |
|---|---|---|---|---|---|---|---|
| 58 | no | 115 | 0.29 | 58 | how | 98 | 0.32 |
| 59 | out | 115 | 0.29 | 59 | replied | 97 | 0.32 |
| 60 | good | 114 | 0.29 | 60 | then | 93 | 0.30 |
| 61 | laughing | 112 | 0.28 | 61 | one | 92 | 0.30 |
| 62 | do | 109 | 0.28 | 62 | no | 91 | 0.30 |
| 63 | Aroma | 108 | 0.27 | 63 | my | 90 | 0.29 |
| 64 | know | 106 | 0.27 | 64 | now | 90 | 0.29 |
| 65 | like | 106 | 0.27 | 65 | here | 85 | 0.28 |
| 66 | from | 104 | 0.26 | 66 | there | 83 | 0.27 |
| 67 | who | 104 | 0.26 | 67 | go | 82 | 0.27 |
| 68 | been | 102 | 0.26 | 68 | when | 80 | 0.26 |
| 69 | very | 101 | 0.26 | 69 | why | 80 | 0.26 |
| 70 | smiling | 95 | 0.24 | 70 | Xiren | 80 | 0.26 |
| 71 | go | 92 | 0.23 | 71 | had | 79 | 0.26 |
| 72 | well | 90 | 0.23 | 72 | Pinger | 79 | 0.26 |
| 73 | Patience | 89 | 0.23 | 73 | too | 76 | 0.25 |
| 74 | see | 89 | 0.23 | 74 | know | 74 | 0.24 |
| 75 | come | 88 | 0.22 | 75 | Tanchun | 72 | 0.24 |
| 76 | oh | 86 | 0.22 | 76 | right | 71 | 0.23 |
| 77 | think | 86 | 0.22 | 77 | remarked | 69 | 0.23 |
| 78 | then | 85 | 0.22 | 78 | Xue | 69 | 0.23 |
| 79 | were | 85 | 0.22 | 79 | Aunt | 67 | 0.22 |
| 80 | here | 84 | 0.21 | 80 | do | 67 | 0.22 |
| 81 | laugh | 83 | 0.21 | 81 | told | 65 | 0.21 |
| 82 | little | 81 | 0.21 | 82 | who | 65 | 0.21 |
| 83 | Xiang-yun | 81 | 0.21 | 83 | put | 64 | 0.21 |
| 84 | back | 78 | 0.20 | 84 | Xiangyun | 64 | 0.21 |
| 85 | lady | 78 | 0.20 | 85 | like | 63 | 0.21 |

（续表）

| 霍译 | 字符 | 字频 | 百分比 | 杨译 | 字符 | 字频 | 百分比 |
|---|---|---|---|---|---|---|---|
| 86 | Xue | 78 | 0.20 | 86 | come | 62 | 0.20 |
| 87 | aunt | 76 | 0.19 | 87 | Li | 62 | 0.20 |
| 88 | by | 75 | 0.19 | 88 | see | 61 | 0.20 |
| 89 | old | 75 | 0.19 | 89 | well | 60 | 0.20 |
| 90 | an | 73 | 0.19 | 90 | about | 59 | 0.19 |
| 91 | Tan-chun | 72 | 0.18 | 91 | cousin | 59 | 0.19 |
| 92 | got | 71 | 0.18 | 92 | by | 58 | 0.19 |
| 93 | right | 71 | 0.18 | 93 | let | 57 | 0.19 |
| 94 | get | 69 | 0.18 | 94 | answered | 56 | 0.18 |
| 95 | would | 69 | 0.18 | 95 | Dowager | 56 | 0.18 |
| 96 | cousin | 68 | 0.17 | 96 | some | 54 | 0.18 |
| 97 | how | 68 | 0.17 | 97 | us | 54 | 0.18 |
| 98 | could | 67 | 0.17 | 98 | Wan | 54 | 0.18 |
| 99 | Li | 67 | 0.17 | 99 | were | 54 | 0.18 |
| 100 | miss | 67 | 0.17 | 100 | back | 51 | 0.17 |

从列举《红楼梦》"笑道"类会话引导语的霍译本和杨译本中的前100位高频词我们可以发现，在霍译本和杨译本中均出现了 said、laughed 和 smiled 三个动词，但在两个译本中的数量和比例差异显著。在霍译本中，said 是排名第1位的词，有1403个，占总文本的3.57%；而在杨译本中，said 虽也是排名第1位的动词，但数量只有374个，占总文本的1.23%。在霍译本中，laughed 排名第19位，有264个，比例为0.67%；smiled 排名第40位，有165个，比例为0.42%。在杨译本中，laughed 排名第27位，有153个，占文本总量的0.50%；smiled 排名第34位，有140个，比例为0.46%。霍译文本和杨译文本中的高频词还都出现了名词 smile。在霍译文本中，smile 排名第38位，有166个，占文本总量的0.42%；在杨译文本中，smile 排名第16位，有280个，占文本总量的0.92%，比例为霍译文本的2倍还多。图4-2可以清晰显示 said、laughed、smiled 和 smile 在两个译本中的差异。

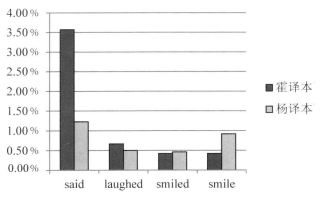

图 4-2 动词 said、laughed、smiled 和名词 smile 在"笑道"类会话引导语两译本中所占比例对比

此外,霍译文本前 100 位高频词中还出现了两个动词的现在分词形式: laughing(排名第 61 位,数量 112,占文本总量的 0.28%)和 smiling(排名第 70 位,数量 95,占文本总量的 0.24%),以及名词 laugh(排名第 81 位,数量 83,占文本总量的 0.21%)。杨译文本前 100 位高频词中还有其他几个动词值得关注:chuckled(排名第 32 位,数量 142,占文本总量的 0.47%)、cried(排名第 52 位,数量 103,占文本总量的 0.34%)、replied(排名第 59 位,数量 97,占文本总量的 0.32%)、remarked(排名第 77 位,数量 69,占文本总量的 0.23%)、told(排名第 81 位,数量 65,占文本总量的 0.21%)和 answered(排名第 94 位,数量 56,占文本总量的 0.18%)。

（二）霍译本与杨译本独特词研究

《红楼梦》里"笑道"类会话引导语的霍译本相对于杨译本的独特词有 2003 个,将人名、地名用词筛除后,词频在 5 次以上的仅有 31 个:

smilingly(29)

smiles(16)

began(13)

ha(11)

perfectly(9)

coz(8)

deprecatingly(8)

drily(8)

moments(8)

amusement(7)

coloured(7)

famous(7)

genially(7)

bless(6)

doubt(6)

dying(6)

good-humouredly(6)

greatly(6)

ho(6)

literary(6)

merely(6)

mistaken(6)

reassuringly(6)

wide(6)

bravo(5)

discussing(5)

enter(5)

graciously(5)

grateful(5)

happily(5)

kotow(5)

《红楼梦》里"笑道"类会话引导语的杨译本相对于霍译本的独特词有 2003 个，将人名、地名用词筛除后，词频在 5 次以上的仅有 23 个：

| | | |
|---|---|---|
| teased(48) | concubine(7) | approached(5) |
| rejoined(29) | meal(7) | bound(5) |
| chortled(16) | scolded(7) | fragrant(5) |
| approved(12) | soothingly(7) | relatives(5) |
| quipped(10) | demanded(6) | sniggered(5) |
| warned(10) | responded(6) | spoilt(5) |
| high(8) | run(6) | tricks(5) |
| priest(8) | scoffed(6) | |

霍译文本的独特词中以-ly 结尾的副词居多，如 smilingly、perfectly、deprecatingly、drily、genially、good-humouredly、greatly、merely、reassuringly、graciously、happily 等。此外名词复数 smiles 也是独特词中频率较高的。杨译文本中的独特词以动词居多，如 teased、rejoined、chortled、approved、quipped、warned、scolded、demanded、responded、scoffed、sniggered 等，说明杨宪益在进行"笑道"类会话引导语翻译时，依然倾向于使用多样化的动词，而不是大量地使用单纯的 said。

（三）霍译本与杨译本特色词研究

《红楼梦》"笑道"类会话引导语的霍译本相对于杨译本的特色词有 335 个，将人名、地名用词筛除后，关键度在 5 以上的特色词有 92 个（见表 4 - 7）。

表 4 - 7 "笑道"类会话引导语霍译本特色词

| 排序 | 词语 | 关键度 | 排序 | 词语 | 关键度 |
|---|---|---|---|---|---|
| 1 | said | 365.392 | 10 | smiles | 17.732 |
| 2 | oh | 49.343 | 11 | think | 16.07 |
| 3 | very | 36.354 | 12 | had | 15.925 |
| 4 | smilingly | 32.14 | 13 | when | 15.033 |
| 5 | at | 23.258 | 14 | ah | 14.653 |
| 6 | laughing | 22.583 | 15 | began | 14.408 |
| 7 | amused | 19.911 | 16 | what | 14.067 |
| 8 | little | 19.395 | 17 | was | 13.456 |
| 9 | got | 18.388 | 18 | about | 13.19 |

（续表）

| 排序 | 词语 | 关键度 | 排序 | 词语 | 关键度 |
|---|---|---|---|---|---|
| 19 | bit | 12.56 | 47 | ladyship | 7.376 |
| 20 | been | 12.122 | 48 | ought | 7.054 |
| 21 | smiling | 11.915 | 49 | seems | 7.016 |
| 22 | that | 10.684 | 50 | doubt | 6.65 |
| 23 | person | 10.317 | 51 | dying | 6.65 |
| 24 | into | 10.176 | 52 | grand | 6.65 |
| 25 | room | 10.08 | 53 | greatly | 6.65 |
| 26 | exactly | 9.975 | 54 | ha | 6.65 |
| 27 | perfectly | 9.975 | 55 | ho | 6.65 |
| 28 | delightedly | 9.472 | 56 | literary | 6.65 |
| 29 | all | 9.208 | 57 | merely | 6.65 |
| 30 | shall | 8.944 | 58 | mistaken | 6.65 |
| 31 | coloured | 8.866 | 59 | reassuringly | 6.65 |
| 32 | coz | 8.866 | 60 | speaking | 6.65 |
| 33 | deprecatingly | 8.866 | 61 | wide | 6.65 |
| 34 | drily | 8.866 | 62 | it | 6.419 |
| 35 | moments | 8.866 | 63 | sort | 6.364 |
| 36 | nice | 8.66 | 64 | her | 6.177 |
| 37 | be | 8.227 | 65 | hurriedly | 6.09 |
| 38 | could | 8.034 | 66 | ones | 6.09 |
| 39 | gave | 8.032 | 67 | seem | 6.09 |
| 40 | from | 7.967 | 68 | stuff | 6.09 |
| 41 | its | 7.958 | 69 | trying | 6.09 |
| 42 | yes | 7.852 | 70 | laughed | 5.929 |
| 43 | amusement | 7.758 | 71 | woman | 5.9 |
| 44 | famous | 7.758 | 72 | of | 5.663 |
| 45 | genially | 7.758 | 73 | but | 5.622 |
| 46 | humouredly | 7.758 | 74 | bless | 5.541 |

（续表）

| 排序 | 词语 | 关键度 | 排序 | 词语 | 关键度 |
|---|---|---|---|---|---|
| 75 | box | 5.541 | 84 | kotow | 5.541 |
| 76 | bravo | 5.541 | 85 | perhaps | 5.541 |
| 77 | discussing | 5.541 | 86 | sir | 5.541 |
| 78 | enter | 5.541 | 87 | have | 5.459 |
| 79 | graciously | 5.541 | 88 | being | 5.365 |
| 80 | grateful | 5.541 | 89 | full | 5.235 |
| 81 | ha | 5.541 | 90 | job | 5.182 |
| 82 | happily | 5.541 | 91 | perhaps | 5.182 |
| 83 | hid | 5.541 | 92 | herself | 5.051 |

　　《红楼梦》里"笑道"类会话引导语的杨译本相对于霍译本的特色词有 414 个,将人名、地名用词筛除后,关键度在 5 以上的特色词有 160 个(见表 4 - 8)。

表 4 - 8　"笑道"类会话引导语杨译本特色词

| 排序 | 词语 | 关键度 | 排序 | 词语 | 关键度 |
|---|---|---|---|---|---|
| 1 | chuckled | 210.485 | 16 | put | 34.387 |
| 2 | cried | 109.075 | 17 | he | 32.577 |
| 3 | remarked | 96.324 | 18 | agreed | 30.309 |
| 4 | lady | 90.084 | 19 | told | 29.664 |
| 5 | teased | 82.046 | 20 | urged | 29.138 |
| 6 | retorted | 78.399 | 21 | countered | 28.868 |
| 7 | smile | 73.754 | 22 | declared | 28.868 |
| 8 | replied | 71.859 | 23 | chortled | 27.349 |
| 9 | answered | 66.669 | 24 | how | 26.813 |
| 10 | rejoined | 49.569 | 25 | with | 26.697 |
| 11 | madam | 45 | 26 | sister | 25.488 |
| 12 | old | 43.175 | 27 | lady | 24.13 |
| 13 | exclaimed | 42.298 | 28 | giggled | 24.04 |
| 14 | asked | 38.074 | 29 | approved | 20.512 |
| 15 | so | 37.034 | 30 | grinned | 19.981 |

（续表）

| 排序 | 词语 | 关键度 | 排序 | 词语 | 关键度 |
|---|---|---|---|---|---|
| 31 | laughingly | 19.723 | 59 | hastily | 11.245 |
| 32 | gaily | 19.713 | 60 | small | 11.245 |
| 33 | cheerfully | 18.588 | 61 | why | 11.096 |
| 34 | she | 18.128 | 62 | demanded | 10.256 |
| 35 | second | 17.69 | 63 | responded | 10.256 |
| 36 | sister | 17.69 | 64 | scoffed | 10.256 |
| 37 | quipped | 17.093 | 65 | proposed | 9.99 |
| 38 | warned | 17.093 | 66 | explained | 9.945 |
| 39 | cousin | 17.091 | 67 | too | 9.721 |
| 40 | announced | 16.992 | 68 | fine | 9.305 |
| 41 | protested | 16.78 | 69 | this | 8.777 |
| 42 | fun | 15.782 | 70 | we | 8.642 |
| 43 | this | 15.767 | 71 | approached | 8.546 |
| 44 | aunt | 14.707 | 72 | bound | 8.546 |
| 45 | that | 14.631 | 73 | brothers | 8.546 |
| 46 | what | 14.631 | 74 | concubine | 8.546 |
| 47 | objected | 14.569 | 75 | fragrant | 8.546 |
| 48 | quite | 14.09 | 76 | relatives | 8.546 |
| 49 | suggested | 14.09 | 77 | run | 8.546 |
| 50 | fine | 13.674 | 78 | sniggered | 8.546 |
| 51 | high | 13.674 | 79 | spoilt | 8.546 |
| 52 | priest | 13.674 | 80 | tricks | 8.546 |
| 53 | begged | 12.744 | 81 | assured | 8.496 |
| 54 | at | 12.614 | 82 | buddha | 8.496 |
| 55 | meal | 11.965 | 83 | the | 8.273 |
| 56 | scolded | 11.965 | 84 | then | 8.237 |
| 57 | soothingly | 11.965 | 85 | observed | 7.992 |
| 58 | blame | 11.499 | 86 | seat | 7.579 |

（续表）

| 排序 | 词语 | 关键度 | 排序 | 词语 | 关键度 |
|------|------|--------|------|------|--------|
| 87 | if | 7.504 | 115 | pay | 5.883 |
| 88 | a | 7.337 | 116 | commented | 5.876 |
| 89 | after | 7.328 | 117 | child | 5.838 |
| 90 | those | 7.328 | 118 | quickly | 5.662 |
| 91 | his | 7.169 | 119 | alike | 5.622 |
| 92 | uncle | 7.169 | 120 | crowed | 5.622 |
| 93 | nonsense | 7.078 | 121 | invite | 5.622 |
| 94 | sight | 7.078 | 122 | ordered | 5.622 |
| 95 | everyone | 7.045 | 123 | promptly | 5.622 |
| 96 | sir | 6.95 | 124 | brother | 5.456 |
| 97 | with | 6.839 | 125 | you | 5.275 |
| 98 | besides | 6.837 | 126 | bring | 5.212 |
| 99 | brother | 6.837 | 127 | lines | 5.212 |
| 100 | duty | 6.837 | 128 | aiya | 5.128 |
| 101 | egg | 6.837 | 129 | amida | 5.128 |
| 102 | fall | 6.837 | 130 | attendant | 5.128 |
| 103 | joked | 6.837 | 131 | bah | 5.128 |
| 104 | overjoyed | 6.837 | 132 | because | 5.128 |
| 105 | smart | 6.837 | 133 | belong | 5.128 |
| 106 | steward | 6.837 | 134 | charge | 5.128 |
| 107 | stewards | 6.837 | 135 | coaxed | 5.128 |
| 108 | twinkle | 6.837 | 136 | delightful | 5.128 |
| 109 | verdict | 6.837 | 137 | disclaimed | 5.128 |
| 110 | versifying | 6.837 | 138 | everybody | 5.128 |
| 111 | volunteered | 6.837 | 139 | fellow | 5.128 |
| 112 | offered | 6.372 | 140 | games | 5.128 |
| 113 | our | 6.013 | 141 | happens | 5.128 |
| 114 | fortune | 5.883 | 142 | hit | 5.128 |

（续表）

| 排序 | 词语 | 关键度 | 排序 | 词语 | 关键度 |
|------|------|--------|------|------|--------|
| 143 | jar | 5.128 | 152 | sighed | 5.128 |
| 144 | opera | 5.128 | 153 | south | 5.128 |
| 145 | osmanthus | 5.128 | 154 | starting | 5.128 |
| 146 | parried | 5.128 | 155 | unicorn | 5.128 |
| 147 | plant | 5.128 | 156 | vulgar | 5.128 |
| 148 | raise | 5.128 | 157 | were | 5.128 |
| 149 | respectfully | 5.128 | 158 | whore | 5.128 |
| 150 | servant | 5.128 | 159 | works | 5.128 |
| 151 | sheepish | 5.128 | 160 | here | 5.064 |

"笑道"类会话引导语的霍译文本相对于杨译文本的第一大特色词是 said，关键度高达 365.392，说明霍克思比杨宪益更倾向于用单纯的 said 来翻译多种多样的"笑道"。smilingly 作为特色词的关键度有 32.14，同时它也是霍译文本中词频最高的独特词。杨译文本的第一大特色词是 chuckled，关键度为 210.485，但 chuckled 并不是杨译文本的独特词，在霍译文本中也有使用，只是数量远远小于杨译文本。位列杨译文本前 100 位高频词的 cried、remarked 和 smile 也有很高的关键度，分别为 109.075、96.324 和 73.754。杨译文本中的独特词如 teased、rejoined、chortled、scolded 等同样也是很重要的特色词。

（四）霍译本与杨译本二词以上搭配

以上笔者分析的都是使用单个动词来翻译《红楼梦》"笑道"类会话引导语的情况。经过进一步检索，笔者发现还有一些二词以上的短语或其他表达形式，如介词短语、动词短语、形容词短语等。现将使用次数在两次以上的表达方式列举如下：

（1）介词短语：with a smile（306）

　　　　　　　with a＋*adj*. smile（61）

　　　　　　　with a laugh（64）

　　　　　　　with a＋*adj*. laugh（10）

　　　　　　　with a grin（16）

　　　　　　　with a chuckle（9）

　　　　　　　with a giggle（4）

　　　　　　　with a twinkle（4）

（2）动词短语：clapped his/her/their hands（32）

           clapping his/her hands(7)

           clapped his/her hands delightedly(7)

           shook his/her head(14)

           gave a+*adj*. laugh(10)

           gave a+*adj*. smile(4)

           laughing in spite of herself(3)

（3）并列动词：laughed and said(6)

           smiled and said(6)

           smiled and nodded(4)

           nodded and smiled(3)

           clapped his/her/their hands and laughed(9)

           laughed and clapped their hands(5)

（4）形容词短语：full of smiles(4)

需要说明的是，laughing in spite of herself 只是动词的现在分词形式加上副词作状语，并不能算是动词短语，此处为了统计方便，权且将此表达方式也放入"动词短语"一类。

以下为这些译文表达方式在"笑道"类会话引导语霍译本和杨译本中的分布情况，其中 with a+*adj*. smile、with a+*adj*. laugh、gave a+*adj*. laugh 和 gave a+*adj*. smile 的使用情况将后续单独列出（见表 4-9）。

表 4-9　短语类表达方式在"笑道"类会话引导语两译本中使用情况统计

| 表达方式 | 总数量 | 霍译文本数量 | 杨译文本数量 |
|---|---|---|---|
| with a smile | 306 | 64 | 242 |
| with a laugh | 64 | 38 | 26 |
| with a grin | 16 | 7 | 9 |
| with a chuckle | 9 | 1 | 8 |
| with a giggle | 4 | 2 | 2 |
| with a twinkle | 4 | 0 | 4 |
| clapped his hands | 16 | 8 | 8 |
| clapped her hands | 9 | 5 | 4 |
| clapped their hands | 7 | 4 | 3 |
| clapped his hands delightedly | 5 | 4 | 1 |
| clapped her hands delightedly | 2 | 2 | 0 |
| clapping his hands | 4 | 2 | 2 |

（续表）

| 表达方式 | 总数量 | 霍译文本数量 | 杨译文本数量 |
|---|---|---|---|
| clapping her hands | 3 | 1 | 2 |
| shook her head | 11 | 5 | 6 |
| shook his head | 3 | 2 | 1 |
| laughing in spite of herself | 3 | 3 | 0 |
| laughed and said | 6 | 4 | 2 |
| smiled and said | 6 | 3 | 3 |
| smiled and nodded | 4 | 4 | 0 |
| nodded and smiled | 3 | 2 | 1 |
| laughed and clapped their hands | 5 | 4 | 1 |
| clapped her hands and laughed | 4 | 2 | 2 |
| clapped his hands and laughed | 3 | 1 | 2 |
| clapped their hands and laughed | 2 | 0 | 2 |
| full of smiles | 4 | 4 | 0 |

通过列举上述表达方式在"笑道"类会话引导语霍译本和杨译本中的使用情况,我们可以发现:

（1）with a smile 的用法是杨译文本的一大特色,杨译文本使用了 242 次,而霍译文本中仅有 64 次,杨译数量是霍译的将近 4 倍。

（2）with a chuckle 也是杨译文本的特色用法,有 8 例,而霍译文本中仅有 1 例。

（3）with a twinkle 和 clapped their hands and laughed 是杨译文本的独特用法,霍译文本中没有出现过。

（4）clapped one's hands delightedly 是霍译文本的特色用法,共出现了 6 次,而杨译文本中仅出现过 1 次。

（5）laughing in spite of herself、smiled and nodded 和 full of smiles 是霍译文本的独特用法,杨译文本中没有出现过。

接下来笔者分别考察了 with a+adj. smile、with a+adj. laugh、gave a+adj. laugh 和 gave a+adj. smile 的使用情况（见表 4-10、表 4-11、表 4-12 和表 4-13）。

表 4－10 "with a＋*adj*. smile"在"笑道"类会话引导语两译本中使用情况统计

| 表达方式 | 数量 | 霍译文本数量 | 杨译文本数量 |
|---|---|---|---|
| 总数量 | 61 | 43 | 18 |
| 总类别 | 41 | 33 | 11 |
| with a conciliatory smile | 5 | 1 | 4 |
| with a disarming smile | 3 | 2 | 1 |
| with a faint smile | 3 | 0 | 3 |
| with a gentle smile | 3 | 3 | 0 |
| with a sheepish smile | 3 | 0 | 3 |
| with a bitter smile | 2 | 2 | 0 |
| with a crushing smile | 2 | 2 | 0 |
| with a dry smile | 2 | 2 | 0 |
| with a gracious smile | 2 | 2 | 0 |
| with a grateful smile | 2 | 2 | 0 |
| with a knowing smile | 2 | 1 | 1 |
| with a pleased smile | 2 | 2 | 0 |
| with a polite smile | 2 | 2 | 0 |
| with a broad smile | 1 | 1 | 0 |
| with a charming smile | 1 | 1 | 0 |
| with a complacent smile | 1 | 1 | 0 |
| with a confident smile | 1 | 1 | 0 |
| with a confidential smile | 1 | 1 | 0 |
| with a courteous smile | 1 | 0 | 1 |
| with a deferential smile | 1 | 0 | 1 |
| with a diplomatic smile | 1 | 1 | 0 |
| with a fond smile | 1 | 0 | 1 |
| with a friendly smile | 1 | 1 | 0 |
| with a good-humoured smile | 1 | 1 | 0 |
| with a knowledgeable smile | 1 | 1 | 0 |

（续表）

| 表达方式 | 数量 | 霍译文本数量 | 杨译文本数量 |
|---|---|---|---|
| with a lubricious smile | 1 | 1 | 0 |
| with a meaningful smile | 1 | 1 | 0 |
| with a mischievous smile | 1 | 1 | 0 |
| with a mocking smile | 1 | 0 | 1 |
| with a modest smile | 1 | 1 | 0 |
| with a mollifying smile | 1 | 0 | 1 |
| with a nonchalant smile | 1 | 1 | 0 |
| with a placatory smile | 1 | 1 | 0 |
| with a pleasant smile | 1 | 0 | 1 |
| with a proud smile | 1 | 1 | 0 |
| with a sarcastic smile | 1 | 1 | 0 |
| with a sly smile | 1 | 1 | 0 |
| with a smug smile | 1 | 1 | 0 |
| with a studied smile | 1 | 1 | 0 |
| with a winning smile | 1 | 1 | 0 |
| with a wry smile | 1 | 1 | 0 |

从表 4-10 我们可以看出，with a+$adj$. smile 这一表达方式是霍译文本的一大特色，总数量有 43 个，是杨译文本的 2.4 倍；表达方式的类别多达 33 种，是杨译文本类别的 3 倍。

表 4-11 "with a+$adj$. laugh"在"笑道"类会话引导语两译本中使用情况统计

| 表达方式 | 数量 | 霍译文本数量 | 杨译文本数量 |
|---|---|---|---|
| 总数量 | 10 | 9 | 1 |
| 总类别 | 10 | 9 | 1 |
| with a delighted laugh | 1 | 1 | 0 |
| with a dismissive laugh | 1 | 1 | 0 |
| with a feigned laugh | 1 | 1 | 0 |
| with a good-natured laugh | 1 | 1 | 0 |

(续表)

| 表达方式 | 数量 | 霍译文本数量 | 杨译文本数量 |
|---|---|---|---|
| with a little laugh | 1 | 1 | 0 |
| with a playful laugh | 1 | 1 | 0 |
| with a rueful laugh | 1 | 1 | 0 |
| with a short laugh | 1 | 1 | 0 |
| with a soft laugh | 1 | 0 | 1 |
| with a strange laugh | 1 | 1 | 0 |

with a＋*adj*. laugh 更加明显是霍译文本的特色表达方式,共有 9 种不同的形式,杨译文本只有 1 种形式,总量只有 1 个,且与霍译文本不同。

表 4‐12　"gave a＋*adj*. laugh"在"笑道"类会话引导语两译本中使用情况统计

| 表达方式 | 数量 | 霍译文本数量 | 杨译文本数量 |
|---|---|---|---|
| 总数量 | 10 | 10 | 0 |
| 总类别 | 5 | 5 | 0 |
| gave a little laugh | 6 | 6 | 0 |
| gave a crapulous laugh | 1 | 1 | 0 |
| gave a deprecatory laugh | 1 | 1 | 0 |
| gave a nervous laugh | 1 | 1 | 0 |
| gave a silly laugh | 1 | 1 | 0 |

gave a＋*adj*. laugh 是霍译文本的独特表达方式,共有 5 个不同类别,总数量为 10 个,其中 gave a little laugh 使用频率最高,有 6 次。杨译文本中没有这一表达方式。

表 4‐13　"gave a＋*adj*. smile"在"笑道"类会话引导语两译本中使用情况统计

| 表达方式 | 数量 | 霍译文本数量 | 杨译文本数量 |
|---|---|---|---|
| 总数量 | 4 | 3 | 1 |
| 总类别 | 4 | 3 | 1 |
| gave a faint smile | 1 | 1 | 0 |
| gave a rueful smile | 1 | 1 | 0 |
| gave a smarmy smile | 1 | 1 | 0 |

（续表）

| 表达方式 | 数量 | 霍译文本数量 | 杨译文本数量 |
|---|---|---|---|
| gave a wan smile | 1 | 0 | 1 |

gave a＋*adj*. smile 是霍译文本的特色表达方式,共有 3 个不同类别,总数量为 3 个,杨译文本只有 1 种形式,总量只有 1 个,且与霍译文本不同。

通过对以上 4 种表达方式:with a＋*adj*. smile、with a＋*adj*. laugh、gave a＋*adj*. laugh 和 gave a＋*adj*. smile 的使用情况的统计,我们可以总结出,虽然 with a smile 是杨译文本的最大特色,但是在 smile 或 laugh 前加上一个形容词的形式却是霍译文本的一大特色。此外,在"动词＋名词"形式的动词短语(如 give a smile/laugh)使用方面,霍译文本的使用数量和种类明显多于杨译文本。这种使用"虚化动词＋名词"结构的动词短语来替代单纯动词的偏好(尽管后面的名词通常是由动词转化而来的动作名词)也是英语中的一大特色,如使用 give a smile 来替代动词 smile,或使用 have a try 来替代动词 try。

### 三、《红楼梦》"笑道"类会话引导语英译案例研究

笔者将在上述对《红楼梦》原文以及译文中的"笑道"类会话引导语分析统计的基础上开展《红楼梦》里"笑道"类会话引导语英译的案例研究。为此笔者将选取霍译文本和杨译文本中均排名前 100 位的高频动词 said、laughed 和 smiled,霍译文本中数量最多的独特词 smilingly 和 smiles,杨译文本中数量最多的独特词 teased 和关键度最高的特色词 chuckled,杨译文本中最为特色介词短语 with a smile,以及霍译文本中特色动词短语 with a＋*adj*. laugh 等进行分析。

(一)"笑道"类英译之 said

said 一词在"笑道"类会话引导语的英译中仍然保持着非常高的数量和百分比。在霍译文本中,said 高居前 100 位高频词第 1 名,有 1404 个,占霍译文本总量的 3.57%；在杨译文本中,said 排在前 100 位高频词的第 10 名,有 374 个,占杨译文本总量的 1.23%。said 也是"笑道"类会话引导语的霍译本相对于杨译本的第一大特色词,关键度高达 365.392。

以下为几个霍译和杨译均使用 said 来翻译"笑道"类会话引导语的例子:

1.【原文】道人笑道:"你就请解。"(第一回)

【霍译】'Please do!' **said** the Taoist.

【杨译】"By all means do," **said** the Taoist.

2.【原文】雨村笑道:"你也算贫贱之交了;此系私室,但坐不妨。"(第四回)

【霍译】'Come,' **said** Yu-cun, 'as a friend of my early, hard-up days you are entitled to. After all，this is a private room. Why not？'

【杨译】"We were friends in the days when I was hard up，" **said** Yucun. "Besides，this is my private office."

3.【原文】贾政笑道："此数处不能游了。虽如此，到底从那一边出去，也可略观大概。"（第十七回）

【霍译】'I can see that we shan't be able to finish today，' **said** Jia Zheng. 'However，if we go out by the way I said，we should at least be able to get some idea of the general layout.'

【杨译】"We can't see the rest of the places，" **said** Jia Zheng. "But by going out the other way we can at least get a general idea，even if we don't see them all."

4.【原文】宝钗笑道："等着，咱们两个一齐儿走，瞧瞧他去。"（第二十回）

【霍译】'Wait！' **said** Bao-chai. 'Let's go and see her together！'

【杨译】"Wait，" **said** Baochai. "Let's go together."

5.【原文】宝玉笑道："起来吃饭去。——就开戏了，你爱听那一出？我好点。"（第二十二回）

【霍译】'Get up and have something to eat！' he **said**. 'The players will be starting shortly. Tell me some play you like so that I shall know which one to choose！'

【杨译】"Come on to breakfast，" he **said**. "The show will soon be starting. Tell me which opera you'd like and I'll ask for it."

6.【原文】黛玉笑道："他不能答就算输了。"（第二十二回）

【霍译】'Failure to answer means defeat，' **said** Dai-yu.

【杨译】"Failure to answer promptly means defeat，" **said** Daiyu.

7.【原文】凤姐笑道："你要爱吃，我那里还有呢。"（第二十五回）

【霍译】'I've still got quite a bit left，' **said** Xi-feng. 'If you really like it，you can have it all.'

【杨译】"If you really like it I've plenty more，" **said** Xifeng.

8.【原文】宝玉笑道："紫鹃，把你们的好茶沏碗我喝。"（第二十六回）

【霍译】'Nightingale，' **said** Bao-yu， ' what about a cup of that excellent tea of yours？'

【杨译】"Zijuan，" **said** Baoyu， "pour a cup of that good tea of yours for me，will you？"

9.【原文】王夫人笑道："到底是宝丫头好孩子，不撒谎。"（第二十八回）

【霍译】'You see! Bao-chai is a good girl. She doesn't tell lies，' **said** Lady Wang.

【杨译】"After all she's good girl，" **said** Lady Wang. "Baochai wouldn't tell a lie."

10.【原文】贾母听说，就笑道："既这么着，我和你去。"（第二十九回）

　　【霍译】'All right then，I'll come，' **said** Grandmother Jia，who had been listening.

　　【杨译】When the Lady Dowager heard of this she **said**，"In that case，I'll go along with you."

11.【原文】湘云忙**笑道**："好姐姐！你这么说，倒不是真心待我了。（第三十七回）

　　【霍译】'My dearest girl！' **said** Xiang-yun. 'Of course I shan't take it amiss! How can you suggest such a thing? If you do so again，I shall begin to think that you aren't really fond of me at all!'

　　【杨译】"My dear cousin，you're being touchy instead if you talk like that，" **said** Xiangyun.

12.【原文】王夫人**笑道**："既在令内，没有站着的理。"（第四十回）

　　【霍译】'If Faithful is going to be our M. C.，' **said** Lady Wang，'we can't possibly have her standing up all the time.'

　　【杨译】"If you're joining in，there's no reason why you should stand，" **said** Lady Wang.

13.【原文】黛玉**笑道**："这可是云丫头闹的。我的卦再不错。"（第四十九回）

　　【霍译】'Yun is at the bottom of this，' **said** Dai-yu. 'Mark my words！'

　　【杨译】'This is all Xiangyun's doing，' **said** Daiyu. 'What did I tell you？'

14.【原文】宝琴**笑道**："在南京收着呢，此时那里去取？"（第五十二回）

　　【霍译】'That's not possible，' **said** Bao-qin. 'I left it behind in Nanking.'

　　【杨译】'I left it in Nanjing，' **said** Baoqin. 'I can't lay my hands on it at a moment's notice.'

15.【原文】紫鹃**笑道**："你也好了，该放我回去瞧瞧我们那一个去了。"（第五十七回）

【霍译】'Now that you're better,' said Nightingale, 'you ought to let me go back to see how my other invalid is getting on.'

【杨译】'Now that you're better you should let me go back to see my own patient,' said Zijuan.

（二）"笑道"类英译之 laughed

laughed 在"笑道"类会话引导语霍译本和杨译本中都位居高频词前列。该词在霍译文本中排第 19 位,数量为 264,占文本总量的 0.67%;在杨译文本中排第 27 位,数量为 153,占文本总量的 0.50%。以下为几个霍译和杨译均使用 laughed 来翻译"笑道"类会话引导语的例子:

1.【原文】雨村笑道:"不妥,不妥。等我再斟酌斟酌,压服得口声才好。"（第四回）

【霍译】Yu-cun laughed. 'Too risky! Let me turn it over in my mind a little longer. The main thing is to think of something that will stop people talking.'

【杨译】"Impossible," Yucun laughed. "I shall have to think this over carefully in order to suppress idle talk."

2.【原文】平儿笑道:"不少就罢了,那里还有多出来的分儿?"（第二十一回）

【霍译】Patience laughed. 'Isn't it enough that there was nothing missing? Why should there be anything extra?'

【杨译】Pinger laughed. "Isn't it enough that nothing's missing? What else could be there?"

3.【原文】坠儿笑道:"他就叫小红。你问他作什么?"（第二十六回）

【霍译】Trinket laughed: 'Yes. Why do you ask?'

【杨译】Zhuier laughed. "That's right. Why do you ask?"

4.【原文】众人听了都笑道:"骂的巧,可不是给了那西洋花点子哈巴儿了!"（第三十七回）

【霍译】The other maids laughed. 'You'd better watch what you say! That's just who she did give them to: Master Bao's little dog, Flower.'

【杨译】The other girls laughed. "You've hit the nail on the head. They were given to this foreign-species, spotted lap-dog of ours."

5.【原文】凤姐儿忙笑道:"这话老祖宗说差了。……"（第五十二回）

【霍译】Xi-feng laughed. 'Now there you are quite wrong, Grannie.'

【杨译】"You're wrong there, Old Ancestress," laughed Xifeng.

6.【原文】宝钗笑道："真真膏粱纨袴之谈！"（第五十六回）

【霍译】Bao-chai laughed. 'There speaks the voice of gilded youth. How typical!'

【杨译】'Truly spoken like a rich young dandy!' laughed Baochai.

7.【原文】众婆子笑道："真真是位呆姑娘，连当票子也不知道！"（第五十七回）

【霍译】The women laughed: 'What a simpleton! Fancy not knowing what a pawn ticket is!'

【杨译】Everybody laughed. 'Little simpleton! She doesn't even know what a pawn ticket is.'

8.【原文】紫鹃笑道："你这个小东西儿，倒也巧。"（第五十七回）

【霍译】Nightingale laughed. 'You're an artful little minx, aren't you?

【杨译】'You imp!' Zijuan laughed.

9.【原文】袭人笑道："我说你是猫儿食。虽然如此，也该上去陪他们，多少应个景儿。"（第六十二回）

【霍译】Aroma laughed: 'You're like a cat: always eating except when you ought to be. You'd better come and sit with them all the same, for appearance's sake.'

【杨译】"I always say you're as bad as a cat," Xiren laughed. "Whatever you smell takes your fancy. Other people's food tastes better to you than your own. Still, you'd better go and keep them company and make a show of eating."

10.【原文】李纨尤氏都笑道："姑娘也别说呆话。难道你是不出门子的吗？"（第七十一回）

【霍译】Li Wan and You-shi both laughed. 'Now you are talking like a simpleton, young lady. Don't you think you will be getting married then as well?'

【杨译】Li Wan and Madam You laughed. "You're talking nonsense too, child. Are you never going to get married? Whom are you trying to fool?"

11.【原文】凤姐笑道："你夏爷爷好小气。这也值的放在心里？"（第七十二回）

【霍译】Xi-feng laughed. 'Your Daddy Xia is an old fuss-pot, tell him. He really shouldn't worry his head over such trifles.'

【杨译】"His Excellency is too scrupulous." Xifeng **laughed**. "He may as well forget it."

12.【原文】尤氏忙**笑**道:"我今儿是那里来的晦气? 偏都碰着你姐儿们气头儿上了。"(第七十五回)

【霍译】You-shi **laughed**. 'I think today must be my unlucky day. I seem to have caught all you young ladies in a thoroughly unpleasant mood.'

【杨译】"I'm certainly out of luck today," Madam You **laughed**, "Finding so many of you girls in a bad temper."

13.【原文】金桂听了**笑**道:"你怎么遭塌起爷们来了!"(第九十一回)

【霍译】Jin-gui **laughed**. 'How dare you insult one of the masters like that…'

【杨译】Jingui **laughed**. "How can you run down a gentleman like that?"

14.【原文】周妈妈**笑**道:"你别哄我。他们什么人家,肯给我们庄家人?"(第一百十九回)

【霍译】Mrs Zhou **laughed**:'Don't go making fun of me! A great family like theirs, stoop to the likes of us!'

【杨译】"Don't make fun of me!" **laughed** Mrs. Zhou. "Such grand people would never agree to marry her to a family like ours."

15.【原文】雨村低了半日头,忽然**笑**道:"是了,是了!"(第一百二十回)

【霍译】Yu-cun lowered his head in thought for a while, then suddenly **laughed**:'Yes! Of course!'

【杨译】Yucun lowered his head in thought, then suddenly **laughed**, "I get it!"

(三)"笑道"类英译之 smiled

smiled 在"笑道"类会话引导语霍译本和杨译本中也均位居高频词前列,只是数量和比例略少于 laughed。在霍译文本中,smiled 排第 40 位,数量为 165,占文本总量的 0.42%;在杨译文本中排第 34 位,数量为 140,占文本总量的 0.46%。

我们通过词典中的释义可以清楚地看到动词 smile 与 laugh 的区别。

(1)《牛津高阶英汉双解词典》(*Oxford Advanced Learner's English-Chinese Dictionary*):

**laugh**：*make the sounds and movements of the face and body that express lively amusement，joy，contempt，etc* 笑；发笑

**smile**：*give an expression of the face，usu with the corners of the mouth turned up，showing happiness，amusement，pleasure，etc* 微笑

（2）《美国传统词典（双解）》（*E-C American Heritage Dictionary*）：

**laugh**：*to express certain emotions，especially mirth，delight，or derision，by a series of spontaneous，usually unarticulated sounds often accompanied by corresponding facial and bodily movements.* 笑：为表达某种情感，尤指高兴、快乐或嘲笑而发的一阵自发的，通常是不清晰的声音，并常伴随着脸部和身体的运动

**smile**：*to have a facial expression characterized by an upward curving of the corners of the mouth and indicating pleasure，amusement，or derision.* 微笑：做出一种面部表情，其特点是嘴角向上弯成曲线，表示舒服、高兴或嘲笑

从以上关于 laugh 与 smile 的释义我们可以推断，laugh 指的是"大笑"，常表示出声的笑，其程度要大于 smile；smile 只是微笑，通常不发出声音。

以下为几个霍译和杨译使用 smiled 来翻译"笑道"类会话引导语的例子，其中有些是霍译和杨译不约而同使用 smiled 来翻译的例子：

1. 【原文】（凤姐）说着，又向小红**笑道**："明儿你伏侍我罢，我认你做干女孩儿。我一调理，你就出息了！"（第二十七回）

   【霍译】She **smiled** at Crimson again. 'How would you like to come and work for me and be my god-daughter? With a little grooming from me you could go far.'

   【杨译】She **smiled** at Xiaohong. "You must come and work for me. I'll make you my adopted daughter and see that you turn out all right."

2. 【原文】小红**笑道**："愿意不愿意？——我们也不敢说。"（第二十七回）

   【霍译】Crimson **smiled**. 'As to being willing or not，madam，I don't think it's my place to say.'

   【杨译】Xiaohong **smiled**. "Willing? As if that were for us to say!"

3. 【原文】琪官接了，**笑道**："无功受禄，何以克当？"（第二十八回）

   【霍译】Bijou **smiled** and accepted it ceremoniously：'I have done nothing to deserve this favour. It is too great an honour.'

   【杨译】"What have I done to deserve this?" Qiguan **smiled**.

4. 【原文】黛玉**笑道**："你死了，别人不知怎么样，我先就哭死了。"（第三十一回）

【霍译】Dai-yu **smiled**. 'If you were to die，I don't know about anyone else，but I know that I should die of grief.'

【杨译】"I can't say what others would do if you died." Daiyu **smiled**. "I'd die first of crying."

5.【原文】妙玉笑道："这更好了。只是你嘱咐他们，抬了水，只搁在山门外头墙根下，别进门来。"（第四十一回）

【霍译】Adamantina **smiled** graciously. 'That would be very nice. But tell them to bring the water only as far as the gate. They can leave it there at the foot of the outer wall. Tell them not to come inside.'

【杨译】"That's a good idea." She **smiled**. "Only make them leave the buckets by the wall outside the gate. They mustn't come in."

6.【原文】宝玉笑着道："满屋里就只是他磨牙。"（第二十回）

【霍译】'Of all the girls in this room she has the sharpest tongue，' said Bao-yu.

【杨译】and Baoyu **smiled**. "She's got the sharpest tongue of you all，" he remarked.

7.【原文】平儿笑道："吃饭么还不请奶奶去?"（第七十一回）

【霍译】Patience **smiled**. 'She wouldn't eat without first asking you，' she said.

【杨译】Pinger **smiled**. "How could we omit to invite you，madam，if we were having a meal?"

8.【原文】袭人笑道："并不是我多话。一个人知书达礼，就该往上巴结才是。就是心爱的人来了，也叫他瞧着喜欢尊敬啊。"（第八十六回）

【霍译】Aroma **smiled**. 'I'm not giving you a lecture. It's just that you know what people say about actors. Now that you're studying the classics and learning all the proper rules of behaviour，you should try to conform and get on in the world. When your sweetheart comes along，surely you'll want to make a good impression then?'

【杨译】"I didn't mean to nag." She **smiled**. "But someone who studies the classics and knows the rules of propriety ought to aim high. Then，when the one you love comes，she'll be pleased and respect you."

9.【原文】贾政看完,笑道:"这里正因人多,甄家倒荐人来。又不好却的。"
(第九十三回)

【霍译】Jia Zheng **smiled** wrily as he reached the end of the letter. 'Here we are overstaffed ourselves,' he mused aloud to himself, 'and the Zhens must send us one of theirs. We shall have to try and find room for him somehow, I suppose.'

【杨译】After reading this Jia Zheng **smiled**. "We were thinking that our staff is too large," he said. "However, we can't turn away someone recommended by the Zhen family."

10.【原文】林家的**笑道**:"不是不耽:头一宗,这件事,老太太和二奶奶办事,我们都不能很明白;再者,又有大奶奶和平姑娘呢。"(第九十七回)

【霍译】Lin's wife **smiled**. 'It is not that I can't take the responsibility. It is just that Her Old Ladyship and Mrs Lian have arranged everything and the likes of us don't really know what's going on. In the circumstances, it seems only right to mention you and Miss Patience.'

【杨译】"It's not that." Mrs. Lin **smiled**. "But we can't be sure what plan the old lady and Madam Lian have; and besides you and Miss Pinger are here, madam."

11.【原文】二仙**笑道**:"此乃玄机,不可预泄。"(第一回)

【霍译】The reverend gentlemen laughed. 'These are heavenly mysteries and may not be divulged.

【杨译】"This is a mystery which we cannot divulge." The two immortals **smiled**.

12.【原文】凤姐**笑道**:"你该去了。"(第十二回)

【霍译】Xi-feng laughed. 'You had better go!'

【杨译】"You had better go now," Xifeng **smiled**.

13.【原文】袭人**笑道**:"你们不用白忙,我自然知道,不敢乱给他东西吃的。"(第十九回)

【霍译】'Now don't you two rush about, Mother,' said Aroma. 'I know how to look after him. There's no point in your giving him a lot of things he won't be able to eat.'

【杨译】"You're just wasting your time. I know him." Xiren **smiled**. "It's no use putting out those sweetmeats. He can't eat just anything."

14.【原文】宝玉**笑道**:"你今年十几岁?"(第二十四回)

【霍译】'How old are you then?' Bao-yu asked him.

【杨译】Baoyu **smiled**. "What age are you?"

15.【原文】两个人正说着,只见紫鹃进来,看见宝玉,**笑说道**:"宝二爷,今日这样高兴!"(第八十六回)

【霍译】While they were talking Nightingale came in, and on seeing Bao-yu in the room, inquired with a smile:'To what are we to attribute this joyful event, Master Bao?'

【杨译】While they were talking Zijuan had come in. She **smiled** at the sight of Baoyu. "So you're in good spirits today, Master Bao!" she remarked.

（四）"笑道"类英译之 smilingly 和 smiles

smilingly 和 smiles 是"笑道"类会话引导语的霍译文本中词频最高的独特词,数量分别为 29 和 16,这两个词在杨译文本中一次都没有出现过。

前文已经探讨过几部权威词典里关于 smilingly 的定义,意思为"微笑着;微笑地;带着微笑地",在句中做伴随状语。下面笔者将列举几个霍译文本中使用 smilingly 来翻译"笑道"类会话引导语的例子,同时考察杨译本中的翻译方法:

1.【原文】贾蓉媳妇秦氏便忙**笑道**:"我们这里有给宝二叔收拾下的屋子,老祖宗放心,只管交给我就是了。"(第五回)

【霍译】but Qin-shi, the little wife of Jia Rong, **smilingly** proposed an alternative. 'We have got just the room here for Uncle Bao. Leave him to me, Grannie dear! He will be quite safe in my hands.'

【杨译】At once Jia Rong's wife Qin Keqing said with a smile:"We have a room ready here for Uncle Baoyu. The Old Ancestress can set her mind at rest and leave him safely to me."

2.【原文】略待半刻,见王夫人无话,方欲退出去,薛姨妈忽又**笑道**:"你且站住。我有一件东西,你带了去罢。"(第七回)

【霍译】Having finished it, she waited for some comment from Lady Wang, but finding that none was forth-coming, was on the point of withdrawing when Aunt Xue **smilingly** enjoined her to stay. 'Just a moment! There is something I should like you to take for me.'

【杨译】It seemed Lady Wang had no further instructions for her，and she was on the point of leaving when Aunt Xue stopped her. "Wait a minute，" she said with a smile. "I've something for you to take back."

3.【原文】二人正说着，只见湘云走来，**笑道**："爱哥哥，林姐姐，你们天天一处玩，我好容易来了，也不理我理儿。"

【霍译】Just then Xiang-yun burst in on them and reproved them **smilingly** for abandoning her："Couthin Bao，Couthin Lin：you can thee each other every day. It'th not often I get a chanthe to come here；yet now I have come，you both ignore me！'

【杨译】They were interrupted by Xiangyun's arrival. "Why，Ai Brother and Sister Lin！" she cried cheerfully. "You can be together every day，but it's rarely I have a chance to visit you；yet you pay no attention to poor little me."

4.【原文】黛玉听了，就欲回去，袭人**笑道**："姑娘请站着，有一个字帖儿，瞧瞧写的是什么话。"（第二十二回）

【霍译】She was on the point of going back again when Aroma **smilingly** detained her：'Just a moment，Miss！There's a note here. Would you like to see what it says？'

【杨译】she was turning to leave when Xiren said with a smile："Just a minute，miss！He wrote something you might like to look at."

5.【原文】凤姐答应着，回头望着玉钏儿**笑道**："大喜，大喜！"（第三十六回）

【霍译】After promising to see that this was done，Xi-feng turned **smilingly** to Silver and congratulated her.

【杨译】Xifeng turned to look at Yuchuan. "Congratulations！" she called with a smile.

6.【原文】贾母听说，指着惜春**笑道**："你瞧我这个小孙女儿，他就会画；等明儿叫他画一张如何？"（第四十回）

【霍译】Grandmother Jia **smilingly** pointed a finger in Xi-chun's direction. 'You see my little great-niece over there？She can paint. Shall we get her to do you a painting of it？'

【杨译】The Lady Dowager pointed to Xichun. "See this young grand-daughter of mine？" she asked. "She can paint. Shall I get her to do a painting for you tomorrow？"

7. 【原文】凤姐儿笑道:"媳妇来接婆婆来了。"(第四十五回)

   【霍译】Xi-feng **smilingly** inquired of Lai Da's wife whether she had come to collect her mother-in-law.

   【杨译】Xifeng remarked with a smile，"the daughter-in-law has come for her mother-in-law."

8. 【原文】探春笑道:"明儿我补一个柬来,请你入社。"(第四十八回)

   【霍译】'I can see I shall soon be writing an invitation asking you to join our poetry club,' said Tan-chun **smilingly**.

   【杨译】Tanchun said，"tomorrow I'll prepare some refreshments and invite you formally to join our poetry club."

9. 【原文】黛玉听了,便知有文章,因笑道:"你念出来我听听。"(第四十九回)

   【霍译】Dai-yu realized that something must lie behind this request; nevertheless she **smilingly** promised that she would do her best.

   【杨译】Sensing something behind this she said archly，"Go on."

10. 【原文】李绮笑道:"恰是了。"(第五十回)

    【霍译】Li Qi acknowledged **smilingly** that this was correct.

    【杨译】"You've hit the nail on the head，" Li Qi told her.

11. 【原文】莺儿便笑道:"你会拿这柳条子编东西不会?"(第五十九回)

    【霍译】'Do you know how to weave things with these?' Oriole **smilingly** asked her companion.

    【杨译】"Can you weave things out of osiers?" Yinger asked.

12. 【原文】黛玉笑道:"你知道我这病,大夫不许多吃茶,这半钟尽够了,难为你想的到。"(第六十二回)

    【霍译】'Oh，you know me,' said Dai-yu **smilingly**. 'I can't drink much tea because of my illness. The doctor says it's bad for me. This half cup will be quite enough for me. Thank you very much，though. It's very kind of you.'

    【杨译】But Daiyu said，"You know the doctor won't let me drink too much tea on account of my illness，so this half cup is plenty. Thank you for bringing it."

13. 【原文】李纨听如此说,便已知道昨夜的事,因笑道:"你这话有因。是谁做的事够使的了?"(第七十五回)

    【霍译】Li Wan realized that she must be referring to the events of the previous night. 'Why do you say that?' she asked **smilingly**. 'What has who got up to that doesn't bear investigating?'

【杨译】Li Wan knew from this that she had heard about the last night's happenings. "Why do you say that?" she laughed. "Who's been carrying on in a scandalous way?"

14.【原文】众人听了,都又笑道:"这原该如此。"(第七十八回)

【霍译】'And very right that they should!' said the literary gentlemen **smilingly**.

【杨译】"So we should," they all agreed, laughing.

15.【原文】只见王爷笑道:"众位只管就请。叫人来给我送出去,告诉锦衣府的官员说:这都是亲友,不必盘查,快快放出。"(第一百五回)

【霍译】The prince, however, seemed unperturbed, and announced **smilingly**: 'Gentlemen, please consider yourselves free to leave. Send for some of my men to escort them out,' he continued, addressing Zhao, 'and tell your own officers that these are all guests and are not to be hindered or subjected to any kind of search, but are to be let through without delay.'

【杨译】"These gentlemen are free to go," the prince said affably. "Have attendants see them out and notify your guards that there is no need to search them as they are all guests. Let them leave at once."

名词 smile 在"笑道"类会话引导语霍译本和杨译本中均拥有较高的词频。该词在霍译文本中有 166 个,占文本总量的 0.42%,在杨译文本中有 280 个,占文本总量的 0.92%,是霍译文本中比例的 2 倍多。但是复数形式 smiles 却是霍译文本中的独特词,词频为 16,在杨译文本中未被使用过。以下为霍译文本中使用 smiles 来翻译"笑道"类会话引导语的例子:

1.【原文】正说着,只见宝钗走进来,笑道:"偏了我们新鲜东西了!"(第二十六回)

【霍译】At that moment Bao-chai walked in, all **smiles**. 'I hear you've made a start on the famous present,' she said.

【杨译】Just then Baochai came in. "So you've been treated to those delicacies of ours," she teased.

2.【原文】只见凤姐儿跑进来,**笑道**:"老太太在那里抱怨天,抱怨地,只叫我来瞧瞧你们好了没有……"(第三十回)

【霍译】They spun round to look just as Xi-feng, full of **smiles**, came bustling into the room. 'Grandmother has been grumbling away something awful,' she said. 'She insisted that I should come over and see if you were both all right…'

【杨译】The two of them started, then turned to see Xifeng sweeping gaily in. "The old lady's fulminating against Heaven and Earth," she informed them. "She insisted I come to see if you'd made it up. ..."

3.【原文】只见贾蔷进去,**笑道**:"你来瞧这个玩意儿。"(第三十六回)

【霍译】'Look! Look what I've brought for you,' said Jia Qiang, full of **smiles**.

【杨译】(Jia Qiang)who had walked in gaily calling out:"Get up and look at this!"

4.【原文】(周瑞家的)说着,一径去了,半日方来,**笑道**:可是老老的福来了,"竟投了这两个人的缘了。"(第三十九回)

【霍译】She left the room and was gone for some considerable time. When she eventually returned, she was full of **smiles**. 'It's Grannie's lucky day,' she said. 'She's struck lucky with both of them.'

【杨译】She went out and reappeared after some time, beaming. "Luck must be with you today, granny," she announced. "The two ladies have taken quite a fancy to you."

5.【原文】话未说完,贾母**笑道**:"可是我老糊涂了!……"(第四十六回)

【霍译】Grandmother Jia was at once all **smiles**. 'Of course not, my dear. I am a silly old woman!…'

【杨译】At once the old lady chuckled, "I'm losing my wits with age," she exclaimed.

6.【原文】平儿忙答应了一声出来,那些媳妇们都悄悄的拉住**笑道**:"那里用姑娘去叫? 我们已有人叫去了。"(第五十五回)

【霍译】Not waiting to be ordered, Patience murmured something and hurried out; but the women outside silently waylaid her and with broad **smiles** prevented her from going. 'We can't let you go, miss: that would never do! In any case, we've already sent someone.'

【杨译】Pinger promptly agreed and went out. The stewards' wives quietly drew her aside and said，"There's no need for you to go，miss. We've already sent someone."

7.【原文】探春李纨都**笑道**："你也留心看出来了!……"(第五十六回)

【霍译】Tan-chun and Li Wan exchanged knowing **smiles**. 'You've noticed，too，then，' said Tan-chun.

【杨译】"So you've noticed that too." Tanchun and Li Wan smiled.

8.【原文】(平儿)说着去了;半日方回来，**笑道**："我说是白走一趟。这样好事，奶奶岂有不依的!"(第五十六回)

【霍译】She was gone for some time，but returned eventually，full of **smiles**："I knew it wasn't necessary to go. Of course she agrees. A good idea like this：how could she do otherwise?'

【杨译】After a while she came back to tell them gaily，"I said there was no need to go. It's such a good idea，of course my mistress approves."

9.【原文】林之孝家的**笑道**："这才好呢，这才是读书知礼的。"(第六十三回)

【霍译】Lin Zhi-xiao's wife was all **smiles**. 'Well，that's all right then. Respectable is what an educated young gentleman ought to be.'

【杨译】"That's good，" approved Mrs. Lin. "That's how someone with education and good manners ought to behave."

10.【原文】众人都**笑说**："前儿在一处看见二爷写的斗方儿，越发好了，多早晚赏我们几张贴贴。"(第八回)

【霍译】The men all relaxed in **smiles**. 'I saw some of your calligraphy in town the other day，Master Bao，' said one of them. 'It's getting really good! When are you going to give us a few sheets for ourselves，to put up on the wall?'

【杨译】while one of the other men said cheerfully："The other day we saw some inscriptions written by you，young master. Your calligraphy's even better than before. When will you give us a few samples to put on our walls?"

11.【原文】那小丫头子应了便走。众媳妇上来**笑说**："嫂子快求姑娘们叫回那孩子来罢。平姑娘来了，可就不好了!"(第五十九回)

【霍译】As the little maid ran off on her errand，the other women in the compound drew round Swallow's mother with interested **smiles**. 'Better ask them to call that child back，' they advised her. 'You don't want Miss Patience coming here.'

【杨译】As the little girl left on this errand，the older servant-maids gathered round Mother He. "Quick，sister!" they urged. "Ask the young ladies to call that child back. If Miss Pinger comes，you're in for trouble."

12.【原文】尤氏贾蓉一齐**笑说**："到底是婶娘宽洪大量，足智多谋！等事妥了，少不得我们娘儿们过去拜谢。"（第六十八回）

【霍译】You-shi and Jia Rong were all **smiles**. 'Very handsome of you，and very resourceful，too. But then you always were both of those things. When this affair is safely out of the way，we shall come round and make you a kotow.'

【杨译】Madam You and Jia Rong responded，"It's most generous and kind of you. How clever you are! Once it's settled，we'll certainly both come to thank you."

13.【原文】两个姑子忙立起身来**笑说**："奶奶素日宽洪大量，今日老祖宗千秋，奶奶生气，岂不惹人议论？"（第七十一回）

【霍译】The two nuns rose to their feet with propitiatory **smiles**. 'Come，Mrs Zhen! You are such a kind，forgiving person as a rule. Surely you are not going to lose your temper on Her Old Ladyship's birthday? Whatever would people say?'

【杨译】The two nuns rose respectfully to their feet to demur，"You're so magnanimous，madam，won't it make for talk if you lose your temper today of all days when our Old Ancestress is celebrating her birthday?"

14.【原文】（那园中人）见他来了，都**笑说**："你这会子又跑到这里做什么？"（第七十一回）

【霍译】They welcomed Faithful with **smiles** and urged her to be seated. 'What are you doing here at this late hour?' they asked her.

【杨译】At sight of her they pressed her to take a seat. "What brings you here at this hour?" they asked.

15.【原文】李十儿便站起，**堆着笑说**："这么不禁玩！几句话就脸急了？"

（第九十九回）

【霍译】Ten stood up，all **smiles**：'Come on now，can't you take a joke? No need to get rattled by a few words...'

【杨译】Li Shier stood up then，smiling. "Can't you take a joke?"he chuckled. "Don't be so thin-skinned."

（五）"笑道"类英译之 teased

teased 是"笑道"类会话引导语的杨译本相对于霍译本的第一大独特词，在杨译文本中出现了 48 次，在霍译文本中一次都没有使用过。

笔者先来考察几部权威词典对于动词 tease 的定义：

（1）《牛津高阶英语词典》（第 6 版）（*Oxford Advanced Learner's Dictionary*）：*to laugh at sb and make jokes about them either in a friendly way or in order to annoy or embarrass them*。

（2）《朗文当代英语词典》（第 4 版）（*Longman Dictionary of Contemporary English*）：*to laugh at someone and make jokes in order to have fun by embarrassing them，either in a friendly way or in an unkind way*。

（3）《柯林斯高阶英语词典》（*Collins COBUILD Advanced Learner's English Dictionary*）：*To tease someone means to laugh at them or make jokes about them in order to embarrass，annoy，or upset them.*

（4）《美国传统词典（双解）》（*E-C American Heritage Dictionary*）：*to make fun of；mock playfully* 取笑；开玩笑地嘲弄。

（5）《牛津高阶英汉双解词典》（*Oxford Advanced Learner's English-Chinese Dictionary*）：*make fun of（sb）in a playful or unkind way；try to provoke（sb）with questions or petty annoyances* 取笑，嘲弄（某人）；逗弄，招惹（某人）。

通过以上几部词典的释义，我们可以推断 tease 表达的是"取笑；戏弄；嘲弄"之意，这种"嘲弄"可以是善意的，亦或许是带有恶意的。以下为杨译文本中使用 teased 的例子：

1.【原文】探春笑道："只怕又是杜撰！"（第三回）

【杨译】"You're making that up，I'm afraid，" **teased** Tanchun.

【霍译】'I expect you made it up，'said Tan-chun scornfully.

2.【原文】宝玉笑道："你学惯了，明儿连你还咬起来呢。"（第二十回）

【杨译】"If you copy her long enough，you'll soon be talking the same way，" Baoyu **teased**.

【霍译】'You'd better not imitate her，'said Bao-yu. 'It'll get to be a habit. You'll be lisping yourself before you know where you are.'

3.【原文】翠缕撇嘴**笑道**:"还是这个毛病儿。"(第二十一回)

【杨译】"Still up to your old tricks," **teased** Cuilu.

【霍译】Kingfisher pursed her lips up derisively: 'You haven't changed much, have you?'

4.【原文】凤姐**笑道**:"你别作梦！你给我们家做了媳妇,少什么?"(第二十五回)

【杨译】"Are you dreaming? What's wrong with being our daughter-in-law?" **teased** Xifeng.

【霍译】Xi-feng laughed: 'What's so irritating about it?'

5.【原文】平儿手里拿着头发,**笑道**:"这是一辈子的把柄儿。"(第二十一回)

【杨译】Dangling the hair in front of him, she **teased**, "I'll have this hold over you for the rest of my life."

【霍译】Patience dangled the hair in front of him. 'You'll have to watch your step from now on,' she said.

6.【原文】宝玉尚未说话,黛玉便先**笑道**:"你看着人家赶蚊子的分上,也该去走走。"(第三十六回)

【杨译】Before Baoyu could answer, Daiyu **teased**, "You should go anyway for the sake of the one who kept away the mosquitoes."

【霍译】'Of course you must go!' said Dai-yu, before he had time to reply. 'Surely you owe a visit to the person who saved you from the mosquitoes?'

7.【原文】众人不知话内有因,都**笑道**:"说的好可怜见儿的！连我们也软了,饶了他罢!"(第四十二回)

【杨译】The others did not know what lay behind this exchange. "How pathetic she sounds," they **teased**. "Our hearts bleed for her. Do let her off!"

【霍译】The others, not knowing what lay behind these words, were greatly amused. 'Do forgive her!' they said, laughing. 'How pitifully she pleads! Even we are melted.'

8.【原文】尤氏**笑道**:"只许你主子作弊,就不许我作情吗?"(第四十三回)

【杨译】"so your mistress is allowed to cheat, but I'm not allowed to bribe you," **teased** Madam You.

【霍译】'Take it,' said You-shi. 'Is your mistress the only one who's allowed to break the rules? Mayn't I do favours too，if I want to?'

9.【原文】晴雯**笑道**："外头有个鬼等着呢。"(第五十一回)

【杨译】"Beware of the ghost out there waiting for you," **teased** Qingwen.

【霍译】'There's a ghost waiting for you out there，' said Skybright.

10.【原文】众人**笑道**："人未见形，先已闻声。"(第五十二回)

【杨译】They **teased**，"Before you see her，you hear her voice."

【霍译】'Ere yet the shape was seen，the voice was heard' said the others，laughing.

11.【原文】紫鹃**笑道**："你也念起佛来，真是新闻!"(第五十七回)

【杨译】"Really，this is news to me! Since when have you started invoking Buddha?" she **teased**.

【霍译】Nightingale looked up at him with amusement：'It's not often we hear you calling on the Lord.'

12.【原文】湘云**笑道**："病也比人家另一样，原招笑儿! 反说起人来。"(第五十八回)

【杨译】"Even in illness you had to be unique，" she **teased**. "How can you blame us for laughing?"

【霍译】'It's your fault for being so comical，' said Xiang-yun. 'Why do you always have to be so different? Even your illnesses are different from everyone else's.'

13.【原文】李纨**笑道**："人家不得贵婿，反捱打，我也不忍得。"(第六十三回)

【杨译】"She hasn't got a noble husband and now you want me to beat her," **teased** Li Wan. "No，I can't bring myself to do it."

【霍译】'Oh，that seems rather hard!' said Li Wan. 'She's not getting a royal husband and now she is to be beaten as well!'

14.【原文】宝玉**笑道**："这样还算不得什么。"(第八十回)

【杨译】"In that case，" Baoyu **teased**，"your plaster doesn't amount to much."

【霍译】'They are not such great shakes after all then，' said Bao-yu，smiling.

15.【原文】凤姐在地下站着，**笑道**："你两个那里象天天在一块儿的? 倒象是客，有这么些套话! 可是人说的'相敬如宾'了。"(第八十五

回）

**【杨译】**Xifeng standing near them smiled. "You two are behaving like guests，not like inseparables，" she **teased**. All these civilities! Well，as the saying goes，'you show each other respect as to a guest.'

**【霍译】**Xi-feng was standing near them and observed sarcastically：'I thought you two were meant to be inseparable? The way you talk anyone would think you were strangers. Still，I suppose His to honour，Hers to obey...'

（六）"笑道"类英译之 chuckled

chuckled 是"笑道"类会话引导语的杨译本相对于霍译本的第一大特色词，关键度为 210.485。chuckled 在杨译文本中的词频为 142，在霍译文本中仅有 4 例。笔者在前文已经考察过 chuckled 的含义，表示"轻声地笑；咯咯笑"之意。chuckled 也是杨译本会话引导语总文本相对于霍译本会话引导语总文本的第一特色词。

下面笔者将列举几个霍译和杨译使用 chuckled 来翻译"笑道"类会话引导语的例子，其中仅有 1 例是霍译和杨译不约而同使用 chuckled 来翻译"笑道"。

1.**【原文】**道士**笑道**："连我也不知道此系何方，我系何人。不过暂来歇脚而已。"（第六十六回）

**【杨译】**The priest **chuckled**，"I myself don't know where we are or who I am. I'm simply putting up here for the time being."

**【霍译】**'And may I know whom I have the honour of addressing?' The Taoist **chuckled**. 'I don't know where this place is any more than you do. Nor who I am. It is a place where I am resting a little while before going on elsewhere.'

2.**【原文】**宝玉**笑道**："你又哄我了。"（第八回）

**【杨译】**"You're making fun of me again." Baoyu **chuckled**.

**【霍译】**'You're just saying that to humour me，' said Bao-yu.

3.**【原文】**宝玉**笑道**："你这里长远了，不怕没八人轿你坐。"（第十九回）

**【杨译】**Baoyu **chuckled**. "If you stay here long enough，you'll have your sedan-chair and eight bearers some day."

**【霍译】**'Oh，come now! Isn't that stretching it a bit?' said Bao-yu with a laugh. 'For eight bearers and a handsome husband I bet you'd go!'

4.**【原文】**凤姐**笑道**："你既吃了我们家的茶，怎么还不给我们家作媳妇

儿?"(第二十五回)

【杨译】Xifeng **chuckled**. "Drink our family's tea，a daughter-in-law to be!"

【霍译】'That's fair enough，' said Xi-feng. 'You know the rule："drink the family's tea，the family's bride-to-be".'

5.【原文】探春笑道:"宝姐姐有心,不管什么他都记得。"(第二十九回)

【杨译】"Cousin Baochai's observant，" **chuckled** Tanchun. "She never forgets anything either."

【霍译】'Cousin Bao is observant，' said Tan-chun. 'No matter what it is，she remembers everything.'

6.【原文】宝玉笑道:"我说你们这几个人难说话,果然不错。"(第三十二回)

【杨译】Baoyu **chuckled**. "I always say you girls are hard to talk with. And this proves it."

【霍译】'Well，I've said that you lot are difficult to talk to，' said Bao-yu，'and I was certainly right！'

7.【原文】宝钗笑道:"就是为那话了。"(第三十六回)

【杨译】"There you are！" Baochai **chuckled**.

【霍译】'There you are！' said Bao-chai. 'That'll be what she wants to see you about.'

8.【原文】刘老老笑道:"老太太留下我,叫我也热闹一天去。"(第四十回)

【杨译】"The old lady made me stay to enjoy myself for a day，" **chuckled** Granny Liu.

【霍译】'It was Her Old Ladyship that kept me，' said Grannie Liu. 'She said she wanted me to enjoy myself for a day or two before I went back.'

9.【原文】众人都笑道:"这却使不得。"(第四十回)

【杨译】"That won't do，" **chuckled** the others.

【霍译】'No，no，we can't have that！ 'said the others，laughing.

10.【原文】宝玉笑道:"我深知道,我也不领你的情,只谢他二人便了。"(第四十一回)

【杨译】"I'm well aware of that." Baoyu **chuckled**. "So I'll thank them instead of you."

【霍译】Bao-yu laughed. 'I fully realize that，and I don't feel in the least indebted to you. I shall offer my thanks to them.'

11.【原文】贾母听了，**笑道**："你不会，等我亲自让他去。"（第四十四回）

【杨译】"If you can't make her drink," **chuckled** the old lady，"I'll go out presently and toast her myself."

【霍译】'If you can't make her，I shall have to come out and deal with her myself，' said Grandmother Jia，laughing.

12.【原文】湘云**笑道**："你们瞧我里头打扮的。"（第四十九回）

【杨译】"You should see what I'm wearing underneath," **chuckled** Xiangyun.

【霍译】'You haven't seen what I am wearing underneath yet，' said Xiang-yun.

13.【原文】（几个老婆子）因又**笑道**："阿弥陀佛！今日天睁了眼，把这个祸害妖精退送了，大家清净些。"（第七十七回）

【杨译】"Buddha be praised!" they chortled. "At last Heaven has opened its eyes. Once this pest is gone we shall have a little peace."

【霍译】She **chuckled**. 'Holy Name! The Lord has opened his eyes at last! With that little pest out of the way，it will be a better place for all of us!'

14.【原文】（宝玉）幸喜还记得，便哈哈的**笑道**："是了，是了!"（第一百十六回）

【杨译】... and pleased that he could still remember it，he laughed aloud and exclaimed，"That's it，that's it!"

【霍译】To his great delight，he found that he could still remember every detail of his dream，and he **chuckled** aloud with satisfaction：'So! So!'

15.【原文】那僧**笑道**："也该还我了。"（第一百十七回）

【杨译】"And so you should!" laughed the monk.

【霍译】'And so you should!' **chuckled** the monk.

（七）"笑道"类英译之 with a smile

with a smile 的用法是杨译文本的一大特色，杨译文本使用了 242 次，而霍译文本中仅有 64 次，杨译数量是霍译的将近 4 倍。以下为几个杨译文本中使用 with a smile 来翻译"笑道"类会话引导语的例子，其中有些例子是霍译和杨译同时使用了 with a smile。

1.【原文】周瑞家的进来，**笑道**："林姑娘，姨太太叫我送花儿来了。"（第七回）

【杨译】Mrs. Zhou greeted her **with a smile** as she entered and said，"Madam Xue asked me to bring you these flowers to wear."

【霍译】'Miss Lin，' said Zhou Rui's wife **with a smile**，'Mrs Xue asked me to give you these flowers.'

2.【原文】贾母笑道："你也别信他。他懂得什么？"（第九十回）

【杨译】"Don't listen to her. What does she know?" said the old lady **with a smile**.

【霍译】Grandmother Jia said to Xi-feng **with a smile**："You shouldn't take what she says so seriously，my dear. She doesn't understand such things.

3.【原文】李纨笑道："老太太和太太说的都是。据我的糊涂想头，必是宝玉有喜事来了，此花先来报信。"（第九十四回）

【杨译】"I'm sure the old lady and mistress are right，" put in Li Wan **with a smile**. "In my foolish opinion，this blossoming shows that something good is coming Baoyu's way."

【霍译】Li Wan spoke next. 'I think you are both right，' she said **with a smile**. 'My own humble suggestion is that they have flowered specially to tell us of some happy event that is about to take place in Bao-yu's life.'

4.【原文】恰好凤姐进来，笑道："老太太姑妈又想着什么了？"（第九十八回）

【杨译】Just then Xifeng came in and asked **with a smile**. "What are you ladies discussing?"

【霍译】Luckily Xi-feng came in at this moment，and inquired **with a smile**：'Grandmother，Auntie，what is troubling you？'

5.【原文】宝玉才要说话，袭人便忙笑说道："原来留的是这个，多谢费心。"（第十九回）

【杨译】Before he could make any comment Xiren interposed **with a smile**，"So that's what you kept for me— thank you."

【霍译】Bao-yu was about to say something when Aroma cut in **with a smile**：'So that's what you were saving for me! It was a very kind thought.'

6.【原文】黛玉笑着道："宝二爷在家么？"（第九十六回）

【杨译】"Is Master Bao in?" Daiyu asked **with a smile**.

【霍译】'Is Master Bao at home？' asked Dai-yu **with a smile**.

7.【原文】秦氏笑道:"我这屋子大约神仙也可以往得了。"(第五回)

【杨译】"This room of mine is probably fit for a god," rejoined Keqing **with a smile**.

【霍译】'My room,' said Qin-shi with a proud smile, 'is fit for an immortal to sleep in.'

8.【原文】秦氏笑道:"任凭他是神仙,'治了病治不了命'。婶子,我知道这病不过是挨日子的。"(第十一回)

【杨译】"Even if he were an immortal, he could cure a disease but not avert my fate," retorted Keqing **with a smile**. "I know it's only a matter of time now, auntie."

【霍译】Qin-shi smiled. 'Even if he's a miracle-man, Auntie, "death's a sickness none can cure", and I know that it's just a question of time now.'

9.【原文】宝玉笑道:"能儿来了。"(第十五回)

【杨译】"Look who's here," said Baoyu **with a smile**.

【霍译】'Here's Sappy,' said Bao-yu with a meaningful smile.

10.【原文】贾母笑道:"老神仙,你好?"(第二十九回)

【杨译】"And are you well, Old Immortal?" she responded **with a smile**.

【霍译】'And how are you, old Holy One?' Grandmother Jia asked him with a pleased smile.

11.【原文】薛姨妈笑道:"你宝姐姐没过来,家里和香菱作活呢。"(第八十四回)

【杨译】"She didn't come," answered Aunt Xue **with a smile**. "She's doing needlework at home with Xiangling."

【霍译】'She couldn't come with me today,' said Aunt Xue, with a rather unconvincing smile. 'She and Caltrop have a lot of sewing to catch up on at home.'

12.【原文】薛蝌被他拿话一激,脸越红了,连忙走过来陪笑道:"嫂子说那里的话?"(第一百回)

【杨译】At this taunt, Xue Ke blushed even redder. Stepping over quickly he countered **with a smile**, "How can you say such a thing, sister-in-law!"

【霍译】Xue Ke felt the sting of her remark and blushed a deeper shade of red. He took a step towards her and said with a polite smile：'Of course not，sister-in-law.'

13. 【原文】黛玉也**微笑道**："大好了。听见说二哥哥身上也欠安，好了么?"（第八十五回）

【杨译】"Yes，much better，" she answered **with a smile**. "I heard you were unwell too. Are you all right now?"

【霍译】'Yes，thank you，' replied Dai-yu，with a hint of a smile. 'And you? I heard that you were not very well yourself.'

14. 【原文】只见邢岫烟赶忙出来，迎着凤姐**陪笑道**："这使不得，没有的事。事情早过去了。"（第九十回）

【杨译】At once Xiuyan came out to greet her **with a smile**. "Please don't，" she said. "It's of no account —over and done with."

【霍译】She greeted Xi-feng and said with an anxious smile：'You mustn't do that! It was nothing really. And it's all over now.'

15. 【原文】贾母拭了拭眼泪，**微笑道**："你又不知要编派谁呢? 你说来，我和姨太太听听。说不笑，我们可不依。"（第九十八回）

【杨译】The old lady wiped her tears and said **with a smile**，"Whom are you making fun of this time I wonder? Go ahead and tell us. But if it isn't funny，lookout!"

【霍译】Grandmother Jia wiped away her tears，and managed a feeble smile. 'Who are you going to make fun of now? Come on，we are listening. If you don't make us laugh，we will not let you off lightly.

从上述例子我们可以发现，许多在杨译文本中使用 with a smile 的时候，霍译选择使用 with a+*adj*. smile 来进一步阐明说话者的姿态和神情，如例 7 中的 with a proud smile、例 9 中的 with a meaningful smile、例 10 中的 with a pleased smile、例 11 中的 with a rather unconvincing smile、例 12 中的 with a polite smile、例 14 中的 with an anxious smile、例 15 中的 with a feeble smile 等。这种 with a+*adj*. smile 的用法是霍译文本的显著特色。

（八）"笑道"类英译之 with a+*adj*. laugh

在"笑道"类会话引导语霍译文本和杨译文本中均出现了不同数量的 with a+*adj*. smile、with a+*adj*. laugh 和 gave a+*adj*. smile 的用法，而 with a+*adj*. laugh 却是霍译文本非常具有特色的表达方式，在杨译文本中极少被使用。

下面笔者将列举霍译文本中使用 with a+*adj*. laugh 来翻译"笑道"类会

话引导语的例子,同时对比杨译文本中的翻译方式。

1.【原文】宝钗也悄悄的**笑道**:"还不快做上去,只姐姐妹妹的! 谁是你姐姐? 那上头穿黄袍的才是你姐姐呢。"(第十八回)

　【霍译】'Sister!' said Bao-chai **with a little laugh**. 'Stop fooling about and get on with your poem! That's your sister, sitting up there in the golden robe. I'm no sister of yours!'

　【杨译】Suppressing a smile Baochai replied, "Hurry up and finish instead of talking such nonsense. Who are you calling 'sister'? That's your sister sitting up there in the golden robes. Why call me your sister?"

2.【原文】袭人**笑道**:"谁哭来着? 才迷了眼揉的。"(第十九回)

　【霍译】'Who's been crying?' said Aroma **with a feigned laugh**. 'I've just been rubbing my eyes.'

　【杨译】"Who's been crying?" she retorted cheerfully. "I've just been rubbing my eyes."

3.【原文】宝玉一面收书,一面**笑道**:"正经快把花儿埋了罢,别提那些个了。"(第二十三回)

　【霍译】Bao-yu took back the book from her **with a good-natured laugh**: 'Never mind about all that now! Let's get on with this flower-burying!'

　【杨译】Laughing he put the book away. "Never mind that. Let's get on with burying the flowers."

4.【原文】那张道士先呵呵**笑道**:"无量寿佛!"(第二十九回)

　【霍译】The abbot prefaced his greeting **with a good deal of jovial laughter**. 'Blessed Buddha of Boundless Life!'

　【杨译】"Buddha of Infinite Longevity!" he exclaimed.

5.【原文】贾母**笑道**:"我年下就要的,你别脱懒儿;快拿出来给我快画!"(第五十回)

　【霍译】Grandmother Jia brushed aside this excuse **with a dismissive laugh**. 'I want that painting ready by the end of the year. Don't be so lazy! Fetch it out at once and get on with it, my girl!'

　【杨译】"I want it for New Year, so don't be lazy!" teased the old lady. "You must fetch it out at once and go on with it."

6.【原文】贾琏搂着他**笑道**:"人人都说我们那夜叉婆俊,如今我看来,给你

拾鞋也不要!"(第六十五回)

【霍译】He hugged her to him **with a delighted laugh**. 'They're always telling me how perfect that termagant wife of mine is,' he said, 'but the way you look tonight, she's not fit to carry your shoes!'

【杨译】Throwing his arms around her, Jia Lian declared, "Everyone calls that shrew of mine good-looking, but to me she isn't fit even to pick up your shoes."

7.【原文】湘云微笑道:"我有个择席的病,况且走了困,只好躺躺儿罢;你怎么也睡不着?"(第七十六回)

【霍译】'I can never get to sleep in a strange bed,' said Xiang-yun **with a rueful laugh**. 'Anyway, I'm too tired to get to sleep. I'll just have to lie and rest. Can't you get to sleep either?'

【杨译】"I can't sleep well in a strange bed — that's my trouble. And I'm no longer sleepy, so I'm just resting. What about you?"

8.【原文】代儒觉得了,笑了一笑道:"你只管说,讲书是没有什么避忌的。"(第八十二回)

【霍译】The Preceptor sensed what was coming and tried to conceal his embarrassment **with a short laugh**: 'Come on boy, come on. What is holding you back?'

【杨译】He broke off here and glanced up at the teacher, who smiled. "Just go ahead. In expounding the classics, as the Book of Ceremony says, nothing is taboo."

9.【原文】他外甥笑道:'一口装不下,得两口才好。'(第九十二回)

【霍译】... and he replied **with a strange laugh** that one would not be enough.

【杨译】He said with a smile, "One's not enough. We need two."

10.【原文】湘云笑道:"扯臊! 老太太还等你告诉? 你打量这些人为什么来? 是老太太请的!"(第一百八回)

【霍译】'Shame on you!' cried Xiang-yun **with a playful laugh**. 'As if Grannie needed you to remind her! Who do you think invited every-one here but Grannie?'

【杨译】"For shame!" retorted Xiangyun playfully. "The old lady doesn't need any reminding. Do you suppose these visitors would have come if she hadn't invited them?"

## 四、《红楼梦》会话引导语"冷笑道"的英译研究

在《红楼梦》"笑道"类会话引导语中，还有一个特殊的表达形式不容忽视，那就是"冷笑道"。"冷笑道"也是曹雪芹在描写人物会话时的神态表情的十分重要的形式之一，几乎原文中的主要人物都曾"冷笑"过。本小节笔者将单独探讨"冷笑道"的用法及其英译。

（一）《红楼梦》原文中的"冷笑道"

《现代汉语词典》里对"冷笑"一词的解释为"含有讽刺、不满意、无可奈何、不屑于、不以为然等意味或怒意的笑"。与"笑道"一样，每一个"冷笑道"出现时的人物、语境、情感不尽相同，对于每个伴随"道"的"笑"究竟有多"冷"，需要读者自己去琢磨揣测。

笔者在自行创建的"《红楼梦》原文—霍译本—杨译本平行语料库"中检索"冷笑*道："，得到110个反馈结果，其中包括"冷笑一声道：""冷笑了两声道："
"冷笑几声道：""冷笑两声道："等，共同构成一个"原文—霍译—杨译"的"冷笑道"会话引导语语料库。在此语料库基础上，笔者分别整理出了"冷笑道"会话引导语的原文、霍译本、杨译本文档，以供研究之用。其中"冷笑道"会话引导语的霍译本（或称霍译文本）容量为1615，"冷笑道"会话引导语的杨译本（或称杨译文本）容量为1404。

（二）《红楼梦》译文中的"冷笑道"

笔者首先对"冷笑道"会话引导语的霍译文本和杨译文本的高频词进行研究。霍译和杨译总文本中排名前100名的词语及其分布如表4-14所示（筛除人名、地名用字）：

表4-14 "冷笑道"会话引导语霍译本和杨译本高频词

| 排序 | 词语 | 总词频 | 霍译文本 | 百分比 | 杨译文本 | 百分比 |
|---|---|---|---|---|---|---|
| 1 | you | 105 | 52 | 3.22 | 53 | 3.77 |
| 2 | a | 85 | 45 | 2.79 | 40 | 2.85 |
| 3 | the | 77 | 42 | 2.60 | 35 | 2.49 |
| 4 | said | 64 | 58 | 3.59 | 6 | 0.43 |
| 5 | I | 62 | 34 | 2.11 | 28 | 1.99 |
| 6 | to | 58 | 33 | 2.04 | 25 | 1.78 |
| 7 | she | 49 | 23 | 1.42 | 26 | 1.85 |
| 8 | of | 46 | 31 | 1.92 | 15 | 1.07 |
| 9 | smiled | 40 | 11 | 0.68 | 29 | 2.07 |

（续表）

| 排序 | 词语 | 总词频 | 霍译文本 | 百分比 | 杨译文本 | 百分比 |
|------|------|--------|----------|--------|----------|--------|
| 10 | that | 39 | 24 | 1.49 | 15 | 1.07 |
| 11 | me | 36 | 20 | 1.24 | 16 | 1.14 |
| 12 | and | 34 | 18 | 1.11 | 16 | 1.14 |
| 13 | it | 33 | 19 | 1.18 | 14 | 1.00 |
| 14 | with | 32 | 18 | 1.11 | 14 | 1.00 |
| 15 | scornfully | 28 | 15 | 0.93 | 13 | 0.93 |
| 16 | what | 26 | 14 | 0.87 | 12 | 0.85 |
| 17 | have | 24 | 12 | 0.74 | 12 | 0.85 |
| 18 | not | 24 | 18 | 1.11 | 6 | 0.43 |
| 19 | be | 23 | 11 | 0.68 | 12 | 0.85 |
| 20 | her | 23 | 14 | 0.87 | 9 | 0.64 |
| 21 | in | 23 | 16 | 0.99 | 7 | 0.50 |
| 22 | is | 23 | 17 | 1.05 | 6 | 0.43 |
| 23 | so | 20 | 9 | 0.56 | 11 | 0.78 |
| 24 | was | 19 | 14 | 0.87 | 5 | 0.36 |
| 25 | gave | 18 | 8 | 0.50 | 10 | 0.71 |
| 26 | he | 18 | 9 | 0.56 | 9 | 0.64 |
| 27 | laugh | 18 | 7 | 0.43 | 11 | 0.78 |
| 28 | sarcastically | 18 | 6 | 0.37 | 12 | 0.85 |
| 29 | smile | 18 | 10 | 0.62 | 8 | 0.57 |
| 30 | for | 17 | 11 | 0.68 | 6 | 0.43 |
| 31 | laughed | 16 | 4 | 0.25 | 12 | 0.85 |
| 32 | your | 16 | 10 | 0.62 | 6 | 0.43 |
| 33 | him | 15 | 9 | 0.56 | 6 | 0.43 |
| 34 | if | 15 | 6 | 0.37 | 9 | 0.64 |
| 35 | know | 15 | 8 | 0.50 | 7 | 0.50 |
| 36 | snorted | 15 | 1 | 0.06 | 14 | 1.00 |
| 37 | all | 14 | 9 | 0.56 | 5 | 0.36 |
| 38 | no | 14 | 5 | 0.31 | 9 | 0.64 |

（续表）

| 排序 | 词语 | 总词频 | 霍译文本 | 百分比 | 杨译文本 | 百分比 |
|---|---|---|---|---|---|---|
| 39 | who | 14 | 7 | 0.43 | 7 | 0.50 |
| 40 | at | 13 | 6 | 0.37 | 7 | 0.50 |
| 41 | coldly | 13 | 11 | 0.68 | 2 | 0.14 |
| 42 | my | 13 | 7 | 0.43 | 6 | 0.43 |
| 43 | on | 13 | 7 | 0.43 | 6 | 0.43 |
| 44 | are | 12 | 7 | 0.43 | 5 | 0.36 |
| 45 | bitterly | 12 | 7 | 0.43 | 5 | 0.36 |
| 46 | do | 12 | 7 | 0.43 | 5 | 0.36 |
| 47 | should | 12 | 7 | 0.43 | 5 | 0.36 |
| 48 | young | 12 | 7 | 0.43 | 5 | 0.36 |
| 49 | lady | 11 | 5 | 0.31 | 6 | 0.43 |
| 50 | scornful | 11 | 4 | 0.25 | 7 | 0.50 |
| 51 | this | 11 | 3 | 0.19 | 8 | 0.57 |
| 52 | way | 11 | 5 | 0.31 | 6 | 0.43 |
| 53 | why | 11 | 6 | 0.37 | 5 | 0.36 |
| 54 | about | 10 | 6 | 0.37 | 4 | 0.28 |
| 55 | as | 10 | 5 | 0.31 | 5 | 0.36 |
| 56 | but | 10 | 7 | 0.43 | 3 | 0.21 |
| 57 | could | 10 | 5 | 0.31 | 5 | 0.36 |
| 58 | how | 10 | 5 | 0.31 | 5 | 0.36 |
| 59 | there | 10 | 6 | 0.37 | 4 | 0.28 |
| 60 | can | 9 | 3 | 0.19 | 6 | 0.43 |
| 61 | his | 9 | 3 | 0.19 | 6 | 0.43 |
| 62 | out | 9 | 2 | 0.12 | 7 | 0.50 |
| 63 | talk | 9 | 3 | 0.19 | 6 | 0.43 |
| 64 | like | 8 | 5 | 0.31 | 3 | 0.21 |
| 65 | sneered | 8 | 2 | 0.12 | 6 | 0.43 |
| 66 | they | 8 | 1 | 0.06 | 7 | 0.50 |
| 67 | too | 8 | 3 | 0.19 | 5 | 0.36 |

（续表）

| 排序 | 词语 | 总词频 | 霍译文本 | 百分比 | 杨译文本 | 百分比 |
|------|------|--------|----------|--------|----------|--------|
| 68 | we | 8 | 4 | 0.25 | 4 | 0.28 |
| 69 | when | 8 | 6 | 0.37 | 2 | 0.14 |
| 70 | from | 7 | 5 | 0.31 | 2 | 0.14 |
| 71 | little | 7 | 5 | 0.31 | 2 | 0.14 |
| 72 | or | 7 | 4 | 0.25 | 3 | 0.21 |
| 73 | them | 7 | 4 | 0.25 | 3 | 0.21 |
| 74 | well | 7 | 6 | 0.37 | 1 | 0.07 |
| 75 | any | 6 | 4 | 0.25 | 2 | 0.14 |
| 76 | had | 6 | 6 | 0.37 | 0 | 0.00 |
| 77 | just | 6 | 3 | 0.19 | 3 | 0.21 |
| 78 | mother | 6 | 2 | 0.12 | 4 | 0.28 |
| 79 | now | 6 | 3 | 0.19 | 3 | 0.21 |
| 80 | oh | 6 | 5 | 0.31 | 1 | 0.07 |
| 81 | other | 6 | 2 | 0.12 | 4 | 0.28 |
| 82 | same | 6 | 2 | 0.12 | 4 | 0.28 |
| 83 | sniffed | 6 | 6 | 0.37 | 0 | 0.00 |
| 84 | think | 6 | 5 | 0.31 | 1 | 0.07 |
| 85 | time | 6 | 3 | 0.19 | 3 | 0.21 |
| 86 | two | 6 | 4 | 0.25 | 2 | 0.14 |
| 87 | were | 6 | 3 | 0.19 | 3 | 0.21 |
| 88 | whether | 6 | 3 | 0.19 | 3 | 0.21 |
| 89 | before | 5 | 3 | 0.19 | 2 | 0.14 |
| 90 | by | 5 | 1 | 0.06 | 4 | 0.28 |
| 91 | does | 5 | 3 | 0.19 | 2 | 0.14 |
| 92 | face | 5 | 4 | 0.25 | 1 | 0.07 |
| 93 | fine | 5 | 0 | 0.00 | 5 | 0.36 |
| 94 | madam | 5 | 0 | 0.00 | 5 | 0.36 |
| 95 | mockingly | 5 | 0 | 0.00 | 5 | 0.36 |
| 96 | ought | 5 | 4 | 0.25 | 1 | 0.07 |

（续表）

| 排序 | 词语 | 总词频 | 霍译文本 | 百分比 | 杨译文本 | 百分比 |
|------|------|--------|----------|--------|----------|--------|
| 97 | place | 5 | 2 | 0.12 | 3 | 0.21 |
| 98 | retorted | 5 | 0 | 0.00 | 5 | 0.36 |
| 99 | see | 5 | 4 | 0.25 | 1 | 0.07 |
| 100 | some | 5 | 4 | 0.25 | 1 | 0.07 |

我们可以看到，在霍译文本和杨译文本排名前 100 位的高频词中，said、smiled 和 gave 位列前 3 名，但数量和比例差别较大。said 在霍译文本中排名第 1 位，数量有 58 个，占文本总量的 3.59%，而霍译文本中大多使用"said＋短语"或"said＋副词"的形式来翻译"冷笑道"；said 在杨译文本中排名第 51 位，数量仅有 6 个，占文本总量的 0.43%，仅为霍译文本比例的 1/8。smiled 在杨译文本中排名第 4 位，是数量最多的动词，数量有 29 个，占文本总量的 2.07%；霍译文本中排名第 26 位，数量有 11 个，占文本总量的 0.68%。gave 在杨译文本中排名第 24 位，数量有 10 个，占文本总量的 0.71%；霍译文本中略少，仅有 8 个，占文本总量的 0.50%。我们通过图 4－3 可以清晰地看到三个动词在两个译本中的差异：

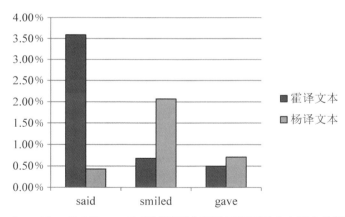

图 4－3　said、smiled 和 gave 在"冷笑道"会话引导语两译本中所占比例对比

"冷笑道"会话引导语的霍译本相对于杨译本的独特词有 306 个，去除人名、地名用词，词频在 2 次以上的有 35 个：

had(6)　　　　　　contemptuously(4)　　　chamberlain(3)

sniffed(6)　　　　　bit(3)　　　　　　　　chilling(3)

look（3）　　　　　　concern（2）　　　　　　moments（2）

malice（3）　　　　　　consequences（2）　　　much（2）

say（3）　　　　　　　dear（2）　　　　　　　right（2）

sneeringly（3）　　　　drily（2）　　　　　　　studies（2）

somewhat（3）　　　　finally（2）　　　　　　temper（2）

suppose（3）　　　　　finished（2）　　　　　turning（2）

very（3）　　　　　　found（2）　　　　　　usher（2）

want（3）　　　　　　into（2）　　　　　　　wife（2）

capable（2）　　　　　looked（2）　　　　　　word（2）

case（2）　　　　　　man（2）

"冷笑道"会话引导语的霍译本相对于杨译本的特色词有 75 个，去除人名、地名用词，关键度在 5 以上的仅有 5 个（见表 4-15）。

表 4-15　"冷笑道"会话引导语霍译本特色词

| 排序 | 词语 | 关键度 |
| --- | --- | --- |
| 1 | said | 39.559 |
| 2 | had | 7.228 |
| 3 | sniffed | 7.228 |
| 4 | when | 7.228 |
| 5 | coldly | 5.261 |

said 是霍译文本相对于杨译文本的第一大特色词，关键度有 39.559。动词 sniffed 既是霍译文本的独特词又是特色词。

"冷笑道"会话引导语的杨译本相对于霍译本的独特词有 240 个，去除人名、地名用词，词频在 2 次以上的有 38 个：

fine（5）　　　　　　father（3）　　　　　　child（2）

madam（5）　　　　　steward（3）　　　　　clear（2）

mockingly（5）　　　　would（3）　　　　　　clothes（2）

retorted（5）　　　　　attendant（2）　　　　company（2）

asked（4）　　　　　both（2）　　　　　　concubine（2）

even（4）　　　　　　care（2）　　　　　　cried（2）

still（4）　　　　　　caustically（2）　　　　cynically（2）

disdainfully（3）　　　chief（2）　　　　　　everyone（2）

| | | |
|---|---|---|
| faint(2) | instead(2) | old(2) |
| feel(2) | ironic(2) | says(2) |
| find(2) | ironically(2) | scent(2) |
| ghost(2) | might(2) | sister(2) |
| hands(2) | nice(2) | |

"冷笑道"会话引导语的杨译本相对于霍译本的特色词有 280 个,去除人名、地名用词,关键度在 5 以上的仅有 7 个(见表 4-16)。

表 4-16 "冷笑道"会话引导语杨译本特色词

| 排序 | 词语 | 关键度 |
|---|---|---|
| 1 | snorted | 16.063 |
| 2 | smiled | 12.196 |
| 3 | fine | 7.931 |
| 4 | mockingly | 7.931 |
| 5 | retorted | 7.931 |
| 6 | asked | 6.345 |
| 7 | laughed | 5.858 |

snorted 和 smiled 是杨译文本相对于霍译文本关键度最高的特色词。mockingly 既是杨译文本的独特词又是特色词。

除了单个词的研究之外,"冷笑道"会话引导语在霍译本和杨译本中还有一些重要的短语与其他表达方式值得我们关注。经笔者检索筛选,霍译总文本和杨译总文本中的二词以上表达方式及分布(使用次数在 2 次以上)如表 4-17 所示。

表 4-17 短语类表达形式在"冷笑道"会话引导语两译本中使用情况统计

| 表达形式 | 数量 | 霍译文本 | 杨译文本 |
|---|---|---|---|
| smiled sarcastically | 9 | 2 | 7 |
| laughed scornfully | 7 | 1 | 6 |
| smiled scornfully | 6 | 1 | 5 |
| smiled bitterly | 5 | 2 | 3 |
| gave a scornful laugh | 3 | 0 | 3 |
| of malice | 3 | 3 | 0 |

（续表）

| 表达形式 | 数量 | 霍译文本 | 杨译文本 |
|---|---|---|---|
| smiled coldly | 3 | 2 | 1 |
| smiled disdainfully | 3 | 0 | 3 |
| smiled mockingly | 3 | 0 | 3 |
| sniffed scornfully | 3 | 3 | 0 |
| with a scornful laugh | 3 | 0 | 3 |
| a chilling smile | 2 | 2 | 0 |
| a cynical laugh | 2 | 0 | 2 |
| a faint smile | 2 | 0 | 2 |
| a scornful smile | 2 | 1 | 1 |
| an ironic smile | 2 | 0 | 2 |
| flush with anger | 2 | 1 | 1 |
| laughed caustically | 2 | 0 | 2 |
| laughed mockingly | 2 | 0 | 2 |
| laughed sarcastically | 2 | 0 | 2 |
| little laugh | 2 | 2 | 0 |
| smiled cynically | 2 | 0 | 2 |
| smiled ironically | 2 | 0 | 2 |
| with a sardonic smile | 2 | 1 | 1 |

其中 smiled sarcastically 是使用次数最多的表达方式,霍译文本 2 次,杨译文本 7 次,共 9 次。of malice、sniffed scornfully、a chilling smile 和 little laugh 是霍译文本的独特用法;gave a scornful laugh、smiled disdainfully、smiled mockingly、with a scornful laugh、a cynical laugh、a faint smile、an ironic smile、laughed caustically、laughed mockingly、laughed sarcastically、smiled cynically 和 smiled ironically 是杨译文本的独特用法。laughed scornfully 和 smiled scornfully 可以看作杨译文本的特色用法。

（三）《红楼梦》"冷笑道"会话引导语英译案例研究

笔者将在上述对《红楼梦》原文以及译文中的"冷笑道"会话引导语分析统计的基础上开展《红楼梦》"冷笑道"会话引导语英译的案例研究。为此笔者将选取霍译文本中的特色词 said 和独特词 sniffed、杨译文本中的特色词 snorted

和独特词 mockingly、霍译和杨译文本中使用最多的短语"smiled sarcastically"等进行相关分析。

**1. "冷笑道"英译之 said**

在"冷笑道"会话引导语的霍译文本和杨译文本中,said 在霍译文本的词频中排名第 1 位,数量有 58 个,占文本总量的 3.59%;在杨译文本中排名第 51 位,数量仅有 6 个,占文本总量的 0.43%,仅为霍译文本比例的 1/8。霍译文本中大多使用"said+短语"或"said+副词"的形式来翻译"冷笑道",但也有 said 单独使用的情况。以下为霍译文本中使用 said 来翻译"冷笑道"的例子:

1. 【原文】贾母**冷笑道**:"你分明使我无立足之地,你反说起你来!"(第三十三回)

   【霍译】'On the contrary,' **said** Grandmother Jia,'it is you who have rejected me.'

   【杨译】The Lady Dowager smiled sarcastically."You're making it clear that there's no place for me,and yet you start complaining."

2. 【原文】宝钗**冷笑道**:"好个千金小姐!好个不出屋门的女孩儿!满嘴里说的是什么? 你只实说罢。"(第四十二回)

   【霍译】'My dear,well-bred young lady!' **said** Bao-chai.'My dear,sheltered young innocent! What were those things I heard you saying yesterday? Come now,the truth!'

   【杨译】"A fine young lady you are,a sheltered,innocent girl!" Baochai snorted."Yet the things you say! Confess now."

3. 【原文】宝钗**冷笑道**:"我说你不中用! ……"(第四十二回)

   【霍译】'Oh,you're just hopeless!' **said** Bao-chai.

   【杨译】"I knew you'd be no use." Baochai smiled mockingly.

4. 【原文】鸳鸯红了脸,向平儿**冷笑道**:"我只想咱们好:……"(第四十六回)

   【霍译】'Thank you,' **said** Faithful when she had finished.'You and I at least are still friends.'

   【杨译】Still blushing,Yuanyang answered bitterly,"What good friends we were,the dozen or so of us."

5. 【原文】宝玉**冷笑道**:"虽如此说,但只我倒替你担心虑后呢!"(第七十九回)

   【霍译】'Hmn,maybe,' **said** Bao-yu.'All the same,I am a bit worried for you.'

【杨译】Baoyu smiled wanly. "Still，I'm rather worried for you."

**2. "冷笑道"英译之 sniffed**

在"冷笑道"会话引导语的霍译文本中出现了 6 次 sniffed 的用法，杨译文本中一次都没有使用过。我们先来考察几部权威词典关于 sniff 一词的释义。

（1）《牛津高阶英语词典》（第 6 版）（*Oxford Advanced Learner's Dictionary*）：*to say sth in a complaining or disapproving way*。

（2）《朗文当代英语词典》（第 4 版）（*Longman Dictionary of Contemporary English*）：*to say something in a way that shows you think something is not good enough*。

（3）《柯林斯高阶英语词典》（*Collins COBUILD Advanced Learner's English Dictionary*）：*You can use sniff to indicate that someone says something in a way that shows their disapproval or contempt*.

（4）《美国传统词典》（双解）（*E-C American Heritage Dictionary*）：*to regard something in a contemptuous or dismissive manner* 鄙视：用瞧不起或不重视的态度看待某物。

（5）《牛津高阶英汉双解词典》（*Oxford Advanced Learner's English-Chinese Dictionary*）：*sniff at sth ignore or show contempt for sth* 嗤之以鼻。

通过以上几部词典的定义，我们可以推断动词 sniff 用来表达"轻蔑地说；鄙视地说；嗤之以鼻"之意。下面列举霍译文本中使用 sniffed 来翻译"冷笑道"的例子：

1. 【原文】宝玉**冷笑道**："我只当是谁的亲戚，原来是璜嫂子侄儿，我就去向他问问！"（第九回）

　【霍译】Bao-yu **sniffed** contemptuously. 'So that's who he is! The nephew of Cousin Huang's wife. I'll go and speak to her about this.'

　【杨译】"So that's who he is!" said Baoyu scornfully. "Cousin Jia Huang's nephew. I shall go and see her about this."

2. 【原文】袭人听了，**冷笑道**："你倒别这么说。从此以后，我是太太的人了，我要走，连你也不必告诉，只回了太太就走。"（第三十六回）

　【霍译】'Huh！' Aroma **sniffed** scornfully. 'That's not at all the way it is. I belong to Her Ladyship now. Now if I want to leave you，I don't have to talk to you about it at all. All I have to do is have a word with Her Ladyship，and off I go！'

　【杨译】"You've no call to talk like that." She gave an ironic smile. "From now on I belong to Her Ladyship. I can leave without so much as a word to you，just by getting permission from her.'

3.【原文】邢夫人**冷笑道**:"大家子三房四妾的也多,偏咱们就使不得?"(第四十六回)

【霍译】Lady Xing **sniffed**. 'Lots of men in well-to-do families like ours have troops of concubines. Why should it be so shameful only in our case?'

【杨译】"Other noble families often have three or four concubines，so why shouldn't we?" retorted Lady Xing coldly.

4.【原文】藕官**冷笑道**:"有什么仇恨? 他们不知足,反怨我们!"(第五十九回)

【霍译】Nénuphar **sniffed**. 'I didn't do anything. It's because she's so greedy. She can't squeeze as much out of me as she used to be able to.'

【杨译】"What feud?" Ouguan snorted. "There's just no satisfying them they're for ever nagging at us."

5.【原文】王夫人**冷笑道**:"这也是个没廉耻的货!"(第七十七回)

【霍译】Lady Wang **sniffed** scornfully. 'Another shameless young baggage!'

【杨译】Lady Wang smiled scornfully. "Another shameless slut!"

6.【原文】紫鹃听了,**冷笑道**:"二爷就是这个话呀! 还有什么?"(第一百十三回)

【霍译】Nightingale **sniffed** scornfully. 'Is that all you had to say? Isn't there anything new?

【杨译】"Is that all，young master?" she asked sarcastically. "Have you nothing else to say?"

**3. "冷笑道"英译之 snorted**

snorted 是"冷笑道"会话引导语的杨译本相对于霍译本的第一大特色词,关键度为 16.063。该词在杨译文本中使用过 14 次,在霍译文本中仅出现过 1 次。

我们首先来看几部权威词典对于动词 snort 的解释:

(1)《牛津高阶英语词典》(第 6 版)(*Oxford Advanced Learner's Dictionary*): *to make a loud sound by breathing air out noisily through your nose，especially to show that you are angry or amused*。

(2)《朗文当代英语词典》(第 4 版)(*Longman Dictionary of Contemporary*

English）：*to make a sudden loud noise through your nose*，*for example because you are angry or laughing*。

（3）《柯林斯高阶英语词典》（*Collins COBUILD Advanced Learner's English Dictionary*）：*When people or animals snort，they breathe air noisily out through their noses. People sometimes snort in order to express disapproval or amusement*.

（4）《美国传统词典》（双解）（*E-C American Heritage Dictionary*）：*to make an abrupt noise expressive of scorn，ridicule，or contempt* 轻蔑地哼：突然发出表现蔑视、嘲笑或自得的声音。

（5）《牛津高阶英汉双解词典》（*Oxford Advanced Learner's English-Chinese Dictionary*）：～（*at sb/sth*）（*of people*）*do this to show impatience，contempt，disgust，amusement，etc*（指人）发哼声（喷鼻息表示不耐烦、蔑视、厌恶、欢娱等）。

通过以上几部词典的释义，我们可以推断 snort 一词传达的是"哼着鼻子说"的含义，通常用来表示"不耐烦、不赞成、轻蔑"等态度。以下为杨译文和霍译文本中使用 snorted 来翻译"冷笑道"的例子：

1.【原文】狗儿**冷笑道**："有法儿还等到这会子呢!"（第六回）

【杨译】"Would I have waited all this time if there was some way out?" Gouer **snorted**.

【霍译】Gou-er **snorted** sarcastically. 'If there were a way, do you suppose I should have waited till now before trying it out?

2.【原文】黛玉听了**冷笑道**："我当是谁，原来是他!"（第二十回）

【杨译】"Oh，her." Daiyu **snorted**. "I wondered whom you meant."

【霍译】'Oh her,' said Dai-yu coldly. 'I wondered whom you could mean.'

3.【原文】袭人**冷笑道**："你问我，我知道吗?"（第二十一回）

【杨译】"How should I know?" Xiren **snorted**.

【霍译】Aroma smiled coldly. 'Why ask me? How should I know?'

4.【原文】晴雯**冷笑道**："我原是糊涂人，那里配和我说话!"（第三十一回）

【杨译】"I'm too silly to be up to talking to you，" **snorted** Qingwen.

【霍译】Skybright gave a harsh little laugh. 'Oh，yes. I'm too stupid to talk to.'

5.【原文】贾母便**冷笑两声**道："你也不必和我赌气，你的儿子，自然你要打就打。"（第三十三回）

【杨译】The old lady **snorted**. "You needn't try to work off your rage on me. It's not for me to stop you beating your son."

【霍译】'Hoity-toity，keep your temper！'said Grandmother Jia.

‘He's your son. If you want to beat him，that's up to you.'

**4. "冷笑道"英译之 mockingly**

副词 mockingly 是"冷笑道"会话引导语在杨译文本里的独特用法，总共有 5 例，在霍译文本中一次都没有出现过。mock 作为动词的意思为"取笑；嘲弄"，mockingly 作为副词主要传达"取笑地；嘲弄地；挖苦地"之意，阐明说话人的态度和方式。

以下为杨译文本中使用 mockingly 的例子，共有 3 例 smiled mockingly 和 2 例 laughed mockingly。

1.【原文】只篦了三五下儿，见晴雯忙忙走进来取钱，一见他两个，便**冷笑道**："哦！ 交杯盏儿还没吃，就上了头了!"（第二十回）

【杨译】Baoyu had just started combing it with a fine comb when Qingwen hurried in to fetch some money. She **laughed mockingly** at the sight of them. "Fancy！ You haven't yet drunk the bridal cup but already you're doing her hair."

【霍译】But he had not drawn it more than four or five times through her hair，when Skybright came bursting in to get some more money. Seeing the two of them together，she smiled sarcastically：'Fancy！ Doing her hair already — before you've even drunk the marriage-cup！'

2.【原文】凤姐听了**冷笑道**："我难道这个也不知道！ 我也这么想来着。"（第二十二回）

【杨译】"As if that hadn't occurred to me too！" Xifeng **smiled mockingly**.

【霍译】'Do you suppose I didn't think of that？' said Xi-feng with scorn. 'I'm not that stupid！'

3.【原文】宝钗**冷笑道**："我说你不中用!"（第四十二回）

【杨译】"I knew you'd be no use." Baochai **smiled mockingly**.

【霍译】'Oh，you're just hopeless！' said Bao-chai.

4.【原文】探春**冷笑道**："正是呢，有别人撵的，不如我先撵!"（第七十五回）

【杨译】"That's the idea." Tanchun **smiled mockingly**. "Better drive them out before getting thrown out by others."

【霍译】'Well，why not？' said Tan-chun bitterly. 'Better be driven out now by me than by someone else later on.'

5.【原文】那丫头听说,便**冷笑一声道**:"爷不认得的也多呢! 岂止我一个!"(第二十四回)

    【杨译】The maid **laughed mockingly**. "There are plenty of us you haven't seen. I'm not the only one by any means."

    【霍译】She replied with some bitterness:'There are quite a few of us you've never seen. I'm not the only one,by any means.'

**5. "冷笑道"英译之 smiled sarcastically**

smiled sarcastically 是"冷笑道"会话引导语在霍译和杨译文本中使用频率较高的短语,共 9 例,其中霍译文本 2 例,杨译文本 7 例。名词 sarcasm 的意思是"讥讽;讽刺;挖苦",其副词形式 sarcastically 表示"讽刺地;挖苦地"之意。

以下为霍译文本和杨译文本中使用 smiled sarcastically 来翻译"冷笑道"的例子:

1.【原文】袭人**冷笑道**:"我那里敢动气呢?"(第二十一回)

    【杨译】"Who am I to be cross?" Xiren **smiled sarcastically**.

    【霍译】Aroma laughed mirthlessly. 'It's not for the likes of me to get into rages.'

2.【原文】王夫人便**冷笑道**:"好个美人儿! 真象个'病西施'了! 你天天作这轻狂样儿给谁看!"(第七十四回)

    【杨译】She **smiled sarcastically**. "What a beauty!" she sneered. "Really like an ailing Xi Shi. Whom are you trying to vamp,going about like this?"

    【霍译】'Good gracious me!' she exclaimed sarcastically. 'What swooning Xi-shi have we here? For whose benefit do you go around in this extraordinary get-up?'

3.【原文】金桂**冷笑道**:"两个人的腔调儿都够使的了。别打量谁是傻子!"(第八十回)

    【杨译】Jingui **smiled sarcastically**. "You're both pretty obvious. Do you take me for a fool?"

    【霍译】Jin-gui hooted at them contemptuously. 'You two really are a comedy! You must think I'm an idiot.'

4.【原文】贾政**冷笑道**:"你要再提'上学'两个字,连我也羞死了。"(第九回)

    【杨译】"Don't make me die of shame with this talk about school." His father laughed scornfully.

    【霍译】Jia Zheng **smiled sarcastically**. 'I think you had better not use that word "studies" again in my hearing, unless you want to make me blush for you.'

5.【原文】凤姐冷笑道:"你们要拣远道儿走!"(第二十四回)

【杨 译】"What a roundabout way of doing things!" She **smiled sarcastically**.

【霍 译】'You have a very devious way of going about things,' said Xi-feng with a hint of malice in her smile.

# 第三节　"哭道"类会话引导语翻译研究

《红楼梦》中除了没完没了的"笑道","哭道"也占有一定的比例。笔者本节研究的"哭道"类会话引导语主要包括两大类别:"哭道:"和"泣道:"。"哭道"类会话引导语兼备"哭"和"道"双重形式和含义。

## 一、《红楼梦》原文中的"哭道"类会话引导语

笔者在自行创建的"《红楼梦》原文—霍译本—杨译本平行语料库"中检索"哭道:"和"泣道:",将检索结果经过筛选确认,合并构成一个"原文—霍译—杨译"的"哭道"会话引导语语料库,其中"哭道:"的用法有50例,"泣道:"有2例。

在此语料库基础上,笔者分别整理出"哭道"类会话引导语的原文、霍译本、杨译本文档,以供研究之用。其中"哭道"类会话引导语的霍译本(或称霍译文本)容量为1000,"哭道"类会话引导语的杨译本(或称杨译文本)容量为758。

## 二、《红楼梦》译文中的"哭道"类会话引导语

笔者将对《红楼梦》"哭道"类会话引导语的霍译本和杨译本进行高频词、独特词以及特色词等方面的分析研究。

### (一)霍译本与杨译本高频词研究

笔者分别对《红楼梦》"哭道"类会话引导语的霍译本和杨译本进行词频分析,将位列前100位的高频词列举如表4-18所示。

表4-18　"哭道"类会话引导语霍译本和杨译本高频词

| 霍译文本 | 词语 | 词频 | 百分比 | 杨译文本 | 词语 | 词频 | 百分比 |
|---|---|---|---|---|---|---|---|
| 1 | to | 45 | 4.50 | 1 | to | 27 | 3.56 |
| 2 | her | 32 | 3.20 | 2 | sobbed | 25 | 3.30 |
| 3 | and | 27 | 2.70 | 3 | you | 25 | 3.30 |

（续表）

| 霍译文本 | 词语 | 词频 | 百分比 | 杨译文本 | 词语 | 词频 | 百分比 |
|---|---|---|---|---|---|---|---|
| 4 | she | 21 | 2.10 | 4 | I | 21 | 2.77 |
| 5 | I | 18 | 1.80 | 5 | her | 20 | 2.64 |
| 6 | the | 18 | 1.80 | 6 | she | 19 | 2.51 |
| 7 | was | 17 | 1.70 | 7 | and | 15 | 1.98 |
| 8 | of | 16 | 1.60 | 8 | he | 12 | 1.58 |
| 9 | said | 16 | 1.60 | 9 | the | 11 | 1.45 |
| 10 | you | 16 | 1.60 | 10 | his | 10 | 1.32 |
| 11 | it | 15 | 1.50 | 11 | him | 8 | 1.06 |
| 12 | tearfully | 14 | 1.40 | 12 | of | 8 | 1.06 |
| 13 | but | 12 | 1.20 | 13 | with | 8 | 1.06 |
| 14 | he | 12 | 1.20 | 14 | madam | 7 | 0.92 |
| 15 | in | 12 | 1.20 | 15 | that | 7 | 0.92 |
| 16 | a | 10 | 1.00 | 16 | was | 7 | 0.92 |
| 17 | that | 10 | 1.00 | 17 | a | 6 | 0.79 |
| 18 | had | 9 | 0.90 | 18 | but | 6 | 0.79 |
| 19 | have | 8 | 0.80 | 19 | for | 6 | 0.79 |
| 20 | his | 8 | 0.80 | 20 | me | 6 | 0.79 |
| 21 | no | 8 | 0.80 | 21 | on | 6 | 0.79 |
| 22 | for | 7 | 0.70 | 22 | sister | 6 | 0.79 |
| 23 | weeping | 7 | 0.70 | 23 | in | 5 | 0.66 |
| 24 | him | 6 | 0.60 | 24 | my | 5 | 0.66 |
| 25 | sobbed | 6 | 0.60 | 25 | tears | 5 | 0.66 |
| 26 | with | 6 | 0.60 | 26 | again | 4 | 0.53 |
| 27 | as | 5 | 0.50 | 27 | as | 4 | 0.53 |
| 28 | Dai-yu | 5 | 0.50 | 28 | called | 4 | 0.53 |
| 29 | from | 5 | 0.50 | 29 | can | 4 | 0.53 |
| 30 | my | 5 | 0.50 | 30 | caught | 4 | 0.53 |
| 31 | now | 5 | 0.50 | 31 | cried | 4 | 0.53 |

| 霍译文本 | 词语 | 词频 | 百分比 | 杨译文本 | 词语 | 词频 | 百分比 |
|---|---|---|---|---|---|---|---|
| 32 | out | 5 | 0.50 | 32 | Daiyu | 4 | 0.53 |
| 33 | say | 5 | 0.50 | 33 | hold | 4 | 0.53 |
| 34 | tears | 5 | 0.50 | 34 | if | 4 | 0.53 |
| 35 | when | 5 | 0.50 | 35 | lady | 4 | 0.53 |
| 36 | Aroma | 4 | 0.40 | 36 | not | 4 | 0.53 |
| 37 | at | 4 | 0.40 | 37 | said | 4 | 0.53 |
| 38 | be | 4 | 0.40 | 38 | siqi | 4 | 0.53 |
| 39 | been | 4 | 0.40 | 39 | then | 4 | 0.53 |
| 40 | began | 4 | 0.40 | 40 | when | 4 | 0.53 |
| 41 | chess | 4 | 0.40 | 41 | child | 3 | 0.40 |
| 42 | hand | 4 | 0.40 | 42 | go | 3 | 0.40 |
| 43 | if | 4 | 0.40 | 43 | had | 3 | 0.40 |
| 44 | Jia | 4 | 0.40 | 44 | hand | 3 | 0.40 |
| 45 | lady | 4 | 0.40 | 45 | here | 3 | 0.40 |
| 46 | me | 4 | 0.40 | 46 | how | 3 | 0.40 |
| 47 | not | 4 | 0.40 | 47 | it | 3 | 0.40 |
| 48 | please | 4 | 0.40 | 48 | more | 3 | 0.40 |
| 49 | so | 4 | 0.40 | 49 | now | 3 | 0.40 |
| 50 | son | 4 | 0.40 | 50 | out | 3 | 0.40 |
| 51 | them | 4 | 0.40 | 51 | see | 3 | 0.40 |
| 52 | then | 4 | 0.40 | 52 | son | 3 | 0.40 |
| 53 | this | 4 | 0.40 | 53 | these | 3 | 0.40 |
| 54 | Wang | 4 | 0.40 | 54 | through | 3 | 0.40 |
| 55 | what | 4 | 0.40 | 55 | wailed | 3 | 0.40 |
| 56 | Xi-feng | 4 | 0.40 | 56 | Wang | 3 | 0.40 |
| 57 | about | 3 | 0.30 | 57 | what | 3 | 0.40 |
| 58 | any | 3 | 0.30 | 58 | who | 3 | 0.40 |
| 59 | Bao-yu | 3 | 0.30 | 59 | Xifeng | 3 | 0.40 |

（续表）

| 霍译文本 | 词语 | 词频 | 百分比 | 杨译文本 | 词语 | 词频 | 百分比 |
|---|---|---|---|---|---|---|---|
| 60 | can | 3 | 0.30 | 60 | Xiren | 3 | 0.40 |
| 61 | child | 3 | 0.30 | 61 | your | 3 | 0.40 |
| 62 | clung | 3 | 0.30 | 62 | all | 2 | 0.26 |
| 63 | could | 3 | 0.30 | 63 | any | 2 | 0.26 |
| 64 | cry | 3 | 0.30 | 64 | arm | 2 | 0.26 |
| 65 | crying | 3 | 0.30 | 65 | back | 2 | 0.26 |
| 66 | down | 3 | 0.30 | 66 | Baoyu | 2 | 0.26 |
| 67 | Er-jie | 3 | 0.30 | 67 | beat | 2 | 0.26 |
| 68 | get | 3 | 0.30 | 68 | been | 2 | 0.26 |
| 69 | go | 3 | 0.30 | 69 | coming | 2 | 0.26 |
| 70 | herself | 3 | 0.30 | 70 | cruel | 2 | 0.26 |
| 71 | into | 3 | 0.30 | 71 | die | 2 | 0.26 |
| 72 | is | 3 | 0.30 | 72 | do | 2 | 0.26 |
| 73 | left | 3 | 0.30 | 73 | done | 2 | 0.26 |
| 74 | Lian | 3 | 0.30 | 74 | good | 2 | 0.26 |
| 75 | little | 3 | 0.30 | 75 | home | 2 | 0.26 |
| 76 | made | 3 | 0.30 | 76 | is | 2 | 0.26 |
| 77 | only | 3 | 0.30 | 77 | just | 2 | 0.26 |
| 78 | Patience | 3 | 0.30 | 78 | know | 2 | 0.26 |
| 79 | tell | 3 | 0.30 | 79 | let | 2 | 0.26 |
| 80 | there | 3 | 0.30 | 80 | lie | 2 | 0.26 |
| 81 | wailed | 3 | 0.30 | 81 | maid | 2 | 0.26 |
| 82 | way | 3 | 0.30 | 82 | mean | 2 | 0.26 |
| 83 | wept | 3 | 0.30 | 83 | name | 2 | 0.26 |
| 84 | your | 3 | 0.30 | 84 | no | 2 | 0.26 |
| 85 | again | 2 | 0.20 | 85 | nothing | 2 | 0.26 |
| 86 | an | 2 | 0.20 | 86 | off | 2 | 0.26 |
| 87 | answered | 2 | 0.20 | 87 | one | 2 | 0.26 |

（续表）

| 霍译文本 | 词语 | 词频 | 百分比 | 杨译文本 | 词语 | 词频 | 百分比 |
|---|---|---|---|---|---|---|---|
| 88 | Aunt | 2 | 0.20 | 88 | over | 2 | 0.26 |
| 89 | back | 2 | 0.20 | 89 | Pinger | 2 | 0.26 |
| 90 | beaten | 2 | 0.20 | 90 | protesting | 2 | 0.26 |
| 91 | bitterly | 2 | 0.20 | 91 | put | 2 | 0.26 |
| 92 | broke | 2 | 0.20 | 92 | second | 2 | 0.26 |
| 93 | burst | 2 | 0.20 | 93 | sir | 2 | 0.26 |
| 94 | clinging | 2 | 0.20 | 94 | so | 2 | 0.26 |
| 95 | coming | 2 | 0.20 | 95 | sobbing | 2 | 0.26 |
| 96 | cried | 2 | 0.20 | 96 | soon | 2 | 0.26 |
| 97 | cruel | 2 | 0.20 | 97 | stay | 2 | 0.26 |
| 98 | did | 2 | 0.20 | 98 | tearfully | 2 | 0.26 |
| 99 | die | 2 | 0.20 | 99 | tell | 2 | 0.26 |
| 100 | face | 2 | 0.20 | 100 | terror | 2 | 0.26 |

通过对比"哭道"类会话引导语在霍译本和杨译本里的高频词我们可以发现，在排名前 100 位的高频词中，霍译本和杨译本均出现的动词有 4 个：said、sobbed、wailed 和 cried，但数量和比例差异显著。said 在霍译文本中是数量最多的动词，有 16 个，占文本总量的 1.60%；而在杨译文本中数量仅有 4 个，占文本总量的 0.53%，仅是霍译文本比例的三分之一。sobbed 在杨译文本中是使用最多的动词，有 25 个，占文本总量的 3.30%；霍译文本中 sobbed 仅有 6 个，占文本总量的 0.60%。wailed 在霍译文本和杨译文本中各有 3 个，分别占文本总量的 0.30% 和 0.40%。cried 在杨译文本中有 4 个，占文本总量的 0.53%；而在霍译文本中仅有 2 个，占文本总量的 0.20%，尚不到杨译文本比例的一半。此外，在霍译文本和杨译文本前 100 位高频词中还共同出现了副词 tearfully 和名词 tears。tearfully 在霍译文本中有 14 个，占文本总量的 1.40%；而在杨译文本中仅出现 2 次，比例仅为 0.26%，尚不到霍译文本比例的五分之一。名词 tears 在霍译文本和杨译文本中各有 5 个，分别占文本总量的 0.50% 和 0.66%。

我们通过下图可以清晰地看出霍译文本和杨译文本共享的高频词及所占比例，其中霍译文本最为突出的是 said 和 tearfully，杨译文本最为突出的是 sobbed（见图 4-4）。

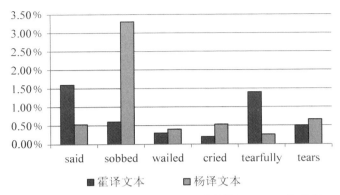

**图 4 - 4  动词 said、sobbed、wailed、cried 与副词 tearfully 和名词 tears
在"哭道"类会话引导语两译本中所占比例对比**

（二）霍译本与杨译本独特词研究

《红楼梦》"哭道"类会话引导语的霍译本相对于杨译本的独特词有 218 个，
将人名、地名用词筛除后，词频在 2 次以上的仅有 27 个：

from(5)          broke(2)          partly(2)
please(4)        clinging(2)       reproached(2)
them(4)          forget(2)         saying(2)
clung(3)         half(2)           such(2)
could(3)         longer(2)         taken(2)
crying(3)        oh(2)             try(2)
way(3)           once(2)           us(2)
answered(2)      other(2)          very(2)
beaten(2)        own(2)            whose(2)

《红楼梦》"哭道"类会话引导语的杨译本相对于霍译本的独特词有 151 个，
将人名、地名用词筛除后，词频在 2 次以上的仅有 14 个：

caught(4)        arm(2)            mean(2)
hold(4)          beat(2)           soon(2)
more(3)          do(2)             want(2)
through(3)       done(2)           yet(2)
who(3)           know(2)

### （三）霍译本与杨译本特色词研究

《红楼梦》"哭道"类会话引导语的霍译本相对于杨译本的特色词有 55 个，将人名、地名用词筛除后，关键度在 5 以上的特色词有 4 个：weeping（关键度 7.770）、tearfully（关键度 6.897）、from（关键度 5.550）和 say（关键度 5.550）。尽管 said 在霍译文本中词频非常高，但它并不是霍译文本的特色词。现在分词形式的 weeping 和副词 tearfully 的用法值得我们关注。

杨译本相对于霍译本的特色词有 182 个，将人名、地名用词筛除后，关键度在 5 以上的特色词有 7 个：sobbed（关键度 18.872）、caught（关键度 6.828）、hold（关键度 6.828）、madam（关键度 5.610）、more（关键度 5.121）、through（关键度 5.121）和 who（关键度 5.121）。sobbed 是杨译文本词频最高的动词，也是相对于霍译文本的第一大特色词。笔者在下文中将对该词做重点分析。

### （四）霍译本与杨译本二词以上搭配

前文所分析的均为使用单个动词来翻译《红楼梦》"哭道"类会话引导语的情况。经过进一步检索，笔者发现还有一些二词以上的短语或其他表达形式，使用次数在 2 次以上的表达方式有：with tears、burst into tears、clung to、clinging to、began to cry、caught hold of 等。这些表达方式在霍译文本和杨译文本中的分布如表 4-19 所示。

表 4-19　短语类表达形式在"哭道"类会话引导语两译本中使用情况统计

| 表达形式 | 总数量 | 杨译文本 | 霍译文本 |
|---|---|---|---|
| with tears | 5 | 3 | 2 |
| began to cry | 3 | 1 | 2 |
| burst into tears | 3 | 1 | 2 |
| caught hold of | 3 | 3 | 0 |
| clung to | 3 | 0 | 3 |
| clinging to | 2 | 0 | 2 |

其中，clung to 和 clinging to 是霍译文本的独特表达方式，caught hold of 是杨译文本的独特表达方式。

## 三、《红楼梦》"哭道"类会话引导语英译案例研究

笔者在上述对《红楼梦》原文以及译文中的"哭道"类会话引导语分析统计的基础上开展《红楼梦》"哭道"类会话引导语英译的案例研究。为此笔者选取霍译文本和杨译文本中均排名前 100 位、但两者比例差异明显的动词 said、sobbed、副词 tearfully、霍译文本中关键度最高的特色词 weeping，以及独特短

语 clung/clinging to 来开展相关分析。

（一）"哭道"类英译之 said

said 在"哭道"类会话引导语霍译文本和杨译文本的高频词中分别排名第 9 位和第 37 位。said 是霍译文本中数量最多的动词，有 16 个，占文本总量的 1.60%；而在杨译文本中数量仅有 4 个，占文本总量的 0.53%，仅为霍译文本比例的 1/3。因此 said 是霍译文本相对于杨译文本的重要特色词之一，关键度为 4.572。冯庆华教授对该词作过相关研究，认为 said 与人名一起使用时，经常出现在会话第一句的中间，而且人名一般后置(冯庆华，2015)。

以下为霍译文本和杨译文本中使用 said 来翻译"哭道"类会话引导语的例子：

1.【原文】宝玉满面泪痕**哭道**："家里姐姐妹妹都没有，单我有，我说没趣儿；……"（第三回）

   【霍译】'None of the girls has got one,' **said** Bao-yu, his face streaming with tears and sobbing hysterically. 'Only I have got one. It always upsets me...'

   【杨译】His face stained with tears，Baoyu sobbed，"None of the girls here has one，only me. What's the fun of that? ..."

2.【原文】晴雯**哭道**："我多早晚闹着要去了？ 饶生了气，还拿话压派我。"（第三十一回）

   【霍译】'When have I ever agitated to leave?' **said** Skybright，weeping now in earnest. 'Even if you're angry with me，you ought not to twist things round in order to get the better of me.'

   【杨译】"When did I insist on leaving?" sobbed Qingwen. "You fly into a rage，then put words into my mouth."

3.【原文】王夫人**哭道**："宝玉虽然该打，老爷也要保重。"（第三十三回）

   【霍译】'No doubt Bao-yu deserved to be beaten,' **said** Lady Wang tearfully, 'but it is bad for you to get over-excited.'

   【杨译】"I know Baoyu deserves a beating," sobbed Lady Wang. "But you mustn't wear yourself out，sir."

4.【原文】小丫头子**哭道**："我原没看见奶奶来，我又惦记着屋里没人，才跑来着。"（第四十四回）

   【霍译】'I didn't see you at first，ma'am,' **said** the little girl tearfully. 'I was running because I'd just remembered that there was no one at home to look after things.'

【杨译】"I didn't see you，madam，" sobbed the maid. "I ran because I remembered there was no one in our apartments."

5.【原文】（藕官）又**哭**道："我也不便和你面说，你只回去，背人悄悄问芳官就知道了。"（第五十八回）

【霍译】She began to cry. 'It's no good，' she **said**. 'I can't say it to your face. After you've got back，when there's no one else around，you can get Parfumée to tell you.'

【杨译】Then，sobbing again，she added，"I can't bring myself to tell you. If you must know，go back and ask Fangguan when no one else is about."

6.【原文】打得春燕又愧又急，因**哭**道："莺儿姐姐玩话，你就认真打我！"（第五十九回）

【霍译】'Oriole was only joking，' said Swallow，weeping — partly from the pain and partly from the humiliation of being beaten in front of the others.

【杨译】Hurt and humiliated，Chunyan sobbed，"Sister Yinger was only joking，yet you believed her and beat me."

7.【原文】尤氏也**哭**道："何曾不是这样？"（第六十八回）

【霍译】'I did try，' **said** You-shi tearfully.

【杨译】"That's how it was，really，" sobbed Madam You.

8.【原文】尤二姐**哭**道："妹妹，我一生品行既亏，今日之报，既系当然，何必又去杀人作孽？"（第六十九回）

【霍译】'Sister，' **said** Er-jie，weeping，'my whole life has been sinful. You yourself say that my present sufferings are a punishment. Why should I add the crime of murder to my other sins?'

【杨译】Second Sister sobbed，"I've already got a bad name，sister. As I deserve my present fate，why should I add to my crimes by killing her?"

9.【原文】入画跪**哭**道："我不敢撒谎，奶奶只管明日问我们奶奶和大爷去，若说不是赏的，就拿我和我哥哥一同打死无怨。"（第七十四回）

【霍译】'I wouldn't dare lie to you，madam，' said Picture，weeping. 'You have only to ask Mr and Mrs Zhen. If they say my brother wasn't given these things，I shan't complain if you beat us both to death.'

【杨译】Kneeling before her Ruhua sobbed，"I dare not lie to you，madam.You can check with Her Ladyship and His Lordship tomorrow. If they say these weren't gifts, I won't complain if you have me and my brother beaten to death."

10.【原文】晴雯又**哭道**："回去他们看见了要问，不必撒谎，就说是我的。既担了虚名，越性如此，也不过这样了。"（第七十七回）

【霍译】'If anyone sees that when you get back and asks you whose it is，' **said** Skybright，weeping，'there's no need to tell them any lies. Tell them it's mine. Since I've got such a bad reputation anyway，I might as well have something to show for it when I'm gone!'

【杨译】"If they see these when you go back and question you，" she sobbed，"there's no need to lie. Just tell them these are mine. Since I've been falsely accused，why shouldn't I at least have this satisfaction?"

11.【原文】（宝玉）因**泣道**："且卸下这个来，等好了再戴上罢。"（第七十七回）

【霍译】'Better take these off，' he **said**（he was crying himself as he spoke）. 'You can put them on again when you are better.'

【杨译】"Better take these off，" he advised. "You can wear them when you're better."

12.【原文】尤二姐拉他**哭道**："姐姐，我从到了这里，多亏姐姐照应。……"（第六十九回）

【霍译】Er-jie clutched her hand. She was crying weakly as she replied. 'Sister，you have been so good to me，ever since I came to this place....'

【杨译】Second Sister took her hand and **said** through tears，"How good you've been to me，sister，since I came here!..."

13.【原文】袭人等急的又**哭道**："小祖宗儿，你看这玉丢了没要紧；要是上头知道了，我们这些人就要粉身碎骨了！"（第九十四回）

【霍译】'Little ancestor，please...' came tearfully from where Aroma stood in the throng of distraught maids. 'It's all very well for you to say "forget about it"！ But what you seem to have forgotten is that if Their Ladyships get to hear，the likes of us will be torn to shreds and ground to powder！'

【杨译】Weeping in desperation Xiren **said**，"You may not care that the jade's lost，Little Ancestor，but if this comes to the mistresses' ears it'll be the death of us!"

14.【原文】平儿**哭道**："如今已经这样，东西去了，不能复来。奶奶这样，还得再请个大夫瞧瞧才好啊！"（第一百六回）

【霍译】Patience **said** to him with tears in her eyes：'Everything's gone! We'll never get any of it back. And look at Mrs Lian，sir. You must send for a doctor.'

【杨译】"What's done is done，" sobbed Pinger. " We can't get back what we've lost. But the mistress is so ill，you must send for a doctor for her."

通过上述例子我们可以发现，霍译本和杨译本中使用 said 来翻译"哭道"时都不是单独使用的，均加入了一些其他修饰成分，如 said XX tearfully、said with tears、said through tears，以及 said XX，weeping 等，说明译者在翻译时将"哭"和"道"分开进行处理，使得内容更清晰，表述更形象。

（二）"哭道"类英译之 sobbed

sobbed 是杨译文本中使用最多的动词，有 25 个，占文本总量的 3.30%，而在霍译文本中仅有 6 个，占文本总量的 0.60%，是杨译文本比例的 1/5 不到。sobbed 也成为杨译文本相对于霍译文本的第一大特色词，关键度为 18.872。

我们先来看几部权威词典对于动词"sob"的解释：

（1）《牛津高阶英语词典》（第 6 版）（*Oxford Advanced Learner's Dictionary*）：*to cry noisily，taking sudden，sharp breaths；～ sth（out）to say sth while you are crying*。

（2）《朗文当代英语词典》（第 4 版）（*Longman Dictionary of Contemporary English*）：*to cry noisily while breathing in short sudden bursts；to say something while you are sobbing*。

（3）《柯林斯高阶英语词典》（*Collins COBUILD Advanced Learner's English Dictionary*）：*If you sob something，you say it while you are crying.*

（4）《美国传统词典》（双解）（*E-C American Heritage Dictionary*）：*to weep aloud with convulsive gasping；cry uncontrollably* 呜咽：抽搐着喘气地大声哭；不能控制地哭。

*to utter with sobs*，呜咽着说。

（5）《牛津高阶英汉双解词典》（*Oxford Advanced Learner's English-Chinese Dictionary*）：*draw in breath noisily and irregularly from sorrow，pain，etc，esp while crying* 啜泣；抽噎。

通过以上几部词典的释义,我们可以推断 sob 一词表达的是"呜咽着说;啜泣着说;哭诉"之意,本身便可包含"哭"和"说"的双重含义。以下为霍译文本和杨译文本中使用 sob 来翻译"哭道"类会话引导语的例子:

1.【原文】秦钟**哭道**:"有金荣在这里,我是不在这里念书的。"(第九回)

   【杨译】"I'm not coming here any more," **sobbed** Qin Zhong, "if Jin Rong is allowed to stay."

   【霍译】'If Jokey Jin stays here,' wailed Qin Zhong tearfully, 'I'm not studying in this school any longer.'

2.【原文】黛玉**哭道**:"我也是白效力,他也不稀罕,自有别人替他再穿好的去呢!"(第二十九回)

   【杨译】"All my work for nothing," **sobbed** Daiyu. "He doesn't care for it.He can get someone else to make him a better one."

   【霍译】'It was a waste of time making it,' she **sobbed**. 'He doesn't really care for it. And there's someone else who'll no doubt make him a better one!'

3.【原文】(黛玉)便**哭道**:"你也不用来哄我! 从今以后,我也不敢亲近二爷,权当我去了。"(第三十回)

   【杨译】"You needn't flatter me," she **sobbed**. "I shall never dare be friends with you again.Behave as if I'd gone."

   【霍译】'You don't have to treat me like a child,' she blurted out tearfully. 'From now on I shall make no further claims on you. You can behave exactly as if I had gone away.'

4.【原文】凤姐儿**哭道**:"我才家去换衣裳,不防琏二爷在家和人说话,……"(第四十四回)

   【杨译】"When I went home just now to change,' Xifeng **sobbed**, 'I heard him talking to someone..."

   【霍译】'When I went home just now to change my clothes,' Xi-feng tearfully related, 'I was surprised to hear Mr Lian indoors talking to somebody...'

5.【原文】袭人定了一回,**哭道**:"不知紫鹃姑奶奶说了些什么话,那个呆子眼也直了,手脚也冷了,话也不说了,李妈妈掐着也不疼了,已死了大半个了!"(第五十七回)

   【杨译】Making an effort to calm herself Xiren **sobbed**, "I don't know what your Miss Zijuan's been telling him, but the silly boy's eyes are staring, his hands and feet are cold; he can't speak, and when Nanny Li pinched him he felt nothing. He's more dead than alive!'"

【霍译】Aroma made an effort to control herself and answered tearfully：'I don't know what Her Ladyship here can have said to him，but that simpleton of ours just stares into space without speaking，his hands and feet are icy-cold，and when Nannie Li pinches him，he doesn't seem to feel anything. He looked half dead when I left.'

6.【原文】凤姐也假意**哭道**："狠心的妹妹！你怎么丢下我去了？辜负了我的心！"（第六十九回）

【杨译】Xifeng put on a show of sobbing，"How cruel of you，sister，to leave me alone like this! What a poor return for my kindness!"

【霍译】Xi-feng made a show of weeping too and hypo-critically reproached Er-jie for her 'cruelty'. 'Hard-hearted sister!' she wailed. 'How could you bear to leave me like this when you knew how much I cared for you?'

7.【原文】司棋一把拉住，**哭道**："我的姐姐！咱们从小儿耳鬓厮磨，……"（第七十二回）

【杨译】Siqi caught her by the arm. "Sister，we've been on good terms since we were children，" she **sobbed**.

【霍译】Chess clung to her hand and wept. 'Dear Faithful! We've known each other now since we were little girls.'

8.【原文】司棋见了这般，知不能免，因跪着**哭道**："姑娘好狠心！哄了我这两日，如今怎么连一句话也没有？"（第七十七回）

【杨译】"How cruel you are，miss!" **sobbed** Siqi，seeing that her fate was sealed. "You've kept me hoping the last two days，yet won't say a good word for me now."

【霍译】When it became clear that her mistress was determined to say nothing and that there was to be no escape for her，Chess fell down on her knees and reproached her tearfully. 'You have a cruel heart，miss! All through these last few days you have allowed me to go on hoping，but now，when the time comes，you won't say a single word to help me!'

9.【原文】黛玉**哭道**："老太太，这是什么事呢!"（第八十二回）

【杨译】"What does that mean，madam?" she **sobbed**.

【霍译】'But what's to become of me，Grannie?' she **sobbed**.

10.【原文】黛玉越听越气，越没了主意，只得拉着宝玉**哭道**："好哥哥! 你叫我跟了谁去?"（第八十二回）

【杨译】Feeling yet more angry and helpless，she gripped his arm. "Good cousin，to whom do you want me to go?" she **sobbed**.

【霍译】Dai-yu listened in despair as this，her very last hope，was taken from her. Clinging to him helplessly，she gave a feverish cry: 'Oh Bao! I've no separate way to go! How could you say such a thing!'

11.【原文】贾环吓得**哭道**："我再不敢嚷了!"（第九十四回）

【杨译】In his terror Huan **sobbed**，"I won't breathe a word about it!"

【霍译】'I promise never to mention it again!' wailed Jia Huan in terror.

12.【原文】平儿气的**哭道**："有话明说，人死了也愿意!"（第一百十三回）

【杨译】"Say plainly what you want，" she **sobbed** angrily. "Then we can die content!"

【霍译】Patience finally broke down. Half angrily，half tearfully she begged Jia Lian: 'Please，won't you tell us what the matter is? It's not fair to keep us in this dreadful suspense...'

13.【原文】贾兰也不及请安，便**哭道**："二叔丢了!"（第一百十九回）

【杨译】Without stopping to pay his respects he **sobbed**，"Uncle Bao has disappeared!"

【霍译】He did not even greet them but burst into tears. 'Lost!' he **sobbed**.

14.【原文】薛姨妈又**哭道**："我也不要命了! 赶到那里见他一面，同他死在一处就完了。"（第八十五回）

【杨译】"I wish I were dead!" wailed Aunt Xue. "I'll go and see my son for the last time，then die together with him!"

【霍译】'What have I left to live for?' **sobbed** Aunt Xue. 'Let me go there and see him once! Then the two of us can die together!'

15.【原文】王夫人**哭道**："他若抛了父母，这就是不孝，怎能成佛作祖?"（第一百十九回）

【杨译】 "If he's so unfilial as to abandon his parents，how can he become a Buddha?" **sobbed** Lady Wang.

【霍译】 'But if he rejects his own mother and father，' **sobbed** Lady Wang，'then he's failing in his duty as a son. And in that case how can he ever hope to become a Saint or a Buddha?'

（三）"哭道"类英译之 tearfully

副词 tearfully 同属"哭道"类会话引导语霍译文本和杨译文本前 100 位高频词，但在两者中的数量和比例差异显著：在霍译文本中有 14 个，占文本总量的 1.40%，而在杨译文本中仅出现 2 次，比例仅为 0.26%，是霍译文本比例的 1/5 不到。tearfully 也是霍译本相对于杨译本的特色词，关键度为 6.897。

《牛津高阶英语词典》（第 6 版）（*Oxford Advanced Learner's Dictionary*）对于 tearful 的解释为：(of a person) crying，or about to cry;《柯林斯高阶英语词典》（*Collins COBUILD Advanced Learner's English Dictionary*）对于 tearful 的解释为：If someone is tearful，their face or voice shows signs that they have been crying or that they want to cry. 因此我们可以推断 tearful 的意思为"含泪的；眼泪汪汪的；带有哭腔的"，其副词 tearfully 传达的是"眼泪汪汪地；含泪地"意义。

以下为霍译文本和杨译文本中使用 tearfully 来翻译"哭道"类会话引导语的例子，其中杨译文本中仅有 2 例：

1.【原文】平儿气怯，忙住了手，**哭道**："你们背地里说话，为什么拉我呢?"（第四十四回）

　【霍译】 Patience，whose gentle nature was easily overawed，at once left off，**tearfully** protesting that it was cruel of them to speak about her in such a way behind her back.

　【杨译】 Pinger fearing that he would beat her promptly left off，protesting **tearfully**，"When you talk behind our backs，why drag me in?"

2.【原文】王夫人也**哭道**："妞儿不用着急！……"（第一百十九回）

　【霍译】 Lady Wang was in tears herself：'Try not to worry，child....'

　【杨译】 "Don't worry，child，" said Lady Wang **tearfully**，...

3.【原文】秦钟**哭道**："有金荣在这里，我是不在这里念书的。"（第九回）

　【霍译】 'If Jokey Jin stays here，' wailed Qin Zhong **tearfully**，'I'm not studying in this school any longer.'

　【杨译】 "I'm not coming here any more，" sobbed Qin Zhong，"if Jin Rong is allowed to stay."

4.【原文】(黛玉)便**哭道**："你也不用来哄我！从今以后,我也不敢亲近二爷,权当我去了。"(第三十回)

　　【霍译】'You don't have to treat me like a child,' she blurted out **tearfully**. 'From now on I shall make no further claims on you. You can behave exactly as if I had gone away.'

　　【杨译】"You needn't flatter me," she sobbed. "I shall never dare be friends with you again. Behave as if I'd gone."

5.【原文】王夫人**哭道**："宝玉虽然该打,老爷也要保重。"(第三十三回)

　　【霍译】'No doubt Bao-yu deserved to be beaten,' said Lady Wang **tearfully**, 'but it is bad for you to get over-excited.'

　　【杨译】"I know Baoyu deserves a beating," sobbed Lady Wang. "But you mustn't wear yourself out, sir."

6.【原文】小丫头子**哭道**："我原没看见奶奶来,我又惦记着屋里没人,才跑来着。"(第四十四回)

　　【霍译】'I didn't see you at first, ma'am,' said the little girl **tearfully**. 'I was running because I'd just remembered that there was no one at home to look after things.'

　　【杨译】"I didn't see you, madam," sobbed the maid. "I ran because I remembered there was no one in our apartments."

7.【原文】那小丫头子先还强嘴,后来听见凤姐儿要烧了红烙铁来烙嘴,方**哭道**："二爷在家里,打发我来这里瞧着奶奶,要见奶奶散了,先叫我送信儿去呢。不承望奶奶这会子就来了。"(第四十四回)

　　【霍译】At first the maid tried sticking to her story, but when she heard that Xi-feng was going to heat an iron red-hot and burn her mouth with it, she broke down and **tearfully** confessed that Jia Lian was at home and had stationed her in the passage-way to look out for her mistress and give him warning of her coming; but as Xi-feng had left the party so much earlier than expected, she had been taken unawares.

　　【杨译】The maid went on protesting her innocence until Xifeng threatened to brand her mouth with a red-hot iron. Then she confessed with tears: 'the master's home. He sent me here to watch out for you and let him know as soon as I saw you coming, madam. He didn't think you would be back so soon.'

8.【原文】袭人定了一回,**哭道**："不知紫鹃姑娘说了些什么话,那个呆子

眼也直了,手脚也冷了,话也不说了,李妈妈掐着也不疼了,已死了大半个了!"(第五十七回)

【霍译】Aroma made an effort to control herself and answered **tearfully**:'I don't know what Her Ladyship here can have said to him,but that simpleton of ours just stares into space without speaking,his hands and feet are icy-cold,and when Nannie Li pinches him,he doesn't seem to feel anything. He looked half dead when I left.'

【杨译】Making an effort to calm herself Xiren sobbed,"I don't know what your Miss Zijuan's been telling him,but the silly boy's eyes are staring,his hands and feet are cold;he can't speak,and when Nanny Li pinched him he felt nothing. He's more dead than alive!"

9.【原文】凤姐儿**哭**道:"我才家去换衣裳,不防琏二爷在家和人说话,……"(第四十四回)

【霍译】'When I went home just now to change my clothes,'Xi-feng **tearfully** related,'I was surprised to hear Mr Lian indoors talking to somebody.'

【杨译】"When I went home just now to change,"Xifeng sobbed,"I heard him talking to someone."

10.【原文】尤氏也**哭**道:"何曾不是这样?"(第六十八回)

【霍译】'I did try,'said You-shi **tearfully**.

【杨译】"That's how it was,really,"sobbed Madam You.

11.【原文】鸳鸯忙要回身,司棋拉住苦求,**哭**道:"我们的性命,都在姐姐身上,只求姐姐超生我们罢了!"(第七十一回)

【霍译】Faithful wanted to turn away,but Chess clung to her **tearfully** and beseechingly.'Our lives are in your hands,Faithful. Be merciful!'

【杨译】Yuanyang wanted to hurry away,but Siqi caught hold of her and begged through her sobs:"Our lives are in your hands,sister. Do,please,let us off!"

12.【原文】司棋见了这般,知不能免,因跪着**哭**道:"姑娘好狠心!哄了我这两日,如今怎么连一句话也没有?"(第七十七回)

【霍译】When it became clear that her mistress was determined to say nothing and that there was to be no escape for her,

Chess fell down on her knees and reproached her **tearfully**. 'You have a cruel heart, miss! All through these last few days you have allowed me to go on hoping, but now, when the time comes, you won't say a single word to help me!'

【杨译】"How cruel you are, miss!" sobbed Siqi, seeing that her fate was sealed. "You've kept me hoping the last two days, yet won't say a good word for me now."

13.【原文】袭人等急的又**哭道**:"小祖宗儿,你看这玉丢了没要紧;要是上头知道了,我们这些人就要粉身碎骨了!"(第九十四回)

【霍译】'Little ancestor, please...' came **tearfully** from where Aroma stood in the throng of distraught maids. 'It's all very well for you to say "forget about it"! But what you seem to have forgotten is that if Their Ladyships get to hear, the likes of us will be torn to shreds and ground to powder!'

【杨译】Weeping in desperation Xiren said, "You may not care that the jade's lost, Little Ancestor, but if this comes to the mistresses' ears it'll be the death of us!"

14.【原文】宝玉片时清楚,自料难保,见诸人散后,房中只有袭人,因唤袭人至跟前,拉着手**哭道**:"我问你:宝姐姐怎么来的? ……"(第九十八回)

【霍译】His brief access of clarity enabled Bao-yu to understand the gravity of his illness. When the others had gone and he was left alone with Aroma, he called her over to his side and taking her by the hand said **tearfully**: 'Please tell me how Cousin Chai came to be here?'

【杨译】Baoyu, now that his mind had cleared, was convinced that he was dying. As the others had gone, leaving only Xiren there, he called her over to him and clasped her hand. "Tell me," he sobbed, "what is Cousin Baochai doing here?"

(四)"哭道"类英译之 weeping 和 wept

weeping 是"哭道"类会话引导语的霍译文本相对于杨译文本的第一特色词,关键度为 7.770。weeping 在霍译文本中有 7 个,占文本总量的 0.70%,而在杨译文本中仅有 1 例。此外,霍译文本中还有 3 例 wept 的用法,杨译文本中也仅有 1 例。

我们先来看几部权威词典对于动词 weep 的解释:

(1)《牛津高阶英语词典》(第 6 版)(*Oxford Advanced Learner's Dictionary*)：~(*at / over sth*)(*formal or literary*)*to cry*，*usually because you are sad*。

(2)《朗文当代英语词典》(第 4 版)(*Longman Dictionary of Contemporary English*)：(*formal or literary*)*to cry*，*especially because you feel very sad*。

(3)《柯林斯高阶英语词典》(*Collins COBUILD Advanced Learner's English Dictionary*)：*If someone weeps*，*they cry*.(*LITERARY*)。

(4)《美国传统词典》(双解)(*E-C American Heritage Dictionary*)：*To shed* (*tears*)*as an expression of emotion* 流(泪)：流(泪)作为感情的一种表达方式。

(5)《牛津高阶英汉双解词典》(*Oxford Advanced Learner's English-Chinese Dictionary*)：~(*for / over sb / sth*)*shed tears*；*cry* 流泪；哭泣。

通过以上几部词典的释义，我们可以看到 weep 一词的用法是比较偏正式性和文学性的，表达的是"(通常因悲伤)哭泣；流泪"之意。

以下为霍译文本和杨译文本中使用 weeping 或 wept 来翻译"哭道"类会话引导语的例子：

1.【原文】金钏儿听见，忙跪下**哭道**："我再不敢了！太太要打要骂，只管发落，别叫我出去，就是天恩了！"(第三十回)

【霍译】Golden threw herself，**weeping**，upon her knees：'No，Your Ladyship，please！Beat me and revile me as much as you like，but please，for pity's sake，don't send me away.'

【杨译】At these words Jinchuan fell on her knees and burst into tears. "I shan't let it happen again，madam，" she cried. "Whip me，scold me or punish me as you please，but for pity's sake don't send me away!"

2.【原文】晴雯**哭道**："我多早晚闹着要去了？饶生了气，还拿话压派我。"(第三十一回)

【霍译】'When have I ever agitated to leave?' said Skybright，**weeping** now in earnest. 'Even if you're angry with me，you ought not to twist things round in order to get the better of me.'

【杨译】"When did I insist on leaving?" sobbed Qingwen. "You fly into a rage，then put words into my mouth."

3.【原文】打得春燕又愧又急，因**哭道**："莺儿姐姐玩话，你就认真打我！"(第五十九回)

【霍译】'Oriole was only joking，' said Swallow，**weeping** — partly from the pain and partly from the humiliation of being beaten in front of the others.

【杨译】Hurt and humiliated，Chunyan sobbed，"sister Yinger was only joking，yet you believed her and beat me."

4.【原文】尤二姐**哭道**："妹妹，我一生品行既亏，今日之报，既系当然，何必又去杀人作孽?"(第六十九回)

【霍译】'Sister，' said Er-jie，**weeping**，'my whole life has been sinful. You yourself say that my present sufferings are a punishment. Why should I add the crime of murder to my other sins?'

【杨译】Second Sister sobbed，"I've already got a bad name，sister. As I deserve my present fate，why should I add to my crimes by killing her?"

5.【原文】凤姐也假意**哭道**："狠心的妹妹! 你怎么丢下我去了? 辜负了我的心!"(第六十九回)

【霍译】Xi-feng made a show of **weeping** too and hypo-critically reproached Er-jie for her 'cruelty'. 'Hard-hearted sister!' she wailed. 'How could you bear to leave me like this when you knew how much I cared for you?'

【杨译】Xifeng put on a show of sobbing，"How cruel of you，sister，to leave me alone like this! What a poor return for my kindness!"

6.【原文】司棋一把拉住，**哭道**："我的姐姐! 咱们从小儿耳鬓厮磨，⋯⋯"(第七十二回)

【霍译】Chess clung to her hand and **wept**. 'Dear Faithful! We've known each other now since we were little girls.'

【杨译】Siqi caught her by the arm. "Sister，we've been on good terms since we were children，" she sobbed.

7.【原文】晴雯又**哭道**："回去他们看见了要问，不必撒谎，就说是我的。既担了虚名，越性如此，也不过这样了。"(第七十七回)

【霍译】'If anyone sees that when you get back and asks you whose it is，' said Skybright，**weeping**，'there's no need to tell them any lies. Tell them it's mine. Since I've got such a bad reputation anyway，I might as well have something to show for it when I'm gone!'

【杨译】"If they see these when you go back and question you，" she sobbed，"there's no need to lie. Just tell them these are mine. Since I've been falsely accused，why shouldn't I at least have this satisfaction?"

8.【原文】司棋见了宝玉，因拉住**哭道**："他们做不得主，好歹求求太太去！"（第七十七回）

【霍译】Chess clung to Bao-yu and **wept**. 'There's nothing they can do. If you want to save me，you'll have to speak to Her Ladyship.'

【杨译】Siqi caught hold of his sleeve. "They can't disobey orders，" she sobbed. "But please go and beg Her Ladyship to let me off."

9.【原文】迎春**哭道**："我不信我的命就这么苦？从小儿没有娘，幸而过婶娘这边来，过了几年心净日子；如今偏又是这么个结果！"（第八十回）

【霍译】Ying-chun **wept**. 'I can't believe that it was my fate to be so unhappy. After losing my mother as a tiny child，it seemed such bliss when you brought me here to live with Cousin Wan and the girls. And now，after just a few years of blessedness，I am to end like this!'

【杨译】"I can't believe I was fated to suffer like this，" sobbed Yingchun. "I lost my mother when I was a child，and was lucky to have a few peaceful years here with you，auntie. But now see what's become of me!"

10.【原文】袭人等急的又**哭道**："小祖宗儿，你看这玉丢了没要紧；要是上头知道了，我们这些人就要粉身碎骨了！"（第九十四回）

【霍译】'Little ancestor，please...' came tearfully from where Aroma stood in the throng of distraught maids. 'It's all very well for you to say "forget about it"! But what you seem to have forgotten is that if Their Ladyships get to hear，the likes of us will be torn to shreds and ground to powder!'

【杨译】**Weeping** in desperation Xiren said，"You may not care that the jade's lost，Little Ancestor，but if this comes to the mistresses' ears it'll be the death of us!"

我们可以看到，几乎所有的 weeping 都是与 said 或其他动词搭配做伴随状语,更加印证了霍译文本倾向于将"哭"和"道"分开来翻译的特点。

（五）"哭道"类英译之 clung/clinging to

在"哭道"类会话引导语的霍译文本中,还出现了独特的短语 clung to 和 clinging to,用来翻译"哭道"类会话引导语中的一类特定表达方式——"拉住哭道"。杨译文本在翻译时多采用 caught hold of 这一短语。以下为几个典型例子:

1. 【原文】话未说了,把个宝钗气怔了,**拉着薛姨妈哭道**:"妈妈,你听哥哥说的是什么话!"（第三十四回）

   【霍译】Anger at first made Bao-chai speechless；then，**clinging to** Aunt Xue，she burst into tears. 'Mamma，listen to what Pan is saying to me！'

   【杨译】Baochai was speechless at first with indignation. Then catching hold of her mother she sobbed："Do you hear what he's saying，mother？"

2. 【原文】鸳鸯忙要回身,司棋**拉住苦求,哭道**:"我们的性命,都在姐姐身上,只求姐姐超生我们罢了!"（第七十一回）

   【霍译】Faithful wanted to turn away，but Chess **clung to** her tearfully and beseechingly. 'Our lives are in your hands，Faithful. Be merciful！'

   【杨译】Yuanyang wanted to hurry away，but Siqi caught hold of her and begged through her sobs："Our lives are in your hands，sister. Do，please，let us off！"

3. 【原文】司棋**一把拉住,哭道**:"我的姐姐! 咱们从小儿耳鬓厮磨,……"（第七十二回）

   【霍译】Chess **clung to** her hand and wept. 'Dear Faithful! We've known each other now since we were little girls.'

   【杨译】Siqi caught her by the arm. "Sister，we've been on good terms since we were children，" she sobbed.

4. 【原文】司棋见了宝玉,因**拉住哭道**:"他们做不得主,好歹求求太太去!"（第七十七回）

   【霍译】Chess **clung to** Bao-yu and wept. 'There's nothing they can do. If you want to save me，you'll have to speak to Her Ladyship.'

   【杨译】Siqi caught hold of his sleeve. "They can't disobey orders，" she sobbed. "But please go and beg Her Ladyship to let me off."

5.【原文】黛玉越听越气,越没了主意,只得**拉着宝玉哭道**:"好哥哥! 你叫我跟了谁去?"(第八十二回)

【霍译】Dai-yu listened in despair as this，her very last hope，was taken from her. **Clinging to** him helplessly，she gave a feverish cry：'Oh Bao! I've no separate way to go! How could you say such a thing!'

【杨译】Feeling yet more angry and helpless，she gripped his arm. "Good cousin，to whom do you want me to go?" she sobbed.

《牛津高阶英汉双解词典》(*Oxford Advanced Learner's English-Chinese Dictionary*)对 cling to sb 的释义为：*hold on tightly to sb* 紧抓住或抱住某人；*be emotionally dependent on sb* 感情上依靠某人。《美国传统词典(双解)》(*E-C American Heritage Dictionary*)对该词的解释为：*to hold fast or adhere to sb* 紧握,粘着；*to remain emotionally attached* 保留感情上的联系。由此我们可以推断 cling to sb 不仅指动作上的"拉"和"靠",还蕴含着心理上的"依附感"和"依靠感",比较符合"拉着哭道"的具体情境和氛围。而杨译文本中使用的 caught hold of sb/sb's sleeve 或 gripped sb's arm 无法传达这种双重含义。

## 第四节 "骂道"类会话引导语翻译研究

《红楼梦》独特的艺术魅力很大程度上在于作者对人物形象的生动塑造,使得各个人物的嬉笑怒骂皆具风韵。《红楼梦》中的人物不仅有笑声和哭声,鉴于森严的社会等级制度和各人物间悬殊的社会地位,骂人的场合也有很多。从作者构思的每一句骂语中,我们可以了解到骂人者的社会地位、性别年龄、文化程度、修养水平等,对于凸显人物性格和各种人物关系,以及推动故事情节发展有非常重要的意义。本节笔者将着重研究《红楼梦》中"骂道"类会话引导语的翻译问题。

### 一、《红楼梦》原文中的"骂道"类会话引导语

《红楼梦》原文中的"骂道"类会话引导语主要有"骂道："和"骂："两类,其中"骂道："有 48 个,"骂："有 10 个。因此,本部分主要考察这两类种类引导语。

笔者将以上两个文本合并成一个总的"骂道"类会话引导语文本(总数量为58 个)统一进行研究,整理出一个"原文—霍译—杨译"的"骂道"类会话引导语语料库,在此语料库的基础上分别整理出"骂道"类会话引导语的原文、霍译本、杨译本文档,以供研究之用。其中"骂道"类会话引导语的霍译本(或称霍译文

本)容量为1102，"骂道"类会话引导语的杨译本(或称杨译文本)容量为814。

## 二、《红楼梦》译文中的"骂道"类会话引导语

笔者将对《红楼梦》"骂道"类会话引导语的霍译本和杨译本进行高频词、独特词以及特色词等方面的分析研究。

### (一)霍译本与杨译本高频词研究

笔者通过分别对《红楼梦》"骂道"类会话引导语的霍译本和杨译本进行词频分析，将位列前100位的高频词列举如表4-20所示。

表4-20 "骂道"类会话引导语霍译本和杨译本高频词

| 霍译文本 | 词语 | 词频 | 百分比 | 杨译文本 | 词语 | 词频 | 百分比 |
|---|---|---|---|---|---|---|---|
| 1 | her | 39 | 3.54 | 1 | you | 39 | 4.79 |
| 2 | she | 36 | 3.27 | 2 | she | 33 | 4.05 |
| 3 | the | 30 | 2.72 | 3 | her | 26 | 3.19 |
| 4 | and | 28 | 2.54 | 4 | the | 25 | 3.07 |
| 5 | of | 24 | 2.18 | 5 | and | 21 | 2.58 |
| 6 | to | 19 | 1.72 | 6 | swore | 19 | 2.33 |
| 7 | you | 19 | 1.72 | 7 | to | 18 | 2.21 |
| 8 | was | 18 | 1.63 | 8 | scolded | 14 | 1.72 |
| 9 | a | 16 | 1.45 | 9 | he | 12 | 1.47 |
| 10 | little | 16 | 1.45 | 10 | in | 12 | 1.47 |
| 11 | with | 16 | 1.45 | 11 | of | 11 | 1.35 |
| 12 | said | 14 | 1.27 | 12 | whore | 9 | 1.11 |
| 13 | in | 13 | 1.18 | 13 | with | 9 | 1.11 |
| 14 | at | 12 | 1.09 | 14 | a | 8 | 0.98 |
| 15 | shouted | 11 | 1.00 | 15 | this | 8 | 0.98 |
| 16 | Xi-feng | 10 | 0.91 | 16 | at | 7 | 0.86 |
| 17 | he | 9 | 0.82 | 17 | Jia | 7 | 0.86 |
| 18 | him | 9 | 0.82 | 18 | what | 7 | 0.86 |
| 19 | it | 9 | 0.82 | 19 | all | 6 | 0.74 |
| 20 | on | 9 | 0.82 | 20 | cursed | 6 | 0.74 |
| 21 | Jia | 8 | 0.73 | 21 | out | 6 | 0.74 |

| 霍译文本 | 词语 | 词频 | 百分比 | 杨译文本 | 词语 | 词频 | 百分比 |
|---|---|---|---|---|---|---|---|
| 22 | so | 8 | 0.73 | 22 | stormed | 6 | 0.74 |
| 23 | that | 8 | 0.73 | 23 | that | 6 | 0.74 |
| 24 | this | 8 | 0.73 | 24 | Xifeng | 6 | 0.74 |
| 25 | angrily | 7 | 0.64 | 25 | are | 5 | 0.61 |
| 26 | by | 7 | 0.64 | 26 | as | 5 | 0.61 |
| 27 | creature | 7 | 0.64 | 27 | face | 5 | 0.61 |
| 28 | face | 7 | 0.64 | 28 | his | 5 | 0.61 |
| 29 | from | 7 | 0.64 | 29 | lady | 5 | 0.61 |
| 30 | had | 6 | 0.54 | 30 | was | 5 | 0.61 |
| 31 | his | 6 | 0.54 | 31 | by | 4 | 0.49 |
| 32 | out | 6 | 0.54 | 32 | for | 4 | 0.49 |
| 33 | when | 6 | 0.54 | 33 | forward | 4 | 0.49 |
| 34 | Patience | 5 | 0.45 | 34 | herself | 4 | 0.49 |
| 35 | wife | 5 | 0.45 | 35 | him | 4 | 0.49 |
| 36 | aunt | 4 | 0.36 | 36 | it | 4 | 0.49 |
| 37 | began | 4 | 0.36 | 37 | little | 4 | 0.49 |
| 38 | Er-jie | 4 | 0.36 | 38 | on | 4 | 0.49 |
| 39 | for | 4 | 0.36 | 39 | spat | 4 | 0.49 |
| 40 | have | 4 | 0.36 | 40 | back | 3 | 0.37 |
| 41 | herself | 4 | 0.36 | 41 | could | 3 | 0.37 |
| 42 | hold | 4 | 0.36 | 42 | disgust | 3 | 0.37 |
| 43 | into | 4 | 0.36 | 43 | fumed | 3 | 0.37 |
| 44 | not | 4 | 0.36 | 44 | ground | 3 | 0.37 |
| 45 | off | 4 | 0.36 | 45 | hard | 3 | 0.37 |
| 46 | spat | 4 | 0.36 | 46 | me | 3 | 0.37 |
| 47 | though | 4 | 0.36 | 47 | mother | 3 | 0.37 |
| 48 | what | 4 | 0.36 | 48 | now | 3 | 0.37 |
| 49 | who | 4 | 0.36 | 49 | off | 3 | 0.37 |

（续表）

| 霍译文本 | 词语 | 词频 | 百分比 | 杨译文本 | 词语 | 词频 | 百分比 |
|---|---|---|---|---|---|---|---|
| 50 | as | 3 | 0.27 | 50 | one | 3 | 0.37 |
| 51 | Bao | 3 | 0.27 | 51 | Pinger | 3 | 0.37 |
| 52 | both | 3 | 0.27 | 52 | Qingwen | 3 | 0.37 |
| 53 | but | 3 | 0.27 | 53 | sister | 3 | 0.37 |
| 54 | er | 3 | 0.27 | 54 | they | 3 | 0.37 |
| 55 | Grandmother | 3 | 0.27 | 55 | up | 3 | 0.37 |
| 56 | mother | 3 | 0.27 | 56 | Wang | 3 | 0.37 |
| 57 | no | 3 | 0.27 | 57 | wife | 3 | 0.37 |
| 58 | old | 3 | 0.27 | 58 | Bao | 2 | 0.25 |
| 59 | one | 3 | 0.27 | 59 | Baoyu | 2 | 0.25 |
| 60 | only | 3 | 0.27 | 60 | bastard | 2 | 0.25 |
| 61 | Skybright | 3 | 0.27 | 61 | before | 2 | 0.25 |
| 62 | Swallow | 3 | 0.27 | 62 | blind | 2 | 0.25 |
| 63 | turned | 3 | 0.27 | 63 | blushing | 2 | 0.25 |
| 64 | wrathfully | 3 | 0.27 | 64 | boxed | 2 | 0.25 |
| 65 | your | 3 | 0.27 | 65 | but | 2 | 0.25 |
| 66 | Zhao | 3 | 0.27 | 66 | Chunyan | 2 | 0.25 |
| 67 | across | 2 | 0.18 | 67 | concubine | 2 | 0.25 |
| 68 | after | 2 | 0.18 | 68 | creatures | 2 | 0.25 |
| 69 | all | 2 | 0.18 | 69 | Crimson | 2 | 0.25 |
| 70 | anger | 2 | 0.18 | 70 | death | 2 | 0.25 |
| 71 | angry | 2 | 0.18 | 71 | ears | 2 | 0.25 |
| 72 | Bao-yu | 2 | 0.18 | 72 | Er | 2 | 0.25 |
| 73 | be | 2 | 0.18 | 73 | eyes | 2 | 0.25 |
| 74 | became | 2 | 0.18 | 74 | Fangguan | 2 | 0.25 |
| 75 | did | 2 | 0.18 | 75 | finger | 2 | 0.25 |
| 76 | do | 2 | 0.18 | 76 | flowers | 2 | 0.25 |
| 77 | doing | 2 | 0.18 | 77 | foul-mouthed | 2 | 0.25 |

| 霍译文本 | 词语 | 词频 | 百分比 | 杨译文本 | 词语 | 词频 | 百分比 |
|---|---|---|---|---|---|---|---|
| 78 | doorway | 2 | 0.18 | 78 | frantic | 2 | 0.25 |
| 79 | exclaimed | 2 | 0.18 | 79 | from | 2 | 0.25 |
| 80 | eyes | 2 | 0.18 | 80 | going | 2 | 0.25 |
| 81 | Faithful | 2 | 0.18 | 81 | grabbed | 2 | 0.25 |
| 82 | few | 2 | 0.18 | 82 | had | 2 | 0.25 |
| 83 | floor | 2 | 0.18 | 83 | hold | 2 | 0.25 |
| 84 | flowers | 2 | 0.18 | 84 | if | 2 | 0.25 |
| 85 | furious | 2 | 0.18 | 85 | into | 2 | 0.25 |
| 86 | fury | 2 | 0.18 | 86 | laughing | 2 | 0.25 |
| 87 | gave | 2 | 0.18 | 87 | Lian | 2 | 0.25 |
| 88 | going | 2 | 0.18 | 88 | look | 2 | 0.25 |
| 89 | good | 2 | 0.18 | 89 | madam | 2 | 0.25 |
| 90 | great | 2 | 0.18 | 90 | made | 2 | 0.25 |
| 91 | half | 2 | 0.18 | 91 | may | 2 | 0.25 |
| 92 | hand | 2 | 0.18 | 92 | monkey | 2 | 0.25 |
| 93 | here | 2 | 0.18 | 93 | no | 2 | 0.25 |
| 94 | horrible | 2 | 0.18 | 94 | old | 2 | 0.25 |
| 95 | if | 2 | 0.18 | 95 | pointing | 2 | 0.25 |
| 96 | indignant | 2 | 0.18 | 96 | rage | 2 | 0.25 |
| 97 | laughed | 2 | 0.18 | 97 | rascal | 2 | 0.25 |
| 98 | leave | 2 | 0.18 | 98 | second | 2 | 0.25 |
| 99 | left | 2 | 0.18 | 99 | several | 2 | 0.25 |
| 100 | Lian | 2 | 0.18 | 100 | smiling | 2 | 0.25 |

从上表我们可以发现，在《红楼梦》里"骂道"类会话引导语霍译本和杨译本前100位的高频词中，核心动词几乎没有一个是重合的，只有一个动词 spat 在霍译文本和杨译文本中均有出现。spat 表示"啐道"之意，时常与"骂道"连用。鉴于笔者在之后的章节中会单独对"啐道"类会话引导语进行研究，在此对 spat 不多做分析。因此我们可以说，霍译文本和杨译文本在翻译"骂道"类会话引导

语时,高频动词完全不一样。

霍译文本中使用最多的动词依然是 said,有 14 个,占文本总量的 1.27%;其次为"shouted",有 11 个,占文本总量的 1.00%。在杨译文本中,said 一次都没有出现,使用最多的动词是 swore 和 scolded,数量分别为 19 和 14,分别占文本总量的 2.33% 和 1.72%。

霍译文本高频词中与"骂道"相关的名词有 anger 和 fury,杨译文本高频词中出现了 rage。霍译文本中还有几个重要的形容词和副词,如 angry、furious、angrily、wrathfully 等,在杨译文本中一次都没有出现。

**(二)霍译本与杨译本独特词研究**

《红楼梦》"骂道"类会话引导语的霍译本相对于杨译本的独特词有 350 个,将人名、地名用词筛除后,词频在 2 次以上的有 42 个:

| | | |
|---|---|---|
| said(14) | exclaimed(2) | red(2) |
| creature(7) | floor(2) | rubbish(2) |
| though(4) | furious(2) | seized(2) |
| who(4) | great(2) | side(2) |
| both(3) | half(2) | snapped(2) |
| turned(3) | here(2) | strumpet(2) |
| wrathfully(3) | horrible(2) | taken(2) |
| across(2) | indignant(2) | there(2) |
| after(2) | laughed(2) | these(2) |
| angry(2) | leave(2) | trying(2) |
| became(2) | left(2) | violently(2) |
| did(2) | man(2) | voice(2) |
| doing(2) | might(2) | which(2) |
| doorway(2) | object(2) | words(2) |

杨译文本相对于霍译文本的独特词有 190 个,将人名、地名用词筛除后,词频在 2 次以上的有 24 个:

| | | |
|---|---|---|
| swore(19) | fumed(3) | boxed(2) |
| scolded(14) | ground(3) | creatures(2) |
| cursed(6) | bastard(2) | death(2) |
| stormed(6) | before(2) | ears(2) |
| lady(5) | blushing(2) | foul-mouthed(2) |

| frantic(2) | monkey(2) | then(2) |
| grabbed(2) | rascal(2) | unable(2) |
| made(2) | smiling(2) | way(2) |

（三）霍译本与杨译本特色词研究

《红楼梦》"骂道"类会话引导语的霍译本相对于杨译本的特色词有 71 个，将人名、地名用词筛除后，关键度在 5 以上的特色词只有 4 个：said（关键度 15.051）、creature（关键度 7.525）、shouted（关键度 6.697）和 when（关键度 5.375）。

杨译文本相对于霍译文本的特色词有 49 个，将人名、地名用词筛除后，关键度在 5 以上的特色词有 10 个：swore（关键度 33.346）、scolded（关键度 24.571）、You（关键度 14.732）、cursed（关键度 10.53）、stormed（关键度 10.53）、whore（关键度 7.514）、foul（关键度 5.265）、fumed（关键度 5.265）、ground（关键度 5.265）和 they（关键度 5.265）。

通过以上对于霍译文本和杨译文本的独特词和特色词的分析我们可以看出，霍译文本在翻译"骂道"类会话引导语时着重使用了 said 和 shouted 两个动词，而杨译文本的用词则比较丰富，以 swore、scolded、cursed、stormed 等为代表和特色。

## 三、《红楼梦》"骂道"类会话引导语英译案例研究

笔者在上述对《红楼梦》原文以及译文中的"骂道"类会话引导语分析统计的基础上开展《红楼梦》"骂道"类会话引导语英译的案例研究。为此笔者将选取霍译文本中的特色词 shouted、位居杨译文本独特词和特色词前列的 swore 和 scolded 等来进行"骂道"类会话引导语英译的分析研究。

（一）"骂道"类英译之 shouted

shouted 是"骂道"类会话引导语霍译本相对于杨译本的特色词，关键度为 6.697。shouted 位列霍译文本高频词第 15 位，数量有 11 个，占文本总量的 1.00%；而杨译文本中仅有 1 例此种用法。

我们先来看几部权威词典对于动词 shout 的解释：

（1）《牛津高阶英语词典》（第 6 版）（Oxford Advanced Learner's Dictionary）：~（at sb to do sth）to say sth in a loud voice；to speak loudly/angrily to sb。

（2）《朗文当代英语词典》（第 4 版）（Longman Dictionary of Contemporary English）：to say something very loudly。

（3）《柯林斯高阶英语词典》（Collins COBUILD Advanced Learner's English Dictionary）：If you shout，you say something very loudly，usually *because you want people a long distance away to hear you or because you are angry.*

(4)《美国传统词典》(双解)(*E-C American Heritage Dictionary*):*to say with or utter a shout.* 大叫着说:高声说或发出喊叫声。

(5)《牛津高阶英汉双解词典》(*Oxford Advanced Learner's English-Chinese Dictionary*):～(*at/to sb*);～(*out*)*speak or call out in a loud voice* 大声说;喊;呼;叫。

通过以上几部词典对于动词 shout 的解释,我们可以推断 shout 有"大叫;呼喊;大声说"的意思,通常是因为生气或希望远方的人能听见时而"大喊大叫"。"《红楼梦》原文引语句里的许多'骂道'大多不是'训斥'的意思,基本上是高声表示不满,有的句子甚至包含了一些谩骂与辱骂的词语。"(冯庆华,2015)因此笔者认为动词 shouted 基本与原文中"骂道"的含义相符。

以下为几个霍译文本和杨译文本中使用 shouted 来翻译"骂道"类会话引导语的例子,其中杨译文本中仅有 1 例:

1. 【原文】急叫醒时,只见(妙玉)眼睛直竖,两颧鲜红,**骂道**:"我是有菩萨保佑,你们这些强徒敢要怎么样?"(第八十七回)

   【霍译】She was woken from this apparent coma, only to fix her eyes into a rigid stare and cry out, her cheeks burning a fierce crimson: 'Buddha is my Protector! Don't touch me, you ruffians!'

   【杨译】Her eyes staring, crimson in the face, she **shouted**, "How dare you thugs attack one under Buddha's protection!"

2. 【原文】凤姐便一扬手,照脸打了个嘴巴,把那小孩子打了一个斤斗,**骂道**:"小野杂种! 往那里跑?"(第二十九回)

   【霍译】Out flew Xi-feng's hand and dealt him a resounding smack on the face that sent him flying. 'Clumsy brat!' she **shouted**. 'Look where you're going!'

   【杨译】She boxed his ears so hard that he pitched to the ground. "Look out where you're going, little bastard!" she swore.

3. 【原文】宝玉还**骂道**:"下流东西们,我素日担待你们得了意,一点儿也不怕,越发拿着我取笑儿了!"(第三十回)

   【霍译】'Worthless lot!' he **shouted**. 'Because I always treat you decently, you think you can get away with anything. I'm just your laughing-stock.'

   【杨译】"You low creatures!" he stormed. "I treat you so well that you've lost all sense of respect. Now you dare make fun of me!"

4.【原文】(凤姐)也不容分说,抓着鲍二家的就撕打。又怕贾琏走了,堵着门站着**骂道**:"好娼妇!你偷主子汉子,还要治死主子老婆!"(第四十四回)

【霍译】There, without more ado, she proceeded to seize hold of Bao Er's wife and belabour her, breaking off only to block the doorway with her body in case Jia Lian might think of escaping. 'Filthy whore!' she **shouted**. 'Stealing a husband isn't enough for you, it seems. You have to murder his wife as well!'

【杨译】Without a word she caught hold of Bao Er's wife and pummelled her, then posted herself at the door to cut off Jia Lian's retreat. "Dirty whore!" she cursed. "You steal your mistress' husband and plot to murder your mistress."

5.【原文】……(贾琏)今见平儿也打,便上来踢**骂道**:"好娼妇!你也动手打人!"(第四十四回)

【霍译】…the sight of Patience doing the same thing so roused his vaLiancy that he **shouted** at her and gave her a kick. 'Little whore! You want to join in too, do you?'

【杨译】…but as soon as Pinger joined in he charged forward and kicked her. "You slut! Who are you to raise your hand against her?"

6.【原文】他娘也正为芳官之气未平,又恨春燕不遂他的心,便走上来打了个耳刮子,**骂道**:"小娼妇,你能上了几年台盘,你也跟着那起轻薄浪小妇学!……"(第五十九回)

【霍译】Swallow's mother was still smarting from her unsuccessful quarrel with Parfumée and was angry with Swallow for not having taken her side. 'Little strumpet!' she **shouted**, bearing down on her wrathfully and slapping her across the head. 'How long now have you been working with those young madams? — it hasn't taken you very long to pick up their airs and graces!'

【杨译】Mother He's tiff with Fangguan still rankled, and Chunyan's waywardness made her even angrier. Stepping forward she boxed her ears. "You whore!" she cried. "A few years in high society and you imitate the ways of those loose women."

7.【原文】二姐儿倒不好意思说什么，只见三姐儿似笑非笑、似恼非恼的**骂道**："坏透了的小猴儿崽子！没了你娘的说了！多早晚我才撕他那嘴呢！"（第六十四回）

【霍译】If so, Er-jie was too embarrassed to answer. Not so her sister, however. 'Little monster!' San-jie **shouted**, half angrily and half in jest. 'Keep your dirty little mouth shut — unless you want me to come over and shut it for you!'

【杨译】She was too embarrassed to say anything, but her sister scolded: "What a devilish monkey you are! Have you nothing else to talk about? Just wait, I'm going to pull out that tongue of yours."

8.【原文】贾赦听了，喝了一声，又**骂**："混账！没天理的囚攮的！偏你这么知道！还不离了我这里！"（第四十六回）

【霍译】'Villain! Parricide!' Jia She **shouted**, in instant fury. 'Trust you to know that! Get out of my sight!'

【杨译】Jia She swore. "You scurvy scoundrel!" he fumed. "Quite a know-all, aren't you? Get out!"

9.【原文】（贾菌）便**骂**："好囚攮的们！这不都动了手了么！"（第九回）

【霍译】'Rotten swine!' he **shouted**. 'If this is a free-for-all, here goes!'

【杨译】"You gaolbirds!" he swore. "If you want a fight, you can have it."

10.【原文】说毕，摔手出去了。急的赵姨娘**骂**："没造化的种子！这是怎么说！"（第六十二回）

【霍译】With those words he flounced out of the room, to the great indignation of his mother, who **shouted** after him angrily. 'Ungrateful little blackguard! What do you mean by it?'

【杨译】With that he stormed out. By this time Concubine Zhao was frantic too. "Ungrateful brat!" she cursed. "Misbegotten monster!"

从以上的例子我们可以看到，当霍译文本使用 shouted 时，杨译分别使用了 cursed、stormed、swore、scolded 等动词来描绘"骂道"的情景。

（二）"骂道"类英译之 swore

swore 是杨译文本中词频最高的独特词，有 19 个，同时也是杨译文本相对于霍译文本的第一大特色词,关键度为33.346。

我们先来看几部权威词典对于动词 swear 的解释:

(1)《牛津高阶英语词典》(第6版)(*Oxford Advanced Learner's Dictionary*):~(*at sb/sth*)*to use rude or offensive language,usually because you are angry*。

(2)《朗文当代英语词典》(第4版)(*Longman Dictionary of Contemporary English*):*to use rude and offensive language*。

(3)《柯林斯高阶英语词典》(*Collins COBUILD Advanced Learner's English Dictionary*):*If someone swears,they use language that is considered to be rude or offensive,usually because they are angry*.

(4)《美国传统词典》(双解)(*E-C American Heritage Dictionary*):*to use profane oaths;curse* 发渎神之语,诅咒。

(5)《牛津高阶英汉双解词典》(*Oxford Advanced Learner's English-Chinese Dictionary*):~(*at sb/sth*)*use rude or blasphemous words in anger,surprise,etc;curse* 咒骂,诅咒。

通过以上几部词典的释义,我们可以推断动词 swear 可以表达"咒骂;诅咒;说脏话"之意。以下为几个杨译文本中使用 swore 来翻译"骂道"类会话引导语的例子:

1.【原文】鸳鸯又是气,又是臊,又是急,**骂道**:"两个坏蹄子,再不得好死的!"(第四十六回)

【杨译】Frantic with rage and embarrassment,Yuanyang **swore**,"You two whorees,you won't come to a good end!"

【霍译】Both embarrassed and exasperated by these taunts,Faithful rounded on her tormentors with some heat. 'You're rotten,both of you,and I hope you both come to bad ends!'

2.【原文】晴雯便冷不防,欠身一把将他的手抓住,向枕边拿起一丈青来,向他手上乱戳,又**骂道**:"要这爪子做什么?

【杨译】Then Qingwen,lunging forward,grabbed one of her hands and began jabbing it with a hairpin from under her pillow. "What use is this claw?" she **swore**.

【霍译】As she did so,Skybright suddenly raised herself from her lying position,snatched hold of her hand,and began jabbing at it violently with an enormous hairpin which she had been keeping concealed under her pillow. 'What do you want this little claw for?' she said.

3.【原文】香菱听了,红了脸,忙要起身拧他,**笑骂道**:"我把你这个烂了嘴的小蹄子! 满口里放屁胡说!"(第六十二回)

　　【杨译】Blushing,Xiangling got ready to spring up to pinch her. "You foul-mouthed whore!" she **swore**, laughing. "What drivel you talk!"

　　【霍译】Caltrop laughed,though her face had turned bright red. 'You horrible little creature! What rubbish you talk!' She had begun getting up,intending to give Cardamome's mouth a good pinch.

4.【原文】二姨娘红了脸,**骂道**:"好蓉小子! 我过两日不骂你几句,你就过不得了,越发连个体统都没了!"(第六十三回)

　　【杨译】Second Sister You blushed. "You rascal!" she **swore** at him. "You can't get by if I don't curse you every other day! You're going from bad to worse,with absolutely no sense of what's proper."

　　【霍译】Er-jie turned red. 'Now look here,young Rong,' she said, 'you behave yourself! I suppose you are one of those people who,if they don't get a good telling-off every once in a while,don't feel comfortable.'

5.【原文】……随后晴雯赶来骂道:"我看你这小蹄子儿往那里去? 输了不叫打! 宝玉不在家,我看有谁来救你!"(第六十四回)

　　【杨译】...and the next minute Qingwen appeared. "Where are you going,you whore?" she **swore**. "You've lost,yet you want to escape a spanking. With Baoyu out who's going to come to your rescue?"

　　【霍译】...and a moment later Skybright burst through the doorway in pursuit. 'Where are you,you little wretch? If you've lost, you have to have a slap. It's no good running to Bao-yu to protect you: he isn't here today.'

6.【原文】贾琏听了,**骂道**:"这个还了得!"(第九十三回)

　　【杨译】"Outrageous!"**swore** Jia Lian.

　　【霍译】'What a preposterous state of affairs!' exclaimed Jia Lian.

7.【原文】贾珍听见,**骂道**:"糊涂东西! 妖怪原是聚则成形,散则成气,如今多少神将在这里,还敢现形吗?"(第一百二回)

　　【杨译】"You fools!" **swore** Jia Zhen. "Monsters take shape or vanish into thin air just as they please. With all the heavenly generals here, how dare they show themselves?"

【霍译】'Fools!' snapped Cousin Zhen, when he heard this. 'Evil spirits don't behave like that at all. At certain times they condense into crude matter, at others they dissolve into the ether. With so many benevolent spirits present of course they wouldn't dare take on material form.'

8.【原文】平儿手里正剥了个满黄螃蟹,听如此奚落他,便拿着螃蟹照琥珀脸上来抹,口内**笑骂**:"我把你这嚼舌根的小蹄子儿……"(第三十八回)

【杨译】Pinger had just scooped out the yellow flesh of a crab, and at this gibe she aimed it at Hupo's face, laughing. "You foul-mouthed whore!" she **swore**.

【霍译】Patience, who had in her hand a crab richly endowed with 'yolk' that she had just finished shelling, held it up when she heard this jibe and advanced on Amber, intending to smear her face with it. 'You nasty, spiteful little creature!' she said, both laughing and indignant. 'I'll—'

9.【原文】凤姐便一扬手,照脸打了个嘴巴,把那小孩子打了一个斤斗,**骂**道:"小野杂种! 往那里跑?"(第二十九回)

【杨译】She boxed his ears so hard that he pitched to the ground. "Look out where you're going, little bastard!" she **swore**.

【霍译】Out flew Xi-feng's hand and dealt him a resounding smack on the face that sent him flying. 'Clumsy brat!' she shouted. 'Look where you're going!'

10.【原文】莺儿赌气将花柳皆掷于河中,自回房去。这里把个婆子心疼的只念佛,又**骂**:"促狭小蹄子! 遭塌了花儿,雷也是要劈的!"(第五十九回)

【杨译】In disgust, Yinger tossed all her flowers and twigs into the stream and went back to her room, while Chunyan's aunt crossly invoked the aid of Buddha. "May a thunderbolt strike the wicked little whore, spoiling all those flowers!" she **swore**.

【霍译】Oriole was by now so disgusted with the whole affair that she threw everything — basket, twigs and flowers — into the water and went off home，leaving the old aunt blessing herself in pious horror at the waste. 'Wicked creature!' she called out after her. 'You ought to be struck by lightning，throwing away good flowers like that!'

鉴于 swore 在霍译文本中一次都没有使用,笔者认为有必要参考一下该词在三部英文原版小说《飘》《名利场》和《大卫·科波菲尔》中的使用情况:

《飘》中有 7 个例句:

| | | |
|---:|:---:|:---|
| leading toward the road and | swore | lustily，with a joy |
| ，worried forehead and Gerald | swore | more frequently than usual and |
| said the two of them | swore | up hill and down dale |
| did not laugh. They | swore | silently as they saw her |
| treasured but which they now | swore | were of no earthly use |
| you threw that vase and | swore | and proved that you weren |
| at one corner and he | swore | with passionate imPatience. |

《名利场》中有 23 个例句:

| | | |
|---:|:---:|:---|
| the 'Necks，and | swore | he would take the law |
| a country accent，and | swore | a great deal at the |
| Sir Pitt in a fury | swore | that if he ever caught |
| remarked that Sir Pitt never | swore | at Lady Crawley while his |
| in this way，he | swore | out loud that I was |
| ，and with dreadful oaths | swore | that if it wasn' |
| power on earth，he | swore | ，would induce him to |
| may consider unmanly. He | swore | that Amelia was an angel |
| a dock，and Osborne | swore | at him from the study |
| chap as that？Osborne | swore | with a great oath that |
| himself as usual，and | swore | he was becoming quite a |
| wild（for Sir Pitt | swore | that no governess should ever |
| should be refused altogether， | swore | solemnly that the young gent |
| with delighted laughter，and | swore | that she was better than |
| of genteel life. He | swore | it was as good as |
| with a horsewhip which he | swore | he would lay across the |
| broken，except when he | swore | and was savage，if |

| | | |
|---|---|---|
| companion afterwards. Her father | **swore** | to her that she should |
| it. He chuckled and | **swore** | to himself behind the sheet |
| years，he said She | **swore** | ，last night only， |
| boy. He growled and | **swore** | at Miss Osborne as usual |
| was disengaged too，and | **swore** | he would be the winner |
| solicitor of the insurance company | **swore** | it was the blackest case |

《大卫·科波菲尔》中有 6 个例句：

| | | |
|---|---|---|
| showed a violent temper or | **swore** | an oath，was this |
| such occasion），and | **swore** | a dreadful oath that he |
| I forgive you！Bob | **swore** | ！- as the Englishman |
| so like English. Bob | **swore** | ，my ducks！' |
| the banisters，' Bob | **swore** | ！' as I went |
| she says. So I | **swore** | tonight，that if she |

通过对比 swore 一词在小说《飘》《名利场》和《大卫·科波菲尔》中的使用情况,笔者发现在 36 例用法里面没有一个 swore 是用来引导直接引语的,仅有几例中 swore 用来引导间接引语,但这几例中的 swear 一词表示的是"发誓;宣誓"之意,例如：

- …he flung down Miss Sharp's bandboxes in the gutter at the ' Necks，and swore he would take the law of his fare.(《名利场》)
- So I swore tonight，that if she didn't go，I'd go to bed at six.(《大卫·科波菲尔》)

swear 表示"咒骂;诅咒"意思时的用法只有作不及物动词,或者用于 swear at sb 中,例如：

- Then his mouth went down violently at one corner and he swore with passionate imPatience.(《飘》)
- "He growled and swore at Miss Osborne as usual，and would smile when George came down late for breakfast."(《名利场》)

（三）"骂道"类英译之 scolded

scolded 也是杨译文本相对于霍译文本的重要独特词和关键词,数量有 14 个,关键度为 24.571。该词在霍译文本中一次都没有出现。

我们先来看几部权威词典对于动词 scold 的解释：

(1)《牛津高阶英语词典》(第 6 版)(*Oxford Advanced Learner's Dictionary*)：
~ *sb*（*for sth ／ for doing sth*）（*formal*）*to speak angrily to sb，especially a child，because they have done sth wrong*。

（2）《朗文当代英语词典》（第 4 版）（*Longman Dictionary of Contemporary English*）：*angrily criticize someone，especially a child，about something they have done*。

（3）《柯林斯高阶英语词典》（*Collins COBUILD Advanced Learner's English Dictionary*）：*If you scold someone，you speak angrily to them because they have done something wrong.*（*FORMAL*）。

（4）《美国传统词典》（双解）（*E-C American Heritage Dictionary*）：*v.tr.*（及物动词）*to reprimand or criticize harshly and usually angrily* 责骂：严厉地且通常愤怒地责备或批评。*v.intr.*（不及物动词）*to reprove or criticize openly* 谩骂：公开谴责或批评。

（5）《牛津高阶英汉双解词典》（*Oxford Advanced Learner's English-Chinese Dictionary*）：～ *sb*（*for sth／doing sth*）*express anger，criticism，etc，esp to a child；rebuke sb* 骂，责骂（尤指对儿童）；叱责某人。

通过以上几部词典的释义，我们可以推断 scold 一词表示"责骂；批评；斥责"之意，对象通常是小孩或儿童，且用法比较正式。以下为几个杨译文本中使用 scolded 来翻译"骂道"类会话引导语的例子：

1.【原文】只见王夫人翻身起来，照金钏儿脸上就打了个嘴巴，指着**骂道**："下作小娼妇儿！好好儿的爷们，都叫你们教坏了!"（第三十回）

【杨译】At this point Lady Wang sat up and slapped Jinchuan's face. "Shameless slut!" she **scolded**. "It's low creatures like you who lead the young masters astray."

【霍译】At this point Lady Wang sat bolt upright and dealt Golden a slap in the face. 'Shameless little harlot!' she cried, pointing at her wrathfully. 'It's you and your like who corrupt our innocent young boys.'

2.【原文】慌的薛姨妈拉住**骂道**："作死的孽障，你打谁去？你先打我来!"（第三十四回）

【杨译】In desperation his mother dragged him back. "You'll be the death of me，you monster，" she **scolded**. "Off to pick a fight，are you? Better kill me first."

【霍译】...but his dis-traught mother clung to him and prevented him from going. 'You stupid creature!' she said. 'Who do you think you're going to hit with that? If you're going to hit anyone，you'd better begin with me!'

3.【原文】贾母笑**骂道**："小蹄子们！还不搀起来，只站着笑!"（第四十回）

【杨译】"You wretches!" **scolded** the Lady Dowager. "Help her up. Don't just stand there laughing."

【霍译】Grandmother Jia laughed too, though trying her hardest to sound cross. 'Little monsters!' she said, 'Don't just stand there laughing. Help her up!'

4.【原文】尤氏笑骂道:"小蹄子们! 专会记得这些没要紧的话!"(第四十三回)

【杨译】"You wretches," **scolded** Madam You, smiling. "You only remember words of no consequence."

【霍译】'Subscriptions!' said You-shi scornfully. 'How eagerly you fasten on the ridiculous word!'

5.【原文】邢夫人王夫人见了,气的忙拦住**骂道**:"这下流东西! 你越发反了! 老太太在这里呢!"(第四十四回)

【杨译】Lady Xing and Lady Wang angrily barred his way. "Have you gone mad, you degenerate?" they **scolded**. "How dare you behave like this in the old lady's presence?"

【霍译】This deliberate flouting of their authority by a licensed favourite greatly incensed the two ladies. They seized hold of him with angry scoldings, one on either side. 'Disgusting creature! Have you no sense of decency left whatever? Can't you see that Grandmother is here?'

6.【原文】二姐便悄悄咬牙**骂道**:"很会嚼舌根的猴儿崽子! 留下我们,给你爹做妈不成?"(第六十三回)

【杨译】Gritting her teeth and smiling, Second Sister You **scolded** softly, "You glib-tongued monkey! Are you keeping us here to be your father's mothers?"

【霍译】Er-jie pretended to grind her teeth angrily, though she was trying not to laugh. 'Glib-tongued little ape!' she said. 'We're to be kept around here as second strings for your father, I suppose?'

7.【原文】探春**骂道**:"你们这些人,如今越发没了王法了! 这里是你骂人的地方儿吗?"(第八十三回)

【杨译】Tanchun **scolded**, "You people are getting too out of hand! Is this the place for you to bawl abuse?"

【霍译】'Have you both taken leave of your senses?' exclaimed Tanchun severely. 'How dare you use language like that here?'

8.【原文】凤姐骂道："胡说！我这里断不兴说神说鬼。我从来不信这些个话，快滚出去罢！"（第八十八回）

【杨译】"Nonsense!" Xifeng **scolded**. "We don't allow talk about ghosts and spirits here. I never believe such tales. Hurry up and get out!"

【霍译】'Stupid creature!' snapped Xi-feng. 'I won't have people talking such superstitious nonsense in my presence! I've never believed in such things. Go on — get out of my sight!'

9.【原文】凤姐便骂："糊涂东西！也不睁开眼瞧瞧，这个样儿，怎么挦着走的？还不快进去把那藤屉子春凳抬出来呢！"（第三十三回）

【杨译】"Stupid creatures!" **scolded** Xifeng. "Have you no eyes? He's in no state to walk. Go and fetch that wicker couch."

【霍译】'Idiots!' said Xi-feng. 'Haven't you got eyes in your heads? Can't you see that he's in no fit state to walk? Go and get that wicker summer-bed from inside and carry him in on that.'

10.【原文】黛玉先骂："又与你这蹄子什么相干！"后来见了这样，也笑道："阿弥陀佛！该，该，该！"（第五十七回）

【杨译】"What has this to do with you?" **scolded** Daiyu, and then laughed too at her discomfiture. "Amida Buddha! Serves her right!"

【霍译】Dai-yu who, when Nightingale intervened, had angrily bidden her to mind her own business, now gloated over her discomfiture: 'Holy Name, it serves you right!'

笔者同样参考了动词 scolded 在三部英文原版小说《飘》《名利场》和《大卫·科波菲尔》中的使用情况：

《飘》中有 7 个例句：

| | scolded | |
|---|---|---|
| all that they criticized and | scolded | and teased her. Not |
| irritable because Mrs Merriwether had | scolded | her sharply for sitting on |
| in a state, he | scolded | . |
| you say them? she | scolded | . If you'd |
| it, Melanie, she | scolded | . You're half |
| , praised, petted, | scolded | . They didn't |
| not a happy day. | Scolded | and for the most part |

《名利场》中有 2 个例句：

             ; that is，George   **scolded**   his wife violently for her

        locataires. Most of them   **scolded**   and grumbled；some of

《大卫·科波菲尔》中只有 1 个例句：

           , and to be violently   **scolded**   by his wife every morning

scolded 一词在小说《飘》《名利场》和《大卫·科波菲尔》中使用不多，且很少用来引导直接引语，只有来自《飘》中的 3 个例子：

- "You young misses ought ter tek shame，gittin' Miss Pitty in a state，" he scolded.
- "Even if you think such things，why do you say them?" she scolded. "If you'd just think what you please but keep your mouth shut，everything would be so much nicer."
- "You'll have to stop it，Melanie，" she scolded. "You're half sick yourself and if you don't eat more，you'll be sick in bed and we'll have to nurse you. Let these men go hungry. They can stand it. They've stood it for four years and it won't hurt them to stand it a little while longer."

# 第五节　"啐道"类会话引导语翻译研究

除了"骂道"类会话引导语之外，《红楼梦》原文中还有一类颇具特色的表示"厌恶""愤怒""轻蔑"等情感的会话引导语——"啐道"。对于动词"啐"，《新华字典》给出的解释是："吐；发出唾声。表示鄙弃或愤怒。如：啐骂（唾骂）；啐了一口痰；啐出一口鲜血"；《现代汉语词典》给出的解释是：①用力从嘴里吐出来；②叹词，表示唾弃、斥责或辱骂。因此，"啐道"一词实际上包含了"啐"和"道"两个动作，传达"唾弃＋责骂"的双重含义。本节笔者将着重分析"啐道"类会话引导语的英译问题。

## 一、《红楼梦》原文中的"啐道"类会话引导语

"啐"是一个非常明显地表示不满和鄙夷的动作，《红楼梦》中"啐道"类会话引导语的使用也都很强烈地表达了人物的思想感情。据冯庆华教授统计，"'啐道'基本上都是女性的行为，唯一的男性是贾琏。"由此我们可以推断"啐道"类会话引导语的使用能够鲜明地展示人物的性格特征。

《红楼梦》原文中的"啐道"类会话引导语主要包括两个类别:单纯的"啐道:"和"啐了一口道:"。其中单纯的"啐道:"有 35 个,"啐了一口道:"有 5 个(含"啐了一口,道:""啐了一口,厉声道:"等)。

笔者将以上两个文本合并成一个总的"啐道"类会话引导语文本(总数量为40)统一进行研究,整理出一个"原文—霍译—杨译"的"啐道"类会话引导语语料库,在此语料库的基础上分别整理出"啐道"类会话引导语的原文、霍译本、杨译本文档,以供研究之用。其中"啐道"类会话引导语的霍译本(或称霍译文本)容量为414,"啐道"类会话引导语的杨译本(或称杨译文本)容量为283。

## 二、《红楼梦》译文中的"啐道"类会话引导语

笔者将对《红楼梦》"啐道"类会话引导语的霍译本和杨译本进行高频词、独特词以及特色词等方面的分析研究。

### (一)霍译本与杨译本高频词研究

笔者通过分别对《红楼梦》"啐道"类会话引导语的霍译本和杨译本进行词频分析,将词频为 2 次以上的词语列举如表 4-21 所示。

表 4-21 "啐道"类会话引导语霍译本和杨译本高频词

| 霍译文本 | 词语 | 词频 | 百分比 | 杨译文本 | 词语 | 词频 | 百分比 |
|---|---|---|---|---|---|---|---|
| 1 | you | 19 | 4.59 | 1 | spat | 14 | 4.95 |
| 2 | said | 14 | 3.38 | 2 | you | 13 | 4.59 |
| 3 | spat | 12 | 2.90 | 3 | in | 12 | 4.24 |
| 4 | the | 9 | 2.17 | 4 | she | 8 | 2.83 |
| 5 | to | 9 | 2.17 | 5 | the | 8 | 2.83 |
| 6 | her | 8 | 1.93 | 6 | disgust | 6 | 2.12 |
| 7 | in | 8 | 1.93 | 7 | and | 5 | 1.77 |
| 8 | that | 8 | 1.93 | 8 | that | 5 | 1.77 |
| 9 | Xi-feng | 8 | 1.93 | 9 | to | 5 | 1.77 |
| 10 | and | 7 | 1.69 | 10 | face | 4 | 1.41 |
| 11 | at | 6 | 1.45 | 11 | her | 4 | 1.41 |
| 12 | a | 5 | 1.21 | 12 | Jia | 4 | 1.41 |
| 13 | face | 5 | 1.21 | 13 | Xifeng | 4 | 1.41 |
| 14 | I | 5 | 1.21 | 14 | cried | 3 | 1.06 |
| 15 | it | 5 | 1.21 | 15 | Daiyu | 3 | 1.06 |

（续表）

| 霍译文本 | 词语 | 词频 | 百分比 | 杨译文本 | 词语 | 词频 | 百分比 |
|---|---|---|---|---|---|---|---|
| 16 | Jia | 5 | 1.21 | 16 | for | 3 | 1.06 |
| 17 | of | 5 | 1.21 | 17 | Lian | 3 | 1.06 |
| 18 | out | 5 | 1.21 | 18 | me | 3 | 1.06 |
| 19 | was | 5 | 1.21 | 19 | on | 3 | 1.06 |
| 20 | your | 5 | 1.21 | 20 | out | 3 | 1.06 |
| 21 | all | 4 | 0.97 | 21 | scoffed | 3 | 1.06 |
| 22 | are | 4 | 0.97 | 22 | snapped | 3 | 1.06 |
| 23 | contemptuously | 4 | 0.97 | 23 | so | 3 | 1.06 |
| 24 | Dai-yu | 4 | 0.97 | 24 | talk | 3 | 1.06 |
| 25 | Lian | 4 | 0.97 | 25 | blame | 2 | 0.71 |
| 26 | not | 4 | 0.97 | 26 | family | 2 | 0.71 |
| 27 | she | 4 | 0.97 | 27 | flushed | 2 | 0.71 |
| 28 | be | 3 | 0.72 | 28 | fool | 2 | 0.71 |
| 29 | but | 3 | 0.72 | 29 | I | 2 | 0.71 |
| 30 | indignantly | 3 | 0.72 | 30 | is | 2 | 0.71 |
| 31 | little | 3 | 0.72 | 31 | it | 2 | 0.71 |
| 32 | Aroma | 2 | 0.48 | 32 | nonsense | 2 | 0.71 |
| 33 | arsehole | 2 | 0.48 | 33 | pah | 2 | 0.71 |
| 34 | aunt | 2 | 0.48 | 34 | Qiuwen | 2 | 0.71 |
| 35 | bear | 2 | 0.48 | 35 | rubbish | 2 | 0.71 |
| 36 | cried | 2 | 0.48 | 36 | snorted | 2 | 0.71 |
| 37 | from | 2 | 0.48 | 37 | stupid | 2 | 0.71 |
| 38 | going | 2 | 0.48 | 38 | swore | 2 | 0.71 |
| 39 | here | 2 | 0.48 | 39 | this | 2 | 0.71 |
| 40 | him | 2 | 0.48 | 40 | what | 2 | 0.71 |
| 41 | lady | 2 | 0.48 | 41 | whore | 2 | 0.71 |
| 42 | me | 2 | 0.48 | 42 | Xiren | 2 | 0.71 |
| 43 | mother | 2 | 0.48 | | | | |

（续表）

| 霍译文本 | 词语 | 词频 | 百分比 | 杨译文本 | 词语 | 词频 | 百分比 |
|---|---|---|---|---|---|---|---|
| 44 | old | 2 | 0.48 | | | | |
| 45 | really | 2 | 0.48 | | | | |
| 46 | Ripple | 2 | 0.48 | | | | |
| 47 | serious | 2 | 0.48 | | | | |
| 48 | silly | 2 | 0.48 | | | | |
| 49 | snorted | 2 | 0.48 | | | | |
| 50 | so | 2 | 0.48 | | | | |
| 51 | take | 2 | 0.48 | | | | |
| 52 | this | 2 | 0.48 | | | | |
| 53 | thought | 2 | 0.48 | | | | |
| 54 | time | 2 | 0.48 | | | | |
| 55 | Wang | 2 | 0.48 | | | | |
| 56 | with | 2 | 0.48 | | | | |
| 57 | woman | 2 | 0.48 | | | | |

"啐道"类会话引导语霍译文本和杨译文本词频在 2 次以上的动词仅有 2 个是相同的：spat 和 snorted。spat 是"啐"字最直接对应的英译,在杨译文本中词频最高,有 14 个,占文本总量的 4.95%,在霍译文本中有 12 个,占文本总量的 2.90%。霍译文本中词频最高的是 said,有 14 个,占文本总量的 3.38%。snorted 在杨译文本和霍译文本中均出现了 2 次,比例分别为 0.71% 和 0.48%。在霍译文本中还出现了动词 cried 以及副词 contemptuously 和 indignantly。杨译文本中还有动词 scoffed、snapped、flushed、swore 等。

（二）霍译本与杨译本独特词研究

《红楼梦》"啐道"类会话引导语的霍译本相对于杨译本的独特词有 145 个,将人名、地名用词筛除后,词频在 2 次以上的只有 18 个：

at(6)　　　　　　be(3)　　　　　　here(2)

was(5)　　　　　indignantly(3)　　old(2)

all(4)　　　　　arsehole(2)　　　really(2)

are(4)　　　　　bear(2)　　　　serious(2)

contemptuously(4)　going(2)　　　take(2)

| | | |
|---|---|---|
| thought(2) | time(2) | woman(2) |

杨译文本相对于霍译文本的独特词有 81 个,将人名、地名用词筛除后,词频在 2 次以上的只有 13 个:

| | | |
|---|---|---|
| disgust(6) | blame(2) | rubbish(2) |
| for(3) | flushed(2) | swore(2) |
| scoffed(3) | fool(2) | whore(2) |
| snapped(3) | nonsense(2) | |
| talk(3) | Pah(2) | |

在霍译文本的独特词中,两个副词 contemptuously 和 indignantly 的用法值得关注。杨译文本的独特词主要集中在几个动词,即 scoffed、snapped、flushed 和 swore。

(三)霍译本与杨译本特色词研究

《红楼梦》"啐道"类会话引导语的霍译本相对于杨译本的特色词有 33 个,将人名、地名用词筛除后,关键度在 5 以上的特色词有 3 个:said(关键度 8.533)、at(关键度 6.008)和 was(关键度 5.006)。

杨译文本相对于霍译文本的特色词有 91 个,将人名、地名用词筛除后,关键度在 5 以上的特色词有 5 个:disgust(关键度 11.181)、for(关键度 5.591)、scoffed(关键度 5.591)、snapped(关键度 5.591)和"talk"(关键度 5.591)。

(四)霍译本与杨译本二词以上搭配

以上笔者分析的都是使用单个动词来翻译《红楼梦》"啐道"类会话引导语的情况。经过进一步检索,笔者发现还有一些二词以上的短语或其他表达形式,使用次数在 2 次以上的表达方式有:spat in disgust、spat in sb's face、spat contemptuously、flushed and spat、rebuked oneself、spat out、spat at sb 等。这些表达方式在霍译文本和杨译文本中的分布如表 4-22 所示。

表 4-22　短语类表达形式在"啐道"类会话引导语两译本中使用情况统计

| 表达方式 | 霍译文本 | 杨译文本 |
|---|---|---|
| spat in disgust | 0 | 6 |
| spat in sb's face | 4 | 4 |
| spat contemptuously | 3 | 0 |
| flushed and spat | 0 | 2 |
| rebuked oneself | 1 | 1 |

（续表）

| 表达方式 | 霍译文本 | 杨译文本 |
|---|---|---|
| spat at sb | 2 | 0 |
| spat out | 0 | 2 |

其中 spat in disgust、flushed and spat 和 spat out 是杨译文本的独特表达方式；spat contemptuously 和 spat at sb 是霍译文本的独特表达方式。spat in sb's face 和 rebuked oneself 的用法在霍译文本和杨译文本中基本持平。

## 三、《红楼梦》"啐道"类会话引导语英译案例研究

笔者在上述对《红楼梦》原文以及译文中的"啐道"类会话引导语分析统计的基础上开展《红楼梦》"啐道"类会话引导语英译的案例研究。为此笔者将选取霍译文本中的特色词 said，杨译文本中的独特词和特色词 scoffed、snapped 和短语 spat in disgust，以及霍译文本和杨译文本中均数量较多的 spat in sb's face 来进行"啐道"类会话引导语英译实例的分析。

（一）"啐道"类英译之 said

said 在霍译文本中词频最高，有 14 个，占文本总量的 3.38%，在杨译文本中仅使用过 1 次。同时，said 也是霍译文本相对于杨译文本的第一大特色词，关键度为 8.533。

以下为霍译文本和杨译文本中使用 said 来翻译"啐道"类会话引导语的例子：

1.【原文】凤姐**照脸啐了一口**，**厉声道**："你少在我跟前唠唠叨叨的！"（第九十回）

　　【霍译】Xi-feng spat straight in the old woman's face and **said** harshly：'Hold your tongue! That's quite enough!'

　　【杨译】Xifeng spat in her face. "Don't give me that talk!" she **said** sternly.

2.【原文】凤姐**啐道**："呸！扯臊！他是'哪吒'我也要见见。别放你娘的屁了！再不带来打你顿好嘴巴子！"（第七回）

　　【霍译】'Fiddlestick!' **said** Xi-feng. 'I don't care if he's a three-faced wonder with eight arms，I still want to see him. Stop farting about and bring him in，or I'll box your ears!'

　　【杨译】"Even if he's a monster，I insist on seeing him. Don't talk like a fool! Fetch him in at once or I'll give you a good slap."

3.【原文】凤姐笑着**啐道**："别放你娘的屁！"（第十六回）

【霍译】'Gracious arsehole!' **said** Xi-feng.

【杨译】"Don't talk rubbish!" Xifeng snorted.

4. 【原文】贾琏听了**啐道**："你们两个人不睦，又拿我来垫喘儿了。我躲开你们就完了。"（第二十一回）

【霍译】'Oh no!' **said** Jia Lian. 'If you two want to quarrel，I'm not going to stand between you and take all the knocks，I'm getting out of here!'

【杨译】"When you two fall out，why put the blame on me? I'd better make myself scarce."

5. 【原文】黛玉便**啐道**："呸！我打量是谁，原来是这个狠心短命的——"（第二十八回）

【霍译】'Pshaw!' she **said** crossly to herself. 'I thought it was another girl，but all the time it was that cruel，hate —'

【杨译】"So that's who it is." She snorted. "That heartless，wretched..."

6. 【原文】黛玉**啐道**："大清早起'死'呀'活'的，也不忌讳！你说有呢就有，没有就没有，起什么誓呢！"（第二十八回）

【霍译】'Hush!' **said** Dai-yu. 'Talking about death at this time of the morning! You should be more careful what you say. If you did，you did. If you didn't，you didn't. There's no need for these horrible oaths.'

【杨译】"Hush! Don't talk about dying so early in the morning. Did you or didn't you? There's no need to swear."

7. 【原文】那婆子**啐道**："呸！放你娘的屁！宝玉如今在园里住着，跟他的人都在园里，你又跑了这里来带信儿了！"（第二十八回）

【霍译】'— your mother's twat!' **said** the old woman. 'Master Bao lives in the Garden now. All his maids are in the Garden. What do you want to come running round here for?'

【杨译】"You farting fool!" she cried. "Master Bao lives in the Garden now and so do all his attendants. Why bring the message here?"

8. 【原文】正说着，只见麝月走过来，瞪了一眼，**啐道**："少作点孽儿罢!"（第三十一回）

【霍译】Just then Musk appeared. She stared at them indignantly. 'Don't do that!' she **said**. 'It's wicked to waste things like that.'

【杨译】Just then along came Sheyue. "What a wicked waste!" she cried. "Stop it."

9.【原文】黛玉一想："这话怎么顺嘴说出来了呢?"反觉不好意思,便**啐道**："你找不找与我什么相干! 倒茶去罢。"(第九十四回)

【霍译】The off-hand manner of her reply came as a shock to Dai-yu,who felt most put out and **said** curtly:'Do as you please,it's all the same to me. Bring me a cup of tea.'

【杨译】Daiyu wondered how she had come to blurt out such a question,and in embarrassment she answered curtly,"I don't care where you go. Fetch me some tea."

10.【原文】绣橘不待说完,便**啐了一口**,道："做什么你白填了三十两? 我且和你算算账! 姑娘要了些什么东西?"(第七十三回)

【霍译】'Thirty taels?' **said** Tangerine indignantly. 'How do you make that out? Just tell me one or two of the things the mistress is supposed to have asked you for.'

【杨译】Not waiting for her to finish,Xiuju spat in disgust. "On what have you spent thirty taels for us? Let's work it out. What has our young lady asked you for?"

在以上例子中我们可以发现,杨译中仅使用了一次 said,且是与 spat in sb's face 连用的。此外,笔者还发现一个现象,那就是杨译中将有些"啐道"会话引导语省略不译,直接翻译人物会话,读者只能通过话轮的转换和上下文语境来推测说话的人物和神态,如上面的例 2、例 4、例 6 等,这也是杨译中的一个显著的特色。

(二)"啐道"类英译之 scoffed 和 snapped

scoffed 和 snapped 是杨译文本相对于霍译文本的独特词和特色词,词频均为 3,关键度均为 5.591。

我们先来看几部权威词典对于动词 scoff 和 snap 的释义:

(1)《牛津高阶英语词典》(第 6 版)(*Oxford Advanced Learner's Dictionary*):

scoff:～(*at sb/sth*)*to talk about sb/sth in a way that makes it clear that you think they are stupid or ridiculous*

snap:～(*at sb*)*to speak or say sth in an impatient,usually angry,voice*

(2)《朗文当代英语词典》(第 4 版)(*Longman Dictionary of Contemporary English*):

scoff：*to laugh at a person or idea，and talk about them in a way that shows you think they are stupid*

snap：*to say something quickly in an angry way*

（3）《柯林斯高阶英语词典》（*Collins COBUILD Advanced Learner's English Dictionary*）：

scoff：*If you scoff at something，you speak about it in a way that shows you think it is ridiculous or inadequate.*

snap：*If someone snaps at you，they speak to you in a sharp，unfriendly way.*

（4）《美国传统词典》（双解）（*E-C American Heritage Dictionary*）：

scoff：*to mock at or treat with derision* 嘲笑或嘲弄

snap：*to speak abruptly or sharply* 呵斥：突然并且严厉地说话

（5）《牛津高阶英汉双解词典》（*Oxford Advanced Learner's English-Chinese Dictionary*）：

scoff：*~（at sb/sth）speak contemptuously（about or to sb/sth）；jeer or mock* 嘲弄；嘲笑

snap：*speak or say（sth）in a sharp（usu angry）voice* 厉声说（话）（通常指生气时）

通过以上几部词典的释义，我们可以推断 scoff 表达的是"嘲笑；嘲讽"之意，该词在我们探讨"笑道"类会话引导语英译时也出现过。snap 传达的是"呵斥；声色俱厉地说"之意，通常指人生气时的"恶声恶气"。这两个动词的实际意义其实与"啐道"传达的字面含义没有重合之处，只能说都表现出了轻蔑或厌恶之情。

以下为杨译文本中使用 scoffed 和 snapped 来翻译"啐道"类会话引导语的例子：

1.【原文】黛玉**啐道**："你这几天还不乏，趁这会子不歇一歇，还嚼什么蛆！"（第五十七回）

【杨译】"Aren't you tired after the last few days?" **scoffed** Daiyu. "Why don't you sleep instead of talking such nonsense?"

【霍译】Dai-yu snorted at her disgustedly. 'Aren't you tired after all your exertions during these last few days? I can't understand why，instead of chattering away to yourself，you don't take this opportunity to get a bit of rest.'

2.【原文】柳氏**啐道**："发了昏的！今年还比往年？"（第六十一回）

【杨译】Mrs. Liu spat. "You're crazy!" she **scoffed.** "This year's not like the old days."

【霍译】'You must be mad！' said the cook. 'We can't do that sort of thing any more now.'

3.【原文】里头袭人便**啐道**："二爷不用理他！"（第九十五回）

【杨译】"Don't listen to him，Master Bao!" **scoffed** Xiren from inside.

【霍译】But Aroma called out jeeringly from within：'You're not going to take any notice of him，are you？'

4.【原文】黛玉**啐道**："呸！你倒来替人派我的不是！我怎么浮躁了？"（第三十回）

【杨译】"So you side with the others and blame me，" **snapped** Daiyu. "In what way was I hasty？"

【霍译】'Poh！' said Dai-yu scornfully. 'You are trying to make out that it was my fault because you have taken his side against me. Of course I wasn't too hasty.'

5.【原文】林之孝家的**啐道**："糊涂攘的！他过去一说，自然都完了。没有单放他妈、又打你妈的礼！"（第七十一回）

【杨译】"How silly can you get？" **snapped** Mrs. Lin. "If she goes and asks，the whole business will blow over. They can't just let her mother off and have yours beaten，can they？"

【霍译】Lin Zhi-xiao's wife shoved her off impatiently. 'You really are a stupid child! Didn't I just say that if she has a word with her sister that will be the end of the matter? That means they'll both be let off. You surely don't think they'd let her mother off and give yours a beating?'

6.【原文】王夫人**啐道**："糊涂东西！你姨妈的死活都不知，你还要走吗？"（第一百十二回）

【杨译】"Stupid creature！" **snapped** Lady Wang. "Your mother may be dying. How can you leave？"

【霍译】'You great booby！' retorted Lady Wang contemptuously （and not a little hypocritically）. 'Would you forsake your own mother when she is at death's door?'

（三）"啐道"类英译之 spat in disgust

spat in disgust 是杨译文本中使用次数最多的独特表达方式，数量有 6 次。以下为杨译文本中使用 spat in disgust 来翻译"啐道"类会话引导语的例子：

1.【原文】赵姨娘**啐道**："谁叫你上高台盘了？下流没脸的东西！那里玩不

得？谁叫你跑了去讨这没意思?"（第二十回）

【杨译】His mother **spat in disgust**. "Shameless little brat! Who told you to put yourself forward? Is there nowhere else for you to play? Why go looking for trouble?"

【霍译】Aunt Zhao spat contemptuously：'Nasty little brat! That's what comes of getting above yourself. Who asked you to go playing with that lot? You could have gone anywhere else to play. Asking for trouble!'

2.【原文】凤姐**啐道**："你早做什么了？这会子我看见你了,你来推干净儿!"（第四十四回）

【杨译】Xifeng **spat in disgust**. "And what have you been doing all this time?" she cried. "You're only trying to clear yourself because I caught you."

【霍译】Xi-feng spat contemptuously. 'You've left it a bit late，haven't you — waiting until you see me and then trying to act the innocent?'

3.【原文】贾母**啐道**："下流东西! 灌了黄汤,不说安分守己的挺尸去,倒打起老婆来了!"（第四十四回）

【杨译】She **spat in disgust** and swore，"You degenerate! After swigging you might at least stretch out on your bed quietly like a corpse instead of beating your wife."

【霍译】Grandmother Jia snorted. 'Disgusting wretch! If you must go filling yourself with liquor，why can't you lie down quietly and sleep it off like a good，sensible creature? Fancy knocking your own wife about!'

4.【原文】鸳鸯**啐道**："什么东西! ——你还说呢! 前儿你主子不是这么混说? 谁知应到今儿了。"（第四十七回）

【杨译】Yuanyang **spat in disgust**. "What rubbish! Your mistress was raving the other day. How can you go repeating that today?"

【霍译】'You too now?' said Faithful angrily. 'You're a nice lot，I must say! It was your mistress who suggested that the other day. I thought we hadn't heard the last of that.'

5.【原文】一时黛玉红了脸,**啐了一口道**："你们都不是好人! 再不跟着好人学,只跟着凤丫头学的贫嘴贱舌的。"（第二十五回）

【杨译】Daiyu flushed and **spat in disgust**. "How horrid you all are! I can't think what end you'll come to. Instead of following the example of good people，you're learning from Xifeng to make vulgar jokes."

【霍译】Dai-yu affected scorn，but was blushing hotly. 'You are all horrid. Instead of following good examples，you all imitate Feng and make nasty，cheap jokes all the time.'

6.【原文】绣橘不待说完，便啐了一口，道："做什么你白填了三十两？我且和你算算账！姑娘要了些什么东西？"（第七十三回）

【杨译】Not waiting for her to finish，Xiuju **spat in disgust**. "On what have you spent thirty taels for us? Let's work it out. What has our young lady asked you for?"

【霍译】'Thirty taels?' said Tangerine indignantly. 'How do you make that out? Just tell me one or two of the things the mistress is supposed to have asked you for.'

这里我们不禁要想，名词 disgust 表示"厌恶；憎恶"之意，而动词 spit 本身就能够传达"因憎恨或轻蔑而吐唾沫"的含义。不知两者的结合是否符合英语里的传统表达习惯呢？

为此笔者考察了 spat in disgust 在 3 部英文原版小说《飘》《名利场》和《大卫·科波菲尔》中的使用情况，结果发现该词在几部小说中一次都没有使用过。事实上，在 3 部原版小说中 spat 仅仅使用过 7 次，且全部出现在小说《飘》里面：

- Rhett! She **spat** on the ground，for the very name tasted bad.
- He returned Scarlett's stare coldly and **spat** across the rail of the banister before he spoke.
- He **spat** again. 'I reckon that's my bizness'，he said.
- While she watched him，Archie turned suddenly toward the fire and **spat** a stream of tobacco juice on it with such vehemence that India，Melanie and Pitty leaped as though a bomb had exploded.
- I reckon I do，he answered coldly and **spat** again.
- Archie grunted and **spat** on the floor.
- But Tom，full of years and irritable at disturbances，switched his tail and **spat** softly.

我们可以看出以上 7 个例子中 spat 都是单独完成的动作，该词后面加介词或者副词来充当状语。这与霍译文本中喜爱使用 spat contemptuous 和 spat at sb 的偏好基本一致。

英国国家语料库中 spat in disgust 的使用仅有 3 例：

- He eyed her for a moment，**spat in disgust**，and ignoring her，turned to his men crowding the galley's...
- He **spat in disgust** and went into his cottage.
- And villagers walking past gave the gathering a wide berth，and **spat in disgust** with disparaging comments.

因此我们可以判定，杨译中特色的表达方式 spat in disgust 并未得到几部英文原版小说和英国国家语料库的有力支持。

（四）"啐道"类英译之 spat in sb's face

spat in sb's face 在霍译文本和杨译文本中均有使用，且数量较多，各有 4 例。该短语的字面意思是"照脸啐道"，应属于"啐道"类动作里面情感最为强烈、颇具侮辱性的表达方式之一。以下为霍译文本和杨译文本中使用 spat in sb's face 来翻译"啐道"类会话引导语的例子：

1.【原文】凤姐照脸一口唾沫，啐道："你尤家的丫头没人要了，偷着只往贾家送！"（第六十八回）

【霍译】Xi-feng **spat in her face**. 'Nobody else wanted that precious sister of yours，so you had to foist her onto our family.'

【杨译】Xifeng **spat in her face**. "Couldn't you find husbands for the girls of your family that you had to smuggle them into the Jia family?" she demanded.

2.【原文】贾琏照脸啐道："我打量什么事，这样慌张！"（第一百十五回）

【霍译】Jia Lian **spat in the servant's face**：'Hng! I thought from the fluster you were in that it was something serious.'

【杨译】Jia Lian **spat in the fellow's face**. "Is that any reason to panic?"

3.【原文】秋纹兜脸啐了一口道："没脸面的下流东西！"（第二十四回）

【霍译】Ripple **spat in her face**：'Nasty，shameless little slut！'

【杨译】Qiuwen **spat in her face**. "Shameless slut！"

4.【原文】宝玉红了脸，啐了一口，道："呸！没趣儿的东西！还不快走呢。"（第八十五回）

【霍译】Bao-yu blushed fiercely and **spat in Jia Yun's face**：'Ugh! Why don't you clear off? You make me sick！'

【杨译】Baoyu flushed and spat. "Clear off，you oaf！"

5.【原文】凤姐照脸啐了一口，厉声道："你少在我跟前唠唠叨叨的！"（第九十回）

【霍译】Xi-feng **spat straight in the old woman's face** and said harshly：

'Hold your tongue! That's quite enough!'

【杨译】Xifeng **spat in her face**. "Don't give me that talk!" she said sternly.

　　本章在前期对于《红楼梦》原文以及霍译本、杨译本中会话引导语研究的基础上，着重分析研究《红楼梦》会话引导语的翻译问题。笔者将《红楼梦》中的会话引导语划分为几个主要的类别分别进行翻译研究："说道"类、"笑道"类、"哭道"类、"骂道"类和"啐道"类会话引导语。在每一个类别的考察中，又分为原文统计、译文分析和英译案例研究几个层面进行。在对英译过程中使用的某些特色词语或短语进行研究时，笔者不但援引几部常用词典中的权威释义，也借助于英文原版小说和英国国家语料库寻求数据支持。

　　在研究过程中我们发现，《红楼梦》会话引导语的英译中出现了对译、增译、转译、合译、分译等多种翻译方法。在考察《红楼梦》会话引导语英译的过程中，笔者也进一步印证了霍译本和杨译本的语言各具特色、翻译风格迥异。这些差异或源于两位译者母语文化的影响以及翻译目的的不同。

# 结　语

本书在前人零星研究的基础上对我国古典白话小说《红楼梦》中会话引导语的英译进行了全面、系统、深入的剖析。在对原文和译文中会话引导语的系统分类与特色分析基础上，对会话引导语的英译进行了深入探寻和案例研究，得到了较为科学的结论。本书在总结本项研究的理论意义及实践意义的基础上，同时实事求是地分析此项研究的局限性并合理探讨后续可能的研究课题。

## 一、研究结论

在前面各章研究结果的基础上，本书的结论大致归结如下：

（1）作为古典白话小说的杰出代表，《红楼梦》中的会话引导语格式固定、数量巨大，基本符合古典白话小说会话引导语的特色，但也有其独特之处，这与《红楼梦》创作的历史背景、社会环境以及作者的写作风格有关。

（2）《红楼梦》英译本的分析研究显示出中西方译者之间以及不同西方译者之间的风格差异，这源于不同的译者文化身份以及译者主体性的发挥。

（3）《红楼梦》会话引导语翻译过程的考察揭示出不同母语文化和翻译目的对于译者与译文的重要影响。

母语文化是译者的第一文化优势，在翻译理论与实践中，译者会潜意识或显意识地发挥自己的母语文化优势。霍克思和杨宪益两位译者出身于不同的社会文化，语言习惯、思维模式必然会受到其母语文化的影响，如笔者在前文研究中提到的"汉语重意合、英语重形合"，英文中存在对于动词短语的偏好等。汉语比较注重语言的整体性、象征性和暗示性，而英语则强调逻辑推理和抽象理性。以英文作为母语的霍克思和闵福德在翻译时具有得天独厚的优势，因此译文能够更加贴近西方读者的语言习惯和思维方式。而从《红楼梦》的杨译本中，我们可以深刻体会到译者为了真实、全面地反映原语文化所付出的艰苦努力。作为汉语是母语的杨宪益先生，在翻译《红楼梦》中的会话引导语时能充分把握具体情境和人物特点，推敲人物心理和人物间的关系,语境关注度较高,从而能够恰如其分地选择词语来诠释不同的内涵,确切地传达原文中的意义。因此杨译本对于会话引导语的处理更加灵活,语言也更加多样化。

此外,翻译目的决定翻译过程。在《红楼梦》的英译中,霍、杨两位译者有着截然不同的追求。霍克思曾在《红楼梦》译者"前言"中写道:"我不认为我一切都做得很好,但是如果我能把我在这部汉语小说中所得到的愉悦甚至是部分愉悦传递给我的读者,也就不虚此生了。"正是这种目的和动机使得他在翻译中以目的语文化为归宿,主动顺应西方读者的认知环境。而杨宪益夫妇译《红楼梦》的目的是想尽可能多地把中国文化介绍给英美读者,满足部分英美读者了解中国文化的愿望。因此在翻译过程中坚持"忠实"为第一要义,力求最大限度地传达中国的传统文化。这种"忠实"体现在他们对于《红楼梦》会话引导语所蕴含的真实意义的解读和传达。

## 二、研究意义

本书的意义主要见于如下几点:

第一,自行创建全新版"《红楼梦》原文—霍译本—杨译本平行语料库",选取上海外语教育出版社 2012 年出版的汉英对照版《红楼梦》里的中文内容为底本,确保霍克思译文与原文的完全对应,将杨译本的相关内容核查后录入,在更大程度上保证了语料选取的精确、客观和公正。

第二,对《红楼梦》中的会话引导语进行了界定和分类,拓宽了《红楼梦》英译研究视角,扩展了《红楼梦》译者风格研究领域,有效改善《红楼梦》会话引导语乃至中国古典白话小说会话引导语英译研究中的匮乏和零散局面。

第三,当人类进入 21 世纪,全球多元化背景下中华文化亟待走出国门,一批优秀中华典籍,其中包括古典白话小说等被划入新时代典籍英译范围,古典白话小说译介越来越受到业内人士关注。正是在此时代背景下,《红楼梦》会话引导语的英译研究具有鲜明时代感和现实意义,试图为 21 世纪我国典籍英译提供一定参考借鉴。

## 三、研究局限性

由于本人知识视野与研究能力等方面的不足,本书无论在内容方面还是方法论上均存在一定的局限性,研究还有进一步推进的空间,具体简述如下:

第一,研究对象涵盖面有待进一步扩大。本书已经在分析《红楼梦》会话引导语数量、特色等层面的基础上将会话引导语分为几个重要类别进行研究。较之先前研究,此次研究对象的覆盖面有一定程度扩大,初步改善了会话引导语英译研究的零散局面,在增强会话引导语研究系统性方面做出了有益尝试。然而,此次研究对象依然不够全面系统,在涵盖面和系统性上还有待进一步扩大。譬如,笔者在第五章开头也提到,《红楼梦》会话引导语的数量众多、形式复杂,仅以"道:"结尾的会话引导语就能分出 75 个以上条目。囿于篇幅以及笔者能力所限,本研究中只将《红楼梦》会话引导语的翻译研究立足在"说道"类、"笑道"类、"哭道"类、"骂道"类和"啐道"类这几个主要的大类别进行。

第二,研究方法的科学性有待进一步提高。本书创建了全新版"《红楼梦》原文—霍译本—杨译本平行语料库",目的是增强语料选取客观性。而鉴于会话引导语汉英表达方式迥异,以及语料检索方式的固定性和机械性,笔者无法得到一个完全纯粹的会话引导语汉英对照语料,只能在最大程度上筛选出一个中英文对应的版本(A 版本)以及《红楼梦》原文中的纯粹会话引导语文本(B 版本)。此外,尽管笔者选取了上海外语教育出版社 2012 年出版的汉英对照版《红楼梦》,可以确保霍克思译文与原文的完全对应,但由于杨译本参照底本的差异,笔者在删除杨译本多余部分的基础上也无法确保两部译本的完全对应,绝不排除其中可能出现版本差异以及部分语料择取偏差。

第三,研究论证有待从文外进一步阐发。本书主要基于文内探讨,文外因素提及不多,在论证上难免显得有些薄弱。后续研究还应当增加阐释维度,从文化等文外层面切入,即从作者创作意图与译者主体性之间的矛盾、源发语受众与译入语读者之间,亦即原语文化传播与译文可接受性之间的矛盾等方面,拓宽研究视野,力求文内、文外相结合,对会话引导语英译进行多维度、宽视角探究。

近年来,树立文化自信,让中华文化走出去是不断升温的话题。作为文化的重要组成部分,中国文学作品"走出去"具有非常重大的意义。中国文学对外传播不仅仅是为了让国外了解中国的文学作品,更要了解文学作品中蕴含的整个中国,它承载着在世界范围内提高中国文化软实力和影响力的使命。然而,就目前情况而言,我国有大量的英译汉文学作品,而汉译英作品数量却相对单薄,浩如烟海的中国传统典籍只有一小部分被译介出去,有些重要典籍甚至还没有外译本,源远流长、光辉灿烂的中国文化并没有被世界广泛认知。

翻译在中国文化"走出去"过程中起着举足轻重的作用,优秀译作是中国文化对外传播取得巨大成就的必由之路。如何在翻译中较好地再现中国文化,既保持原作的文学性,又符合国外读者的阅读习惯,这对译者是一个巨大的挑战,文化差异是首先需要克服的问题之一。译者不仅需要具备深厚的文学功底、扎实的外语能力,更需要拥有较强的跨文化意识,谙熟双方文化,可先尝试用国外读者的语言习惯和思维方式去讲述中国故事,让国外读者能够读懂并欣赏译文中的中国文化。

　　本书是笔者对于《红楼梦》会话引导语英译研究的初步尝试,希望本次细微、粗浅的研究能为中国典籍的英译提供些许借鉴和启示。鉴于时间、篇幅、个人能力等多方面限制,本研究存在诸多不足之处和局限性,但同时也为后续研究留下充分的探讨空间。在今后的研究中将进一步精简和优化《红楼梦》原文和译文中的会话引导语文本、适当考虑引入其他语种以增加对比考察的维度,并尝试将研究结果应用到翻译教学及英语写作教学领域。

# 参考文献

中文类：

[1] 巴金:《家》,北京,人民文学出版社,1962年。

[2] 蔡俊杰:《现代汉语言说类动词考察》,上海,上海师范大学硕士论文,2008年。

[3] 蔡义江:《〈红楼梦〉是怎样写成的》,北京,北京图书馆出版社,2004年。

[4] 曹雪梅、沈映梅:《黄新渠〈红楼梦〉译本中"笑道"的译法——基于汉英平行语料库的研究》,《疯狂英语(教师版)》,2010年第4期。

[5] 曹雪芹:《红楼梦八十回校本》,俞平伯校订、王惜时参校,北京,人民文学出版社,1958年。

[6] 曹雪芹:《戚蓼生序本石头记》,北京,人民文学出版社,1975年。

[7] 曹雪芹:《脂砚斋重评石头记(庚辰本)》,北京,人民文学出版社,1975年。

[8] 曹雪芹:《红楼梦(校注本程甲)》,北京,北京师范大学出版社,1987年。

[9] 曹雪芹:《红楼梦(蔡义江校注)》,杭州,浙江文艺出版社,1994年。

[10] 曹雪芹:《红楼梦(八十回石头记)》,北京,北京师范大学出版社,1995年。

[11] 曹雪芹:《脂砚斋全评石头记》,北京,东方出版社,2006年。

[12] 曹雪芹:《绣像全本红楼梦(程甲本)》,北京,华文出版社,2009年。

[13] 曹雪芹、高鹗:《红楼梦(程乙本)》,北京,人民文学出版社,1964年。

[14] 曹雪芹、高鹗:《程甲本红楼梦》,北京,书目文献出版社,1992年。

[15] 曹雪芹、高鹗:《红楼梦(程甲本底本)》,北京,中华书局,2005年。

[16] 曹雪芹、高鹗:《红楼梦(庚辰本底本)》,北京,金盾出版社,2006年。

[17] 曹雪芹、高鹗:《红楼梦(汉英双语精简本)》,黄新渠改写、黄新渠译,北京,外语教学与研究出版社,2008年。

[18] 陈宏薇、江帆:《难忘的历程——〈红楼梦〉英译事业的描写性研究》,《中国翻译》,2003年第5期。

[19] 陈建林:《基于语料库的引述动词研究及其对英语写作教学的启示》,《外语界》,2011年第6期。

［20］陈琳:《基于语料库的〈红楼梦〉说书套语英译研究》,上海,上海外国语大学博士论文,2012 年。

［21］陈明:《新闻语料库中的转述动词》,大连,大连海事大学硕士论文,2002 年。

［22］陈平原:《中国小说叙事模式的转变》,北京,北京大学出版社,2003.

［23］陈润:《引述及其使用策略——兼谈引述在外汉教学中的应用》,上海,上海外国语大学硕士论文,2007 年。

［24］杜学敏:《〈论语〉中说类动词的翻译对比研究》,大连,大连海事大学硕士论文,2009 年。

［25］戴连云:《直接引语模式及其在小说中的作用》,《青海师专学报》,2004 年第 6 期。

［26］范圣宇:《〈红楼梦〉管窥》,北京,中国社会科学出版社,2004 年。

［27］范圣宇:《浅析霍克思译〈石头记〉中的版本问题》,《明清小说研究》,2005 年第 1 期。

［28］范昕:《中国古典小说〈红楼梦〉中的元语言》,《安徽教育学院学报》,2007 年第 4 期。

［29］范一文:《现代汉语“说”的传信功能》,上海,上海师范大学硕士论文,2013 年。

［30］方梅:《北京话里“说”的语法化——从言说动词到从句标记》,《中国方言学报》,2006 年第 1 期。

［31］方梦之:《中国译学大辞典》,上海,上海外语教育出版社,2011 年。

［32］方寅、夏燕舞:《言说动词研究述评》,《安庆师范学院学报(社会科学版)》,2012 年第 5 期。

［33］冯梦龙:《全像古今小说·序》,福州,福建人民出版社,1980 年。

［34］冯庆华:《文体翻译论》,上海,上海外语教育出版社,2002 年。

［35］冯庆华:《红译艺坛——〈红楼梦〉翻译艺术研究》,上海,上海外语教育出版社,2006 年。

［36］冯庆华:《母语文化下的译者风格》,上海,上海外语教育出版社,2008 年。

［37］冯庆华:《实用翻译教程(第三版)》,上海,上海外语教育出版社,2010 年。

［38］冯庆华:《思维模式下的译文词汇》,上海,上海外语教育出版社,2012 年。

［39］冯庆华:《思维模式下的译文句式》,上海,上海外语教育出版社,2015 年。

［40］冯全功:《〈红楼梦〉中“笑道”翻译的对比研究》,《天津外国语大学学报》,2011 年第 6 期。

［41］〔德〕弗雷格:《论涵义和所指》,牟博中等译,见 A.P.马蒂尼奇编《语言哲学》,北京,商务印书馆,1998 年。

[42] 高淮生、李春强:《十年来〈红楼梦〉叙事学研究述评》,《咸阳师范学院学报》,2004 年第 3 期。

[43] 高磊:《韩礼德系统功能模式下引述动词翻译的制约因素》,长沙,中南大学硕士论文,2009 年。

[44] 高磊:《引述动词"道"英译显化的标记理论阐释》,《湖南工业大学学报(社会科学版)》,2013 年第 8 期。

[45] 高天霞:《从"曰＋直接引语"到"说＋直接引语"的演变历程及原因分析》,《陇东学院学报》,2010 年第 4 期。

[46] 高小丽:《汉英报纸新闻语篇中转述言语的比较研究》,南京,南京师范大学博士论文,2013 年。

[47] 耿强:《文学译介与中国文学"走向世界"——"熊猫丛书"英译中国文学研究》,上海,上海外国语大学博士论文,2010 年。

[48] 顾晓波:《〈红楼梦〉杨译本"冷笑"翻译研究》,《河南科技学院学报》,2011 年第 5 期。

[49] 海洋:《〈红楼梦〉儿化词初探》,《中南民族学院学报》,1994 年第 5 期。

[50] 何金松:《虚词历时词典》,武汉,湖北人民出版社,1994 年。

[51] 何心:《汉英"言说类"词语对比研究》,昆明,云南师范大学硕士论文,2008 年。

[52] 何自然、冉永平:《语用与认知》,北京,外语教学与研究出版社,2001 年。

[53] 贺灿文等:《英语科研论文中综述性动词的语料库研究》,《外语学刊》,2001 年第 4 期。

[54] 贺显斌:《英汉翻译过程中的明晰化现象》,《解放军外国语学院学报》,2003 年第 4 期。

[55] 胡开宝:《跨学科视域下的当代译学研究》,北京,外语教学与研究出版社,2009 年。

[56] 胡开宝:《语料库翻译学概论》,上海,上海交通大学出版社,2011 年。

[57] 胡开宝、朱一凡:《基于语料库的莎剧〈哈姆雷特〉汉译文本中显化现象及其动因研究》,《外语研究》,2008 年第 2 期。

[58] 胡启好:《评析〈红楼梦〉杨译本关于"笑道"的翻译》,《延边党校学报》,2009 年第 2 期。

[59] 胡文彬:《〈红楼梦〉在国外》,北京,中华书局,1993 年。

[60] 胡振明:《对话中的道德建构——十八世纪英国小说中的对话性》,北京,对外经贸大学出版社,2007 年。

[61] 胡志清:《中外英语硕士论文转述动词对比研究》,《语言研究》,2007 年第 3 期。

［62］胡壮麟等:《系统功能语法概论》,长沙,湖南教育出版社,1989年。

［63］胡壮麟等:《系统功能语言学概论》,北京,北京大学出版社,2005年。

［64］黄冠颖:《直接引语现象分析》,北京,北京语言大学硕士论文,2007年。

［65］黄国文:《唐诗英译文中的引述现象分析》,《外语学刊》,2002年第3期。

［66］黄国文:《翻译研究的语言学探索》,上海,上海外语教育出版社,2006年。

［67］黄国文、葛达西:《功能语篇分析》,上海,上海外语教育出版社,2006年。

［68］黄金贵:《古代文化词义集类辨考》,上海,上海教育出版社,1995年。

［69］黄立波:《英汉翻译中人称代词主语的显化:基于语料库的考察》,《外语教学与研究》,2008年第6期。

［70］黄勤:《批评性话语分析视角下的新闻翻译分析——以转述话语的翻译为例》,《外语与外语教学》,2008年第3期。

［71］黄谊军:《科技论文引言中综述动词的主谓搭配》,《外语教育》,2001年第1期。

［72］黄映琼:《浅析梅县方言的一组言说动词——"说"、"学"、"话"、"讲"》,《嘉应学院学报》,2013年第6期。

［73］黄友:《转述话语研究》,上海,复旦大学博士论文,2009年。

［74］〔英〕霍克思:《〈红楼梦〉英译笔记》,香港,香港岭南大学文学与翻译研究中心,2000年。

［75］贾影:《"零翻译"还是"不可译"——试与邱懋如教授商榷》,《中国翻译》,2002年第4期。

［76］贾中恒:《转述语及其语用功能初探》,《外国语》,2000年第2期。

［77］江帆:《他乡的石头记:〈红楼梦〉百年英译史研究》,上海,复旦大学博士论文,2007年。

［78］姜菲、董洪学:《翻译中的显化思维和方法》,《外语学刊》,2009年第4期。

［79］姜其煌:《〈红楼梦〉霍克思英文全译本》,《红楼梦学刊》,1980年第1期。

［80］姜秋霞:《文学翻译与社会文化的相互作用关系研究》,北京,外语教育与研究出版社,2009年。

［81］蒋绍愚:《白居易诗中与"口"有关的动词》,《语言研究》,1993年第1期。

［82］蒋骁华:《典籍英译中的"东方情调化翻译倾向"研究——以英美翻译家的汉籍英译为例》,《中国翻译》,2010年第4期。

［83］金岳霖:《形式逻辑》,北京,人民出版社,2006年。

［84］柯飞:《翻译中的隐和显》,《外语教学与研究》,2005年第4期。

［85］兰陵笑笑生:《金瓶梅》,济南,齐鲁书社,1989年。

［86］李根亮:《〈红楼梦〉的传播与接受》,武汉,武汉大学博士论文,2005年。

［87］李秀明:《汉语元话语标记语研究》,北京,中国社会科学出版社,2011年。

［88］李发根:《语言理论与翻译研究》,合肥,中国科学技术大学出版社,2004 年。

［89］廖七一:《当代西方翻译理论探索》,南京,译林出版社,2000 年。

［90］廖秋忠:《廖秋忠文集》,北京,北京语言学院出版社,1992 年。

［91］刘大为:《言语行为与言说动词句》,《汉语学习》,1991 年第 6 期。

［92］刘丹青:《汉语里的一个内容宾语标句词—从“说道”的“道”说起》,见《庆祝〈中国语文〉创刊周年学术论文集》,北京,商务印书馆,2004 年。

［93］刘丹青:《汉语是一种动词型语言——试说动词型语言和名词型语言的类型差异》,《世界汉语教学》,2010 年第 1 期。

［94］刘国波:《杨宪益夫妇英译〈红楼梦〉的叙事学视角研究》,重庆,四川外国语大学硕士论文,2011 年。

［95］刘晋锋、孙巧稚、杨宪益:《述说翻译二三事》,《人民日报海外版》,2005 年 4 月 18 日。

［96］刘克强:《〈水浒传〉四英译本翻译特征多维度对比研究》,上海,上海外国语大学博士论文,2013 年。

［97］刘宓庆:《翻译与语言哲学》,北京,中国对外翻译出版公司,2004 年。

［98］刘宓庆:《新编当代翻译理论》,北京,中国对外翻译出版公司,2005 年。

［99］刘宓庆:《中西翻译思想比较研究》,北京,中国对外翻译出版公司,2005 年。

［100］刘士聪:《红楼译评——〈红楼梦〉翻译研究论文集》,天津,南开大学出版社,2004 年。

［101］刘泽权:《〈红楼梦〉中英文语料库的创建及应用研究》,北京,光明日报出版社,2010 年。

［102］刘泽权、侯羽:《国内外显化研究概述》,《中国翻译》,2008 年第 5 期。

［103］刘泽权、田璐、刘超朋:《〈红楼梦〉中英文语料库的创建》,《当代语言学》,2008 年第 4 期。

［104］刘泽权、田璐:《〈红楼梦〉叙事标记语及其英译——基于语料库的对比分析》,《外语学刊》,2009 年第 1 期。

［105］刘泽权、谭晓平:《面向汉英平行语料库建设的四大名著中文底本研究》,《河北大学学报（哲学社会科学版）》,2010 年第 1 期。

［106］刘泽权、闫继苗:《基于语料库的译者风格与翻译策略研究——以〈红楼梦〉中报道动词及英译为例》,《解放军外国语学院学报》,2010 年第 4 期。

［107］刘泽权、刘超朋、朱虹:《〈红楼梦〉四个英译本的译者风格初探——基于语料库的统计与分析》,《中国翻译》,2011 年第 1 期。

［108］刘泽权、刘艳红:《初识庐山真面目——邦斯尔英译〈红楼梦〉研究（之

一)》,《红楼梦学刊》,2011 年第 4 期。

[109] 刘重德:《西方译论研究》,北京,中国对外翻译出版公司,2003 年。

[110] 卢惠惠:《古代白话小说句式运用研究》,上海,复旦大学博士论文,2004 年。

[111] 卢惠惠:《古代白话小说语言形式的程式化特征》,《明清小说研究》,2007 年第 1 期。

[112] 鲁迅:《鲁迅全集》,北京,人民文学出版社,1973 年。

[113] 栾妮:《〈红楼梦〉中的修辞造词研究》,济南,山东大学博士论文,2009 年。

[114] 罗贯中:《三国演义》,北京,人民文学出版社,1973 年。

[115] 罗国青:《零翻译研究》,上海,上海交通大学出版社,2011 年。

[116] 罗小东:《话本小说叙事研究》,北京,学苑出版社,2002 年。

[117] 罗新璋:《翻译论集》,北京,商务印书馆,1984 年。

[118] 罗竹风等:《汉语大词典(第十册)》,上海,汉语大词典出版社,1986 年。

[119] 吕晶晶:《转述事件框架与转述的多维研究》,《外语研究》,2011 年第 2 期。

[120] 吕俊、侯向群:《翻译批评学引论》,上海,上海外语教育出版社,2009 年。

[121] 马丁:《当代叙事学》,北京,北京大学出版社,1990 年。

[122] 马云霞:《从身体行为到言说行为——修辞动因下言说动词的扩展》,《当代修辞学》,2010 年第 5 期。

[123] 茅盾:《子夜》,北京,人民文学出版社,1960 年。

[124] 米婷婷:《〈生经〉"言说类词"连用情况研究》,《学行堂语言文字论丛》,2011 年第一辑。

[125] 莫言:《丰乳肥臀》,上海,上海文艺出版社,2012 年。

[126] 倪广妍:《〈歧路灯〉引语研究》,武汉,华中师范大学硕士论文,2014 年。

[127] 聂绀弩:《中国古典小说论集》,上海,复旦大学出版社,2005 年。

[128] 聂志军:《西晋以前汉译佛经中"说类词"使用情况及其发展演变研究》,长沙,湖南师范大学硕士论文,2004 年。

[129] 潘继成:《〈红楼梦〉标点浅析》,北京,商务印书馆国际有限公司,2005 年。

[130] 裴文娟:《框架语义学视角下〈哈利·波特与魔法石〉中言说类动词的翻译研究》,广州,广州大学硕士论文,2010 年。

[131] 彭爱民:《忠实于源语文化——〈红楼梦〉文化翻译研究》,上海,上海外国语大学博士论文,2011 年。

[132] 彭建武:《语言转述现象的认知研究》,上海,复旦大学博士论文,2003 年。

[133] 彭宣维:《语言与语言学概论—汉语系统功能语法》,北京,北京大学出版社,2011 年。

[134] 钱钟书:《翻译术开宗明义》,见罗新璋《翻译论集》,北京,商务印书馆,1984 年。

[135] 〔法〕热拉尔·热奈特:《叙事话语新叙事话语》,王文融译,北京,中国社会科学出版社,1990 年。

[136] 申丹:《小说中人物话语的不同表达方式》,《外语教学与研究》,1991 年第 1 期。

[137] 申丹:《有关小说中人物话语表达形式的几点思考》,《外语与外语教学》,1997 年第 1 期。

[138] 申丹:《视角》,《外国文学》,2004 年第 5 期。

[139] 申丹:《叙述学与小说文体学研究》,北京,北京大学出版社,2001 年。

[140] 申丹:《也谈"叙事"还是"叙述"》,《外国文学评论》,2009 年第 3 期。

[141] 施耐庵、罗贯中:《水浒传(汉英对照)》,沙博理译,北京,外文出版社,1999 年。

[142] 施耐庵、罗贯中:《水浒全传(120 回)》,长沙,岳麓书社,2001 年。

[143] 司显柱:《功能语言学与翻译研究—翻译质量评估模式建构》,北京,北京大学出版社,2007 年。

[144] 宋丽娟:《〈今古奇观〉:最早译成西文的中国古典小说》,《明清小说研究》,2009 年第 2 期。

[145] 随利芳:《语法标记"说"和"道"》,《解放军外国语学院学报》,2007 年第 4 期。

[146] 孙逊:《红楼梦鉴赏辞典》,上海,汉语大词典出版社,2006 年。

[147] 孙雁冰:《译不完的"笑道"——杨宪益和霍克思对〈红楼梦〉中"笑道"的翻译》,《沈阳教育学院学报》,2008 年第 2 期。

[148] 谭邦和:《明清小说史》,上海,上海古籍出版社,2006 年。

[149] 谭载喜:《西方翻译简史》,北京,商务印书馆,2006 年。

[150] 唐青叶:《学术语篇中的转述现象》,《外语与外语教学》,2004 年第 2 期。

[151] 田源:《汉语"说"类动词研究》,武汉,华中师范大学硕士论文,2007 年。

[152] 王东风:《文化差异与读者反应——评 Nida 的读者同等反应论》,见郭建中《文化与翻译》,北京,中国对外翻译出版公司,2000 年。

[153] 王东风:《文化缺省与翻译补偿》,见郭建中《文化与翻译》,北京,中国对外翻译出版公司,2000 年。

[154] 王凤阳:《古辞辨》,长春,吉林文史出版社,1993 年。

[155] 王虹:《戏剧文体分析——话语分析的方法》,上海,上海外语教育出版社,2006 年。

[156] 王宏印:《中国文化典籍英译》,北京,外语教学与研究出版社,2009 年。

[157] 王克非、胡显耀：《汉语文学翻译中人称代词的显化和变异》，《中国外语》，2010 年第 4 期。

[158] 王健：《一些南方方言中来自言说动词的意外范畴标记》，《方言》，2013 年第 2 期。

[159] 王凌：《形式与细读：古代白话小说文体研究》，北京，人民出版社，2010 年。

[160] 王三：《语料库基础上对〈红楼梦〉"笑道"一词的英译评析》，《长城》，2012 年第 12 期。

[161] 王文斌、周慈波：《英汉"看"类动词的语义及词化对比分析》，北京，外语教学与研究，2004 年第 2 期。

[162] 王艺：《言语行为和引语》，上海，华东师范大学硕士论文，2004 年。

[163] 王展：《汉语交际框架下的言说类动词研究》，北京，北京大学硕士论文，2008 年。

[164] 汪立荣：《隐义显译与显义隐译及其认知的阐释》，《外语与外语教学》，2006 年第 4 期。

[165] 汪榕培、王宏：《中国典籍英译》，上海，上海外语教育出版社，2009 年。

[166] 汪维辉：《东汉——隋常用词演变研究》，南京，南京大学出版社，2000 年。

[167] 汪维辉：《汉语"说类词"的历时演变与共时分布》，《中国语文》，2003 年第 4 期。

[168] 温秀颖，王颖：《呈现"他者"：文学翻译者的核心责任——以埃杰顿英译〈金瓶梅〉为例》，《外国语言与文学研究》，2012 年第 5 期。

[169] 翁林颖：《"爱笑"凤姐的笑态艺术特色与霍克思的细节显化翻译》，《东北农业大学学报（社会科学版）》，2014 年第 6 期。

[170] 吴承恩：《西游记》，北京，人民文学出版社，1980 年。

[171] 吴剑锋：《现代汉语言说动词研究概观》，《现代语文（语言研究版）》，2009 年第 2 期。

[172] 肖珊：《基于概念语义的言说动词系统研究》，武汉，武汉大学博士论文，2011 年。

[173] 肖维青：《没完没了的"笑道"》，《海外英语》，2006 年第 9 期。

[174] 肖维青：《语料库在〈红楼梦〉译者风格研究中的应用——兼评〈母语文化下的译者风格〉》，《红楼梦学刊》，2009 年第 6 期。

[175] 谢军：《霍克思英译〈红楼梦〉细节化的认知研究》，长沙，湖南师范大学博士论文，2009 年。

[176] 谢天振：《译介学》，上海，上海外语教育出版社，2003 年。

[177] 谢天振等：《中西翻译简史》，北京，外语教学与研究出版社，2009 年。

［178］谢天振、查明建：《中国现代翻译文学史》，上海，上海外语教育出版社，2004 年。

［179］谢耀基：《汉语语法欧化综述》，《语文研究》，2001 年第 1 期。

［180］辛斌：《新闻语篇转述引语的批评性分析》，《外语教学与研究》，1998 年第 2 期。

［181］辛斌：《批评语言学：理论与应用》，上海，上海外语教育出版社，2004 年。

［182］辛斌：《汉英新闻语篇中转述动词的比较分析———以〈中国日报〉和〈纽约时报〉为例》，《四川外语学院学报》，2008 年第 5 期。

［183］辛斌：《引语研究：理论与问题》，《外语与外语教学》，2009 年第 1 期。

［184］邢福义：《〈红楼梦〉里的"因 Y，因 G"》，《湖北大学学报》（哲学社会科学版），1993 年第 4 期。

［185］徐剑平、梁金花：《从接受理论视角看赛珍珠的〈水浒传〉翻译》，《中国翻译》，2003 年第 6 期。

［186］徐赳赳：《叙述文中直接引语分析》，《语言教学与研究》，1996 年第 1 期。

［187］徐珺：《古典小说英译与中国传统文化传承———〈儒林外史〉汉英语篇对比与翻译研究》，长春，吉林出版集团有限责任公司，2005 年。

［188］徐默凡：《言说动词的隐现规律》，《修辞学习》，2008 年第 1 期。

［189］玄玥：《"说"的一种新用法———客观叙述标记词》，《汉语学报》，2011 年第 2 期。

［190］杨大磊：《汉语标句词研究》，上海，上海师范大学硕士论文，2011 年。

［191］杨凤仙：《言说类动词词义演变规律探析》，《励耘学刊（语言卷）》，2006 年第 2 期。

［192］杨凤仙：《古汉语"言说类"动词的演变规律之探析》，《中国政法大学学报》，2011 年第 6 期。

［193］杨为珍、郭荣光：《〈红楼梦〉辞典》，济南，山东文艺出版社，1986 年。

［194］杨义：《中国古典小说史论》，北京，中国社会科学出版社，2004 年。

［195］杨颖莉等：《英语转述句的功能及语用解析》，《东北师大学报（哲学社会科学版）》，2008 年第 1 期。

［196］姚毅：《语言转述中转述动词的认知语用解析》，《湖北经济学院学报（人文社会科学版）》，2012 年第 2 期。

［197］叶常青：《析评〈红楼梦〉中"笑道"的翻译》，广州，华南师范大学硕士论文，2002 年。

［198］叶露：《〈红楼梦〉语篇体裁标记语的英译》，《华中师范大学研究生学报》，2006 年第 2 期。

［199］叶造就：《〈红楼梦〉中"笑道"英译种种》，《广东民族学院学报（社会科学

版)》,1988 年第 1 期。

[200] 易丹：《对象类介词"跟、向、对"与言说类动词搭配使用的分析》,《语文学刊》,2009 年第 8 期。

[201] 尹雪姣：《从〈红楼梦〉英译本对比看中国古代小说典型视角的传译》,《科技信息》,2008 年第 4 期。

[202] 余光中：《翻译和创作》,见罗新璋《翻译论集》,北京,商务印书馆,1984 年。

[203] 禹一奇：《东西方思维模式的交融——杨宪益翻译风格研究》,上海,上海外国语大学博士论文,2009 年。

[204] 袁夕娣：《〈红楼梦〉中"笑道"的译法》,《武汉电力职业技术学院学报》,2008 年第 2 期。

[205] 翟雪艳：《〈国语〉谓语动词研究》,南京,南京大学硕士论文,2013 年。

[206] 詹丹：《〈红楼梦〉与中国古代小说研究》,上海,东华大学出版社,2003 年。

[207] 张德禄、刘汝山：《语篇连贯与衔接理论的发展及应用》,上海,上海外语教育出版社,2003 年。

[208] 张蕾：《明清至 20 世纪四十年代长篇白话小说中人物心理描写的演进轨迹初探》,上海,复旦大学硕士论文,2008 年。

[209] 张明晗：《语境顺应论下〈红楼梦〉前五十六回"笑道"三译本翻译对比分析》,秦皇岛,燕山大学硕士论文,2012 年。

[210] 张荣建：《管领词的引述功能与话语功能》,《外国语》,1998 年第 1 期。

[211] 张荣建：《英语中的管领词：功能分析》,《外语学刊》,2000 年第 1 期。

[212] 张荣建：《书面语和会话中的引语分析》,《外国语》,2000 年第 2 期。

[213] 张荣建：《英语引语的多视角分析》,《重庆师范大学学报》,2007 年第 2 期。

[214] 张迎海：《从〈红楼梦〉中"笑道"的翻译对比看主、被动顺应》,《内蒙古农业大学学报(社会科学版)》,2009 年第 2 期。

[215] 章振邦：《新编英语语法教程》,上海,上海外语教育出版社,2003 年。

[216] 赵朝永：《基于语料库的邦译本〈红楼梦〉译者风格研究》,上海,上海外国语大学博士论文,2014 年。

[217] 赵毅衡：《小说叙述中的转述语》,《文艺研究》,1987 年第 5 期。

[218] 赵毅衡：《苦恼的叙述者——中国小说的叙述形式与中国文化》,北京,北京十月文艺出版社,1994 年。

[219] 赵毅衡：《当说者被说的时候》,北京,中国人民大学出版社,1997 年。

[220] 赵询思：《"说"一字在现代汉语中的虚化情况》,《广西大学学报(哲学社会科学版)》,2006 年第 2 期。

［221］郑敏宇:《叙事类型视角下的小说翻译研究》,上海,上海外语教育出版社,2007 年。

［222］郑青:《汉日言说动词"说"和「言ら」的语法化对比研究》,福州,福建师范大学硕士论文,2011 年。

［223］周汝昌:《红楼梦辞典》,广州,广东人民出版社,1987 年。

［224］周定一:《红楼梦语言词典》,北京,商务印书馆,1995 年。

［225］朱邦国:《〈红楼梦〉人物对话艺术》,乌鲁木齐,新疆人民出版社,1995 年。

［226］朱永生、严世清:《系统功能语言学多维思考》,上海,上海外语教育出版社,2001 年。

［227］朱永生等:《功能语言学导论》,上海,上海外语教育出版社,2004 年。


**外文类:**

［1］Ardekani，M.A.M. *The Translation of Reporting Verbs in English and Persian*，Babel，2002(2).

［2］Baker，Mona. *In Other Words：A Coursebook on Translation*，Shanghai：Shanghai Foreign Language Education Press，2000.

［3］Baker，Mona. *Towards a Methodology for Investigating the Style of a Literary Translator*，Amsterdam & Philadelphia：John Benjamins，2000（12）.

［4］Baker，Mona. *Routledge Encyclopedia of Translation Studies*，Shanghai：Shanghai Foreign Language Education Press，2004.

［5］Baker，Mona. *Translation and Conflict — A Narrative Account*，New York & London：Routledge，2006.

［6］Baker，Mona. Francis G. & Tognini-Bonelli，E.（ed.），*Text and Technology：In Honour of John Sinclair*，Amsterdam & Philadelphia：John Benjamins，1993.

［7］Bassnett，Susan. *Translation Studies*（3rd edition），Shanghai：Shanghai Foreign Language Education Press，2004.

［8］Bergler，S. *Evidential Analysis of Reported Speech*，Boston：Brandeis University，1992.

［9］Biber，D. et al. *Corpus Linguistics*，Beijing：Foreign Language Teaching and Research Press，2000.

［10］Biber，D. et al. *Longman Grammar of Spoken and Written English*，Beijing：Foreign Language Teaching and Research Press，2000.

［11］Cao，Xueqin. *Hung Lou Meng，or，The Dream of the Red Chamber*.

Joly，H. B.（trans.），HongKong：Kelly and Walsh，1892-3.

[12] Cao，Xueqin. *The Dream of the Red Chamber*. Florence & Isabel Mchugh（trans.），New York：Pantheon Books Inc.，1958.

[13] Cao，Xueqin. *A Dream in Red Mansions*（A simplified English Version）. Huang，Xinqu（trans.），Beijing：Foreign Language Teaching and Research Press，1991.

[14] Cao，Xueqin & Gao，E. *A Dream of Red Mansions*. Yang Hsien-yi & Gladys Yang（trans.），Beijing：Foreign Languages Press，1978-1982.

[15] Cao，Xueqin & Gao，E. *The Story of the Stone*. David Hawkes & John Minford（trans.），Shanghai：Shanghai Foreign Language Education Press，2012.

[16] Collins，D. E. *Reanimated Voices：Speech Reporting in a Historical-Pragmatic Perspective*，Amsterdam & Philadelphia：John Benjamins，2001.

[17] Coulmas，Florian. *Direct and Indirect Speech*，Berlin：Mouton，1986.

[18] Englund-Dimitrova，B. *Expertise and Explicitation in the Translation Process*，Amsterdam & Philadelphia：John Benjamins，2005.

[19] Geis，M. L. *The language of politics*，New York：Springer-Verlag，1987.

[20] Halliday，M. A. K. *An Introduction to Functional Grammar*，Beijing：Foreign Language Teaching and Research Press，2000.

[21] Halliday，M. A. K. *Language as Social Semiotic：The Social Interpretation of Language and Meaning*，London：Arnold，1978/Beijing：Foreign Language Teaching and Research Press，2001.

[22] Heine，B. et al. *Grammaticalization：A Conceptual Framework*，Chicago and London：The University of Chicago Press，1991.

[23] Hyland，K. *Disciplinary Discourse：Social Interactions in Academic Writing*，London：Pearson Education Limited，2000.

[24] Klaudy，K. & Karoly，K. *Implicitation in Translation：Empirical Evidence for Operational Asymmetry in Translation*，Across Lauguage and Cultures，2005，6(1).

[25] Klaudy，K.，Lambert J. & Sohar A.，*Translation Studies in Hungary*，Budapest：Scholastica，1996.

[26] Laviosa S. "Core Patterns of Lexical Use in a Comparable Corpus of English Narrative Prose"，*Translators' Journal*，1998，43(4).

[27] Laviosa S. *Corpus-based Translation Studies*：*Theory*，*Findings*，*Applications*，Amsterdam：Rodopi，2002.

[28] Leech，G. N. & M. Short. *Style in Fiction*，Beijing：Foreign Language Teaching and Research Press，2001.

[29] Lefevere，A. *Translating Poetry*：*Seven Strategies and a Blueprint*，Amsterdam：Van Gorcum，1975.

[30] Liu，Z. Q. & Hong，H. Q. "A Corpus-Based Study of Reporting Verbs in Fictions：A Translational Perspective"，*US-China Foreign Language*，2004，2(8).

[31] Lu，Hsun. *A Brief History of Chinese Fiction*. Yang Hsien-yi & Gladys Yang（trans.），Beijing：Foreign Languages Press，2009.

[32] Matejka，L. & Pomorska，K. *Readings in Russian Poetics*，Cambridge：MTI Press，1978.

[33] Martin，J. R. *English Text System and Structure*，Beijing：Peking University Press，2004.

[34] Martin，Wallace. *Recent Theories of Narrative*，Beijing：Peking University Press，2006.

[35] Norrick，N. R. *Conversational Storytelling*. D. Herman（ed.），*The Cambridge Companion to Narrative*，Cambridge：Cambridge University Press，2007.

[36] Newmark，Peter. *Approaches to Translation*，Shanghai：Shanghai Foreign Language Education Press，2002.

[37] Nida，E. *Language*，*Culture and Translation*，Shanghai：Shanghai Foreign Language Education Press，1993.

[38] Nida，E. & C. Taber. *The Theory and Practice of Translation*，Leiden：Brill，1969.

[39] Nida，E. & W. Reyburn. *Meaning across Cultures*，New York：Orbis Books，1993.

[40] Nord，Christiane. *Translating as a Purposeful Activity*，Shanghai：Shanghai Foreign Language Education Press，2002.

[41] Olga，Dontcheva. *Reporting Verbs as Indicators of Stance in Academic Discourse*，Debrecen：Porta Lingea，2008.

[42] Olohan，M. *Introducing Corpora in Translation Studies*，London：Routledge，2004.

[43] Page，Norman. *Forms of Speech in Fiction*. N. Page（ed.），*The*

*Language of Literature*，London，1973.

[44] Page，Norman. *Speech in the English Novel*，London：Macmillan，1988.

[45] Perego，E. "Evidence of Explicitation in Subtitling: Towards a Categorization"，*Across Languages and Cultures*，2003，4(1).

[46] Quirk，R. et al. *A Comprehensive Grammar of the English Language*，London/New York：Longman，1985.

[47] Shen，Dan. *Literary Stylistics and Fictional Translation*，Beijing：Peking University Press，1995.

[48] Somers H. *Terminology*，*LSP and Translation*：*Studies in Language Engineering in Honour of Juan C. Sager*，Amsterdam & Philadelphia：John Benjamins，1996.

[49] Swales，J. *Genre Analysis*：*English in Academic and Research Settings*，Cambridge：Cambridge University Press，1990.

[50] Tannen，Deborah. *Talking Voices*，Cambridge：Cambridge University Press，1989.

[51] Thompson，G. *Introducing Functional Grammar*，Beijing：Foreign Language Teaching and Research Press，2000.

[52] Thompson，G. & Ye，Y. "Evaluation in the Reporting Verbs Used in Academic Papers"，*Applied Linguistics*，1991(4).

[53] Triki，M. & Bahloul，M. "The Reported Speech Revisited: A Question of Self and Expression"，*Academic Research*，2001(1-2).

[54] Tsao，Hsueh-chin. *Dream of the Red Chamber* (Abridged). Chin-Chen Wang (trans.)，New York：Twayne Publishers，1958.

[55] Van Peer，Willie & Seymour，Chatman. *New Perspectives on Narrative Perspective*，Albany：State University of New York Press，2001.

[56] Venuti，Lawrence. *The Translator's Invisibility*，Shanghai：Shanghai Foreign Language Education Press，2004.

[57] Voloshinov，V. *Reported Speech*. Matejka，L & Pomorska，K (ed.)，*Readings in Russian Poetics*，Cambridge：MTI Press，1978.

[58] Weissberg，R. & Buker，S. *Writing up Research*：*Experimental Research Report Writing for Students of English*，Hoboken：Prentice Hall，1990.

[59] Winters，M. "A Corpus-Based Study of Speech-Act Report Verbs as a Feature of Translator's Style"，*Meta*，2007，52(3).

[60] Wong，Laurence. *A Study of the Literary Translations of the "Hong Lou Meng"*：*With Special Reference to David Hawkes's English Version*，

Toronto：University of Toronto，1992.

［61］Wu Shih-Ch'ang. *On the Red Chamber Dream*，Oxford：Oxford University Press，1961.

［62］Yang，Winston L. Y. & Peter Li & Nathan K. Mao. *Classical Chinese Fiction—A Guide to Its Study and Appreciation Essays and Bibliographies*，Boston：G. K. Hall Co.，1978.

［63］Zhang，Jing. *Playing with Desire：Reading Short Vernacular Fiction in 16th and 17th Century China*，St. Louis：Washington University，2006.

# 索　引